Lecture Notes in Computer Science 14977

Founding Editors

Gerhard Goos
Juris Hartmanis

Editorial Board Members

Elisa Bertino, *Purdue University, West Lafayette, IN, USA*
Wen Gao, *Peking University, Beijing, China*
Bernhard Steffen ⓘ, *TU Dortmund University, Dortmund, Germany*
Moti Yung ⓘ, *Columbia University, New York, NY, USA*

The series Lecture Notes in Computer Science (LNCS), including its subseries Lecture Notes in Artificial Intelligence (LNAI) and Lecture Notes in Bioinformatics (LNBI), has established itself as a medium for the publication of new developments in computer science and information technology research, teaching, and education.

LNCS enjoys close cooperation with the computer science R & D community, the series counts many renowned academics among its volume editors and paper authors, and collaborates with prestigious societies. Its mission is to serve this international community by providing an invaluable service, mainly focused on the publication of conference and workshop proceedings and postproceedings. LNCS commenced publication in 1973.

Kazuhiko Minematsu · Mamoru Mimura
Editors

Advances in Information and Computer Security

19th International Workshop on Security, IWSEC 2024
Kyoto, Japan, September 17–19, 2024
Proceedings

Editors
Kazuhiko Minematsu ⓘ
NEC and Yokohama National University
Kawasaki, Japan

Mamoru Mimura ⓘ
National Defense Academy
Yokosuka, Japan

ISSN 0302-9743   ISSN 1611-3349 (electronic)
Lecture Notes in Computer Science
ISBN 978-981-97-7736-5   ISBN 978-981-97-7737-2 (eBook)
https://doi.org/10.1007/978-981-97-7737-2

© The Editor(s) (if applicable) and The Author(s), under exclusive license
to Springer Nature Singapore Pte Ltd. 2024

This work is subject to copyright. All rights are solely and exclusively licensed by the Publisher, whether the whole or part of the material is concerned, specifically the rights of translation, reprinting, reuse of illustrations, recitation, broadcasting, reproduction on microfilms or in any other physical way, and transmission or information storage and retrieval, electronic adaptation, computer software, or by similar or dissimilar methodology now known or hereafter developed.
The use of general descriptive names, registered names, trademarks, service marks, etc. in this publication does not imply, even in the absence of a specific statement, that such names are exempt from the relevant protective laws and regulations and therefore free for general use.
The publisher, the authors and the editors are safe to assume that the advice and information in this book are believed to be true and accurate at the date of publication. Neither the publisher nor the authors or the editors give a warranty, expressed or implied, with respect to the material contained herein or for any errors or omissions that may have been made. The publisher remains neutral with regard to jurisdictional claims in published maps and institutional affiliations.

This Springer imprint is published by the registered company Springer Nature Singapore Pte Ltd.
The registered company address is: 152 Beach Road, #21-01/04 Gateway East, Singapore 189721, Singapore

If disposing of this product, please recycle the paper.

Preface

The 19th International Workshop on Security (IWSEC 2024) was held at Kyoto International Conference Center, Kyoto, Japan between September 17–19, 2024. The workshop was co-organized by the Technical Committee on Information Security (ISEC) of the Engineering Sciences Society of the Institute of Electronics, Information and Communication Engineers (IEICE) and the Special Interest Group on Computer Security (CSEC) of the Information Processing Society of Japan (IPSJ).

Following IWSEC's tradition, we classified the topics of interest into two tracks, namely, the Cryptography Track (Track A) and the Cybersecurity and Privacy Track (Track B); each track was formed by separate Program Committee members. We received 47 submissions in total, 29 papers in Track A and 18 papers in Track B, each of which was then reviewed in a double-blind fashion by three or four experts in the pertinent fields. After comprehensive reviews, we accepted 17 papers, nine papers in Track A and eight papers in Track B, out of which three papers were accepted as short papers, and included their revised and refined versions in this publication. Among them, we selected two best paper awards and one student paper award. The best paper awards went to "Efficient Card-Based Protocols with a Standard Deck of Playing Cards Using Partial Opening" by Yoshiaki Honda and Kazumasa Shinagawa and "Few Edges Are Enough: Few-Shot Network Attack Detection with Graph Neural Networks" by Tristan Bilot, Nour El Madhoun, Khaldoun Al Agha and Anis Zouaoui. The best student paper award went to "Race condition vulnerabilities in WordPress plug-ins" by Rin Miyachi, Konan Nagashima and Taiichi Saito.

Three keynote talks were presented by Dustin Moody (National Institute of Standards and Technology, USA) on "The First PQC Standards", Thomas Peyrin (Nanyang Technological University, Singapore) on "Automated Analysis for Pushing Performance Limits in Symmetric-Key Cryptography", and Andreas Rauber (Vienna University of Technology, Austria and Vienna Scientific Cluster Research Center, Austria) on "Securely Working with Confidential Data: Threats and Mitigations across Layers from Infrastructure to AI Models".

We express our sincere appreciation to all those who contributed to the remarkable success of IWSEC 2024. We are grateful to the authors who submitted their studies to the workshop. We are thankful to the Program Committee members and external reviewers for their diligent reviews and insightful discussions, which led to the creation of an outstanding program. Last but not least, we would like to thank the general co-chairs, Junji Shikata and Koji Chida, for their exceptional leadership, as well as the Organizing Committee members for their great work resulting in a successful event.

September 2024

Kazuhiko Minematsu
Mamoru Mimura

Organization

General Co-chairs

Junji Shikata — Yokohama National University, Japan
Koji Chida — Gunma University, Japan

Program Committee Co-chairs

Kazuhiko Minematsu — NEC, Japan and Yokohama National University, Japan
Mamoru Mimura — National Defense Academy, Japan

Poster Chair

Naoto Yanai — Panasonic, Japan

Publication Chair

Ryoma Ito — National Institute of Information and Communications Technology, Japan

Local Organizing Committee

Yujie Gu — Kyushu University, Japan
Akiko Inoue — NEC, Japan
Kazuki Iwahana — NTT Social Informatics Laboratories, Japan
Motohiro Kambashi — Sumitomo Mitsui Banking Corporation, Japan
Daiki Miyahara — The University of Electro-Communications, Japan
Misato Nakabayashi — NTT Social Informatics Laboratories, Japan
Shohei Satake — Kumamoto University, Japan
Shingo Sato — Yokohama National University, Japan
Miyoko Shinmizu — IQVIA, Japan
Yohei Watanabe — The University of Electro-Communications, Japan
Sven Wohlgemuth — SECOM Intelligent Systems Laboratory, Japan

Kyosuke Yamashita Osaka University, Japan
Rei Yamagishi Hitachi, Ltd., Japan

Program Committee

Track A: Cryptography Track

Miguel Ambrona	Nomadic Labs, France
Kazumaro Aoki	Bunkyo University, Japan
Yoshinori Aono	National Institute of Information and Communications Technology, Japan
Frederik Armknecht	University of Mannheim, Germany
Andrea Caforio	EPFL, Switzerland
Chen-Mou Cheng	BTQ AG, Liechtenstein
Sherman S. M. Chow	Chinese University of Hong Kong, China
Carlos Cid	Simula UiB, Norway and OIST, Japan
Bernardo David	IT University of Copenhagen, Denmark
Antonio Faonio	EURECOM, France
Junqing Gong	East China Normal University, China
Keisuke Hara	AIST, Japan
Yasuhiko Ikematsu	Kyushu University, Japan
Takanori Isobe	University of Hyogo, Japan
Mitsugu Iwamoto	University of Electro-Communications, Japan
Yuichi Komano	Chiba Institute of Technology, Japan
Noboru Kunihiro	University of Tsukuba, Japan
Kirill Morozov	University of North Texas, USA
Khoa Nguyen	University of Wollongong, Australia
Siang Meng Sim	DSO National Laboratories, Singapore
Daniel Slamanig	University of the Bundeswehr Munich, Germany
Willy Susilo	University of Wollongong, Australia
Katsuyuki Takashima	Waseda University, Japan
Serge Vaudenay	EPFL, Switzerland
Damien Vergnaud	Sorbonne Université/Institut Universitaire de France, France
Damian Vizár	CSEM, Switzerland
Yuntao Wang	University of Electro-Communications, Japan
Yuyu Wang	University of Electronic Science and Technology of China, China

Track B: Cybersecurity and Privacy Track

Josep Balasch	KU Leuven, Belgium
Gregory Blanc	Télécom SudParis, France
Eyasu Getahun Chekole	Singapore University of Technology and Design, Singapore
Hervé Debar	Télécom SudParis, France
Pieter Hartel	Technische Universiteit Delft, Netherlands
Harsha Kalutarage	Robert Gordon University, UK
Panayiotis Kotzanikolaou	University of Piraeus, Greece
Hiroki Kuzuno	Kobe University, Japan
Tianyu Li	Technische Universiteit Delft, Netherlands
Frédéric Majorczyk	DGA-MI/CentraleSupélec, France
Weizhi Meng	Technical University of Denmark, Denmark
Alexios Mylonas	University of Hertfordshire, UK
Kazumasa Omote	University of Tsukuba, Japan
Toshiki Shibahara	NTT, Japan
Dario Stabili	University of Bologna, Italy
Rui Tanabe	Juntendo University, Japan
Raylin Tso	National Cheng-Chi University, Taiwan
Rei Ueno	Kyoto University, Japan
Giorgos Vasiliadis	Hellenic Mediterranean University and FORTH-ICS, Greece
Naoto Yanai	Panasonic, Japan
Kuo-Hui Yeh	National Dong Hwa University, Taiwan
Behrouz Zolfaghari	Miami University, USA

Additional Reviewers

Daichi Aoki
Toshiyuki Isshiki
Hyungrok Jo
Yi-Fu Lai
Linjie Li
Jack P. K. Ma
Tezuka Masayuki
Shigeo Mitsunari
Daiki Miyahara
Marzio Mula
Koji Nuida

Shinya Okumura
Ying-Yu Pan
Edoardo Persichetti
Mostafizar Rahman
Suthee Ruangwises
Sebastian Spindler
Bénédikt Tran
Leizhang Wang
Huangting Wu
Kyosuke Yamashita

Contents

Authenticated Encryption

Bit-Wise Analysis for Forgery Attacks on AES-Based AEAD Schemes 3
  Takuro Shiraya, Kosei Sakamoto, and Takanori Isobe

Cryptanalysis of Authenticated Encryption Modes for Wireless
and Real-Time Systems 23
  Alexander Bille and Elmar Tischhauser

Symmetric-key Cryptanalysis

Higher-Order Mixture Differentials for AES-Based Block Ciphers
and Applications to TweAES 45
  Eik List

Weak Keys of the Full MISTY1 Recovered in Practical Time 65
  Bungo Taga, Norimitsu Ito, and Takako Okano

Protocols

Efficient Card-Based Protocols with a Standard Deck of Playing Cards
Using Partial Opening 85
  Yoshiaki Honda and Kazumasa Shinagawa

Attribute-Based Inner Product Functional Encryption in Key-Policy
Setting from Pairing 101
  Anushree Belel and Ratna Dutta

Analysis of Public-key Cryptosystems

Formal Verification of Emulated Floating-Point Arithmetic in Falcon 125
  Vincent Hwang

Experimental Analysis of Integer Factorization Methods Using Lattices 142
  Arata Sato, Aurélien Auzemery, Akira Katayama, and Masaya Yasuda

Sieving Method for SDP with the Zero Window: An Improvement in Low
Memory Environments 158
  Naoki Yoshiguchi, Yusuke Aikawa, and Tsuyoshi Takagi

Vulnerability

Race Condition Vulnerabilities in WordPress Plug-ins 179
    Rin Miyachi, Konan Nagashima, and Taiichi Saito

Finding (and Exploiting) Vulnerabilities on IP Cameras: The Tenda CP3
Case Study 195
    Dario Stabili, Tobia Bocchi, Filip Valgimigli, and Mirco Marchetti

Malware Countermeasure

File System Shield (FSS): A Pass-Through Strategy Against Unwanted
Encryption in Network File Systems 213
    *Arash Mahboubi, Seyit Camtepe, Keyvan Ansari, Marcin Pawłowski,
Paweł Morawiecki, Jarek Duda, and Josef Pieprzyk*

Implementation for Malicious Software Using ChatGPT-4 234
    Nobuyuki Sugio and Hokuto Ito

A Markov Game Model for Evaluating Cybersecurity Attacks on Cloud 244
    *Hooman Alavizadeh, Julian Jang-Jaccard, Hootan Alavizadeh,
and Tansu Alpcan*

Network Security and Privacy

Few Edges are Enough: Few-Shot Network Attack Detection with Graph
Neural Networks 257
    Tristan Bilot, Nour El Madhoun, Khaldoun Al Agha, and Anis Zouaoui

Information Leakage Through Packet Lengths in RTC Traffic 277
    Jaiden Fairoze and Peitong Duan

A Study on Anonymization Through Participation in iPWS Cup 2023 297
    Kabuto Okajima and Koji Chida

Author Index 307

Authenticated Encryption

Bit-Wise Analysis for Forgery Attacks on AES-Based AEAD Schemes

Takuro Shiraya[1], Kosei Sakamoto[2], and Takanori Isobe[1(✉)]

[1] University of Hyogo, Kobe, Japan
takanori.isobe@ai.u-hyogo.ac.jp
[2] Mitsubishi Electric Corporation, Kamakura, Japan

Abstract. We examine the security of AES-based authenticated encryption schemes, including the AEGIS family, Tiaoxin-346, Rocca and Rocca-S. Existing studies evaluated the security against forgery attacks, focusing on state collisions in the encryption phase. These studies estimated the lower bounds for the number of active S-boxes by a byte-wise search. However, this approach might underestimate these bounds, as it potentially include invalid characteristics. In this paper, we conduct a bit-wise evaluation of the AEGIS family, Tiaoxin-346, Rocca, and Rocca-S against forgery attacks based on state collision by Boolean satisfiability problem (SAT) tools. This approach enables us to derive tighter bounds for the minimum number of active S-boxes. Besides, for AEGIS-128L, Tiaoxin-346, and Rocca, we incorporate values of differential distribution tables of S-boxes to obtain the exact differential characteristics probability, which directly lead to actual forgery attacks on AEGIS-128L, Tiaoxin-346, and Rocca. These results reveal that AEGIS-128L cannot claim 256-bit security for forgery attacks, even with a 256-bit tag. Furthermore, for the first time, we perform a security evaluation against forgery attacks exploiting tag collisions in the tag generation phase.

Keywords: AEAD · Forgery attack · differential characteristics probability · SAT solver

1 Introduction

1.1 Background

At SAC 2013, Wu and Preneel proposed an AES-based Authenticated Encryption with an Associated Data (AEAD) scheme called AEGIS-128/128L/256, designed to a high-speed encryption in software [23]. To realize high-speed encryption, the AEGIS family utilizes the AES New Instructions (AES-NI) [4,8], a particular instruction set for single instruction multiple data (SIMD). The AEGIS family was submitted to the CAESAR competition [1], and AEGIS-128 was selected as the final portfolio for high-performance applications. AEGIS-128L/256 has been submitted as an Internet Draft to the RFC [5], featuring the introduction of a 256-bit tag. Nikolić proposed an efficient AEAD scheme called

Tiaoxin-346 using AES-NI in 2014 [15], which was chosen as a third-round candidate in the CAESAR competition. At FSE 2022, Sakamoto et al. proposed an AES-based AEAD scheme called Rocca [16,17] for B5G systems. At ESORICS 2023, Ravi et al. proposed Rocca-S, an AEAD scheme for 6G [2], which supports a 256-bit tag. These ciphers consist of four phases. In the initialization phase, a key and nonce are loaded into a state. An associated data is used to update the state in the authenticated data phase. In the encryption phase, a plaintext is loaded into the state, and a ciphertext is generated. In the finalization phase, a tag is generated.

Forgery attacks are a powerful form of attack against AEAD. In recent years, automatic methods have been utilized to search for distinguishers in cryptanalysis. One such method is based on mixed-integer linear programming (MILP), as proposed by Mouha et al. [14]. This method aims to estimate the lower bound on the number of active S-boxes. Another significant method in automatic search is based on the Boolean satisfiability problem (SAT) or its extension called satisfiability modulo theories (SMT). Sun et al. have proposed an SAT-based automatic search tool for differential characteristics that efficiently evaluates the optimal differential characteristics [20,21].

1.2 Existing Work

Minaud constructed linear biases in the keystream of AEGIS-256 and showed that it is possible to recover information from partially known encrypted plaintext, regardless of the keys involved [13]. Eichlseder et al. proposed improved keystream approximations for the AEGIS family and proved upper bounds for the squared correlation contribution of any suitable linear characteristic [7]. At FSE 2022, Liu et al. showed distinguishing and key recovery attacks for the encryption phase of AEGIS-128 and Tiaoxin-346 by exploiting some algebraic properties in a class of weak keys [12]. Hosoyamada et al. conducted a key-recovery attack on Rocca, showing that despite the designers' claims of 256-bit security, it actually possesses only 128-bit security [9]. This issue has been fixed by introducing a key forward operation in the initialization phase [17]. In this paper, we consider this variant as Rocca. Derbez et al. assessed the key commitment security of the AEGIS family, considering various existing frameworks, and culminated in developing an $O(1)$ attack applicable to all variants of AEGIS [6].

Regarding forgery attacks, existing research focuses on a class of forgery attacks that exploit state collisions by introducing differences during the encryption phase. These roughly estimate the upper bounds of differential characteristics probability for state collisions in the encryption phase by a byte-wise active S-box search [2,15,17,22,23]. The byte-wise estimation potentially underestimates the lower bounds for the number of active S-boxes due to the inclusion of invalid differential characteristics, as this evaluation cannot cover bit-level behaviors. Especially, the estimated bounds for the AEGIS family are particularly rough, even as the IETF considers their standardization. To our

Table 1. Summary of forgery attacks based on state collision in the encryption phase.

Target	Tag Size	Probability	Bounds	Reference
AEGIS-128L	128/256 bits	2^{-216}	Exact	**Our** (Fig. 3)
Tiaoxin-346	128 bits	2^{-180}	Exact	**Our**
Rocca	128 bits	2^{-150}	Exact	**Our** (Fig. 4)

knowledge, no bit-wise evaluation of forgery attacks based on state collisions has been conducted during the encryption phase for AEGIS, Tiaoxin-346, Rocca, and Rocca-S.

1.3 Our Contribution

In this paper, we conduct a bit-wise evaluation against forgery attacks based on state collisions using the Boolean satisfiability problem (SAT) tools [20,21]. This enables us to derive more accurate bounds of AES-based AEAD schemes. Specifically, we estimate the minimum number of active S-boxes by considering bit-level transitions of differential characteristics to exclude invalid characteristics of existing byte-wise searches. Besides, for AEGIS-128L, Tiaoxin-346, and Rocca, we incorporate differential distribution tables of S-boxes, i.e. take the actual differential probabilities via S-box operations into consideration to derive the exact differential characteristics probability. These directly lead to actual forgery attacks on AEGIS-128L, Tiaoxin-346, and Rocca.

Furthermore, for the first time, we perform a security evaluation against forgery attacks that exploit a tag collision in the finalization phase. This assumes that the adversary introduces differences into the plaintext, which canceled out during the finalization phase. Then, we show that forgery attacks are feasible on reduced variants in the finalization of target ciphers. Our results reveal the security margin of the finalization phases. Our contributions are summarized as follows.

Forgery Attacks Based on State Collisions. As shown in Table 1, our bit-wise approach significantly improves the upper bounds of differential characteristics probability of these ciphers. Especially, we significantly improve the upper bounds of differential characteristics probability for AEGIS-128/128L/256. Our results indicate that AEGIS-128/256 could claim a 256-bit forgery security by differential attacks if it supports a 256-bit tag. Additionally, these confirm that Rocca-S achieves 256-bit security for forgery attacks.

For AEGIS-128L, Tiaoxin-346, and Rocca, we succeeded in deriving the exact differential characteristics probability, which directly leads to actual forgery attacks. More precisely, forgery attacks are feasible with time complexity of 2^{216}, 2^{180} and 2^{150} for AEGIS-128L, Tiaoxin-346, and Rocca, respectively. These results reveal that these cannot claim 256-bit security for forgery attacks even with a 256-bit tag.

Table 2. Summary of forgery attacks based on tag collision in the finalization phase.

Target	Tag Size	Attacked Round (Full)	Time
AEGIS-128	128 bits	2 (6)	2^{125}
AEGIS-128L	128/256 bits	2/3 (6/6)	$2^{72}/2^{158}$ (Fig. 5)
AEGIS-256	128 bits	2 (6)	2^{125}
Tiaoxin-346	128 bits	3 (1+20)	2^{36}
Rocca	128 bits	4 (20)	2^{125}
Rocca-S	256 bits	4 (16)	2^{214}

Forgery Attacks Based on Tag Collisions. Table 2 shows that forgery attacks exploiting tag collision are feasible to 2/3/2, 3, 4, and 4-round in the finalization phase of AEGIS-128/128L/256, Tiaoxin-346, Rocca, and Rocca-S, respectively. On the other hand, we find that the finalization phase of AEGIS-128/128L/256, Tiaoxin-346, Rocca, and Rocca-S are secure against forgery attacks based on tag collision after 3/4/3, 4, 5, and 5 rounds, respectively. As far as we know, these are the first evaluation results for tag collision attacks in the finalization phase.

2 Preliminaries

In this section, we first describe forgery attacks. Then, we explain differential characteristics, the security evaluation using the automatic method, and the specifications of AEGIS-128/128L/256, Tiaoxin-346, Rocca, and Rocca-S, respectively.

2.1 Forgery Attacks

The goal of the forgery attacks is to generate the same tag when different messages are input. It has been shown in [15] that the forgery attack is a main threat to the constructions like Tiaoxin-346 and AEGIS as only one-round updates are used to absorb each block of associated data and plaintext.

To proceed with the forgery attacks, we request the encryption of some messages, nonce, and the associated data. The contents of the message, the nonce, and the associated data are not of concern to us. If an internal collision occurs during the cipher operations under these conditions, it becomes possible to forge the tag. We utilize differential characteristics to implement the forgery attacks. The evaluation method of this research is described in Sect. 4.3, while the differential characteristics are explained in Sect. 2.2.

2.2 Differential Characteristics

In this paper, We consider that based on the AES round function, we must regard only an S-box in AES as a non-linear function. In general, differential propagation can be probabilistic only when the differences pass a non-linear function.

Therefore, the differential probability decreases only when the differences pass an S-box. The S-box with a non-zero input difference is called an "active S-box." Basically, when all S-boxes are independent of each other, we can estimate the differential probability of the entire round function by the product of the differential probability of all active S-boxes. We can apply this method to our round function because, for differential propagation, all S-boxes are independent of each other [11,16]. Let DP_{F_R} and DP_s be the differential probabilities of the whole round function and S-box, respectively. We can calculate DP_{F_R} as follows.

$$DP_{F_R} = \prod_{i=1}^{n} DP_s, \qquad (1)$$

where n is the number of active S-boxes in this differential characteristic, which indicates a certain differential propagation. DP_{F_R} is equivalent to the probability of an internal collision in a certain round of F_R.

When evaluating security against an internal collision on t rounds of F_R, the maximum differential probability must be evaluated such that the differences in states at t rounds will all be 0. This can be calculated by searching for the differential characteristics with the minimum number of active S-boxes among all the differential characteristics. Conversely, the maximum differential probability of F_R can be estimated by searching for the lower bound for the number of active S-boxes. Let DP_{F_Rmax} and DP_{smax} be the maximum differential probabilities of the differential characteristics with the minimum number of active S-boxes on F_R and the S-box, respectively. DP_{F_Rmax} can be calculated as follows.

$$DP_{F_Rmax} = \prod_{i=1}^{m} DP_{smax}, \qquad (2)$$

where m is the lower bound of the number of active S-boxes.

2.3 Automatic Search Tools for Differential Cryptanalysis

The automatic search method showed incredible performances in the search for various distinguishers in cryptanalysis. The first category of automatic search is based on mixed integer linear programming (MILP). Another important automatic search is based on the Boolean satisfiability problem (SAT) or the more general extension called satisfiability modulo theories (SMT). Let's consider an example of security evaluation against differential attacks using an active S-box. In the search using MILP, binary variables are assigned to the input and output of each operation, and the differential propagation of each operation is represented in a linear form. Minimizing the number of active S-boxes in the objective function, the lower bound for the active S-boxes is derived. In the search using SAT, binary variables are assigned to the input and output of each operation, and the differential propagation of each operation is represented in CNF. By adding a CNF to minimize the number of active S-boxes, the SAT problem is repeatedly solved to derive the lower bound for the active S-boxes. In this paper, we adopt the SAT method.

3 Our Targets

We explain the encryption phase and the finalization phase, as the other phases are not involved in our evaluation.

3.1 AEGIS Family

A family of AEGIS, including AEGIS-128/128L/256, consists of four phases: initialization, processing the authenticated data, encryption, and finalization [23].

AEGIS-128. The input of the round function $R(S, X_r)$ consists of the state S and one block (X_r). The round function of AEGIS-128 is given as follows:

$$S'[0] = A(S[4], S[0] \oplus X_r), \quad S'[1] = A(S[0], S[1]), \quad S'[2] = A(S[1], S[2]),$$
$$S'[3] = A(S[2], S[3]), \quad S'[4] = A(S[3], S[4]).$$

Let A be one AES round function, $A(X, K)$ are defined as follows:

$$A(X, K) = (\text{MixColumns} \circ \text{ShiftRows} \circ \text{SubBytes}(X)) \oplus K.$$

Encryption Phase. Let $msglen$ be the length of plaintext in bits, and the number of 128-bit plaintext blocks v is expressed as $v = \lceil \frac{msglen}{128} \rceil$. Let P_i and C_i ($0 \leq i \leq v-1$) be the 128-bit plaintext/ciphertext block, respectively. The data X_r inserted in r rounds is expressed as $X_r = P_r$. The ciphertext C_i is expressed as follows:

$$C_i = P_i \oplus S[1] \oplus S[4] \oplus (S[2] \& S[3]), \qquad (0 \leq i \leq v-1).$$

In the encryption phase, $v-1$ iterations of the round function are applied to the state S, and the ciphertext block C_i is generated.

Finalization Phase. Let $adlen$ be the length of the associated data, tmp is expressed as $tmp = S[3] \oplus (adlen || msglen)$, where $adlen$ and $msglen$ are expressed as 64-bit integers. In the finalization phase, 6 iterations of the round function $R(S, tmp)$ are applied to the state S. After 6 iterations of the round function, the 128-bit tag T is generated as follows:

$$T = S[0] \oplus S[1] \oplus S[2] \oplus S[3] \oplus S[4].$$

AEGIS-128L. The input of the round function $R(S, X_{r,a}, X_{r,b})$ consists of the state S and two blocks $(X_{r,a}, X_{r,b})$. The round function of AEGIS-128L is given as follows:

$$S'[0] = A(S[7], S[0] \oplus X_{r,a}), \quad S'[1] = A(S[0], S[1]),$$
$$S'[2] = A(S[1], S[2]), \quad S'[3] = A(S[2], S[3]),$$
$$S'[4] = A(S[3], S[4] \oplus X_{r,b}), \quad S'[5] = A(S[4], S[5]),$$
$$S'[6] = A(S[5], S[6]), \quad S'[7] = A(S[6], S[7]).$$

Encryption Phase. Let $msglen$ be the length of plaintext in bits, the number of 256-bit plaintext blocks v is expressed as $v = \lceil \frac{msglen}{256} \rceil$. Let $P_i = P_i^0 || P_i^1$ and $C_i = C_i^0 || C_i^1 (0 \leq i \leq v-1)$ be the 256-bit plaintext/ciphertext block, respectively. The data $X_r = X_{r,a} || X_{r,b}$ inserted in r rounds is expressed as $X_{r,a} = P_i^0, X_{r,b} = P_i^1$. The ciphertext C_i is expressed as follows:

$$C_i^0 = P_i^0 \oplus S[1] \oplus S[6] \oplus (S[2] \& S[3]),$$
$$C_i^1 = P_i^1 \oplus S[2] \oplus S[5] \oplus (S[6] \& S[7]), \qquad (0 \leq i \leq v-1).$$

In the encryption phase, $v-1$ iterations of the round function are applied to the state S, and the ciphertext block C_i is generated.

Finalization Phase. Let $adlen$ be the length of the associated data, tmp is expressed as $tmp = S[2] \oplus (adlen || msglen)$, where $adlen$ and $msglen$ are expressed as 64-bit integers. In the finalization phase, 6 iterations of the round function $R(S, tmp, tmp)$ are applied to the state S. After 6 iterations of the round function, the 128-bit tag T is generated as follows:

$$T = S[0] \oplus S[1] \oplus S[2] \oplus S[3] \oplus S[4] \oplus S[5] \oplus S[6] \oplus S[7].$$

In the finalization phase of RFC's Draft [5], 7 iterations of the round function are applied to the state S. If the tag size is 128 bits, the tag is generated using the same method as described in the proposed paper. Otherwise, if the tag size is 256 bits, the tag T is generated as follows:

$$T = S[0] \oplus S[1] \oplus S[2] \oplus S[3] \; || \; S[4] \oplus S[5] \oplus S[6] \oplus S[7].$$

AEGIS-256. The input of the round function $R(S, X_r)$ consists of the state S and one block (X_r). The round function of AEGIS-256 is given as follows:

$$S'[0] = A(S[5], S[0] \oplus X_r), \quad S'[1] = A(S[0], S[1]), \quad S'[2] = A(S[1], S[2]),$$
$$S'[3] = A(S[2], S[3]), \quad S'[4] = A(S[3], S[4]), \quad S'[5] = A(S[4], S[5]).$$

Encryption Phase. Let $msglen$ be the length of plaintext in bits, and the number of 128-bit plaintext blocks v is expressed as $v = \lceil \frac{msglen}{128} \rceil$. Let P_i and C_i $(0 \leq i \leq v-1)$ be the 128-bit plaintext/ciphertext block, respectively. The data X_r inserted in r rounds is expressed as $X_r = P_r$. The ciphertext C_i is expressed as follows:

$$C_i = P_i \oplus S[1] \oplus S[4] \oplus S[5] \oplus (S[2] \& S[3]), \qquad (0 \leq i \leq v-1).$$

In the encryption phase, $v-1$ iterations of the round function are applied to the state S, and the ciphertext block C_i is generated.

Finalization Phase. Let $adlen$ be the length of the associated data, tmp is expressed as $tmp = S[3] \oplus (adlen || msglen)$, where $adlen$ and $msglen$ are expressed as 64-bit integers. In the finalization phase, 6 iterations of the round function $R(S, tmp)$ are applied to the state S. After 6 iterations of the round function, the 128-bit tag T is generated as follows:

$$T = S[0] \oplus S[1] \oplus S[2] \oplus S[3] \oplus S[4] \oplus S[5].$$

3.2 Tiaoxin-346

Tiaoxin-346 consists of four phases: initialization, processing associated data, encryption, and finalization/tag production [15]. The input of the round function $R(T_3, T_4, T_6, X_{r,0}, X_{r,1}, X_{r,2})$ consists of the state (T_3, T_4, T_6) and three blocks $(X_{r,0}, X_{r,1}, X_{r,2})$. The round function of Tiaoxin-346 is given as follows:

$T'_3[0] = A(T_3[2], T_3[0]) \oplus X_{r,0}, \quad T'_3[1] = A(T_3[0], \text{const}_a), \quad T'_3[2] = T_3[1],$
$T'_4[0] = A(T_4[3], T_4[0]) \oplus X_{r,1}, \quad T'_4[1] = A(T_4[0], \text{const}_a), \quad T'_4[2] = T_4[1],$
$T'_4[3] = T_4[2], \quad T'_6[0] = A(T_6[5], T_6[0]) \oplus X_{r,2},$
$T'_6[1] = A(T_6[0], \text{const}_a), \quad T'_6[2] = T_6[1], \quad T'_6[3] = T_6[2],$
$T'_6[4] = T_6[3], \quad T'_6[5] = T_6[4].$

Encryption Phase. Let $msglen$ be the length of plaintext in bits, and the number of 256-bit plaintext blocks v is expressed as $v = \lceil \frac{msglen}{256} \rceil$. Let $P_i = P_i^0 \| P_i^1$ and $C_i = C_i^0 \| C_i^1$ ($0 \leq i \leq v-1$) be the 256-bit plaintext/ciphertext block, respectively. The data X_r inserted in r rounds is expressed as $X_{r,0} = P_i^0, X_{r,1} = P_i^1, X_{r,2} = P_i^0 \oplus P_i^1$. The ciphertext C_i is expressed as follows:

$C_i^0 = T_3[0] \oplus T_3[2] \oplus T_4[1] \oplus (T_6[3] \& T_4[3]),$
$C_i^1 = T_6[0] \oplus T_4[2] \oplus T_3[1] \oplus (T_6[5] \& T_3[2]), \qquad (0 \leq i \leq v-1).$

In the encryption phase, $v-1$ iterations of the round function are applied to the state S, and the ciphertext block C_i is generated.

Finalization Phase. Let $adlen$ be the length of the associated data, 1 iteration of the round function $R(T_3, T_4, T_6, adlen, msglen, adlen \oplus msglen)$ is applied to the state S. Then, 20 iterations of the round function $R(T_3, T_4, T_6, \text{const}_b, \text{const}_a, \text{const}_b)$ are applied to the state S. After 20 iterations of the round function, the 128-bit tag T is generated as follows:

$$T = T_3[0] \oplus T_3[1] \oplus T_3[2] \oplus T_4[0] \oplus T_4[1] \oplus T_4[2] \oplus T_4[3]$$
$$\oplus T_6[0] \oplus T_6[1] \oplus T_6[2] \oplus T_6[3] \oplus T_6[4] \oplus T_6[5].$$

3.3 Rocca

Rocca consists of four phases: initialization, processing the associated data, encryption, and finalization [16,17]. The input of the round function $R(S, X_{r,a}, X_{r,b})$ consists of the state S and two blocks $(X_{r,a}, X_{r,b})$. The round function of Rocca is given as follows:

$S'[0] = S[7] \oplus X_{r,a}, \quad S'[1] = A(S[0], S[7]), \quad S'[2] = S[1] \oplus S[6],$
$S'[3] = A(S[2], S[1]), \quad S'[4] = S[3] \oplus X_{r,b}, \quad S'[5] = A(S[4], S[3]),$
$S'[6] = A(S[5], S[4]), \quad S'[7] = S[0] \oplus S[6].$

Encryption Phase. Let $msglen$ be the length of plaintext in bits, and the number of 256-bit plaintext blocks v is expressed as $v = \lceil \frac{msglen}{256} \rceil$. Let $P_i = P_i^0 \| P_i^1$ and $C_i = C_i^0 \| C_i^1$ ($0 \leq i \leq v-1$) be the 256-bit plaintext/ciphertext block, respectively. The data X_r inserted in r rounds is expressed as $X_{r,a} = P_i^0, X_{r,b} = P_i^1$. The ciphertext C_i is expressed as follows:

$$C_i^0 = A(S[1], S[5]) \oplus P_i^0,$$
$$C_i^1 = A(S[0] \oplus S[4], S[2]) \oplus P_i^1, \qquad (0 \leq i \leq v-1).$$

In the encryption phase, $v-1$ iterations of the round function are applied to the state S, and the ciphertext block C_i is generated.

Finalization Phase. Let $adlen$ be the length of the associated data, 20 iterations of the round function $R(S, adlen, msglen)$ are applied to the state S. After 20 iterations of the round function, the 128-bit tag T is generated as follows:

$$T = S[0] \oplus S[1] \oplus S[2] \oplus S[3] \oplus S[4] \oplus S[5] \oplus S[6] \oplus S[7].$$

3.4 Rocca-S

Rocca-S consists of four phases: initialization, processing the associated data, encryption, and finalization [2]. The input of the round function $R(S, X_{r,a}, X_{r,b})$ consists of the state S and two blocks $(X_{r,a}, X_{r,b})$. The round function of Rocca-S is given as follows:

$$S'[0] = S[6] \oplus S[1], \quad S'[1] = A(S[0], X_{r,a}), \quad S'[6] = A(S[1], S[0]),$$
$$S'[3] = A(S[2], S[6]), \quad S'[6] = A(S[3], X_{r,b}), \quad S'[5] = A(S[4], S[3]),$$
$$S'[6] = A(S[5], S[4]).$$

Encryption Phase. Let $msglen$ be the length of plaintext in bits, the number of 256-bit plaintext blocks v is expressed as $v = \lceil \frac{msglen}{256} \rceil$. Let $P_i = P_i^0 \| P_i^1$ and $C_i = C_i^0 \| C_i^1$ ($0 \leq i \leq v-1$) be the 256-bit plaintext/ciphertext block, respectively. The data X_r inserted in r rounds is expressed as $X_{r,a} = P_i^0, X_{r,b} = P_i^1$. The ciphertext C_i is expressed as follows:

$$C_i^0 = A(S[3] \oplus S[5], S[0]) \oplus P_i^0,$$
$$C_i^1 = A(S[4] \oplus S[6], S[2]) \oplus P_i^1, \qquad (0 \leq i \leq v-1).$$

In the encryption phase, $v-1$ iterations of the round function are applied to the state S, and the ciphertext block C_i is generated.

Finalization Phase. Let $adlen$ be the length of the associated data, 16 iterations of the round function $R(S, adlen, msglen)$ are applied to the state S. After 16 iterations of the round function, the 256-bit tag T is generated as follows:

$$T = S[0] \oplus S[1] \oplus S[2] \oplus S[3] \;\|\; S[4] \oplus S[5] \oplus S[6].$$

4 Methods of SAT-Aided Security Evaluations

In this section, we recall the pure SAT-based method to evaluate differential characteristics shown in Sun et al.'s work [20,21]. Then, we explain the tag- and state-collision-based forgery attacks.

4.1 Security Evaluation of SAT

The Boolean satisfiability problem (SAT) is the problem of determining whether there exists an evaluation for the binary variables such that the value of the given Boolean formula equals one. The SAT is formulated with Boolean variables, the operators AND($\land$), OR($\lor$), NOT($\neg$), and parentheses. Every Boolean formula can be converted into an equivalent formula that is in conjunctive normal form (CNF), which is a propositional formula of the form $\bigwedge_{i=0}^{n} \bigvee_{j=0}^{m_i} C_{ij}$, where each $C_{ij} (0 \leq i \leq n, 0 \leq j \leq m_i)$ is either an atomic formula, i.e., a variable or constant, or the negation of an atomic formula, and each disjunction $\bigvee_{j=0}^{m_i} C_{ij}$ is called a clause. In this study, we generate CNF using PySAT [10] and derive solutions using the parkissat-rs [24] and mallob-kicaliglu [18, 19] solvers.

4.2 SAT-Based Automatic Search for Differential Characteristics

Since our targets are constructed by an S-box, matrix, and XOR operations, it is sufficient to describe these modeling methods. Note that the modeling of a matrix can be implemented by an XOR operation as a matrix is decomposed by multiple XOR operations.

- **XOR.** For a bit-wise XOR operation, s.t., $\alpha \oplus \beta = \gamma$. Differential propagation is valid over XOR if the following clauses hold

$$\left. \begin{array}{l} \alpha \lor \beta \lor \overline{\gamma} = 1, \ \alpha \lor \overline{\beta} \lor \gamma = 1, \\ \overline{\alpha} \lor \beta \lor \gamma = 1, \ \overline{\alpha} \lor \overline{\beta} \lor \overline{\gamma} = 1. \end{array} \right\}$$

- **S-box.** Let $\boldsymbol{a} = (a_0, a_1, \ldots, a_{i-1})$, $\boldsymbol{b} = (b_0, b_1, \ldots, b_{i-1})$, and $\boldsymbol{p} = \sum_{i=0}^{j-1} p_i$ be the input and output differences of an i-bit S-box and boolean variables expressing the weight in an S-box where j is the maximum weight of the differential propagation, respectively. To express the differential propagation and its weight in an S-box, we construct the following Boolean formula:

$$f(\boldsymbol{a}, \boldsymbol{b}, \boldsymbol{p}) = \begin{cases} 1 & \text{if } \Pr(\boldsymbol{a} \to \boldsymbol{b}) = 2^{-p}, \\ 0 & \text{otherwise}. \end{cases}$$

A set A, which contains all the vectors satisfying $f(\boldsymbol{x}, \boldsymbol{y}, \boldsymbol{z}) = 0$, is expressed as follows:

$$A = \{(\boldsymbol{x}, \boldsymbol{y}, \boldsymbol{z}) \in \mathbb{F}_2^{2i+j} \mid f(\boldsymbol{x}, \boldsymbol{y}, \boldsymbol{z}) = 0\},$$

where $\boldsymbol{x} = (x_0, x_1, \ldots, x_{i-1})$, $\boldsymbol{y} = (y_0, y_1, \ldots, y_{i-1})$, and $\boldsymbol{z} = (z_0, z_1, \ldots, z_{j-1})$. We need to exclude the propagation expressed A because it is equivalent to a set of invalid propagation patterns as follows:

$$\bigvee_{c=0}^{i-1}(a_c \oplus x_c) \vee \bigvee_{d=0}^{i-1}(b_d \oplus y_d) \vee \bigvee_{e=0}^{j-1}(p_e \oplus z_e) = 1, \ (\boldsymbol{x}, \boldsymbol{y}, \boldsymbol{z}) \in A. \qquad (3)$$

These clauses exactly extract the differential propagation with the corresponding weight in an i-bit S-box. We can convert Eq. (3) to

$$g(\boldsymbol{a},\boldsymbol{b},\boldsymbol{p}) = \bigwedge_{(\boldsymbol{x},\boldsymbol{y},\boldsymbol{z}) \in \mathbb{F}_2^{2i+j}} \left(f(\boldsymbol{x},\boldsymbol{y},\boldsymbol{z}) \vee \bigvee_{c=0}^{i-1}(a_c \oplus x_c) \vee \bigvee_{d=0}^{i-1}(b_d \oplus y_d) \vee \bigvee_{e=0}^{j-1}(p_e \oplus z_e) \right).$$

This equation is called the *product-of-sum* of g. We can reduce the number of clauses in g by several tools, such as Espresso logic minimizer[1]. For the modeling of an S-box to count the number of S-boxes, we simply replace $\boldsymbol{p}$ to a, expressing whether an S-box is active.

- **Boolean cardinality constraints.** Lastly, we need to give an objective function to search the lower bounds for the number of Active S-boxes/the exact differential characteristics probability. Such a function can be implemented by Boolean cardinality constraints. In SAT, it is necessary to model the problem of searching the lower bounds for the number of Active S-boxes/the exact differential characteristics probability, and we utilize Boolean cardinality constraints. Boolean cardinality constraints put numerical restrictions on the number of propositional variables that are allowed to be true at the same time. The following constitute a typical construct of the Boolean cardinality constraints,

$$\sum_{i=1}^{n} x_i \le k,$$

where $(x_1, ..., x_n)$ are Boolean variables (0 or 1), and k define the maximum number of variables. In searching for the lower bounds for the number of Active S-boxes and the exact differential characteristics probability, the variable x_i corresponds to the binary variable $a/\boldsymbol{p}$ as previously described in the context of S-box modeling for AS/DCP. We utilized the better encoding method proposed by Bailleux et al. [3], which is implemented in the CardEnc module from the PySAT for Boolean cardinality constraints.

4.3 Our Analysis of Forgery Attacks

We consider two types of approaches for forgery attacks. In the following, we explain details of our evaluations.

State Collision. The first one exploits state collisions in which the adversary inserts differences into a plaintext, causing state collisions during the encryption phase, as shown in Fig. 1. This approach is the same as existing work [22] and designer's evaluations [2,15,17,23].

In this setting, using the modeling explained in Sect. 4.2, we estimate the lower bounds for the number of active S-boxes by considering the bit-level behaviors of differentials during the search. Additionally, by exploiting the properties

---

[1] https://ptolemy.berkeley.edu/projects/embedded/pubs/downloads/espresso/index.htm.

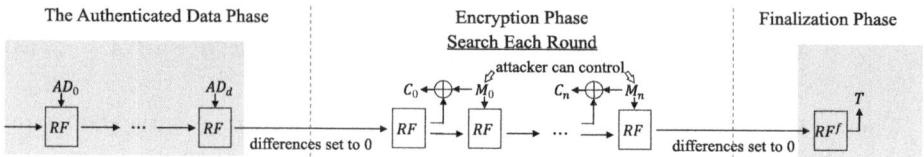

Fig. 1. Overview of forgery attacks based on state collisions.

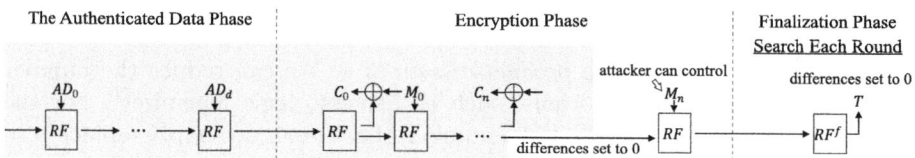

Fig. 2. Overview of forgery attacks based on tag collisions.

of the differential distribution table of the S-box, we find optimal differential characteristic probabilities instead of the upper bounds.

Tag Collision. The second approach exploits tag collisions in which the adversary inserts differences into a plaintext in the last round of the encryption phase so that a state collision occurs in the finalization phase, as shown in Fig. 2. This approach has not been explored in existing work.

In this setting, we also aim to estimate the lower bounds for the number of active S-boxes and, furthermore, derive optimal differential characteristic probabilities, leading to tag collisions.

Table 3. The differential characteristics probability for forgery attacks based on state collisions in the encryption phase (lower bounds for the number of active S-boxes) $[-\log_2]$.

Target	Tag Size (bits)	4R	5R	6R	7R	8R	9R	10R	Reference
AEGIS-128	128 bits			156 (26)	156 (26)	156 (26)	156 (26)	156 (26)	[23]
		–	–	336 (56)	336 (56)	336 (56)	336 (56)	336 (56)	Section 5.1
AEGIS-128L	128/256 bits		150 (25)	150 (25)	150 (25)	150 (25)	150 (25)	150 (25)	[23]
		–	210 (35)	210 (35)	210 (35)	210 (35)	210 (35)	210 (35)	Section 5.1
		–	216	216	216	216	216	216	Section 5.2
AEGIS-256	128 bits	156(26)	156(26)	156(26)	156(26)	156(26)	156(26)	156(26)	[23]
		–	–	–	420 (70)	420 (70)	420 (70)	420 (70)	Section 5.1
Tiaoxin-346	128 bits				180 (30)	180 (30)	180 (30)	180 (30)	[15]
		–	–	–	180 (30)	180 (30)	180 (30)	180 (30)	Section 5.1
					180	180	180	180	Section 5.2
Rocca	128 bits	144 (24)	144 (24)	144 (24)	144 (24)	144 (24)	144 (24)	144 (24)	[17]
		216 (36)	150 (25)	150 (25)	150 (25)	144 (24)	144 (24)	144 (24)	[22]
		234 (39)	216 (36)	180 (30)	150 (25)	150 (25)	150 (25)	150 (25)	Section 5.1
					150	150	150	150	Section 5.2
Rocca-S	256 bits	276 (46)	276 (46)	276 (46)	276 (46)	276 (46)	276 (46)	276 (46)	[2]
		300 (50)	276 (46)	276 (46)	276 (46)	276 (46)	276 (46)	276 (46)	Section 5.1

5 Results of Forgery Attacks Based on State Collisions

In this section, we show results of bit-level analysis for forgery attacks based on state collisions with a comparison to existing results. In Sect. 5.1, we estimate the minimum number of active S-boxes by considering bit-level transitions of differential characteristics to exclude invalid characteristics of byte-wise searches. In Sect. 5.2, we incorporate differential distribution tables of S-boxes for AEGIS-128L, Tiaoxin-346, and Rocca. Due to computational complexity issues, it was not feasible to obtain these results for AEGIS-128/256 and Rocca-S.

5.1 Lower Bounds for the Number of Active S-Boxes

Table 3 shows the lower bounds for the number of active S-boxes, considering bit-wise differential transitions, while existing work focuses on byte-wise truncated characteristics. By using the maximum differential probability of the S-box, namely 2^{-6} as the differential probability of each active S-box, we estimate the upper bounds of the differential characteristic probabilities.

AEGIS-128/128L/256. For the encryption phase of AEGIS-128, AEGIS-128L, and AEGIS-256, we identify differential characteristics that lead to state collisions after 6, 5, and 7 rounds, respectively. As a result, we significantly improve the upper bounds compared to the results provided by the designers. Our findings suggest that AEGIS-128 and AEGIS-256 could claim 256-bit forgery security by differential attacks, provided they support a 256-bit tag.

Tiaoxin-346. For the encryption phase of Tiaoxin-346, we identify differential characteristics that lead to state collisions after 7 rounds. According to Table 1, our evaluation is the same as the byte-wise evaluation by the designer [15]. Thus, unlike AEGIS-128 and AEGIS-256, our results show that Tiaoxin-346 cannot claim 256-bit forgery security, even if supporting a 256-bit tag.

Rocca. For the encryption phase of Rocca, we identify differential characteristics that lead to state collisions after 4 rounds. According to Table 1, our results improve the bounds by a byte-wise evaluation [17]. Our results also show that Rocca cannot claim 256-bit forgery security, even if supporting a 256-bit tag.

Rocca-S. For the encryption phase of Rocca-S, we identify differential characteristics that lead to state collisions after 4 rounds. According to Table 1, our evaluation matches with the byte-wise evaluation by the designer [2].

5.2 Exact Differential Characteristics Probability

Table 3 also shows the exact bounds of differential characteristic probabilities for AEGIS-128L, Tiaoxin-346, and Rocca by exploiting the properties of the differential distribution table of the S-box, namely properly choosing the probability of 2^{-6} or 2^{-7} in each S-box.

Table 4. The differential characteristics probability for forgery attacks based on tag collisions in the finalization phase (lower bounds for the number of active S-boxes) $[-\log_2]$.

Target	Tag Size	1R	2R	3R	4R	5R	6R	Reference
AEGIS-128	128 bits	48 (8)	114 (19)	144 (24)	210 (35)	288 (48)	348 (58)	Section 6.1
		52	125	158	–	–	–	Section 6.2
AEGIS-128L	128/256 bits	12 (2)	72 (12)	144 (24)	210 (35)	288 (48)	360 (60)	Section 6.1
		12	72	158	–	–	–	Section 6.2
AEGIS-256	128 bits	48 (8)	114 (19)	144 (24)	210 (35)	288 (48)	360 (60)	Section 6.1
		52	125	158	–	–	–	Section 6.2
Tiaoxin-346	128 bits	12 (2)	24 (4)	36 (6)	198 (33)	258 (43)	300 (50)	Section 6.1
		12	24	36	203 or more	–	–	Section 6.2
Rocca	128 bits	12 (2)	12 (2)	114 (19)	114 (19)	186 (31)	354 (59)	Section 6.1
		12	12	125	125	190	–	Section 6.2
Rocca-S	256 bits	48 (8)	114 (19)	186 (31)	210 (35)	450 (75)	–	Section 6.1
		52	125	198	214	437 or more	–	Section 6.2

AEGIS-128L. For the encryption phase of AEGIS-128L, we find optimal differential characteristics for forgery attacks after 5 rounds. Our results reveal that forgery attacks are possible with a time complexity of 2^{216}. The differential characteristic for the 5-round forgery attack is shown in Fig. 3.

Tiaoxin-346. For the encryption phase of Tiaoxin-346, we find optimal differential characteristics for forgery attacks after 7 rounds. Our results reveal that forgery attacks are possible with a time complexity of 2^{180}.

Rocca. For the encryption phase of Rocca, we find optimal differential characteristics for forgery attacks after 7 rounds. Our results reveal that forgery attacks are possible with a time complexity of 2^{150}. The differential characteristic for the 7-round forgery attack is shown in Fig. 4.

6 Results of Forgery Attacks Based on Tag Collisions

In this section, we show the results of a bit-level search for forgery attacks exploiting tag collisions. In Sect. 6.1, we estimate the minimum number of active S-boxes by considering bit-level transitions of differential characteristics, which lead to tag collisions. In Sect. 6.2, we utilize differential distribution tables of S-boxes to accurately derive the exact probabilities of differential characteristics for tag collisions.

6.1 Lower Bounds for the Number of Active S-Boxes

Table 4 shows the lower bounds for the number of active S-boxes, which lead to tag collisions. These can be converted into the upper bounds for the differential characteristics probability for each round.

AEGIS-128/128L/256. As the tag length of AEGIS-128/128L/256 is 128/128 or 256/128 bit [23], the lower bounds for the number of active S-boxes should be 22/22 or 43/22 or more in the finalization phase, respectively. According to Table 4, for the finalization phase of AEGIS-128/128L/256, the estimated number of rounds required to be secure against forgery attacks based on tag collisions is estimated as 3/5/3 rounds, respectively.

Tiaoxin-346. As the tag length of Tiaoxin-346 is 128 bits [15], the lower bounds for the number of active S-boxes should be 22 or more in the finalization phase. According to Table 4, for the finalization phase of Tiaoxin-346, the estimated number of rounds required to be secure against forgery attacks based on tag collisions is estimated as 4 rounds.

Rocca. As the tag length of Rocca is 128 bits [16,17], the lower bounds for the number of active S-boxes should be 22 or more in the finalization phase. According to Table 4, for the finalization phase of Rocca, the estimated number of rounds required to be secure against forgery attacks based on tag collisions is estimated as 5 rounds.

Rocca-S. As the tag length of Rocca-S is 256 bits [2], the lower bounds for the number of active S-boxes should be 43 or more in the finalization phase. According to Table 4, for the finalization phase of Rocca-S, the estimated number of rounds required to be secure against forgery attacks based on tag collisions is estimated as 5 rounds.

6.2 Exact Differential Characteristics Probability

Table 4 shows the exact differential characteristics probability for forgery attacks based on tag collisions for each round.

AEGIS-128/128L/256. For the finalization phase of AEGIS-128/128L/256, we find optimal differential characteristics up to 3/3/3 rounds, respectively. For AEGIS-128/128L/256, forgery attacks based on tag collisions are feasible with 2/2/2 rounds, respectively. The optimal differential characteristic for the 2 rounds of tag collisions is shown in Fig. 5.

Tiaoxin-346. For the finalization phase of Tiaoxin-346, we find optimal differential characteristics up to 3 rounds. For Tiaoxin-346, a forgery attack based on tag collisions is feasible with 3 rounds.

Rocca. According to Table 4, for the finalization phase of Rocca, we find optimal differential characteristics up to 5 rounds. For Rocca, a forgery attack based on tag collisions is feasible with 4 rounds.

Rocca-S. According to Table 4, for the finalization phase of Rocca-S, we find optimal differential characteristics up to 4 rounds. For Rocca-S, the maximum number of rounds that can be attacked in forgery attacks based on tag collisions is 4 rounds.

7 Conclusion

In this paper, we conducted a bit-wise evaluation of the AEGIS family, Tiaoxin-346, Rocca, and Rocca-S, against forgery attacks based on state collision and tag collision. We utilized the Boolean satisfiability problem (SAT) tools to obtain exact lower bounds for the number of active S-boxes. Moreover, we derived the optimal differential characteristics in both the encryption phase and the finalization phase. As a result, we obtained the lower bounds for the number of active S-boxes in certain rounds for each target and derived the probability of optimal differential characteristics for the first time.

Acknowledgments. This research was in part conducted under a contract of "Research and development on new generation cryptography for secure wireless communication services" among "Research and Development for Expansion of Radio Wave Resources (JPJ000254)", which was supported by the Ministry of Internal Affairs and Communications, Japan. This work was also supported by JSPS KAKENHI Grant Number JP24H00696.

A Details of Differential Characteristics for Forgery Attacks

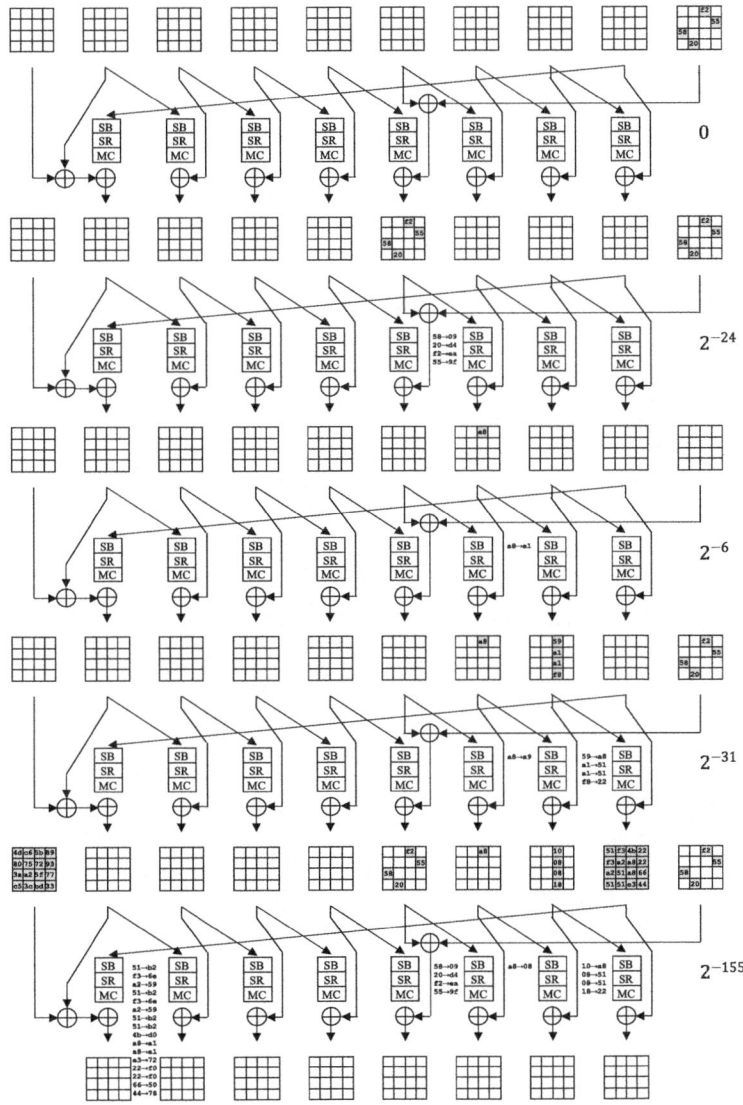

Fig. 3. Optimal differential characteristic for 5-rounds of AEGIS-128L for the forgery attack based on a state collision.

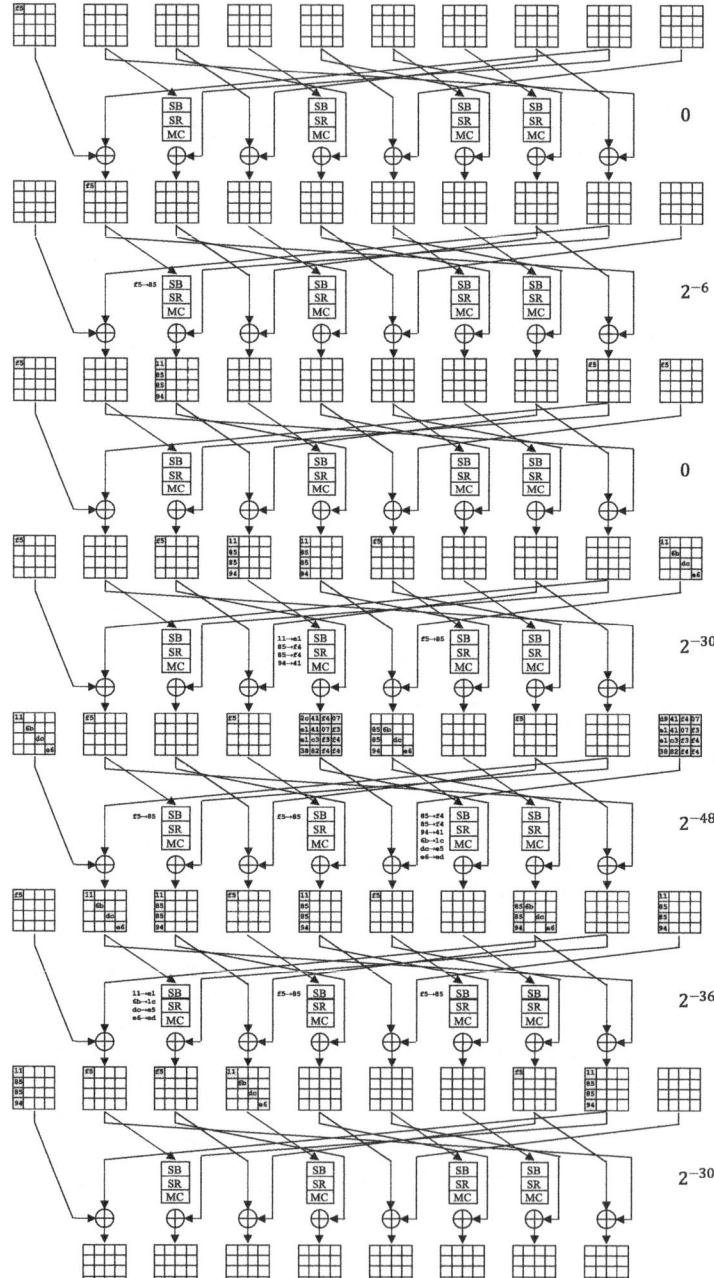

Fig. 4. Optimal differential characteristic for 7-rounds of Rocca for the forgery attack based on a state collision.

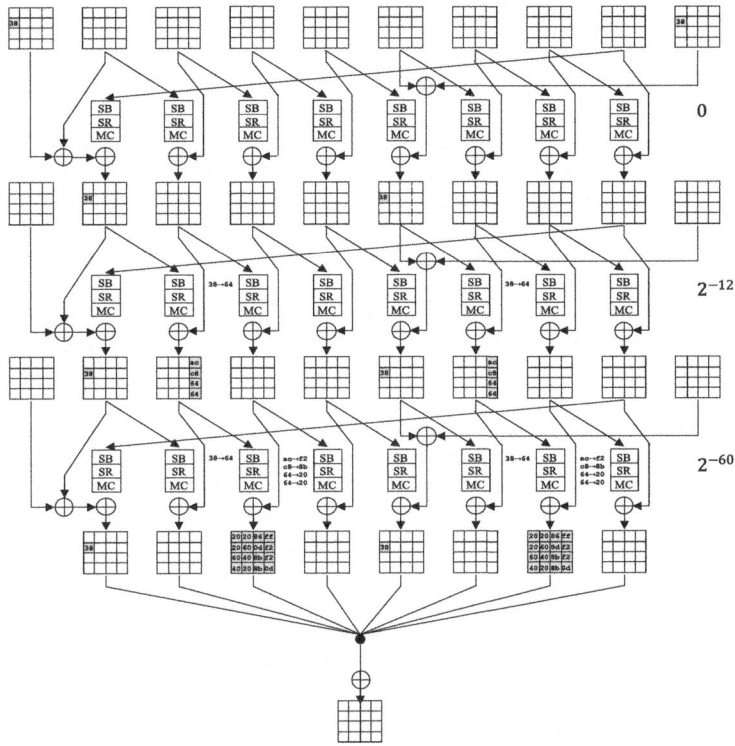

Fig. 5. Optimal differential characteristic for 2-rounds for forgery attack based on tag collision of AEGIS-128L.

References

1. CAESAR: Competition for Authenticated Encryption: Security, Applicability, and Robustness (2018). https://competitions.cr.yp.to/caesar.html
2. Anand, R., et al.: An ultra-high throughput AES-based authenticated encryption scheme for 6G: design and implementation. In: Tsudik, G., Conti, M., Liang, K., Smaragdakis, G. (eds.) ESORICS 2023. LNCS, vol. 14344, pp. 229–248. Springer, Cham (2023). https://doi.org/10.1007/978-3-031-50594-2_12
3. Bailleux, O., Boufkhad, Y.: Efficient CNF encoding of Boolean cardinality constraints. In: Rossi, F. (ed.) CP 2003. LNCS, vol. 2833, pp. 108–122. Springer, Heidelberg (2003). https://doi.org/10.1007/978-3-540-45193-8_8
4. Intel Corporation: Intel® Intrinsics Guide (2024). https://software.intel.com/sites/landingpage/IntrinsicsGuide/. Accessed 03 July 2024
5. Denis, F., Lucas, S.: The AEGIS Family of Authenticated Encryption Algorithms. Internet-Draft draft-irtf-cfrg-aegis-aead-10, Internet Engineering Task Force (2024). Work in Progress
6. Derbez, P., Fouque, P., Isobe, T., Rahman, M., Schrottenloher, A.: Key committing attacks against AES-based AEAD schemes. IACR Trans. Symmetric Cryptol. **2024**(1), 135–157 (2024)

7. Eichlseder, M., Nageler, M., Primas, R.: Analyzing the linear keystream biases in AEGIS. IACR Trans. Symmetric Cryptol. **2019**(4), 348–368 (2019)
8. Gueron, S.: Intel Advanced Encryption Standard (AES) New Instructions Set (2010)
9. Hosoyamada, A., et al.: Cryptanalysis of Rocca and feasibility of its security claim. IACR Trans. Symmetric Cryptol. **2022**(3), 123–151 (2022)
10. Ignatiev, A., Morgado, A., Marques-Silva, J.: PySAT: a Python toolkit for prototyping with SAT oracles. In: Beyersdorff, O., Wintersteiger, C.M. (eds.) SAT 2018. LNCS, vol. 10929, pp. 428–437. Springer, Cham (2018). https://doi.org/10.1007/978-3-319-94144-8_26
11. Jean, J., Nikolić, I.: Efficient design strategies based on the AES round function. In: Peyrin, T. (ed.) FSE 2016. LNCS, vol. 9783, pp. 334–353. Springer, Heidelberg (2016). https://doi.org/10.1007/978-3-662-52993-5_17
12. Liu, F., Isobe, T., Meier, W., Sakamoto, K.: Weak keys in reduced AEGIS and tiaoxin. IACR Trans. Symmetric Cryptol. **2021**(2), 104–139 (2021)
13. Minaud, B.: Linear biases in AEGIS keystream. In: Joux, A., Youssef, A. (eds.) SAC 2014. LNCS, vol. 8781, pp. 290–305. Springer, Cham (2014). https://doi.org/10.1007/978-3-319-13051-4_18
14. Mouha, N., Wang, Q., Gu, D., Preneel, B.: Differential and linear cryptanalysis using mixed-integer linear programming. In: Wu, C.-K., Yung, M., Lin, D. (eds.) Inscrypt 2011. LNCS, vol. 7537, pp. 57–76. Springer, Heidelberg (2012). https://doi.org/10.1007/978-3-642-34704-7_5
15. Nikolic, I.: Tiaoxin-346. Submission to the CAESAR competition (2014)
16. Sakamoto, K., Liu, F., Nakano, Y., Kiyomoto, S., Isobe, T.: Rocca: an efficient AES-based encryption scheme for beyond 5G. IACR Trans. Symmetric Cryptol. **2021**(2), 1–30 (2021)
17. Sakamoto, K., Liu, F., Nakano, Y., Kiyomoto, S., Isobe, T.: Rocca: an efficient AES-based encryption scheme for beyond 5G (full version). IACR Cryptology ePrint Archive, p. 116 (2022)
18. Sanders, P., Schreiber, D.: Decentralized online scheduling of malleable NP-hard jobs. In: Cano, J., Trinder, P. (eds.) Euro-Par 2022. LNCS, vol. 13440, pp. 119–135. Springer, Cham (2022). https://doi.org/10.1007/978-3-031-12597-3_8
19. Schreiber, D., Sanders, P.: Scalable SAT solving in the cloud. In: Li, C.-M., Manyà, F. (eds.) SAT 2021. LNCS, vol. 12831, pp. 518–534. Springer, Cham (2021). https://doi.org/10.1007/978-3-030-80223-3_35
20. Sun, L., Wang, W., Wang, M.: More accurate differential properties of LED64 and Midori64. IACR Trans. Symmetric Cryptol. **2018**(3), 93–123 (2018)
21. Sun, L., Wang, W., Wang, M.: Accelerating the search of differential and linear characteristics with the SAT method. IACR Trans. Symmetric Cryptol. **2021**(1), 269–315 (2021)
22. Takeuchi, N., Sakamoto, K., Isobe, T.: On optimality of the round function of Rocca. IEICE Trans. Fundam. Electron. Commun. Comput. Sci. **106**(1), 45–53 (2023)
23. Wu, H., Preneel, B.: AEGIS: a fast authenticated encryption algorithm. In: Lange, T., Lauter, K., Lisoněk, P. (eds.) SAC 2013. LNCS, vol. 8282, pp. 185–201. Springer, Heidelberg (2014). https://doi.org/10.1007/978-3-662-43414-7_10
24. Zhang, X., Chen, Z., Cai, S.: ParKissat-RS (2022). https://github.com/songfu1983/ParKissat-RS

Cryptanalysis of Authenticated Encryption Modes for Wireless and Real-Time Systems

Alexander Bille and Elmar Tischhauser[(✉)]

Department of Mathematics and Computer Science, University of Marburg,
Marburg, Germany
{bille,tischhauser}@informatik.uni-marburg.de

Abstract. Authenticated encryption (AE) plays a central role in building secure channels for wireless systems, with well-established AE schemes such as CCM or GCM being widely used in security protocols for wireless networks based on IEEE 802.11 (Wi-Fi), IEEE 802.15.4 (such as Zigbee), as well as LTE and 5G mobile networks. Having been proposed as general-purpose AE schemes, they leave optimization potential for new algorithms specifically designed for wireless applications. In this paper, we analyze the security of three such AE algorithm families, namely PFX, PFC and IAR, which were designed to guarantee confidentiality and authenticity in a single-pass process while reducing the number of block cipher calls and avoiding expensive operations like finite field multiplications. As such, they were proposed as alternatives to CCM or GCM for wireless systems, lightweight wireless sensor networks, and real-time wireless applications.

In this paper, we describe universal forgery attacks on all three algorithm families, allowing an adversary to compute valid ciphertexts and authentication tags for any message of their choice without knowledge of the secret key. All attacks only have linear complexity in the length of the target message and as such are entirely practical, essentially as fast as the encryption itself. Our attacks imply that the affected schemes should not be used in practice, despite their attractive performance characteristics.

Keywords: Symmetric cryptography · authenticated encryption · cryptanalysis · universal forgery attacks · wireless network security

1 Introduction

1.1 Motivation and Background

Wireless and mobile networks have become integral components of modern communication systems, playing a central role in connecting individuals, devices, and applications. Since it is common for such networks to handle sensitive and private information, ensuring secure communication to protect transmitted data against unauthorized access is of great importance.

In order to achieve these security objectives, one usually uses authenticated encryption (AE) schemes, which provide both confidentiality and authenticity and integrity in one combined cryptographic primitive [4,24]. In many applications, e.g. secure software updates, healthcare IoT or smart grid management, data authentication is arguably even more important than confidentiality.

Authenticated encryption schemes can broadly be divided into two main categories: the generic composition [4] of an encryption scheme and a message authentication code (MAC), and dedicated constructions aimed at integrating both with more attractive performance or implementation characteristics. Many AE schemes are modes of operation for a block cipher, meaning they can be instantiated with any desired block cipher (for instance, the AES or GIFT [3]) as the underlying cryptographic primitive.

Authenticated encryption for wireless networks is implemented in the IEEE 802.11 (Wi-Fi) family of protocols. The WPA2 and WPA3 protocols employ CCM for confidentiality and integrity [15]. CCM, a mode of operation for block ciphers combining Counter (CTR) mode with CBC-MAC, requires two passes over the message and hence two block cipher calls per message block.

In the context of low-power and resource-constrained wireless sensor networks, the IEEE 802.15.4 standard, used in applications like Zigbee, also uses authenticated encryption in the form of CCM mode [16]. One main concern and design restriction in the context of wireless sensor networks is extending the operational lifespan of battery-powered devices.

In more recent wireless communication protocols such as Long-Term Evolution (LTE) and 5G networks as well as in WPA3, Galois/Counter Mode (GCM) [10,23] has gained prominence due to its parallelizable nature and efficiency for high-speed data transmission, both to secure user data and control plane signaling [11,15]. However, due to the use of large finite field multiplications in addition to block cipher calls, GCM is not particularly suited for resource-constrained environments.

Another particularly efficient scheme is the OCB mode [21,26,27], which is widely standardized [17,22] and in the final portfolio of the NIST-sponsored CAESAR competition [5]. It has the advantage of being a single-pass scheme, requiring only one block cipher call per message block and being completely parallelizable. Its patent status and large internal state however mean that OCB has not found as widespread use as one might expect. However, OCB has been considered in scenarios where minimizing overhead and achieving low-latency communication are critical, such as in real-time applications within mobile networks.

1.2 New AE Designs for Wireless and Real-Time Systems

Design constraints in wireless networks, including limited bandwidth, variable channel conditions, and power constraints, necessitate the careful selection of authenticated encryption schemes. The resulting trade-offs between security, computational efficiency, and energy consumption are central for the inclusion of these schemes in current and future wireless network protocols. As the landscape of wireless communication evolves with emerging technologies like the Internet of Things (IoT) and 6G, it remains an active research topic to improve upon existing authenticated encryption schemes to better meet these specific design constraints.

One particular need for resource-constrained platforms is to minimize the amount of state (e.g., the number of keys or tweaks derived from the master key and nonce) and auxiliary routines (such as finite field multiplication) beyond simple block cipher calls. It is also important to achieve secure AE within a single pass over the data and ideally with only one block cipher call per message block.

These requirements have led to the proposal of several new AE schemes specifically designed for use in wireless and real-time systems. In this paper, we consider the PFX, PFC and IAR families of AE algorithms. PFX [13] is a family of authenticated encryption modes designed to achieve single-pass AE with only $n+1$ block cipher calls for an n-block message. It relies on the idea of plaintext feedback and consists of three individual variants, plain PFX as the basic algorithm, and the two main new variants PFX-CTR and PFX-INC combining ideas from CTR mode and GCM and OCB, respectively. Its main application area are general-purpose wireless networks. The PFC [14] family of AE schemes follows similar design ideas as PFX, but is tailored towards more lightweight platforms such as wireless sensor networks and comes in two variants based on CTR and OCB mode. Finally, IAR [12] is family of two AE modes IAR-CTR and IAR-CFB developed for use in applications with real-time constraints. It caters for a maximum acceptable system delay by using multiple authentication tags.

All three families are designed to improve upon the state of the art in Wi-Fi security by providing superior performance characteristics compared to existing modes such as CCM or GCM. They are also accompanied by security proofs, meaning that they are designed to offer confidentiality and authenticity up to the standard birthday bound of $2^{n/2}$ provided the underlying n-bit block cipher is secure. They also have in common that they are based upon widely used and standardized secure building blocks such as the CTR, CFB and OCB modes of operation.

We finally note that all AE schemes discussed in this section depend on the uniqueness of a nonce for their security guarantees. The same holds for the standard AE schemes such as CCM, GCM, and OCB. All of our attacks respect this setting and never repeat nonces for queries with the same key.

1.3 Contributions

In this paper, we present universal forgery attacks on several authenticated encryption schemes proposed for wireless and real-time systems, in particular the PFX, PFC and IAR families of algorithms. These attacks allow the adversary to create valid ciphertexts and tags for any message of their choice without knowledge of the secret key in a chosen plaintext attack (CPA). We note that the CPA setting is the standard security model in symmetric cryptography, and all schemes attacked in this paper actually come with a security proof in this model. Our attacks hence also invalidate these proofs.

The basic attack strategy is to simulate the calls to block cipher encryptions with the fixed but unknown key by auxiliary chosen plaintext queries. The results from these queries can then be used by the attacker to compute ciphertext and tag for an arbitrary message, resulting in universal forgery attacks. The complexity of our attacks is also very low, namely linear in the length of the target message of the forgery. This means that the effort to universally forge a message for these schemes is basically equivalent to the effort of actually carrying out the authenticated encryption algorithm with knowledge of the secret key.

Altogether, our attacks imply that the affected schemes do not provide the claimed security guarantees and, despite their attractive performance characteristics, should not be used in practice.

Outline of the Paper. We first describe the three algorithm families analyzed in this paper in Sects. 2 to 4. Section 5 outlines the attack model and the general strategy for the universal forgery attacks, then presents our attacks on the PFX, PFC and IAR families of authenticated encryption schemes. Section 6 concludes. A detailed description of our notation can be found in Appendix A.1.

2 The PFX Family of Authenticated Encryption Schemes

The scheme PFX and its advanced modes PFX-CTR, PFX-INC and PFX-CBC are authenticated encryption (AE) protocols designed by Hwang and Gope [13]. Their goal was to perform encryption and authentication with only $n+1$ block encryption calls and in one natural single process (referred to as "authencryption"). The main idea of this family is the use of plaintext feedback as seen in Fig. 1. Each mode has two variants for certifying the integrity of the message. The first works with a so called indicator I which is a preshared value between sender and receiver. This indicator "may not be confidentia" [13] and therefore may be known to the adversary in an attack scenario. The second variant encrypts the last block with a second key K'. Since the basic version of PFX has some limitations compared to AE schemes such as CCM, its designers only recommend this mode for improved authenticity and integrity over conventional encryption-only modes such as CTR. For a full replacement of standard AE schemes, they propose three advanced modes building on PFX: PFX-CTR and PFX-CBC are a fusion of PFX with counter mode [6] and CBC mode [25], respectively, whereas PFX-INC is a fusion with schemes including a incrementing function. The authors mention to use the incremental interface of GCM, OCB, IAPM [19] or CWC [20] for their incremental function. Detailed algorithmic descriptions and illustrations for the encryption process of PFX, PFX-CTR and PFX-INC are provided in Algorithms 1 and 2 and Figs. 1, 3 and 4 in Sect. 5 for easier cross-reference with the attack procedures.

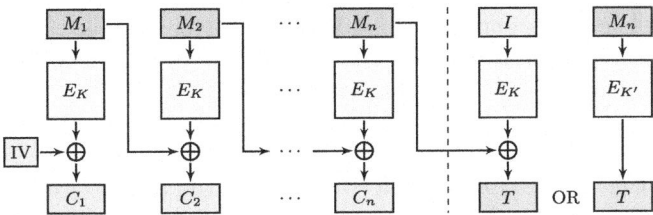

Fig. 1. The PFX authenticated encryption algorithm.

3 The PFC Family of Authenticated Encryption Algorithms

The modes PFC-CTR and PFC-OCB [14] are authenticated encryption schemes. Their motivation is to guarantee integrity and confidentiality with a small additional computation cost. Their schemes work with only $n + 2$ encryption block calls for an n-block message and no other expensive functions, aiming at resource-constrained platforms such as wireless sensor networks. The main idea consists of plaintext feedback, the truncation of block cipher outputs to some most significant bits and a double encryption for the tag. The scheme PFC-OCB is illustrated in Fig. 7 and is a fusion of the well-known OCB mode with the general framework of PFC. This variant follows the OCB standard quite closely, and as such is not affected by our analysis. When instantiated with a p-bit block cipher, the plaintext and ciphertext blocks are r bits long and the tag consists of ℓ bits with $r < \ell \leq p$. The tag is computed by a double encryption where the number of blocks (NOB) of the message is xored between the encryptions. The authors specifically propose the PFC schemes for use in the context of wireless sensor networks, Global Mobility Networks and cloud computing environments because of their attractive computational properties. Detailed algorithmic descriptions and illustrations for PFC-CTR are provided in Algorithm 3 and Fig. 5 in Sect. 5 alongside the corresponding attack procedures.

4 The IAR Family of Authenticated Encryption Schemes

The authenticated encryption modes IAR-CTR and IAR-CFB [12] have been developed for the use in real-time applications, in particular low-latency wireless real-time networks. As for the other families a major focus is the efficiency. Hence IAR-CTR and IAR-CFB use only $n + 2t$ and $n + t$ respectively many block cipher calls for an n-block message. Both modes are designed to cater for a system delay of t encryption blocks. This delay can be adjusted according to the time a message block is processed in a concrete application. The procedure of the IAR schemes can be separated in three parts, as illustrated in Fig. 2. The first part is t blocks long without the plaintext feedback. The input of the block cipher is not message dependent and could in principle be preprocessed. In the second part, the remaining message blocks are encrypted where the input is xored with the t previous (zero padded) plaintexts. The last part creates the t authentication tags. Note that the IAR family use a p-bit block cipher, message blocks of r bits and t many ℓ-bit tags with $r < \ell \leq p$.

The first proposed mode IAR-CTR has its focus on the use of a counter and double encryption for the tags, similar to the PFC family. The second mode IAR-CFB makes use of ciphertext feedback after the initial t ciphertext blocks, meaning a ciphertext block is concatenated to the last one shifted by r bits in a ciphertext feedback shift register (or in other words, the $p - r$ least significant bits are taken). For the first shift operation (during the computation of C_{t+1}), the last counter value from the first part is used instead. A detailed description and illustration of the encryption algorithm for IAR-CTR and IAR-CFB can be found in Algorithm 4 and Figs. 2 and 6 in Sect. 5 alongside the corresponding attack procedures.

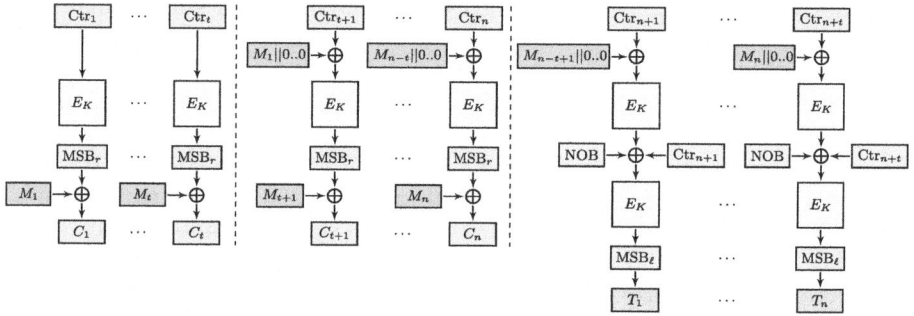

Fig. 2. The IAR-CTR authenticated encryption algorithm.

5 Attacks

In this section, we present several universal forgery attacks on the PFX, PFC and IAR families of authenticated encryption modes. All these attacks allow an adversary to produce valid ciphertexts and tags for an arbitrary message of their choice in a standard chosen plaintext attack setting. Their complexity is always at most linear in the length of the target message, which makes them completely practical, essentially as efficient as running the encryption algorithm itself on the same message.

5.1 Attack Model

We assume the adversary to be able to make chosen plaintext queries to the scheme with an unknown but fixed key K, which is the exact model used for the security proofs of PFX, PFC and IAR [12–14]. In detail, the rules for the adversary are the following: The adversary does not know the key(s). The adversary can make chosen plaintext queries by asking for the encryption of some messages of their choice. Extra parameters such as IV or nonce may be set by the adversary. To respect the design constraints of the modes, the adversary is not allowed to ask for messages with repeating values for an extra parameter, e.g. the adversary may not ask for two message encryptions with the same nonce. In the indicator version of the modes of the PFX family, we assume that the indicator is not known. When making requests, the correct but secret indicator is used for the encryption.

The goal is to build a valid ciphertext-tag pair $C_1, \ldots, C_n, T$ for an arbitrary message $M = M_1, \ldots, M_n$ of our choice out of these queries. When making auxiliary chosen plaintext queries, these auxiliary messages need to be different from M itself. Such a procedure constitutes a *universal forgery attack* on the authenticated encryption scheme, since the adversary is able to forge arbitrary messages of their choice without knowledge of the secret key.

5.2 General Strategy

Most of our forgery attacks are based on the general approach of simulating valid encryptions through carefully crafted auxiliary queries, which we summarize in the following observation:

Observation 1. *Obtaining a block cipher oracle $E_K(X)$ through one or more requests to the authenticated encryption mode is equivalent to being able to perform the encryption and authentication process without knowing the secret key K since the subsequent operations then depend only on values known to the adversary.*

The algorithm which implements such a block cipher oracle through auxiliary chosen plaintext queries to the scheme is referred to as a *gadget G* which has the property that $G(X) = E_K(X)$ without knowledge of the secret key K.

In some schemes, the outputs of the block cipher calls are immediately truncated to the most b significant bits. In these cases we create a gadget simulating the combined process. We mark this property in the superscript of the gadget, i.e. $G^b(X) = \text{MSB}_b(E_K(X))$.

5.3 Attack on PFX

We present a universal forgery attack on PFX in this section. Assume we want to forge the authenticated encryption $C_1, \ldots, C_n, T^*$ of the message $M = M_1, \ldots, M_n$ with initial value IV^*.

We use the strategy described in Observation 1. In the case of PFX, the inputs to the encryption query interface only consist of the IV and plaintext and, depending on the variant, the indicator. We create a gadget G_{PFX} simulating calls to the block cipher $E_K(\cdot)$ by auxiliary chosen plaintext queries to the PFX_K authenticated encryption scheme. To obtain $E_K(X)$ the gadget requests

$$\text{PFX}_K^{\overline{IV}}(X) = C_1', T'$$

with an arbitrary, unused $\overline{\text{IV}} \neq \text{IV}^*$. The block C'_1 is one-block result and T' is the tag which is of no interest. Since $C'_1 = E_K(X) \oplus \overline{\text{IV}}$ the gadget returns $G_{\text{PFX}}(X) := C'_1 \oplus \overline{\text{IV}} = E_K(X)$.

Observation 2. *With G_{PFX} one can get $E_K(X)$ for an arbitrary X without knowledge of the key.*

Now we can forge the ciphertext of our message by the following algorithm.

1. Use G_{PFX} to obtain $E_K(M_1), \ldots, E_K(M_n)$.
2. Compute $C_i = E_K(M_i) \oplus M_{i-1}$ with $M_0 = \text{IV}^*$.
3. Request any j-block message $M' = \overline{M}_1, \ldots, \overline{M}_{j-1}, M_n$ with M_n as the last block. The tag T' of $\text{PFX}_K^{\text{IV}'}(M') = C'_1, \ldots, C'_j$, T' fits the demands since
   (a) (indicator variant) $T' = E_K(I) \oplus M_n = T^*$.
   (b) (two key variant) $T' = E_{K'}(M_n) = T^*$.

The use of single-block auxiliary queries to PFX in the gadget means that the above method cannot be used for forging single block messages. For this special case, we can use an insertion variant which works for messages of length 1 (as well as also for longer messages). This variant requests

$$\text{PFX}_K^{\overline{\text{IV}}}(IV^*, M_1, \ldots, M_n) = C'_0, C_1, \ldots, C_n, T^*$$

for some arbitrary $\overline{\text{IV}}$, obtaining all the necessary ciphertext blocks for our forgery. Only the block C'_0 is of no use and is discarded. In both the indicator and the two-key variants of PFX, the token T^* is valid as shown in the last step of the above forgery algorithm.

Algorithm 1: Encryption $\text{PFX}_K^{\text{IV}}(M_1, \ldots, M_n)$

$C_1 \leftarrow E_K(M_1) \oplus \text{IV}$
for $i = 2$ *to* n **do**
  $\quad C_i \leftarrow E_K(M_i) \oplus M_{i-1}$
if $I \neq NULL$ **then** // indicator version
  $\quad T \leftarrow E_K(I) \oplus M_n$
else
  $\quad T \leftarrow E_{K'}(M_n)$
return $C_1, \ldots, C_n, T$

5.4 Attack on PFX-CTR

We now describe a universal forgery attack on PFX-CTR. Assume we want to forge the encryption $C_1, \ldots, C_n, T^*$ of the message $M = M_1, \ldots, M_n$ with starting value for the counter SV^* and initial value IV^*. First note that Observation 1 also holds for PFX-CTR, we therefore create a gadget $G_{\text{PFX-CTR}}$ simulating $E_K(X)$. The use of a starting value gives us more possibilities for the gadget. To simulate $E_K(X)$ the gadget requests

$$\text{PFX}_K^{\overline{\text{SV}},\overline{\text{IV}}}(X \oplus \overline{\text{SV}}) = C_1', T'$$

with an unused $\overline{\text{IV}} \neq \text{IV}^*$ and an unused $\overline{\text{SV}} \neq \text{SV}^*$. The block C_1' is a one-block result and T' is the tag which is of no interest. Since $C_1' = E_K((X \oplus \overline{\text{SV}}) \oplus \overline{\text{SV}}) \oplus \overline{\text{IV}}$ the gadget returns $G_{\text{PFX-CTR}}(X) := C_1' \oplus \overline{\text{IV}}$.

Observation 3. *For a given X the gadget $G_{PFC\text{-}CTR}$ returns $E_K(X)$ without knowledge of the key K.*

The universal forgery attack procedure is then as follows. Note that the indicator I is not known to the attacker and that $T^* = E_K(I \oplus \text{Ctr}_{n+1})$ where $\text{Ctr}_{n+1} = \text{SV}^* + n$ is the counter value on I when M is encrypted.

1. Use $G_{\text{PFX-CTR}}$ to obtain $A_1, \ldots, A_n = E_K(M_1 \oplus \text{SV}^*), E_K(M_2 \oplus (\text{SV}^* + 1))$, $\ldots, E_K(M_n \oplus (\text{SV}^* + n - 1))$.
2. Compute $C_i = A_i \oplus M_{i-1}$ with $M_0 = \text{IV}^*$.
3. Request any j-block message $M' = \overline{M}_1, \ldots, \overline{M}_{j-1}, M_n$ with M_n as the last block and let $\text{SV}' = \text{SV}^* + n - j$. The tag T' of $\text{PFX}_K^{\text{SV}',\overline{\text{IV}}}(M') = C_1', \ldots, C_j', T'$ with an arbitrary $\overline{\text{IV}} \neq \text{IV}^*$ fits the demands since
   (a) (indicator variant) the starting value $\text{SV}^* + n - j$ is so chosen that the counter value for the indicator is $(\text{SV}^* + n - j) + j = \text{SV}^* + n$. Hence, $T' = E_K(I \oplus (\text{SV}^* + n)) \oplus M_n = T^*$.
   (b) (two key variant) $T' = E_{K'}(M_n) = T^*$.

Due to the freedom provided by choosing the starting value, the same procedure also works for one block messages, so no special variant is required for this case as was necessary for PFX.

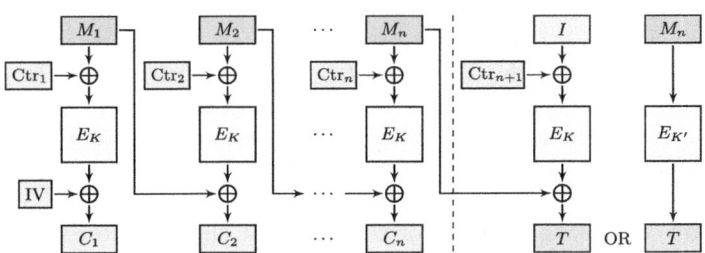

Fig. 3. The PFX-CTR authenticated encryption algorithm.

5.5 Attack on PFX-INC

In this section, we show a universal forgery attack on PFX-INC for the two key variant. Furthermore, we present a universal forgery attack when the indicator is known to the adversary, which is within the security model of PFX-INC. Since PFX-INC follows the pattern of increment-based schemes, we assume that a nonce is part of the scheme and incorporated into the first increment as indicated

Algorithm 2: Encryptions of PFX-CTR and PFX-INC

PFX-CTR$_K^{SV,IV}(M_1, \ldots, M_n)$:
$Ctr_1 \leftarrow SV$
$O_1 \leftarrow E_K(M_1 \oplus Ctr_1)$
$C_1 \leftarrow IV \oplus O_1$
for $i = 2$ *to* n **do**
$\quad Ctr_i \leftarrow Ctr_{i-1} + 1$
$\quad O_i \leftarrow E_K(M_i \oplus Ctr_i)$
$\quad C_i \leftarrow M_{i-1} \oplus O_i$
if $I \neq NULL$ **then** // indicator version
$\quad Ctr_{n+1} \leftarrow Ctr_n + 1$
$\quad O_{n+1} \leftarrow E_K(I \oplus Ctr_{n+1})$
$\quad T \leftarrow M_n \oplus O_{n+1}$
else
$\quad T \leftarrow E_{K'}(M_n)$
return $C_1, \ldots, C_n, T$

PFX-INC$_K^{Nonce}(M_1, \ldots, M_n)$:
$\Delta \leftarrow Init(Nonce)$
$\Delta_1 \leftarrow Inc_1(\Delta)$
$O_1 \leftarrow E_K(M_1 \oplus \Delta_1)$
$C_1 \leftarrow O_1 \oplus \Delta_1$
for $i = 2$ *to* n **do**
$\quad \Delta_i \leftarrow Inc_i(\Delta)$
$\quad O_i \leftarrow E_K(M_i \oplus \Delta_i)$
$\quad C_i \leftarrow M_{i-1} \oplus O_i \oplus \Delta_i$
if $I \neq NULL$ **then** // indicator version
$\quad \Delta_{n+1} \leftarrow Inc_{n+1}(\Delta)$
$\quad O_{n+1} \leftarrow E_K(I \oplus \Delta_{n+1})$
$\quad T \leftarrow M_n \oplus O_{n+1} \oplus \Delta_{n+1}$
else
$\quad T \leftarrow E_{K'}(M_n)$
return $C_1, \ldots, C_n, T$

in Algorithm 2. First, assume we want to forge the encryption $C_1, \ldots, C_n, T^*$ of the message $M = M_1, \ldots, M_n$ with nonce N^* in the two key variant. Since the tag depends only on the last block, the adversary asks for a message with a doubled last block. This means that one can ask for

$$\text{PFX-INC}_K^{N^*}(M_1, \ldots, M_n, M_n) = C_1, \ldots, C_n, C'_{n+1}, T'.$$

Since the tag $T' = E_{K'}(M_n)$ is the same for all messages with equal last block the equation, $T^* = T'$ holds. The block C'_{n+1} is of no use and can be discarded. The remaining blocks are our valid ciphertext-tag pair.

Now, for the indicator variant of PFX-INC, assume that the pre-shared indicator I is known to the adversary. Again, we want to forge the encryption $C_1, \ldots, C_n, T^*$ of the message $M = M_1, \ldots, M_n$ with nonce N^* in the indicator variant. We take advantage of the fact that the indicator is encrypted in the same way as the other blocks. Hence, we request the extended message

$$\text{PFX-INC}_K^{N^*}(M_1, \ldots, M_n, I) = C_1, \ldots, C_n, C'_{n+1}, T'.$$

In this scenario the tag T' is of no use for us. But the block C'_{n+1} fulfills the demands for the tag because $C'_{n+1} = E(I \oplus \Delta_{n+1}) \oplus \Delta_{n+1} \oplus M_n$. Hence, $T^* = C'_{n+1}$ and we get the desired ciphertext with its valid tag.

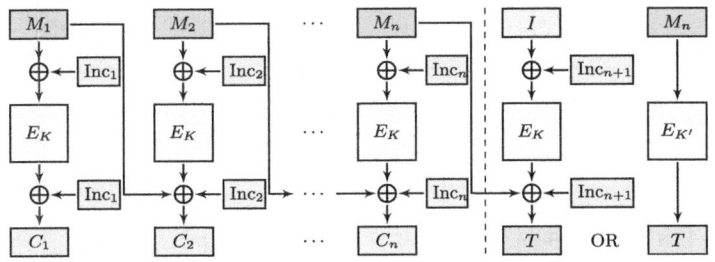

Fig. 4. The PFX-INC authenticated encryption algorithm.

5.6 Attack on PFC-CTR

We demostrate a universal forgery attack on PFC-CTR. Assume we want to forge the encryption $C_1, \ldots, C_n, T^*$ of the message $M = M_1, \ldots, M_n$ with initial value IV^*. Again, we create a gadget $G^r_{\text{PFC-CTR}}$ simulating $\text{MSB}_r(E_K(X))$. To obtain the result of $\text{MSB}_r(E(X))$, $G^r_{\text{PFC-CTR}}$ asks for

$$\text{PFC-CTR}_K^{\overline{IV}}(M'_1, \overline{M}_2) = C'_1, C'_2, T'$$

with an arbitrary block $\overline{M}_2$, an unused $\overline{IV} \neq IV^*$ and $M'_1 = X \oplus (\overline{IV} + 1)$. The idea of this gadget is to get the result from the second ciphertext block because of the freedom provided by the choice of $\overline{IV}$ and M'_1 in the equation $(\overline{IV} + 1) \oplus M'_1 = X$. Hence, the gadget returns $G^r_{\text{PFC-CTR}}(X) := C'_2 \oplus \overline{M}_2$.

The tag now needs to be computed in a different way than the ciphertext blocks. We will take the advantage of the fact that the tag depends only on the length of the message NOB, the last block and the initial value. This means that the tag remains the same as long as the last block, the number of blocks and the initial value are the same. We can then forge our message by the following procedure:

1. Use $G^r_{\text{PFC-CTR}}$ to obtain $A_1, \ldots, A_n = \text{MSB}_r(E_K(\text{Ctr}_1))$, $\text{MSB}_r(E_K(\text{Ctr}_2 \oplus M_1)), \ldots, \text{MSB}_r(E_K(\text{Ctr}_n \oplus M_{n-1}))$ with $\text{Ctr}_i = IV^* + i - 1$.
2. Compute $C_i = A_i \oplus M_i$.
3. To get the tag request $\text{PFC-CTR}^{IV^*}(\overline{M}_1, \ldots, \overline{M}_{n-1}, M_n) = C'_1, \ldots, C'_n, T$ with arbitrary $\overline{M}_1, \ldots, \overline{M}_{n-1}$.

Note that the ciphertext blocks $C_1, \ldots, C_n$ can be also obtained by only one request via an insertion variant of the above algorithm. In this case, we ask for $\text{PFC-CTR}_K^{IV^*-1}(\overline{M}_0, M_1, \ldots, M_n) = C'_0, C_1, \ldots, C_n, T'$ with an arbitrary block $\overline{M}_0$. This gives us all the necessary blocks for the forgery.

5.7 Attack on IAR-CTR

Assume we want to forge the encryption $C_1, \ldots, C_n, T_1, \ldots, T_t$ of the message $M = M_1, \ldots, M_n$ with initial value IV^*. To achieve this we create a gadget $G^r_{\text{IAR-CTR}}$ to simulate $\text{MSB}_r(E_K(X))$ and get the tags by a special request.

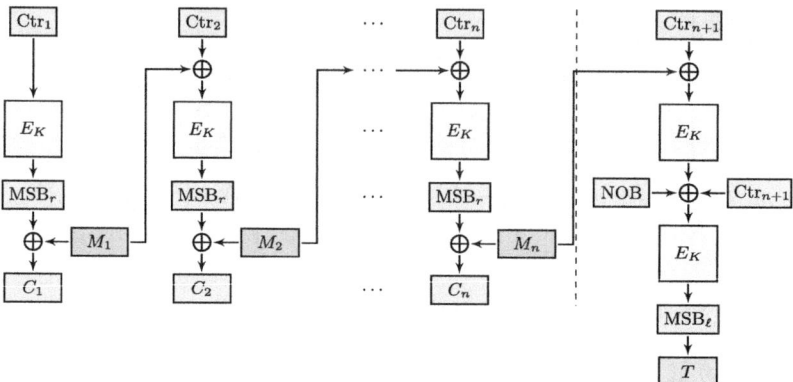

Fig. 5. The PFC-CTR authenticated encryption algorithm.

Algorithm 3: Encryption PFC-CTR$_K^{\text{IV}}(M_1, \ldots, M_n)$

Ctr$_1 \leftarrow$ IV
$O_1 \leftarrow E_K(\text{Ctr}_1)$
$C_1 \leftarrow M_1 \oplus \text{MSB}_r(O_1)$
for $i = 2$ *to* n **do**
$\quad$ Ctr$_i \leftarrow$ Ctr$_{i-1} + 1$
$\quad O_i \leftarrow E_K(M_{i-1} \oplus \text{Ctr}_i)$
$\quad C_i \leftarrow M_i \oplus \text{MSB}_r(O_1)$

Ctr$_{n+1} \leftarrow$ Ctr$_n + 1$
$\tau \leftarrow E_K(M_n \oplus \text{Ctr}_{n+1})$
$O_{n+1} \leftarrow E_K(\text{NOB} \oplus \tau \oplus \text{Ctr}_{n+1})$
$T \leftarrow \text{MSB}_\ell(O_{n+1})$
return $C_1, \ldots, C_n, T$

The simplest option for such a gadget would be to set the initial vector such that the first output block is used for the simulation. However, this does not work whenever one block M_i happens to equal IV$^* + 1$. To avoid this scenario we prepare a message such that the j-th ciphertext output block will be used with $j > t$. To obtain MSB$_r(E_K(X))$ the gadget picks a (preferably small) $j > t$ and chooses some M'_{j-t} and an unused IV$' \neq$ IV* subject to the constraint

$$X = (M'_{j-t} \| 0..0) \oplus (\text{IV}' + j).$$

Let $M' = \overline{M}_1, \ldots, M'_{j-t}, \ldots, \overline{M}_j, \ldots, \overline{M}_q$ a new q-block message with M'_{j-t} as the $(j-t)$-th block. The other blocks can be set to arbitrary values. The gadget $G^r_{\text{IAR-CTR}}$ then asks for

$$\text{IAR-CTR}_K^{\text{IV}'}(M') = C'_1, \ldots, C'_j, \ldots, C'_q, T'_1, \ldots, T'_t.$$

At last, $G^r_{\text{IAR-CTR}}$ returns $G^r_{\text{IAR-CTR}}(X) := C'_j \oplus \overline{M}_j$.

Observation 4. *For a given X the gadget $G^r_{IAR\text{-}CTR}$ simulates $MSB_r(E_K(X))$.*

To obtain the tags we take advantage of the fact that the tags depend only on the counter, the number of blocks and the last t message blocks. Let $M_{\text{TAG}} =$

$\overline{M}_1, \ldots, \overline{M}_{n-t-1}, M_{n-t+1}, \ldots, M_n$ be the message with the same t last blocks as M and some arbitrary ones for the other blocks. Hence we get the tags by the request

$$\text{IAR-CTR}_K^{\text{IV}^*}(M_{\text{TAG}}) = C'_1, \ldots, C'_n, T_1, \ldots, T_t. \qquad (1)$$

A problem occurs when $n = t$ because then $M = M_{\text{TAG}}$ and a request of the message M is not allowed by attack model. To handle this issue, we create another gadget $G_{\text{IAR-CTR}}^\ell$ to obtain a desired tag. Consider the following calculations. Let $\text{Ctr}_i = \text{IV}^* + i$. One tag T_i is constructed by the formula

$$T_i = \text{MSB}_\ell(E_K(n \oplus \text{Ctr}_{n+i} \oplus E_K(\text{Ctr}_{n+1} \oplus M_{n-t+i}||0..0)).$$

The task is to find another initial value IV', number of blocks n' and some message blocks such that we get the same T_i. Let $\text{Ctr}'_i = \text{IV}' + i$. By

$$T_i = \text{MSB}_\ell(E_K(n' \oplus \text{Ctr}'_{n'+i} \oplus E_K(\text{Ctr}'_{n'+1} \oplus M'_{n'-t+i}||0..0))$$

we get the following constraints:

$$\text{Ctr}_{t+i} \oplus M_{n-t+i}||0..0 = \text{Ctr}'_{n'+i} \oplus M'_{n'-t+i}||0..0,$$
$$n \oplus \text{Ctr}_{n+i} = n' \oplus \text{Ctr}'_{n'+1}$$

By transforming these equations we get

$$\text{Ctr}_{t+i} \oplus \text{Ctr}'_{n'+i} = M_{n-t+i}||0..0 \oplus M'_{n'-t+i}||0..0,$$
$$\text{Ctr}_{n+i} \oplus \text{Ctr}'_{n'+i} = n \oplus n',$$
$$\Rightarrow d := \text{Ctr}_{t+i} \oplus \text{Ctr}'_{n'+i} = M_{n-t+i}||0..0 \oplus M'_{n'-t+i}||0..0 = n \oplus n'.$$

It follows that difference d has to be greater or equal to 2^{p-r} because of $d = M_{n-t+i}||0..0 \oplus M'_{n'-t+i}||0..0$. By choosing d one gets the necessary variables n', $M'_{n'-t+i}$, and IV'. Let M_{T_i} be the message

$$\overline{M}_1, \ldots, \overline{M}_{n'-t+i-1}, M_{n-t+i} \oplus \text{MSB}_r(d), \overline{M}_{n'-t+i+1}, \ldots, \overline{M}_{n'}$$

with the desired block at the $(n'-t+i)$-th position and the remaining blocks set to arbitrary values. Hence we can get the tag T_i by the following request

$$\text{IAR-CTR}_K^{\text{IV}^* \oplus d}(M_{T_i}) = C'_1, \ldots, C'_{n'}, T'_1, \ldots, T_i, \ldots, T'_t$$

Observation 5. *With given p-bit integers n, c and r-bit block Z_0 the gadget $G_{IAR-CTR}^\ell$ returns $MSB_\ell(E_K(n \oplus c \oplus E_K(c \oplus Z_0||0..0)))$. This can be used to simulate a tag for IAR-CTR.*

We can now forge the desired message by the following procedure:
1. Use $G_{\text{IAR-CTR}}^r$ to obtain $A_1, \ldots A_t = \text{MSB}_r(E_K(\text{IV}^* + 1)), \ldots, \text{MSB}_r(E_K(\text{IV}^* + t))$.
2. Use $G_{\text{IAR-CTR}}^r$ to obtain $A_{t+1}, \ldots, A_n = \text{MSB}_r(E_K((\text{IV}^* + t + 1) \oplus M_1)), \ldots, \text{MSB}_r(E_K((\text{IV}^* + n) \oplus (M_{n-t})))$.
3. Compute $C_i = A_i \oplus M_i$.
4. Get the tags $T_1, \ldots, T_t$ by the above-mentioned request (1) if $n \neq t$. Otherwise use the gadget $G_{\text{IAR-CTR}}^\ell$ to obtain the tags.

Algorithm 4: Encryptions of IAR-CTR and IAR-CFB

IAR-CTR$_K^{IV}(M_1,\ldots,M_n)$:
Ctr$_0 \leftarrow$ IV
for $i = 1$ *to* t **do**
  | Ctr$_i \leftarrow$ Ctr$_{i-1} + 1$
  | $O_i \leftarrow E_K(\text{Ctr}_i)$
  | $C_i \leftarrow M_i \oplus \text{MSB}_r(O_i)$
for $i = t+1$ *to* n **do**
  | Ctr$_i \leftarrow$ Ctr$_{i-1} + 1$
  | $O_i \leftarrow E_K((M_{i-t}||0..0) \oplus \text{Ctr}_i)$
  | $C_i \leftarrow M_i \oplus \text{MSB}_r(O_i)$
for $i = n+1$ *to* $n+t$ **do**
  | Ctr$_i \leftarrow$ Ctr$_{i-1} + 1$
  | $\tau_i \leftarrow E_K((M_{i-t}||0..0) \oplus \text{Ctr}_i)$
  | $O_i \leftarrow E_K(\text{NOB} \oplus \tau_i \oplus \text{Ctr}_{n+1})$
  | $T_{i-n} \leftarrow \text{MSB}_\ell(O_i)$
return $C_1,\ldots,C_n, T_1,\ldots,T_t$

IAR-CFB$_K^{IV}(M_1,\ldots,M_n)$:
Ctr$_0 \leftarrow$ IV
for $i = 1$ *to* t **do**
  | Ctr$_i \leftarrow$ Ctr$_{i-1} + 1$
  | $O_i \leftarrow E_K(\text{Ctr}_i)$
  | $C_i \leftarrow M_i \oplus \text{MSB}_r(O_i)$
$Y_i = \text{Ctr}_i$
for $i = t+1$ *to* n **do**
  | $Y_i \leftarrow \text{LSB}_{p-r}(Y_{i-1})||C_{i-t}$
  | $O_i \leftarrow E_K((M_{i-t}||0..0) \oplus Y_i)$
  | $C_i \leftarrow M_i \oplus \text{MSB}_r(O_i)$
for $i = n+1$ *to* $n+t$ **do**
  | $Y_i \leftarrow \text{LSB}_{p-r}(Y_{i-1})||C_{i-t}$
  | $O_i \leftarrow E_K((M_{i-t}||0..0) \oplus Y_i)$
  | $T_{i-n} \leftarrow \text{MSB}_\ell(O_i)$
return $C_1,\ldots,C_n, T_1,\ldots,T_t$

5.8 Attack on IAR-CFB

In this section, we present a universal forgery attack on IAR-CFB for the case where $t \geq \lceil \frac{p}{r} \rceil$. This scenario is not only within the specified requirements for these parameters but also entirely practical (see e.g. the experiments in [12]), considering that if r is relatively small compared to p, the number of block cipher calls per message increases, reducing the efficiency of the scheme.

Assume we want to forge the encryption $C_1,\ldots,C_n,T_1,\ldots,T_t$ of the message $M = M_1,\ldots,M_n$ with initial value IV^*. Note that the input for the block cipher is not known immediately since the delayed ciphertext is used as part of the input. We create two gadgets $G_{\text{IAR-CFB}}^r$ and $G_{\text{IAR-CFB}}^\ell$ to simulate $\text{MSB}_r(E(X))$ and $\text{MSB}_\ell(E(X))$, respectively. The first gadget $G_{\text{IAR-CFB}}^r$ makes use of one of the first t encryptions. Let $1 \leq j \leq t$ be the desired index position. To obtain $\text{MSB}_r(E_K(X))$ on the j-th position the gadget $G_{\text{IAR-CFB}}^r$ asks for

$$\text{IAR-CFB}_K^{X-j}(\overline{M}_1,\ldots,\overline{M}_t) = C_1',\ldots,C_t',T_1',\ldots,T_t'$$

with an arbitrary $\overline{M}_i$. Since $C_i' = \text{MSB}_r(E_K(X)) \oplus \overline{M}_i$ this gadget returns $G_{\text{IAR-CFB}}^r(X) := C_j' \oplus \overline{M}_j$. We do not fix one position j due to the freedom of initial vectors we can choose. This comes in quite handy for the next gadget.

Observation 6. *The gadget $G_{IAR-CFB}^r$ returns $\text{MSB}_r(E_K(X))$ for a given X.*

In the following the idea behind the second gadget $G_{\text{IAR-CFB}}^\ell$ is explained. We take advantage of the fact that the chained value Y_i (see Algorithm 4) which is used as the input for the ciphertext is updated by the delayed ciphertext blocks. Let $g = \lceil \frac{p}{r} \rceil$. After g blocks we have full control of this chained value.

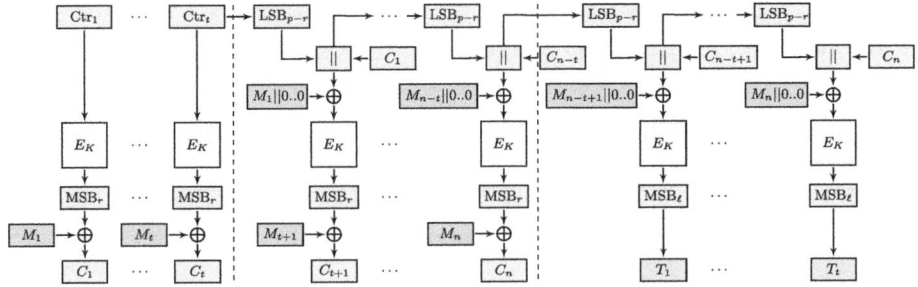

Fig. 6. The IAR-CFB authenticated encryption algorithm.

For the sake of simplicity we assume that $r|p$. The adjustment for the case $r \nmid p$ is described in Appendix A.3. Hence $g = \frac{p}{r}$. Furthermore, let X be the desired message. We split X into g equal sized parts $X_1, \ldots, X_g$. The gadget $G^{\ell}_{\text{IAR-CFB}}$ uses the g-th tag as the result of a t-block message. Before X is used as the input of E_K it will be xored with $M_g \| 0..0$. Thus, we have to set the ciphertexts as $X_1 = C_1 \oplus M_g$ and $X_i = C_i$ for $2 \leq i \leq g$. Due to $C_i = M_i \oplus \text{MSB}_r(E_K(\text{Ctr}_i))$ we know that

$$M_1 = X_1 \oplus M_g \oplus \text{MSB}_r(E_K(\text{Ctr}_1)), \quad (2)$$
$$M_i = X_i \oplus \text{MSB}_r(E_K(\text{Ctr}_i)). \quad (3)$$

By the following we obtain a procedure for computing the auxiliary message which has to be requested to obtain $\text{MSB}_\ell(E_K(X))$:

1. Find unused IV' such that all of $\{\text{Ctr}_1, \ldots, \text{Ctr}_g\}$ and IV' $- j$ for $1 \leq j < t$ are unused as the initial vector with $\text{Ctr}_i = \text{IV}' + i$.
2. Obtain $A_i = \text{MSB}_r(E_K(\text{Ctr}_i))$ by $G^r_{\text{IAR-CFB}}$ such that IV' is still unused for a request.
3. For $2 \leq i \leq g$ set $M'_i = X_i \oplus A_i$ (because of (3)).
4. Set $M'_1 = X_1 \oplus A_1 \oplus M'_g$ (because of (2)).

Now, to obtain $\text{MSB}_\ell(E_K(X))$ we ask for

$$\text{IAR-CFB}^{\text{IV}'}_K(M'_1, \ldots, M'_g, \overline{M}_{g+1}, \ldots, \overline{M}_t) = C'_1, \ldots, C'_t, T'_1, \ldots, T'_n$$

where $M'_1, \ldots, M'_g$ and IV' are obtained by the above procedure and the other blocks are arbitrary. Finally return $G^{\ell}_{\text{IAR-CFB}}(X) := T'_g = \text{MSB}_\ell(E_K(X))$.

Observation 7. *With $G^{\ell}_{\text{IAR-CFB}}$ one can get $\text{MSB}_\ell(E_K(X))$ without knowledge of the key by g many calls of $G^r_{\text{IAR-CFB}}$ and one oracle request.*

We now have all the required tools for our universal forgery attack:

1. Obtain $O_i = \text{MSB}_r(\text{IV}^* + i)$ by $G^r_{\text{IAR-CFB}}$ for $1 \leq i \leq t$.
2. Compute $C_i = M_i \oplus O_i$.

3. Let $Y_t = \text{Ctr}_t$, for $t + 1 \leq i \leq n$
   (a) Compute $Y_i = \text{LSB}_{p-r}(Y_{i-1}) || C_{i-t}$
   (b) Obtain $O_i = \text{MSB}_r(M_{i-t} || 0..0 \oplus Y_i)$ by $G^r_{\text{IAR-CFB}}$.
   (c) $C_i = M_i \oplus O_i$.
4. For $n + 1 \leq i \leq n + t$
   (a) Compute $Y_i = \text{LSB}_{p-r}(Y_{i-1}) || C_{i-t}$
   (b) Obtain $T_{i-n} = \text{MSB}_\ell(M_{i-t} || 0..0 \oplus Y_i)$ by $G^\ell_{\text{IAR-CFB}}$.

The resulting ciphertext blocks and tags yield the desired forgery.

6 Conclusion

In this paper, we have analyzed the security of three AE algorithm families, namely PFX, PFC and IAR, which were designed as improvements to general-purpose well-established AE schemes such as CCM, GCM or OCB which are widely used in security protocols for wireless networks based on IEEE 802.11 (Wi-Fi), IEEE 802.15.4 (such as Zigbee), as well as LTE and 5G mobile networks. The design objective of PFX, PFC and IAR was to guarantee confidentiality and authenticity in a single-pass process while reducing the number of block cipher calls and avoiding expensive operations like finite field multiplications. As such, they appeared to be well-suited alternatives to standard modes such as CCM or GCM for wireless systems, lightweight wireless sensor networks, and real-time wireless applications.

Our analysis however indicates that these AE schemes cannot provide their claimed security guarantees. We described universal forgery attacks on all three algorithm families, allowing an adversary to compute valid ciphertexts and authentication tags for any message of their choice without knowledge of the secret key. All of our attacks only have linear complexity in the length of the target message and as such are entirely practical. Overall, our analysis implies that the affected schemes should not be used in practice, despite their attractive performance characteristics in the context of wireless and real-time networks.

It remains an interesting open problem to adapt existing well-established and secure cryptographic primitives for authenticated encryption more to the specific requirements of wireless network applications, especially in the context of lightweight wireless sensor nodes or real-time constraints. The forgery attacks on PFX, PFC and IAR illustrate the need for thorough and long-term security analysis of new cryptographic algorithms before considering their deployment, emphasizing the importance of adhering to well-established standardized cryptographic algorithms. For applications where standard solutions such as CCM or GCM are not ideal, a promising line of research would be to comparatively evaluate the NIST lightweight cryptography standard Ascon [7–9] as well as algorithms from the CAESAR final portfolio, which besides Ascon include ACORN [28] with a lighweight focus, AEGIS [29] and OCB for high-throughput networks, and Deoxys [18] and COLM [1,2] for scenarios where defense in depth against e.g. nonce misuse is required. These algorithms have already received extensive cryptanalytic scrutiny over a couple of years and could potentially be included in future versions of standards for wireless encryption.

Acknowledgements. We would like to thank the anonymous reviewers for their insightful comments.

A Appendix

A.1 Notation

In the following we briefly define some notation used in this article. Let M and C respectively denote the bit strings containing the plaintext message and its encryption in some mode by a block cipher E_K with the secret key K. Subscripts for M or C, like M_i, denote the i-th block of M or C respectively. The size of each block depends on the used block cipher (typically 64 or 128 bits). The operator $A \oplus B$ is the bitwise xor operation on two bit strings A and B. The output of a MAC is called tag and denoted by the variable T. The selection of the b most or b least significant bits of a bit string is written as $\text{MSB}_b(\cdot)$ and $\text{LSB}_b(\cdot)$, respectively. The total number of blocks of a message is referred to as NOB. The operator $\|$ denotes concatenation of two bit strings. We use $0..0$ to abbreviate the repetition of zeros up to a number (such as the block size) which is clear from the context.

A.2 PFC-OCB Scheme

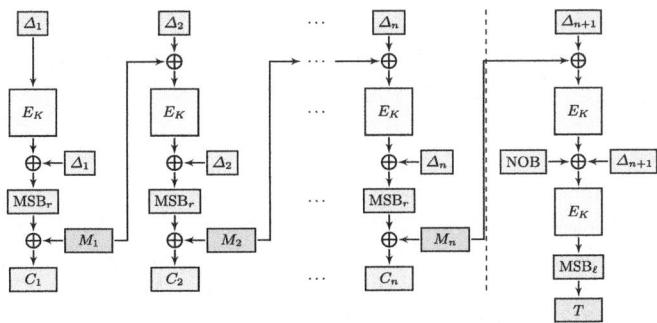

Fig. 7. The PFC-OCB authenticated encryption algorithm.

A.3 Adjustment for $G^\ell_{\text{IAR-CFB}}$ for the Case $r \nmid p$

In the following we explain how to adjust the gadget $G^\ell_{\text{IAR-CFB}}$ for the case $r \nmid p$. Let $g = \lceil \frac{p}{r} \rceil$ and let $q = p \mod r$. First, we consider the case for $g > 2$. Then, the case $g = 2$ will be discussed. We split the input X in the parts $X_1, \ldots, X_g$ where only X_1 consists of q bits and all other blocks of r bits. In this case, the message block M_g influences X_1 and X_2, see Fig. 8a for a visualization. This yields the equations

$$X_1 = \text{LSB}_q(C_1) \oplus \text{MSB}_q(M_g), \tag{4}$$
$$X_2 = C_2 \oplus \text{LSB}_{r-q}(M_g)||0..0, \tag{5}$$
$$X_i = C_i. \tag{6}$$

By combining these equations with $C_i = M_i \oplus \text{MSB}_r(E_K(\text{Ctr}_i))$ we obtain the following relations:

$$\text{LSB}_q(M_1) = X_1 \oplus \text{MSB}_q(M_g) \oplus \text{LSB}_q(\text{MSB}_r(E_K(\text{Ctr}_1))), \tag{7}$$
$$M_2 = X_2 \oplus \text{LSB}_{r-q}(M_g)||0..0 \oplus \text{MSB}_r(E_K(\text{Ctr}_2)), \tag{8}$$
$$M_i = X_i \oplus \text{MSB}_r(E_K(\text{Ctr}_i)), \tag{9}$$

from which we can replace the last two steps (3 and 4) of the message creation step of $G^\ell_{\text{IAR-CFB}}$ with three ones above.

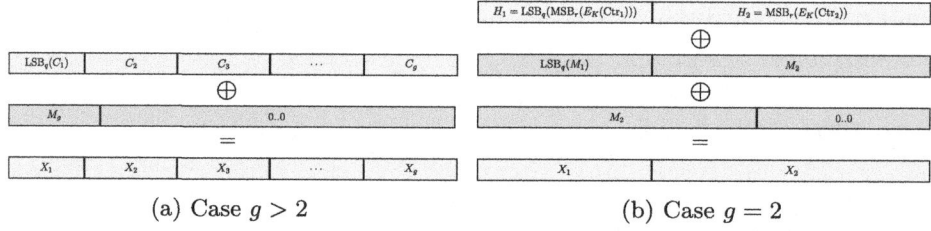

(a) Case $g > 2$ (b) Case $g = 2$

Fig. 8. Illustration of the computation of X in the message creation part for $G_{\text{IAR-CFB}}$ in the case $r \nmid p$. Note that M_g is r bits long while X_1 and $\text{LSB}_q(C_1)$ consist of $q = p \mod r$ bits.

Now we consider the case $g = 2$. Similar to the above case we replace the formulas for the message creation part. Let $s := r - q$. See Fig. 8b for the dependencies in this case. Note that the ciphertexts C_1 and $\text{LSB}_q(C_1)$ are replaced with $\text{LSB}_q(M_1) \oplus \text{LSB}_q(\text{MSB}_r(E_K(\text{Ctr}_1)))$ and $M_2 \oplus \text{MSB}_r(E_K(\text{Ctr}_2))$ respectively because of $C_i = M_i \oplus \text{MSB}_r(E_K(\text{Ctr}_i))$. For ease of presentation, let $H_1 := \text{LSB}_q(\text{MSB}_r(E_K(\text{Ctr}_1)))$ and $H_2 := \text{MSB}_r(E_K(\text{Ctr}_2))$. For the s most significant bits of X_2 there is an "overlap" of two different parts of M_2 as seen in the equations:

$$\text{LSB}_q(X_2) = \text{LSB}_q(M_2) \oplus \text{LSB}_q(H_2), \tag{10}$$
$$\text{MSB}_s(X_2) = \text{LSB}_s(M_2) \oplus \text{MSB}_s(M_2) \oplus \text{MSB}_s(H_2), \tag{11}$$
$$X_1 = \text{MSB}_q(M_2) \oplus \text{LSB}_q(M_1) \oplus H_1. \tag{12}$$

For this overlap we will define $\text{MSB}_s(M_2)$ bitwise. Let $P[i]$ denote the i-th bit of P. For $q \leq i < q + s$ we compute

$$M_2[i] := X_2[i] + M_2[i - q] + H_2[i]. \tag{13}$$

The q least significant bits of M_2 can be computed directly by (10). After the computation of M_2 the desired bits of M_1 are obtainable by (12). The adjustment is done by replacing the last 2 formulas in the auxiliary message creation part of $G^{\ell}_{\text{IAR-CFB}}$ by these ones for M_1 and M_2. This concludes the universal forgery for this case.

References

1. Andreeva, E., et al.: AES-COPA v2. Submission to the CAESAR competition (2016)
2. Andreeva, E., Bogdanov, A., Luykx, A., Mennink, B., Tischhauser, E., Yasuda, K.: Parallelizable and authenticated online ciphers. In: Sako, K., Sarkar, P. (eds.) ASIACRYPT 2013. LNCS, vol. 8269, pp. 424–443. Springer, Heidelberg (2013). https://doi.org/10.1007/978-3-642-42033-7_22
3. Banik, S., Pandey, S.K., Peyrin, T., Sasaki, Yu., Sim, S.M., Todo, Y.: GIFT: a small present. In: Fischer, W., Homma, N. (eds.) CHES 2017. LNCS, vol. 10529, pp. 321–345. Springer, Cham (2017). https://doi.org/10.1007/978-3-319-66787-4_16
4. Bellare, M., Namprempre, C.: Authenticated encryption: relations among notions and analysis of the generic composition paradigm. In: Okamoto, T. (ed.) ASIACRYPT 2000. LNCS, vol. 1976, pp. 531–545. Springer, Heidelberg (2000). https://doi.org/10.1007/3-540-44448-3_41
5. CAESAR Committee: CAESAR: Competition for Authenticated Encryption: Security, Applicability, and Robustness (2019). http://competitions.cr.yp.to/caesar.html
6. Diffie, W., Hellman, M.E.: Privacy and authentication: an introduction to cryptography. Proc. IEEE **67**(3), 397–427 (1979)
7. Dobraunig, C., Eichlseder, M., Mendel, F., Schläffer, M.: Ascon v1.2: lightweight authenticated encryption and hashing. J. Cryptol. **34**(3), 33 (2021)
8. Dobraunig, C., Eichlseder, M., Mendel, F., Schläffer, M.: Ascon v1.2. Submission to the CAESAR competition (2016)
9. Dobraunig, C., Eichlseder, M., Mendel, F., Schläffer, M.: Ascon v1.2. Submission to the NIST Lightweight Cryptography competition (2019)
10. Dworkin, M.J.: SP 800-38D. Recommendation for block cipher modes of operation: Galois/Counter Mode (GCM) and GMAC. Technical report, Gaithersburg, MD, United States (2007)
11. 3rd Generation Partnership Project (3GPP): Security architecture and procedures for 5G System. 3GPP TS 33.501 (2018)
12. Hwang, T., Gope, P.: IAR-CTR and IAR-CFB: integrity aware real-time based counter and cipher feedback modes. Secur. Commun. Netw. **8**(18), 3939–3952 (2015)
13. Hwang, T., Gope, P.: PFX: an essence of authencryption for block-cipher security. Secur. Commun. Netw. **9**(10), 1186–1197 (2016)
14. Hwang, T., Gope, P.: Robust stream-cipher mode of authenticated encryption for secure communication in wireless sensor network. Secur. Commun. Netw. **9**(7), 667–679 (2016)
15. IEEE: IEEE Standard for Information Technology–Telecommunications and Information Exchange between Systems - Local and Metropolitan Area Networks–Specific Requirements - Part 11: Wireless LAN Medium Access Control (MAC)

and Physical Layer (PHY) Specifications. IEEE Std 802.11-2020/Cor 1-2022 (Corrigendum to IEEE Std 802.11-2020 as amended by IEEE Std 802.11ax-2021, IEEE Std 802.11ay-2021, and IEEE Std 802.11ba-2021), pp. 1–18 (2022)
16. IEEE: IEEE Standard for Low-Rate Wireless Networks. IEEE Std 802.15.4-2020/Cor 1-2022 (Corrigendum to IEEE Std 802.15.4-2020 as amended by IEEE Std 802.15.4z-2020, IEEE Std 802.15.4w-2020, IEEE Std 802.15.4y-2021, and IEEE Std 802.15.4aa-2022), pp. 1–22 (2023)
17. ISO 19772:2009. Information technology – Security techniques – Authenticated encryption (2009)
18. Jean, J., Nikolic, I., Peyrin, T., Seurin, Y.: The deoxys AEAD family. J. Cryptol. **34**(3), 31 (2021)
19. Jutla, C.S.: Encryption modes with almost free message integrity. In: Pfitzmann, B. (ed.) EUROCRYPT 2001. LNCS, vol. 2045, pp. 529–544. Springer, Heidelberg (2001). https://doi.org/10.1007/3-540-44987-6_32
20. Kohno, T., Viega, J., Whiting, D.: CWC: a high-performance conventional authenticated encryption mode. In: Roy, B., Meier, W. (eds.) FSE 2004. LNCS, vol. 3017, pp. 408–426. Springer, Heidelberg (2004). https://doi.org/10.1007/978-3-540-25937-4_26
21. Krovetz, T., Rogaway, P.: The software performance of authenticated-encryption modes. In: Joux, A. (ed.) FSE 2011. LNCS, vol. 6733, pp. 306–327. Springer, Heidelberg (2011). https://doi.org/10.1007/978-3-642-21702-9_18
22. Krovetz, T., Rogaway, P.: The OCB authenticated-encryption algorithm. RFC 7253 (2014). https://www.rfc-editor.org/info/rfc7253
23. McGrew, D.A., Viega, J.: The security and performance of the Galois/Counter Mode (GCM) of operation. In: Canteaut, A., Viswanathan, K. (eds.) INDOCRYPT 2004. LNCS, vol. 3348, pp. 343–355. Springer, Heidelberg (2004). https://doi.org/10.1007/978-3-540-30556-9_27
24. Namprempre, C.: Secure channels based on authenticated encryption schemes: a simple characterization. In: Zheng, Y. (ed.) ASIACRYPT 2002. LNCS, vol. 2501, pp. 515–532. Springer, Heidelberg (2002). https://doi.org/10.1007/3-540-36178-2_32
25. NIST: DES modes of operation. FIPS PUB 81 (1980)
26. Rogaway, P.: Efficient instantiations of tweakable blockciphers and refinements to modes OCB and PMAC. In: Lee, P.J. (ed.) ASIACRYPT 2004. LNCS, vol. 3329, pp. 16–31. Springer, Heidelberg (2004). https://doi.org/10.1007/978-3-540-30539-2_2
27. Rogaway, P., Bellare, M., Black, J., Krovetz, T.: OCB: a block-cipher mode of operation for efficient authenticated encryption. In: ACM Conference on Computer and Communications Security, pp. 196–205 (2001)
28. Wu, H.: Acorn: a lightweight authenticated cipher (v3). Submission to the CAESAR competition (2016)
29. Wu, H., Preneel, B.: Aegis: a fast authenticated encryption algorithm (v1.1). Submission to the CAESAR competition (2016)

Symmetric-key Cryptanalysis

Higher-Order Mixture Differentials for AES-Based Block Ciphers and Applications to TweAES

Eik List[✉][iD]

Independent Researcher, Singapore, Singapore
elist@posteo.de

Abstract. In ToSC 2/2018, Grassi introduced mixture differentials for the AES. A mixture takes a pair of texts and derives a second pair from mixing parts of the first one. The conditional probability of the second pair to follow a certain (truncated) differential is then strongly influenced by that of the first pair. Mixtures found various follow-up applications for attacks, leading to Bar-On et al.'s fastest key-recovery attacks on 5-round AES, the fastest boomerangs on up to 6-round AES, or to Bardeh and Rønjom's 6-round distinguisher. However, mixtures are not limited to the AES. Among the recent proposals of AES-based ciphers, TweAES augments the AES by a tiny tweak that is expanded with a simple code and added to the first two rows. Inspired by the observation that the tweak-expansion code of TweAES effectively thwarts tweak-induced mixtures, we propose higher-order mixtures as a generalization. To demonstrate their applicability, we describe a 6-round distinguisher and a 7-round key recovery attack on TweAES.

Keywords: Secret-key cryptography · Differential cryptanalysis · AES

1 Introduction

Recent Distinguishers on the AES. The recent years had seen much cryptanalysis on round-reduced AES, where the community has identified several novel distinguishers, such as mixture differentials [18], yoyos [32], multiple-of-n properties [20], and truncated differentials with small probability distance to an ideal permutation [19]. In the sequel, they were refined and led to more efficient attacks on round-reduced AES, such as more efficient five-round attacks [3], six-round distinguishers [5,6], and six-round attacks [16].

Mixture-Differential Cryptanalysis. Mixture differentials represent a powerful variant of conditional differentials. Given a pair of texts (x, x') that differ in at least two distinct cells $x_i \neq x'_i$ and $x_j \neq x'_j$, one can build a mixture pair $(u, u') \neq (x, x')$ such that $(u_i, u_j) = (x_i, x'_i)$ and $(u'_i, u'_j) = (x'_i, x_j)$. Then, one considers the differential propagation of $\Delta x = x \oplus x'$ to an output difference Δy through the cipher and the propagation of the difference

$\Delta u = u \oplus u'$ to some difference Δv, conditioned on $\Delta x \to \Delta y$. If the probability of $\Pr[\Delta u \to \Delta v | \Delta x \to \Delta y]$ is higher or lower than that for an ideal permutation, it can produce a distinguisher.

For the AES, Grassi [18] showed that four-round AES exhibits deterministic mixture-differential trails, which was derived from the observation in [20] that the set of all eight mixture pairs in a column or diagonal space guarantees that the cardinality of truncated differentials is a multiple of eight. This fact that had been generalized by Boura et al. [9].

The properties for high-probability mixture differentials in the AES stem from its SPN structure and linear layer. Bardeh and Rønjom [5,6] extended them to probabilistic distinguishers on up to six rounds of the AES. Bardeh and Rijmen [4] outlined the relation to related differences; Xie and Tian showed the absence of six-round deterministic mixtures on AES [35]; Qiao et al. [29–31] automated the search for mixtures with a MILP-based approach.

Towards Higher-Order Mixtures. The previous works on AES mixtures had considered the difference between pairs, although they had already studied the cardinality of the set of such conditioned pairs. However, there are AES-based primitives and settings where forming mixture pairs is obstructed. One good example is TweAES that served as instantiation in the NIST LwC candidate ESTATE [11,12]. TweAES is an instantiation of their ElasticTweak framework that extended the AES by a tiny tweak that allowed to derive a small family of independent block ciphers for efficient domain-separation in authenticated encryption schemes. In its tiniest variants, TweAES adds only a four-bit tweak for this purpose. While the AES round function still possesses the structural properties that allow mixtures, the tweak expansion seems to efficiently prohibit mixtures induced by tweak differences, which could allow to pass two rounds for free. For such and similar cases, we propose higher-order mixture differentials that study differences between 2^k pairs for $k \geq 2$. While higher-order mixtures naturally represent a special case of higher-order conditional differentials, it seems to be an interesting subcase that may invite further research.

Outline. In what follows, we provide the necessary notions and descriptions of mixtures, the AES, and TweAES. We show the inapplicability of conventional (first-order) mixtures to induce mixtures from tweak differences for TweAES with four-bit tweaks in Sect. 3. For comparison, we describe partial mixtures and the application to TweAES as an alternative avenue in Sect. 4. We define higher-order mixtures in general in Sect. 5 before we show a distinguisher on six rounds of TweAES with four-bit tweaks that we extend to a seven-round key-recovery attack in Sect. 6. We conclude in Sect. 7.

2 Preliminaries

General Notations. For a non-negative integer k, we write $[k] = \{1, \ldots, k\}$, and $[0..k] = \{0, 1, 2, \ldots, k\}$. We denote by $\mathbb{Z}_q$ the ring of non-negative integers modulo q and by $\mathbb{F}_{q^k}$ the finite field of characteristic q and power k. We represent functions and variables by upper case letters and indices by lowercase letters, sets by calligraphic letters. Moreover, we use bold variables for vectors and matrices.

We employ typewriter font for hexadecimal values or values in fields. Let $X, Y \in \mathbb{F}_2^n$ for some positive integer n in the following. Then, we denote by $X||Y$ the concatenation of X and Y, by $X \oplus Y$ their bitwise XOR. For all $X \in \mathbb{F}_2^n$, we index the bits $X = (X_{n-1} \ldots X_1 X_0)$ where X_{n-1} is the most significant and X_0 the least significant bit of X. We write $\mathsf{wt}(X)$ for the hamming weight of a vector X and $[i..j]$ for the integer interval $\{i, i+1, \ldots, j\}$. For all-zero or all-one-element vectors of m elements each, we write $\mathbf{0}^m = (0, 0, \ldots, 0)$ and $\mathbf{1}^m = (1, 1, \ldots, 1)$, respectively. For a set $\mathcal{X}$, we denote by $X \leftarrow \mathcal{X}$ that X is sampled independently and uniformly at random from $\mathcal{X}$. For vectors $x, y, \ldots$, we write $\mathbf{span}\,(x, y, \ldots)$ for their span.

2.1 Brief Overview of The AES

Brief Definition. We recall only those details of the AES that are necessary for understanding in this work. The AES [13,27] is a substitution-permutation network that transforms 16-byte plaintexts through 10, 12, or 14 rounds in its version with 128, 192, or 256-bit key, respectively, where each byte is interpreted as an element of a field $\mathbb{F}_{2^8}$, and the state as being in $\mathbb{F}_{2^8}^{16}$ or $\mathbb{F}_{2^8}^{4 \times 4}$; we will refer to them also as cells. We will write $\mathtt{i}$ for constants to highlight that they refer to elements of $\mathbb{F}_{2^8}$.

Almost every round consists of the operations SubBytes (SB), ShiftRows (SR), MixColumns (MC), and a round-key addition with a round key K^i. Before the first round, an additional whitening key K^0 is XORed to the state; the final round omits the linear MixColumns operation.

We write S^i for the state after Round i, and $S^i[j]$ for the j-th byte, for $0 \le i \le 10$ and $0 \le j \le 15$. Though, we interchangeably also use the indices for a matrix $x \in \mathbb{F}_{2^8}^{4 \times 4}$ with the usual byte ordering of either

$$\begin{bmatrix} x_0 & x_4 & x_8 & x_{12} \\ x_1 & x_5 & x_9 & x_{13} \\ x_2 & x_6 & x_{10} & x_{14} \\ x_3 & x_7 & x_{11} & x_{15} \end{bmatrix} \quad \text{or} \quad \begin{bmatrix} x_{0,0} & x_{0,1} & x_{0,2} & x_{0,3} \\ x_{1,0} & x_{1,1} & x_{1,2} & x_{1,3} \\ x_{2,0} & x_{2,1} & x_{2,2} & x_{2,3} \\ x_{3,0} & x_{3,1} & x_{3,2} & x_{3,3} \end{bmatrix}.$$

When using two-dimensional indices, we assume, all indices are modulo four.

We denote by $\mathsf{R}[K^i] \stackrel{\text{def}}{=} \mathsf{AK}[K^i] \circ \mathsf{MC} \circ \mathsf{SR} \circ \mathsf{SB}$ one application of the AES round function and by S^r_{SB}, S^r_{SR}, and S^r_{MC} the states in the r-th round directly after the application of SubBytes, ShiftRows, and MixColumns, respectively. We denote by $\widehat{\mathsf{R}} \stackrel{\text{def}}{=} \mathsf{AK}[K^i] \circ \mathsf{SR} \circ \mathsf{SB}$ the reduced final round and $\widehat{K}^i = \mathsf{MC}^{-1}(K^i)$ an equivalent key of K^i transformed through the (bijective) inverse MixColumns operation. Later, we will also use the overline notation such as $\overline{\mathsf{MC}}$ to refer to inverse operations. Finally, $\mathbf{M}$ denotes the MixColumns matrix.

Spaces in the AES. Grassi et al. [21] introduced column, diagonal, anti-diagonal, and mixed spaces that will alleviate our descriptions. Let $\{e_{0,0}, \ldots, e_{3,3}\}$ be unit vectors of $\mathbb{F}_{2^8}^{4 \times 4}$, where $e_{i,j}$ has a single 1 in Row i and Column j.

The column spaces $\mathcal{C}_i$ are defined as the span of unit-cell vectors in the i-th column, i.e. $\mathcal{C}_i = \textbf{span}\,(e_{0,i}, e_{1,i}, e_{2,i}, e_{3,i})$ for $i \in [0..3]$, e.g. $\mathcal{C}_0$ corresponds to

$$\mathcal{C}_0 = \left\{ \begin{bmatrix} x_0 & 0 & 0 & 0 \\ x_1 & 0 & 0 & 0 \\ x_2 & 0 & 0 & 0 \\ x_3 & 0 & 0 & 0 \end{bmatrix} \middle| \, \forall x_0, x_1, x_2, x_3 \in \mathbb{F}_{2^8} \right\} \equiv \begin{bmatrix} x_0 & 0 & 0 & 0 \\ x_1 & 0 & 0 & 0 \\ x_2 & 0 & 0 & 0 \\ x_3 & 0 & 0 & 0 \end{bmatrix}.$$

The diagonal spaces $\mathcal{D}_i$, anti-diagonal spaces $\mathcal{ID}_i$, and mixed spaces are defined as $\mathcal{D}_i = \mathsf{SR}^{-1}(\mathcal{C}_i)$, $\mathcal{ID}_i = \mathsf{SR}(\mathcal{C}_i)$, and $\mathcal{M}_i = \mathsf{MC}(\mathcal{ID}_i)$, respectively:

$$\mathcal{D}_0 \equiv \begin{bmatrix} x_0 & 0 & 0 & 0 \\ 0 & x_1 & 0 & 0 \\ 0 & 0 & x_2 & 0 \\ 0 & 0 & 0 & x_3 \end{bmatrix}, \; \mathcal{ID}_0 \equiv \begin{bmatrix} x_0 & 0 & 0 & 0 \\ 0 & 0 & 0 & x_1 \\ 0 & 0 & x_2 & 0 \\ 0 & x_3 & 0 & 0 \end{bmatrix}, \; \mathcal{M}_0 \equiv \begin{bmatrix} 2 \cdot x_0 & x_3 & x_2 & 3 \cdot x_1 \\ x_0 & x_3 & 3 \cdot x_2 & 2 \cdot x_1 \\ x_0 & 3 \cdot x_3 & 2 \cdot x_2 & x_1 \\ 3 \cdot x_0 & 2 \cdot x_3 & x_2 & x_1 \end{bmatrix}.$$

For $\mathcal{I} \subseteq [0..3]$, $\mathcal{C}_\mathcal{I}$, $\mathcal{D}_\mathcal{I}$, $\mathcal{ID}_\mathcal{I}$, and $\mathcal{M}_\mathcal{I}$ are defined as

$$\mathcal{C}_\mathcal{I} = \bigoplus_{i \in \mathcal{I}} \mathcal{C}_i, \quad \mathcal{D}_\mathcal{I} = \bigoplus_{i \in \mathcal{I}} \mathcal{D}_i, \quad \mathcal{ID}_\mathcal{I} = \bigoplus_{i \in \mathcal{I}} \mathcal{ID}_i, \quad \text{and} \quad \mathcal{M}_\mathcal{I} = \bigoplus_{i \in \mathcal{I}} \mathcal{M}_i.$$

By slight abuse of notation, we will use $\mathcal{D}_i(S)$ or $\mathcal{D}_\mathcal{I}(S)$ for some state $S \in \mathbb{F}_{2^8}^{4 \times 4}$ and $\mathcal{I} \subseteq [0..3]$ to refer to the i-th diagonal or the union of i-th diagonals of S for all $i \in \mathcal{I}$, respectively. This generalizes to columns, inverse diagonals, and mixed spaces of S in a natural manner.

2.2 Mixtures

Activity-Pattern Function. Let $x \in \mathbb{F}_{q^b}^m$ be a vector of field elements, e.g. an AES state for $(q, b, m) = (2, 8, 16)$. Following [32], the activity-pattern function activity $: \mathbb{F}_{q^b}^m \to \mathbb{F}_2^m$, maps $x = (x_0, \ldots, x_{m-1})$ to a vector $\alpha = (\alpha_0, \alpha_1, \ldots, \alpha_{m-1})$ where $\alpha_i = 1$ if $x_i \neq 0$ and 0 otherwise for all $i \in [0..m-1]$. We call α the activity vector of x. Later, we will use similar vectors for column-, diagonal-, anti-diagonal-, and mixed-space activity patterns.

Exchange Function. Given two distinct vectors $x^0, x^1 \in \mathbb{F}_{q^b}^m$ and an activity vector $\alpha \in \mathbb{F}_2^m$, we define exchange $: \mathbb{F}_2^m \times \mathbb{F}_{q^b}^m \times \mathbb{F}_{q^b}^m \to \mathbb{F}_{q^b}^m$ as

$$\mathsf{exchange}_\alpha(x^0, x^1) = (y_0, \ldots, y_{m-1}) \in \mathbb{F}_{q^b}^m \text{ where } y_i = x_i^{\alpha_i} \text{ for all } i \in [0..m-1].$$

Note that $\mathsf{exchange}_\alpha(x^1, x^0) = \mathsf{exchange}_{\alpha \oplus 1^m}(x^0, x^1)$. For vectors $x \in \mathbb{F}_{q^b}^m$, we use $\mathsf{wt}(x)$ for the number of non-zero cells in x:

$$\mathsf{wt}(x) \stackrel{\text{def}}{=} \sum_{i=0}^{m-1} \alpha_i \quad \text{where} \quad \alpha = \mathsf{activity}(x).$$

Definition 1 (Mixtures and Mixture Pairs). Let $x^0, x^1 \in \mathbb{F}_{q^b}^m$ be distinct. The set of all mixtures (that is, mixed texts) of (x^0, x^1) is defined as

$$\mathsf{mixtures}(x^0, x^1) = \left\{ y \in \mathbb{F}_{q^b}^m : \exists \alpha \in \mathbb{F}_2^m \text{ such that } y = \mathsf{exchange}_\alpha(x^0, x^1) \right\}.$$

The elements y are called mixtures of (x^0, x^1). A text y is called a trivial mixture of (x^0, x^1) iff $\alpha \in \{\mathbf{0}^m, \mathsf{activity}(x^0 \oplus x^1)\}$, i.e. if $y \in \{x^0, x^1\}$; otherwise, y is a non-trivial mixture. The set of all mixture pairs of (x^0, x^1) is defined as

$$\mathsf{mixturepairs}(x^0, x^1) = \Big\{ (y^0, y^1) \in \mathbb{F}_{q^b}^m \times \mathbb{F}_{q^b}^m : \exists \alpha \in \mathbb{F}_2^m \text{ such that}$$
$$y^0 = \mathsf{exchange}_\alpha(x^0, x^1) \text{ and } y^1 = \mathsf{exchange}_\alpha(x^1, x^0) \Big\}.$$

The pairs (y^0, y^1) are called mixture pairs of (or induced by) (x^0, x^1). A pair (y^0, y^1) is called a trivial mixture pair of (x^0, x^1) iff $(y^0, y^1) \in \{(x^0, x^1), (x^1, x^0)\}$ and a non-trivial mixture pair otherwise.

2.3 The Need for Small Tweaks and TweAES

Tweak Lengths. Various block-cipher modes of operation employ the primitive for several purposes, e.g. for authentication, encryption, producing an authentication tag, masks for distinct treatment of messages and associated data, etc. Tweakable block ciphers (TBCs) [24] add a tweak as an additional public input that can allow the use of different tweaks for different sub-applications in modes, for security and clarity of description. However, tweak lengths are often as large as block lengths or even longer, e.g. in CRAFT [8], QARMA [1] and QARMAv2 [2], or T-TWINE [33]; the TWEAKEY framework mixes keys and tweaks e.g. in Deoxys-BC and Joltik-BC [22], Skinny and MANTIS [7]. Before 2019, only Kiasu-BC [22] differed in that sense, which is a tweakable block cipher proposed alongside the TWEAKEY framework as an example of how one could transform the AES into a TBC with minimal modifications. It is almost identical to the AES-128 and only adds an unchanged 64-bit tweak to the topmost two rows of the state whenever a round-key addition is performed. Still, this 64-bit tweak is more than what would suffice in many modes for domain separation, which comes at a non-negligible price of implementation costs.

TweAES. To address this need, Chakraborti et al. [10,12] introduced the ElasticTweak framework to augment existing SPN block ciphers with tiny tweaks. They employed a linear code to expand such a tiny tweak to affect a significant portion of the state.[1] They defined a flexible transformation of a block cipher BC into a tweakable block cipher $\mathsf{tBC}[t, t_e, \mathsf{tic}, \mathsf{gap}]$, with t as the tweak length, t_e the expanded tweak length, tic the number of S-boxes affected by a tweak addition, and gap as the number of rounds between two tweak additions. In terms of

---
[1] An $[n, k, d]$-linear code over a field $\mathbb{F}$ is defined by a $k \times n$-element generator matrix $\mathbf{G}$ such that for all nonzero vectors $v \in \mathbb{F}^k$, $v \cdot \mathbf{G}$ has at least d nonzero elements.

instantiations, Chakraborti et al. proposed TweAES, TweGIFT-64, and TweGIFT-128, which tweaked AES-128, GIFT-64, and GIFT-128, respectively. For ESTATE, their second-round candidate to the NIST LightWeight Competition, the authors employed TweAES and TweGIFT as TweGIFT-128 as well as TweAES-6 as a six-round variant [11]. Hereafter, we consider only their variant of tweaked AES with four-bit tweaks, which corresponds to AES[4, 8, 8, 2] in their representation. We call this variant TweAES hereafter, consistent to [11]. TweAES enriches the AES with a tweak addition after Rounds 2, 4, 6, and 8. It takes a four-bit tweak $T = (t_0, t_1, t_2, t_3)$ and expands it to eight bits as $T_e = (t_0, \ldots, t_7)^\top = \mathbf{J} \cdot T^\top$ with a code $\mathbf{G} = [\mathbf{I}|\mathbf{I} \oplus \mathbf{J}]$ that consists of the identity $\mathbf{I}$ and an all-one matrix $\mathbf{J}$. Given that each entry of T_e contains only t_e/tic bits, we define $\widehat{T} \in \mathbb{F}_{2^8}^{16}$ such that $(\widehat{T}^\top)[i] = \widehat{t}_i = 0^{b-t_e/\text{tic}} \| t_i$ for $i \in [0..7]$ and 0^b for $i \in [8..15]$ for the expanded tweak, i.e. for AES[4, 8, 8, 2]:

$$\widehat{T} = \begin{bmatrix} \widehat{t}_0 & \widehat{t}_1 & \widehat{t}_2 & \widehat{t}_3 \\ \widehat{t}_4 & \widehat{t}_5 & \widehat{t}_6 & \widehat{t}_7 \\ 0^8 & 0^8 & 0^8 & 0^8 \\ 0^8 & 0^8 & 0^8 & 0^8 \end{bmatrix} \quad \text{where} \quad \begin{bmatrix} t_4 \\ t_5 \\ t_6 \\ t_7 \end{bmatrix} = (\mathbf{I} \oplus \mathbf{J}) \cdot T^\top = \begin{bmatrix} 0 & 1 & 1 & 1 \\ 1 & 0 & 1 & 1 \\ 1 & 1 & 0 & 1 \\ 1 & 1 & 1 & 0 \end{bmatrix} \cdot \begin{bmatrix} t_0 \\ t_1 \\ t_2 \\ t_3 \end{bmatrix}.$$

We can write $t_{i+4} = s \oplus t_i$ for all $i \in [0..3]$ with the sum $s = t_0 \oplus t_1 \oplus t_2 \oplus t_3$. $\mathbf{I} \oplus \mathbf{J}$ ensures at least four active bits for any nonzero input tweak difference. In TweAES, each tweak bit is XORed to the least significant bit of a byte in the two top rows, i.e., the first bytes in the topmost row are XORed with t_0, t_1, t_2, t_3, respectively. The bytes in the second row are XORed with t_4, t_5, t_6, and t_7, respectively. In combination with the XOR into the second row and the ShiftRows operation after a tweak addition, a non-zero tweak difference will affect at least three pairwise distinct columns of the state.

3 Inapplicability of Tweak-Induced First-Order Mixtures to TweAES with Four-Bit Tweaks

This section explains why the four-round mixture distinguisher by Grassi [17,18] cannot be started from tweak differences for TweAES with four-bit tweaks. Prior, we provide a short overview of the four-round mixture distinguisher.

3.1 Mixture Distinguisher on Four-Round AES

Grassi [18] introduced mixtures as simple structural recombination of bytes of two texts x and x' for deriving a second pair of texts y and y' out of x and x' for AES-like ciphers. He observed that if the bytes of the plaintexts are not mixed inside diagonals, the difference between the mixed pair will match that of the first pair after two rounds:

$$\mathsf{R}^2(x) \oplus \mathsf{R}^2(x') = \mathsf{R}^2(y) \oplus \mathsf{R}^2(y').$$

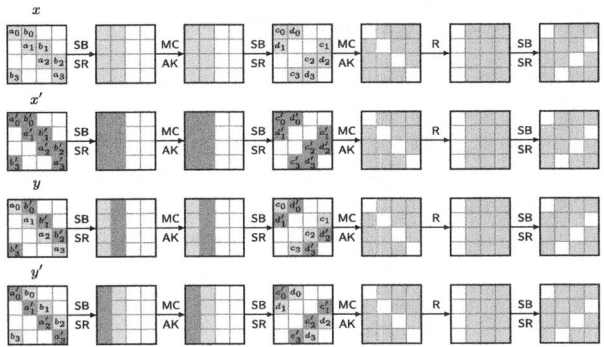

Fig. 1. A mixture-differential distinguisher on four-round AES. Colored bytes are active differences, white bytes are inactive; equal variables mean equal values. (Color figure online)

Thus, if the difference of the first pair will lie in a certain byte-aligned subspace after two rounds, the same will hold for the second pair. Given that if $x \oplus x' \in \mathcal{D}_\mathcal{J}$ for some set $\mathcal{J} \subset [0..3]$ and $|\mathcal{J}| \leq 3$, it holds that

$$\mathsf{R}^2(x) \oplus \mathsf{R}^2(x') \in \mathcal{D}_\mathcal{J} \Leftrightarrow \mathsf{R}^4(x) \oplus \mathsf{R}^4(x') \in \mathcal{M}_\mathcal{J}, \quad \text{which leads to}$$
$$\mathsf{R}^4(y) \oplus \mathsf{R}^4(y') \in \mathcal{M}_\mathcal{J} \Leftrightarrow \mathsf{R}^4(x) \oplus \mathsf{R}^4(x') \in \mathcal{M}_\mathcal{J},$$

i.e., the conditional-differential probability for the second pair is significantly different from that for a random permutation.

Figure 1 illustrates an example. The diagonal activity vector of two plaintexts (x, x'), with two active diagonals in $x \oplus x'$, could be $\mathsf{activity}(x \oplus x') = (1, 1, 0, 0)$. A mixture of two new texts (y, y') with $y \oplus y' = x \oplus x'$ can be derived by mixing the active diagonals of x and x': $y = \mathsf{exchange}_{(1,0,0,0)}(x, x')$ and $y' = \mathsf{exchange}_{(0,1,0,0)}(x, x')$.

The four-round mixture distinguisher above also applies to four-round TweAES when the starting differences are injected into the plaintexts. However, the more interesting aspects in the cryptanalysis of TweAES lie in evaluating how the additional tweak affects its security compared to that of the plain AES. If the mixture differential above could be started from a difference in the tweak only, it could yield an eight-round attack. An adversary could try to cancel a difference in the plaintext with the tweak after the first two rounds, bypass the next two rounds with a zero difference, and inject the differences for two mixture pairs after Round 4 for an eight-round key-recovery attack or even distinguisher. Such bypassing rounds for free by canceling the state difference with the tweak has been used extensively in previous attacks. For example, existing integral, impossible-differential, boomerang, and Demirci-Selçuk meet-in-the-middle attacks on the AES could be extended by one round when applied to Kiasu-BC [14,15,25,34]. Thus, one is naturally interested in methods that make dedicated use of the tweak for more effective attacks also on TweAES.

3.2 On Tweak-Induced Mixtures in TweAES

Tweak-induced mixture differentials can be found for Kiasu-BC straightforwardly since the 64-bit tweak undergoes no transformations. For TweAES, we would have to find four pairwise distinct text-tweak tuples (P, T^0), (P, T^1), (P, T^2), and (P, T^3) such that the diagonals of the extensions $\widehat{T}^2$ and $\widehat{T}^3$ are mixtures of the diagonals of $\widehat{T}^0$ and $\widehat{T}^1$. We can show that the code used for tweak expansion in TweAES, in the way it is combined with ShiftRows, prevents such mixtures. We cannot derive a tweak $\widehat{T}^2$ such that its diagonals are a mixture of those of $\widehat{T}^0$ and $\widehat{T}^1$. Theorem 1 captures this statement. We slightly abuse notation $\mathcal{D}_j(\widehat{T}^i)$ to refer to the j-th diagonal of $\widehat{T}^i$, for $j \in [0..3]$, in the remainder of this section.

Theorem 1. Let $T^0, T^1, T^2 \in (\{0,1\}^4)^3$ be three pairwise distinct tweaks for TweAES and $\widehat{T}^i \in \mathbb{F}_{2^8}^{4 \times 4}$ for $i \in [0..2]$ their corresponding expanded tweaks. Then, there exists a diagonal-space index $j \in [0..3]$ s. t. $\mathcal{D}_j(\widehat{T}^2) \notin \{\mathcal{D}_j(\widehat{T}^0), \mathcal{D}_j(\widehat{T}^1)\}$.

Proof. We denote the expanded tweaks as $T_e^i \in \{0,1\}^8 = (t_0^i, \ldots, t_7^i)$ and the non-expanded tweaks as $T^i = (t_0^i, \ldots, t_3^i)$. Note that $\widehat{T}^i \in \mathbb{F}_{2^8}^{4 \times 4}$ are expanded AES states. Recall that $t_{j+4}^i = s^i \oplus t_j^i$ for $s^i = \bigoplus_{j=0}^{3} t_j^i$ and all $j \in [0..3]$. We will treat all column and diagonal indices j modulo four in the remainder. We define $s^{i,i'} = s^i \oplus s^{i'}$. In the following, we consider four cases that cover all possibilities.

Case (1): $\mathrm{wt}(T^0 \oplus T^1) = 1$. In this case, there must exist exactly one bit $j \in [0..3]$ such that $t_j^0 \neq t_j^1$. If $t_j^2 = t_j^0$, $\widehat{T}^2$ would be identical to $\widehat{T}^0$. Otherwise, if $t_j^2 = t_j^1$, all other bits are identical to that of $\widehat{T}^0$ and $\widehat{T}^1$, producing $\widehat{T}^2 = \widehat{T}^1$ and not a distinct mixed text. Hence, the case is invalid.

Case (2): $\mathrm{wt}(T^0 \oplus T^1) = 2$. Here, it holds that $s^0 = s^1$. In the following, we distinguish between two subcases.

Subcase (2.1): there exists $j \in [0..3]$ such that $t_j^1 \neq t_j^0$, $t_{j+1}^1 \neq t_{j+1}^0$. Thus, both non-expanded tweak bits that differ in $\widehat{T}^1$ from $\widehat{T}^0$ are adjacent. To be a mixture, $\widehat{T}^2$ must share exactly one of the non-expanded tweak bits with $\widehat{T}^0$ and one with $\widehat{T}^1$, i.e. $(t_j^2, t_{j+1}^2) \in \{(t_j^0, t_{j+1}^1), (t_j^1, t_{j+1}^0)\}$ and therefore $s^{0,2} = s^{1,2} = 1$. It follows that $t_{j+6}^2 = t_{j+6}^0 \oplus 1 = t_{j+6}^1 \oplus 1$. Thus, $\mathcal{D}_{j+1}(\widehat{T}^2)$ can never be identical to $\mathcal{D}_{j+1}(\widehat{T}^0)$ or $\mathcal{D}_{j+1}(\widehat{T}^1)$.

Subcase (2.2): there exists $j \in [0..3]$ such that $t_j^1 \neq t_j^0$, $t_{j+2}^1 \neq t_{j+2}^0$. In this case, the non-expanded tweak bits wherein $\widehat{T}^1$ differs from $\widehat{T}^0$ are non-adjacent. For $\widehat{T}^2$ to be a mixture of $\widehat{T}^0$ and $\widehat{T}^1$, it must share exactly one of the non-expanded tweak bits with $\widehat{T}^0$ and one with $\widehat{T}^1$, i.e. $(t_j^2, t_{j+2}^2) \in \{(t_j^0, t_{j+2}^1), (t_j^1, t_{j+2}^0)\}$ and again $s^{0,2} = s^{1,2} = 1$. It follows that $t_{j+5}^2 = t_{j+5}^0 \oplus 1 = t_{j+5}^1 \oplus 1$. Thus, $\mathcal{D}_j(\widehat{T}^2)$ can never be identical to $\mathcal{D}_j(\widehat{T}^0)$ or $\mathcal{D}_j(\widehat{T}^1)$.

Case (3): wt$(T^0 \oplus T^1) = 3$. In this case, it holds that $s^0 \neq s^1$. There exists a single $j \in [0..3]$ such that $t_j^1 = t_j^0$. Again, we distinguish between two subcases.

Subcase (3.1): $s^2 = s^0$. Since $\widehat{T}^2$ shall be a mixture, there must exist some bit j' that $\widehat{T}^2$ shares with $\widehat{T}^0$. Since $s^2 = s^0$, $t_{j'+4}^2 = t_{j'+4}^0$ must hold. Thus, for the diagonal $\mathcal{D}_{j'-1}(\widehat{T}^2) \in \{\mathcal{D}_{j'-1}(\widehat{T}^0), \mathcal{D}_{j'-1}(\widehat{T}^1)\}$, $t_{j'+4}^2 = t_{j'+4}^0$ implies that $t_{j'-1}^2$ must be $t_{j'-1}^0$. For $\widehat{T}^2$ to be a mixture, there must exist a bit $j'' \in \{j'+1, j'+2\}$ that is shared with $\widehat{T}^1$. However, from $s^2 = s^0 \neq s^1$, it follows that $t_{j''+4}^2 = t_{j''}^2 \oplus s^2 \neq t_{j''+4}^1 = t_{j''+4}^0$. Thus, the expanded value of $t_{j''+4}^2$ occurred in neither $\widehat{T}^0$ nor $\widehat{T}^1$ and therefore the diagonal $\mathcal{D}_{j''-1}(\widehat{T}^2) \notin \{\mathcal{D}_{j''-1}(\widehat{T}^0), \mathcal{D}_{j''-1}(\widehat{T}^1)\}$.

Subcase (3.2): $s^2 = s^1$. Similarly, since $\widehat{T}^2$ shall be a mixture, there must exist some bit j' that $\widehat{T}^2$ shares with $\widehat{T}^0$. Since $s^2 = s^1$, $t_{j'+4}^2 = t_{j'+4}^1$ must hold. The diagonal $\mathcal{D}_{j'-1}(\widehat{T}^2)$ can only be $\{\mathcal{D}_{j'-1}(\widehat{T}^0), \mathcal{D}_{j'-1}(\widehat{T}^1)\}$ if $j' = j$, i.e. the bit where the non-expanded tweaks $t_j^0 = t_j^1$ were identical. Then, the diagonal demands that $t_{j-1}^2 = t_{j-1}^1$ and therefore $t_{j+3}^2 = t_{j+3}^1$. Thus, $\widehat{T}^2$ shares two columns with $\widehat{T}^1$. For $\widehat{T}^2$ to be a mixture, there must exist a bit $j'' \in \{j+1, j+2\}$ that is shared with $\widehat{T}^0$. However, from $s^2 = s^1 \neq s^0$, it follows that $t_{j''+4}^2 = t_{j''}^2 \oplus s^2 \neq t_{j''+4}^0 = t_{j''+4}^1$. Thus, the expanded value of $t_{j''+4}^2$ occurred in neither $\widehat{T}^0$ nor $\widehat{T}^1$ and therefore the diagonal $\mathcal{D}_{j''-1}(\widehat{T}^2) \notin \{\mathcal{D}_{j''-1}(\widehat{T}^0), \mathcal{D}_{j''-1}(\widehat{T}^1)\}$.

Case (4): wt$(T^0 \oplus T^1) = 4$. It holds that $s^0 = s^1$ in the following two subcases.

Subcase (4.1): $s^2 = s^0 = s^1$. For $\widehat{T}^2$ to be a mixture of $\widehat{T}^0$ and $\widehat{T}^1$, there must exist some $j \in [0..3]$ such that $t_j^2 = t_j^1$ and $t_{j+1}^2 = t_{j+1}^0$. Since $s^2 = s^0 = s^1$, it holds that $t_{j+5}^2 = t_{j+5}^0$. This implies $\mathcal{D}_j(\widehat{T}^2) = (t_j^1, t_{j+5}^0) \notin \{\mathcal{D}_j(\widehat{T}^0), \mathcal{D}_j(\widehat{T}^1)\}$.

Subcase (4.2): $s^2 \neq s^0 = s^1$. For $\widehat{T}^2$ to be a mixture of $\widehat{T}^0$ and $\widehat{T}^1$, there must exist some $j \in [0..3]$ such that $t_j^2 = t_j^1$ and $t_{j+1}^2 = t_{j+1}^0$. Since $s^2 \neq s^0 = s^1$, it holds that $t_{j+4}^2 = t_{j+4}^0$ and $t_{j+5}^2 = t_{j+5}^1$. Thus, $\mathcal{D}_j(\widehat{T}^2) = \mathcal{D}_j(\widehat{T}^1)$. To have $\mathcal{D}_{j+1}(\widehat{T}^2) \in \{\mathcal{D}_{j+1}(\widehat{T}^0), \mathcal{D}_{j+1}(\widehat{T}^1)\}$, and $\mathcal{D}_{j-1}(\widehat{T}^2) \in \{\mathcal{D}_{j-1}(\widehat{T}^0), \mathcal{D}_{j-1}(\widehat{T}^1)\}$, it follows that $t_{j+6}^2 = t_{j+6}^0$ and $t_{j+3}^2 = t_{j+3}^0$. From an iterated argument, the only solution for the non-expanded parts of $\widehat{T}^2$ is $(t_0^2, \ldots, t_7^2) \in \{(t_0^0, t_1^1, t_2^0, t_3^1, t_4^1, t_5^0, t_6^1, t_7^0), (t_0^1, t_1^0, t_2^1, t_3^0, t_4^1, t_5^1, t_6^0, t_7^1)\}$. However, both solutions have $t_{j+4}^2 \neq t_j^2$ for all $j \in [0..3]$ but $s^2 = 0$, which cannot occur. □

Thus, we cannot induce mixtures from only tweak differences in TweAES. In the following, we study two alternative directions for constructing mixtures induced by tweak differences: (1) partial mixtures and (2) higher-order mixtures.

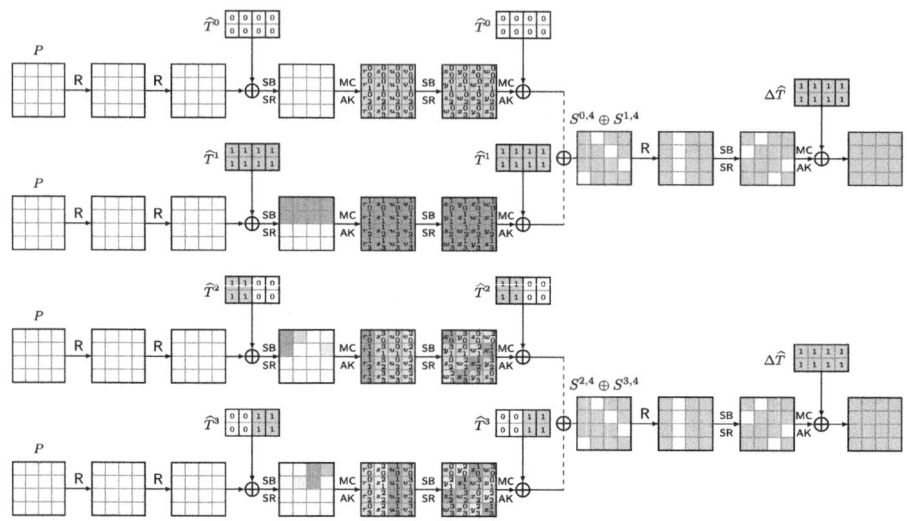

Fig. 2. Six-round trails of TweAES with expanded tweaks from a partial mixture.

4 Partial Mixtures

We can define partial mixtures straightforwardly. Prior, we have to define a generalized variant of the exchange function.

Definition 2 (Second-order exchangeFunction). Let $\mathbf{x} = (x^0, x^1, x^2, x^3) \in (\mathbb{F}_{q^b}^m)^4$ be pairwise distinct with $x^0 \oplus x^1 = x^2 \oplus x^3$ and $\alpha \in (\mathbb{Z}_4)^m$. We define exchange$^{(2)} : (\mathbb{Z}_4)^m \times (\mathbb{F}_{q^b}^m)^4 \to \mathbb{F}_{q^b}^m$ as

$$\text{exchange}_\alpha^{(2)}(\mathbf{x}) = (y_0, \ldots, y_{m-1}) \in \mathbb{F}_{q^b}^m \, , \text{ where } y_i = x_i^{\alpha_i} \text{ for all } i \in [0..m-1].$$

Definition 3 (ε-partial Mixture). Let $\mathbf{x}$ and α be defined as in Definition 2. We call a pair of texts $y^0 = \text{exchange}_\alpha^{(2)}(\mathbf{x})$ and $y^1 = \text{exchange}_{\alpha \oplus \mathbf{1}^m}^{(2)}(\mathbf{x})$ an ε-partial mixture of (x^0, x^1) if $|\{i \in [0..m-1] : \alpha_i \notin \{0,1\}\}| \leq \varepsilon$. Thus, at most ε elements in y^0 and y^1 do not originate from x^0 or x^1.

The lowest ε for a tweak-difference-induced ε-partial mixture of TweAES is two. Figure 2 shows an attempt of a six-round distinguisher from partial mixtures. Let $P \in (\mathbb{F}_{2^8})^{16}$ be a 16-byte plaintext and assume $T^0 = (0,0,0,0)$, $T^1 = (1,1,1,1)$, $T^2 = (1,1,0,0)$, $T^3 = (0,0,1,1)$. Let $\widehat{T}^i$ denote the corresponding expanding tweaks or $i \in [0..3]$ as before. We denote by $S^{i,r}$ the states after r-round encryption of (P, T^i), for $i \in [0..3]$, under a random secret key. The diagonals of T^1 are all $(1,1)$, so that all columns of $S^{0,3}$ differ from those of $S^{1,3}$. For the second pair, it holds that $\mathcal{D}_0(\widehat{T}^2) = \mathcal{D}_0(\widehat{T}^1)$, $\mathcal{D}_2(\widehat{T}^2) = \mathcal{D}_2(\widehat{T}^0)$, $\mathcal{D}_0(\widehat{T}^3) = \mathcal{D}_0(\widehat{T}^0)$, and $\mathcal{D}_2(\widehat{T}^3) = \mathcal{D}_2(\widehat{T}^1)$. Thus, the first and third columns of $S^{2,3}$ and $S^{3,3}$ are inherited from $S^{0,3}$ and $S^{1,3}$, respectively. However, the second and fourth diagonals, $\mathcal{D}_j$, for $j \in \{1,3\}$, are fresh and therefore, the corresponding columns in $S^{2,3}$ and $S^{3,3}$ differ from those of $S^{0,3}$ and $S^{1,3}$.

Define $\mathcal{I} \subset [0..3]$ and let $d = 4 - |\mathcal{I}| \in \{1,2,3\}$. We will derive the probabilities that both pairs lie in a mixed space $\mathcal{M}_\mathcal{I}$ after almost six rounds, with the final tweak addition inverted. As an example, Fig. 2 shows $\mathcal{I} = \{0,2,3\}$. For a random permutation, the probability for this event is approximately $(2^{-4.8d})^2 = 2^{-64d}$. For TweAES, we need d inactive diagonals after Round 4 in both pairs:

$$S^{0,4} \oplus S^{1,4} \in \mathcal{D}_\mathcal{I} \quad \text{and} \quad S^{2,4} \oplus S^{3,4} \in \mathcal{D}_\mathcal{I}$$

since they propagate through two rounds to the mixed space with probability one as $\mathsf{R}^2(x) \oplus \mathsf{R}^2(y) \in \mathcal{M}_\mathcal{I} \Leftrightarrow x \oplus y \in \mathcal{D}_\mathcal{I}$ holds for two-round AES [21]:

$$\Pr\left[\begin{matrix} \mathsf{R}^2(S^{0,4}) \oplus \mathsf{R}^2(S^{1,4}) \in \mathcal{M}_\mathcal{I}, \\ \mathsf{R}^2(S^{2,4}) \oplus \mathsf{R}^2(S^{3,4}) \in \mathcal{M}_\mathcal{I} \end{matrix} \middle| \begin{matrix} S^{0,4} \oplus S^{1,4} \in \mathcal{D}_\mathcal{I} \\ S^{2,4} \oplus S^{3,4} \in \mathcal{D}_\mathcal{I} \end{matrix}\right] = 1.$$

In the following, we assume that the cipher behaves like a first-order Markov cipher, that the S-box is close to being APN (cf. [19]), and the keys are chosen uniformly at random. The probability that the first pair of TweAES has d inactive diagonals is approximately $(2^{-4.8})^d$. The probability for the second pair's difference to be in $\mathcal{D}_\mathcal{I}$ after four rounds conditioned on the event that the first pair's difference after four rounds is in $\mathcal{D}_\mathcal{I}$ is a little more sophisticated. In each column, d bytes must share the same difference of $S^{2,4} \oplus S^{3,4} = S^{0,4} \oplus S^{1,4}$. It has to hold in each column $i \in [0..3]$ that

$$\alpha_{j_1}(y^2_{1-i} \oplus y^3_{1-i}) \oplus \beta_{j_1}(w^2_{3-i} \oplus w^3_{3-i}) = \alpha_{j_1}(y^0_{1-i} \oplus y^1_{1-i}) \oplus \beta_{j_1}(w^0_{3-i} \oplus w^1_{3-i})$$

$$\vdots \quad \vdots \quad \vdots$$

$$\alpha_{j_d}(y^2_{1-i} \oplus y^3_{1-i}) \oplus \beta_{j_d}(w^2_{3-i} \oplus w^3_{3-i}) = \alpha_{j_d}(y^0_{1-i} \oplus y^1_{1-i}) \oplus \beta_{j_d}(w^0_{3-i} \oplus w^1_{3-i}).$$

where the α's and β's are coefficients in the MixColumns matrix and the variables of y^j and w^j refer to the variables in the states after almost four rounds (without the final MixColumns operation) in Fig. 2. If $d \leq 2$, the probability is lower bounded by $2^{-4.8d}$. However, if $d = 3$, the probability in each column i is at least

$$\Pr\left[S^{2,4} \oplus S^{3,4} \in \mathcal{D}_\mathcal{I} | S^{0,4} \oplus S^{1,4} \in \mathcal{D}_\mathcal{I}\right]$$
$$\geq \Pr\left[\begin{matrix} y^2_{1-i} \oplus y^3_{1-i} = y^0_{1-i} \oplus y^1_{1-i} \\ w^2_{3-i} \oplus w^3_{3-i} = w^0_{3-i} \oplus w^1_{3-i} \end{matrix} \text{ for all } i \in [0..3]\right] \geq 2^{-64}.$$

Thus, the conditional probability for $d = 3$ inactive diagonals is at least $2^{-4.16}$ given that the first pair has d inactive diagonals, under our assumptions. It follows in the real world that for $d \in [1..3]$

$$\Pr\left[S^{2,6} \oplus S^{3,6} \in \mathcal{M}_\mathcal{I} \wedge S^{0,6} \oplus S^{1,6} \in \mathcal{M}_\mathcal{I}\right] \simeq 2^{-(32d + \min(32d, 64))}.$$

Thus, such a distinguisher based on a partial mixture seems to require three active diagonals so that the probability of two pairs conforming to the mixture can be substantially higher than the probability for a random permutation.

However, the associated probability of 2^{-160} would imply that the number of necessary pairs was impossible to collect for TweAES with four-bit tweaks since there exist at most $\binom{16}{3} \cdot 2^{128} / \simeq 2^{137.1}$ unordered plaintext-tweak tuples (P, T^0), (P, T^1), and (P, T^2) (which would define $T^3 = T^0 \oplus T^1 \oplus T^2$) for a fixed key. Therefore, we study higher-order mixtures in the following sections.

5 Higher-Order Mixtures

For first-order mixtures, the set of all mixture texts was derived from a single base pair, and an activity vector determined both mixed texts of the tuple. For higher-order mixtures, one can derive texts from more than two texts but from 2^k-tuples instead. For this purpose, we generalize activity vectors $\alpha \in \mathbb{F}_2^m$ to *selection vectors* for generating mixed texts and $\sigma \in \mathbb{Z}_{2^k}$ and *permutation vectors* ψ for generating (i.e. to permuting the values in) mixture tuples. We will extend the earlier Definition 2 of exchange$^{(2)}$ to exchange$^{(k)}$. Moreover, we define generatemixturetuple$^{(k)}$ since exchange cannot define 2^k-tuples for $k > 1$.

For definitional purposes, let Perm$(\mathcal{X})$ be the set of all permutations over a set $\mathcal{X}$. We define two specific applications in the following. We define

$$\mathsf{NbPerm}(\mathbb{Z}_{2^k}) \stackrel{\text{def}}{=} \{\pi \in \mathsf{Perm}(\mathbb{Z}_{2^k}) : |\pi(2i) - \pi(2i+1)| = 1, i \in [0..2^{k-1}-1]\}.$$

Moreover, we extend it to $\mathsf{NbPerm}_0(\mathbb{Z}_{2^k}) \stackrel{\text{def}}{=} \mathsf{NbPerm}(\mathbb{Z}_{2^k}) \cup \mathbf{0}^{2^k}$. The constant element $\mathbf{0}^{2^k}$ will be necessary to cover the space spanned by those vector elements that are constant over all base texts.

Definition 4 (2^k-tuple-derived Mixtures). Define $\mathbf{x} = (x^0, \ldots, x^{2^k-1}) \in (\mathbb{F}_{q^b}^m)^{2^k}$ such that for all $s \in [0..2^{k-1}-1]$, $x^{2s} \oplus x^{2s+1} = \Delta x$ is constant and nonzero. For $\sigma \in (\mathbb{Z}_{2^k})^m$, we define exchange$^{(k)} : (\mathbb{Z}_{2^k})^m \times (\mathbb{F}_{q^b}^m)^{2^k} \to \mathbb{F}_{q^b}^m$ as

$$\mathsf{exchange}_\sigma^{(k)}(\mathbf{x}) = (y_0, \ldots, y_{m-1}) \in \mathbb{F}_{q^b}^m, \text{ where } y_i = x_i^{\sigma_i} \text{ for all } i \in [0..m-1].$$

We call y a trivial mixture of $\mathbf{x}$ if $y \in \mathbf{x}$ i.e., $\sigma_0 = \cdots = \sigma_{2^k-1}$ and a non-trivial mixture of $\mathbf{x}$ otherwise. The set of all k-th-order mixtures is defined as

$$\mathsf{mixtures}^{(k)}(\mathbf{x}) = \left\{ y \in \mathbb{F}_{q^b}^m : \exists \sigma \in (\mathbb{Z}_{2^k})^m \text{ such that } y = \mathsf{exchange}_\sigma^{(k)}(\mathbf{x}) \right\}.$$

Let $\boldsymbol{\psi} = (\psi^0, \ldots, \psi^{2^k-1}) \in \mathsf{NbPerm}_0(\mathbb{Z}_{2^k})^m$. We define generatemixturetuple$^{(k)}$: $\mathsf{NbPerm}_0(\mathbb{Z}_{2^k})^m \times (\mathbb{F}_{q^b}^m)^{2^k} \to (\mathbb{F}_{q^b}^m)^{2^k}$ as

$$\mathsf{generatemixturetuple}_{\boldsymbol{\psi}}^{(k)}(\mathbf{x}) = (y^0, \ldots, y^{2^k-1}) \text{ where } y_i^j = x_i^{\psi^i(j)},$$

for all $j \in [0..2^k - 1]$ and $i \in [0..m - 1]$. A mixture tuple $\mathbf{y}$ is called a trivial mixture of $\mathbf{x}$ iff it is a permutation of $\mathbf{x}$, i.e. $\exists \psi \in \mathsf{NbPerm}_0(\mathbb{Z}_{2^k})$ such that

$y^j = x^{\psi(j)}$ for all $j \in [0..2^k - 1]$. **y** is called a non-trivial mixture tuple of **x** otherwise. The set of all k-th-order mixture tuples is given by

$$\mathsf{mixturetuples}^{(k)}(\mathbf{x}) = \left\{ (y^0, \ldots, y^{2^k-1}) \in (\mathbb{F}_{q^b}^m)^{2^k} : \exists \psi \in \mathsf{NbPerm}_0(\mathbb{Z}_{2^k})^m \text{ s.t.} \right.$$
$$\left. (y^0, \ldots, y^{2^k-1}) = \mathsf{generatemixturetuple}_\psi^{(k)}(\mathbf{x}) \right\} .$$

Example 1. Consider the following 2^2 base texts from two base pairs with $m = 4$:

$$\mathbf{x} = (x^0, x^1, x^2, x^3) = \left(\begin{bmatrix} a_0 \\ b_0 \\ c_0 \\ d_0 \end{bmatrix}, \begin{bmatrix} a_1 \\ b_1 \\ c_1 \\ d_0 \end{bmatrix}, \begin{bmatrix} a_2 \\ b_2 \\ c_2 \\ d_0 \end{bmatrix}, \begin{bmatrix} a_3 \\ b_3 \\ c_3 \\ d_0 \end{bmatrix} \right)$$

and the four derived mixtures:

$$\mathbf{y} = (y^0, y^1, y^2, y^3) = \left(\begin{bmatrix} a_2 \\ b_1 \\ c_3 \\ d_0 \end{bmatrix}, \begin{bmatrix} a_3 \\ b_0 \\ c_2 \\ d_0 \end{bmatrix}, \begin{bmatrix} a_0 \\ b_3 \\ c_1 \\ d_0 \end{bmatrix}, \begin{bmatrix} a_1 \\ b_2 \\ c_0 \\ d_0 \end{bmatrix} \right) .$$

The texts in **y** are mixtures of **x** since there exist corresponding selection vectors σ^i for all $i \in [0..2^k - 1]$. **y** is also a mixture 4-tuple of **x** since there exist permutation vectors ψ^j $j \in [0..m-1]$:

$$\boldsymbol{\sigma} = (\sigma^0, \sigma^1, \sigma^2, \sigma^3) = ((2,1,3,0), (3,0,2,0), (0,3,1,0), (1,2,0,0))$$
$$\boldsymbol{\psi} = (\psi^0, \psi^1, \psi^2, \psi^3) = ((2,3,0,1), (1,0,3,2), (3,2,1,0), \mathbf{0}^4) .$$

Impact on Conditional Probability. In contrast to their first-order variants, mixtures derived from more than one pair may not follow a (truncated) differential trail only because the base pairs do. For example, Grassi [18] exploited that, whenever a base pair followed a truncated differential through four-round AES, its mixtures would also follow this differential. However, the texts y^i in Example 1 above are generated from two pairs each, which defines more equations in addition to those of the base pairs. Still, since all defining vectors ψ^i are permutations or all-constant vectors, their equation system cannot have full rank. This means, that whenever all base pairs and all but one of the mixture pairs follow the same (truncated) differential, this is guaranteed for the remaining pair. Consequently, higher-order mixtures can be a tool for settings where first-order mixtures are inapplicable. Plus, one may construct considerably more sets of higher-order mixture tuples than of the first order. However, higher-order mixtures may come at the price of a significantly reduced probability that all pairs fulfill a certain difference later.

We can define a further extension that can become helpful. Let $\mathsf{NbPerm}_{0,c}(\mathbb{Z}_{2^k}) \stackrel{\text{def}}{=} \mathsf{NbPerm}(\mathbb{Z}_{2^k}) \cup \mathbf{0}^{2^k} \cup (2^{k-1})^{2^k}$. This means that the set of 2^{k-1} mixture texts can define constants not defined by the 2^{k-1} base texts. In Example 1, this could be the case when replacing ψ^3 with $\mathbf{2}^4$, i.e. replacing d_0 in each mixture y^i by a new value $d_1 \neq d_0$. This does not change the differences between pairs and yields more flexibility while preserving a non-full rank of the equation system.

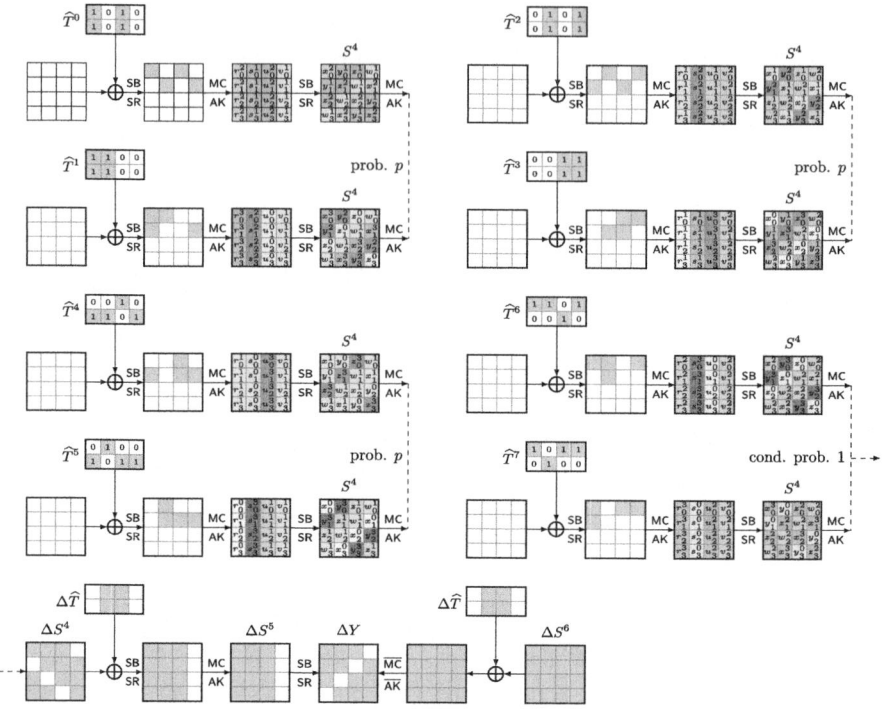

Fig. 3. Second-order mixture distinguisher on six rounds of TweAES. Top: Rounds 3 and 4. Bottom: Truncated differential between state pairs $(2j, 2j+1)$ through Rounds 5 and 6, here for a difference in $\mathcal{D}_{0,1,2}$ after four rounds.

6 Second-Order Mixtures for TweAES

In the following, we construct a second-order mixture distinguisher on six-round TweAES before we extend it to a seven-round key-recovery attack.

6.1 Six-Round Distinguisher

Assume a set of eight plaintext-tweak pairs (P, T^j) for $j \in [0..7]$. Let C^i be the ciphertexts after six rounds and by Y^i the states with the final tweak addition and the MixColumns operation inverted over all text-tweak tuples i. For all $j \in [0..3]$, we need $\Delta T = T^{2j} \oplus T^{2j+1}$ to be constant, where for concreteness, we choose $\Delta T = (0, 1, 1, 0)$. In the following, we describe a second-order mixture distinguisher on six-round TweAES, which is visualized in Fig. 3. We assume that we obtain the same inactive diagonal after the tweak addition at the end of the fourth round between the texts of each of the first three pairs with some probability $p \simeq 2^{-32}$. We want $\mathcal{ID}_\mathcal{I}$ for $|\mathcal{I}| = 3$, i.e. a single inactive anti-diagonal after six rounds without the final MixColumns operation and tweak addition.

Distinguisher Procedure. The distinguisher proceeds as follows:

1. Fix eight pairwise distinct tweaks T^j with $T^{2j} \oplus T^{2j+1} = \Delta T$ for all $j \in [0..3]$.
2. For all $i \in [0..2^{94}-1]$ and $j \in [0..7]$, choose P^i randomly but pairwise distinct and collect the encryptions $C^{i,j}$ of $(P^i, T^{i,j})$. For all $C^{i,j}$, invert the final Mix-Columns operation and tweak addition: $Y^{i,j} = \mathsf{MC}^{-1}(C^{i,j} \oplus \widehat{T}^{i,j})$.
3. If there exist i and $\mathcal{I} \subset \{0,1,2,3\}$, i.e. $|\mathcal{I}| \leq 3$, such that $Y^{i,2j} \oplus Y^{i,2j+1} \in \mathcal{ID}_\mathcal{I}$ holds for all $j \in [0..3]$, then output real and output random otherwise.

Complexity. Since we can choose any of the four anti-diagonals to be inactive in the four pairs, the distinguisher needs $2^{96}/4 = 2^{94}$ chosen plaintexts plus $2^{94} \cdot 8$ inverse MixColumns operations for each octet of eight texts. The memory complexity is negligible, given that at most eight states must be stored at a time. The success probability for the real six-round TweAES is approximately $1 - e^{-1}$ whereas that of a random four-tuple of pairs to have the same inactive anti-diagonal in all pairs is roughly $4 \cdot (2^{-32})^4 \simeq 2^{-126}$, and approximately $2^{94-126} = 2^{-32}$ over all encrypted octets.

6.2 Deriving a Seven-Round Key-Recovery Attack

The distinguisher from Sect. 6.1 can be turned into a key-recovery attack on seven rounds in the spirit of the six-round attacks in [3]. Figure 4 illustrates the appended round and variables. Prior to the attack description, we define precomputation tables $\mathcal{H}_c^t$ for $c \in [0..3]$ and $t \in \{0,1\}$:

1. Initialize an empty table $\mathcal{Z}$.
2. For all columns $y = (y_0, y_1, y_2, y_3) \in \mathbb{F}_{2^8}^4$ and all 2^{24} differences $\Delta y = (\Delta y_0, \Delta y_1, \Delta y_2, \Delta y_3) \in \mathbb{F}_{2^8}^4$ such that $\Delta y_c = 0^7 \| t$:
   - Compute $z \leftarrow \mathsf{SB}(\mathsf{MC}(y))$ and $z' \leftarrow \mathsf{SB}(\mathsf{MC}(y \oplus \Delta y))$, derive $\Delta z \leftarrow z \oplus z'$ and add z to $\mathcal{Z}[\Delta z]$. Note that SB and MC operate on a single column here. We expect on average $2^{32+24-32} = 2^{24}$ entries per Δz.
3. For each $\Delta z, \Delta x \in (\mathbb{F}_{2^8}^4)^2$:
   - For all entries $z \in \mathcal{Z}[\Delta z]$ and $x \in \mathcal{Z}[\Delta x]$, determine $\Delta a = z \oplus x$. Store x in $\mathcal{H}_c^t[\Delta x, \Delta z, \Delta a]$. There will be on average $2^{32+32+24+24-96} = 2^{16}$ values x per index.

The time complexity for the tables $\mathcal{Z}$ is $2 \cdot 4 \cdot 2^{32+24} = 2^{59}$ single-column partial encryption and decryptions through one round and all combinations of t and c each. The complexity for the eight tables $\mathcal{H}_c^t$ is $2 \cdot 4 \cdot 2^{32+32+24+24} = 2^{115}$ memory accesses. We approximate the complexity of an encryption through seven-round TweAES by $7 \cdot 16 = 112 \simeq 2^{6.7}$ S-box lookups in the spirit of e.g. [3,19]. Thus, we consider the creation of the tables to be equivalent to roughly $2^{59} \cdot \frac{2}{4} \cdot \frac{1}{7} + 2^{115-6.7} \simeq 2^{108.3}$ encryption equivalents. The memory costs are $2^{32} \cdot 2^{24}$ for a temporary table $\mathcal{Z}$ and $2 \cdot 4 \cdot 2^{96} \cdot 2^{16}$ four-byte values or 2^{113} AES states over all tables $\mathcal{H}_c^t$.

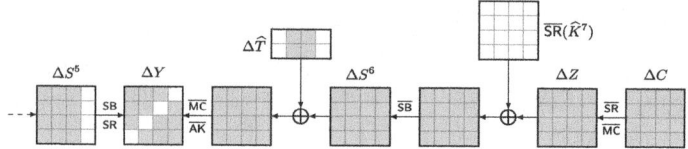

Fig. 4. Final round of the key-recovery attack on seven-round TweAES. Gray bytes are active bytes in differences. (Color figure online)

Attack Procedure. The attack over the first seven rounds proceeds as follows:

1. Initialize empty lists $\mathcal{C}$ and $\mathcal{K}$ and precompute the hash tables $\mathcal{H}_c^t$.
2. Choose 2^s random but pairwise distinct plaintexts and form structures of $8 \cdot 2^s$ plaintext-tweak tuples (P^i, T^j) for $i \in [0..2^s - 1]$ with $T^{2j} \oplus T^{2j+1} = \Delta T$ for $j \in [0..3]$.
3. Collect all ciphertexts $C^{i,j}$ corresponding to (P^i, T^j) for $j \in [0..7]$ from the encryption oracle, invert the final MixColumns and ShiftRows operations to derive $Z^{i,j}$, and store the resulting eight-tuples into $\mathcal{C}$.
4. For all eight-tuples i, all four inverse diagonals (in Y, i.e. S_{SR}^6), and all columns $c \in [0..3]$:
   - For all pairs $Z^{i,0}, Z^{i,1}, Z^{i,2}, Z^{i,3}$, define $\Delta x = Z^{i,0} \oplus Z^{i,1}$, $\Delta z = Z^{i,2} \oplus Z^{i,3}$, and $\Delta a = Z^{i,0} \oplus Z^{i,2}$. Lookup $\mathcal{H}_c^t[\Delta x, \Delta z, \Delta a]$ to obtain 2^{16} values z on average that yield 2^{16} key candidates $k = Z^{i,0} \oplus z$ that produce a difference of t in the byte at the intersection of column c and a fixed inverse diagonal d. Note that whether t should be zero or one depends on the column and diagonal.
   - Repeat the process, redefining $\Delta x = Z^{i,4} \oplus Z^{i,5}$, $\Delta z = Z^{i,6} \oplus Z^{i,7}$, and $\Delta a = Z^{i,4} \oplus Z^{i,6}$. Lookup $\mathcal{H}_c^t[\Delta x, \Delta z, \Delta a]$ to obtain 2^{16} values z' on average that yield 2^{16} key candidates $k' = Z^{i,4} \oplus z'$.
   - For all 2^{16} candidates k, look up if there exists $k' = k$. We expect one candidate on average per column and therefore one 128-bit key candidate for $\widehat{K}^7$ on average per ciphertext tuple and considered inverse diagonal. Store the candidates into $\mathcal{K}$.
5. Finally, sort $\mathcal{K}$ and output all candidates that occur at least 2^{s-95} times.

Complexity. Consider a structure of $8 \cdot 2^s$ plaintext-tweak tuples and their corresponding ciphertexts. The distinguisher had a probability of approximately 2^{-94} to occur, i.e. we expect 2^{s-94} eight-tuples that satisfy our distinguisher on average. We suggest $s = 102$ for our attack, which corresponds to $8 \cdot 2^{102} = 2^{105}$ chosen plaintext-tweak tuples and 2^8 eight-tuples expected to satisfy our distinguisher on average. They cost 2^{105} encryptions and $2^{105} \cdot \frac{1}{7} \simeq 2^{102.2}$ partial decryptions. For each eight-tuple and column, we have to lookup 2^{16} candidates for the first two pairs and 2^{16} candidates for the next two pairs with $4 \cdot 4 \cdot 2^{s+16} = 2^{122}$ memory accesses over four columns and possible inverse diagonals, that yields approximately $2^{115.3}$ encryptions. Merging them needs again 2^{16} lookups

Table 1. Distinguishers and key-recovery attacks on TweAES. Memory = #16-byte states, tw. = #tweaks, rds. = #rounds, KP/CP = known/chosen plaintext(s), trunc. = truncated, imp. = impossible, negl. = negligible.

Rds.	Attack type	Tw.	Complexities			Reference
			Time	Data	Memory	
Distinguishers						
6	Imp. differential	2	2^{127}	2^{127} CP	negl.	[11]
6	2nd-order Mixture	2^3	2^{97}	2^{94} CP	negl.	Sect. 6.1
Key-recovery attacks						
5	Trunc. differential	2	2^{26}	2^5 CP	2^{28}	[11]
6	Integral	2^4	2^{45}	2^5 KP	negl.	[11]
6	Imp. differential	2	2^{119}	2^{119} CP	2^{72}	[11]
7	2nd-order Mixture	2^3	$2^{116.3}$	2^{102} CP	2^{113}	Sect. 6.2
7	Imp. differential	2	2^{100}	2^{100} CP	2^{66}	[28]
8	Imp. differential	2	$2^{124.4}$	$2^{124.3}$ CP	$2^{111.8}$	[28]
8	Imp. differential	2	$2^{120.8}$	$2^{122.1}$ CP	2^{109}	[23]

each i.e. $4 \cdot 4 \cdot 2^s \cdot 2^{16} = 2^{122}$ memory accesses. Storing the candidates takes on average $4 \cdot 2^s = 2^{104}$ memory accesses or $2^{97.3}$ encryptions. Sorting and counting in a list of $4 \cdot 2^s$ key candidates in $O(n \log n)$ takes approximately $2^{110.2}$ memory accesses or 2^{104} encryptions. In total, the time complexity is approximately

$$2^{108.3} + 2^{105} + 2^{102.2} + 2^{115.3} + 2^{115.3} + 2^{97.3} + 2^{104} + 2^{110.2} \simeq 2^{116.3}$$

encryption equivalents. We assume that the key candidates are randomly distributed, which allows us to use the following well-studied lemma. The proof for $K = N$ can be found e.g. in [26], the case for $K < N$ follows easily.

Lemma 1 (Maximum Load of Bins and Balls). *Consider the setting of throwing K balls into N bins uniformly and independently at random. Let ℓ_i denote the load of the i-th bin. For positive $K \leq N$, it holds that*

$$\Pr\left[\exists i \in [1..N] : \ell_i \geq \frac{3 \ln N}{\ln \ln N}\right] \leq \frac{1}{N}.$$

We have $K = 2^{104}$ key candidates on average and $N = 2^{128}$ bins representing the possible key values. Even for $K = N$, the probability that any key will be suggested more than $\frac{3 \ln N}{\ln \ln N} < 60$ times is therefore upper bounded by 2^{-128} under the assumptions of uniform and independent key suggestions. In contrast, we expect that the correct key is suggested 2^8 times on average. Therefore, we expect only the correct key to occur at least $2^{s-95} = 2^7$ times. We compare our attack on TweAES to others on that primitive in the literature in Table 1. However, we emphasize that our goal was not to provide better attacks on the particular primitive but to propose a generalization of an established technique.

7 Conclusion

We proposed higher-order mixtures for settings where conventional (first-order) mixtures were inapplicable. One such setting was the case of **TweAES**, whose tweak-expansion code prevented tweak-induced mixture differentials. We outlined the application for a six-round mixture distinguisher on **TweAES** and derived a seven-round key-recovery attack in the spirit of [3] under the Markov-cipher and black-box S-box assumption. Our result does not threaten the security **TweAES** but points out a property of its tweak expansion. We propose a general technique with potentially broader applicability to other primitives that allows more and more flexible mixtures at the cost of a lower probability of the differential propagation of all pairs. Future work can study further applications on AES-based and other primitives.

Acknowledgments. We thank the reviewers of IWSEC 2024 for their fruitful comments. Eik List has been supported by Deutsche Forschungsgemeinschaft (DFG, German Research Foundation) – LI 4223/1-1.

References

1. Avanzi, R.: The QARMA block cipher family. Almost MDS matrices over rings with zero divisors, nearly symmetric even-mansour constructions with non-involutory central rounds, and search heuristics for low-latency s-boxes. IACR Trans. Symmetric Cryptology **2017**(1), 4–44 (2017). https://doi.org/10.13154/TOSC.V2017.I1.4-44
2. Avanzi, R., et al.: The QARMAv2 family of tweakable block ciphers. IACR Trans. Symmetric Cryptology **2023**(3), 25–73 (2023). https://doi.org/10.46586/TOSC.V2023.I3.25-73
3. Bar-On, A., Dunkelman, O., Keller, N., Ronen, E., Shamir, A.: Improved key recovery attacks on reduced-round AES with practical data and memory complexities. In: Shacham, H., Boldyreva, A. (eds.) CRYPTO 2018. LNCS, vol. 10992, pp. 185–212. Springer, Cham (2018). https://doi.org/10.1007/978-3-319-96881-0_7
4. Bardeh, N.G., Rijmen, V.: New key-recovery attack on reduced-round AES. IACR Trans. Symmetric Cryptology **2022**(2), 43–62 (2022). https://doi.org/10.46586/tosc.v2022.i2.43-62
5. Bardeh, N.G., Rønjom, S.: Practical attacks on reduced-round AES. In: Buchmann, J., Nitaj, A., Rachidi, T. (eds.) AFRICACRYPT 2019. LNCS, vol. 11627, pp. 297–310. Springer, Cham (2019). https://doi.org/10.1007/978-3-030-23696-0_15
6. Bardeh, N.G., Rønjom, S.: The exchange attack: how to distinguish six rounds of AES with $2^{88.2}$ chosen plaintexts. In: Galbraith, S.D., Moriai, S. (eds.) ASIACRYPT 2019. LNCS, vol. 11923, pp. 347–370. Springer, Cham (2019). https://doi.org/10.1007/978-3-030-34618-8_12
7. Beierle, C., Jean, J., Kölbl, S., Leander, G., Moradi, A., Peyrin, T., Sasaki, Yu., Sasdrich, P., Sim, S.M.: The SKINNY family of block ciphers and its low-latency variant MANTIS. In: Robshaw, M., Katz, J. (eds.) CRYPTO 2016. LNCS, vol. 9815, pp. 123–153. Springer, Heidelberg (2016). https://doi.org/10.1007/978-3-662-53008-5_5

8. Beierle, C., Leander, G., Moradi, A., Rasoolzadeh, S.: CRAFT: lightweight tweakable block cipher with efficient protection against DFA attacks. IACR Trans. Symmetric Cryptology **2019**(1), 5–45 (2019). https://doi.org/10.13154/tosc.v2019.i1.5-45
9. Boura, C., Canteaut, A., Coggia, D.: A general proof framework for recent AES distinguishers. IACR Trans. Symmetric Cryptology **2019**(1), 170–191 (2019). https://doi.org/10.13154/tosc.v2019.i1.170-191
10. Chakraborti, A., Datta, N., Jha, A., Mancillas-López, C., Nandi, M., Sasaki, Y.: Elastic-tweak: a framework for short tweak tweakable block cipher. IACR Cryptology ePrint Arch. **2019**, 440 (2019)
11. Chakraborti, A., Datta, N., Jha, A., Mancillas-López, C., Nandi, M., Sasaki, Y.: ESTATE: a lightweight and low energy authenticated encryption mode. IACR Trans. Symmetric Cryptology **2020**(S1), 350–389 (2020). https://doi.org/10.13154/tosc.v2020.iS1.350-389
12. Chakraborti, A., Datta, N., Jha, A., Mancillas-López, C., Nandi, M., Sasaki, Yu.: Elastic-tweak: a framework for short tweak tweakable block cipher. In: Adhikari, A., Küsters, R., Preneel, B. (eds.) INDOCRYPT 2021. LNCS, vol. 13143, pp. 114–137. Springer, Cham (2021). https://doi.org/10.1007/978-3-030-92518-5_6
13. Daemen, J., Rijmen, V.: The Design of Rijndael: AES - The Advanced Encryption Standard. Springer (2002). https://doi.org/10.1007/978-3-662-04722-4
14. Dobraunig, C., Eichlseder, M., Mendel, F.: Square attack on 7-round Kiasu-BC. In: Manulis, M., Sadeghi, A.-R., Schneider, S. (eds.) ACNS 2016. LNCS, vol. 9696, pp. 500–517. Springer, Cham (2016). https://doi.org/10.1007/978-3-319-39555-5_27
15. Dobraunig, C., List, E.: Impossible-differential and boomerang cryptanalysis of round-reduced Kiasu-BC. In: Handschuh, H. (ed.) CT-RSA 2017. LNCS, vol. 10159, pp. 207–222. Springer, Cham (2017). https://doi.org/10.1007/978-3-319-52153-4_12
16. Dunkelman, O., Keller, N., Ronen, E., Shamir, A.: The retracing boomerang attack. In: Canteaut, A., Ishai, Y. (eds.) EUROCRYPT 2020. LNCS, vol. 12105, pp. 280–309. Springer, Cham (2020). https://doi.org/10.1007/978-3-030-45721-1_11
17. Grassi, L.: MixColumns properties and attacks on (round-reduced) AES with a single secret S-Box. In: Smart, N.P. (ed.) CT-RSA 2018. LNCS, vol. 10808, pp. 243–263. Springer, Cham (2018). https://doi.org/10.1007/978-3-319-76953-0_13
18. Grassi, L.: Mixture differential cryptanalysis: a new approach to distinguishers and attacks on round-reduced AES. IACR Trans. Symmetric Cryptology **2018**(2), 133–160 (2018). https://doi.org/10.13154/tosc.v2018.i2.133-160
19. Grassi, L., Rechberger, C.: Truncated differential properties of the diagonal set of inputs for 5-round AES. In: Nguyen, K., Yang, G., Guo, F., Susilo, W. (eds.) ACISP. Lecture Notes in Computer Science, vol. 13494, pp. 24–45. Springer, Cham (2022). https://doi.org/10.1007/978-3-031-22301-3_2
20. Grassi, L., Rechberger, C., Rønjom, S.: A new structural-differential property of 5-round AES. In: Coron, J., Nielsen, J.B. (eds.) EUROCRYPT II. Lecture Notes in Computer Science, vol. 10211, pp. 289–317 (2017). https://doi.org/10.1007/978-3-319-56614-6_10
21. Grassi, L., Rechberger, C., Rønjom, S.: Subspace trail cryptanalysis and its applications to AES. IACR Trans. Symmetric Cryptology **2016**(2), 192–225 (2017). https://doi.org/10.13154/tosc.v2016.i2.192-225
22. Jean, J., Nikolić, I., Peyrin, T.: Tweaks and keys for block ciphers: the TWEAKEY framework. In: Sarkar, P., Iwata, T. (eds.) ASIACRYPT 2014. LNCS, vol. 8874, pp. 274–288. Springer, Heidelberg (2014). https://doi.org/10.1007/978-3-662-45608-8_15

23. Jiang, Z., Jin, C.: Related-tweak multiple impossible differential attack for TweAES. J. Electron. Inf. Technol. **45**(1), 344–352 (2023). https://doi.org/10.11999/JEIT211147
24. Liskov, M., Rivest, R.L., Wagner, D.: Tweakable block ciphers. In: Yung, M. (ed.) CRYPTO. Lecture Notes in Computer Science, vol. 2442, pp. 31–46. Springer (2002). https://doi.org/10.1007/s00145-010-9073
25. Liu, Y., et al.: Improved meet-in-the-middle attacks on reduced-round Kiasu-BC and Joltik-BC. Comput. J. **62**(12), 1761–1776 (2019). https://doi.org/10.1093/comjnl/bxz059
26. Mitzenmacher, M., Upfal, E.: Probability and Computing: Randomized Algorithms and Probabilistic Analysis. Cambridge University Press (2005). https://doi.org/10.1017/CBO9780511813603
27. National Institute of Standards and Technology: FIPS 197, pp. 1–51. National Institute of Standards and Technology (2001)
28. Niu, C., Li, M., Wang, M., Wang, Q., Yiu, S.-M.: Related-tweak impossible differential cryptanalysis of reduced-round TweAES. In: AlTawy, R., Hülsing, A. (eds.) SAC 2021. LNCS, vol. 13203, pp. 223–245. Springer, Cham (2022). https://doi.org/10.1007/978-3-030-99277-4_11
29. Qiao, K.: Quadruple differential distinguishers and an automatic searching tool. techrxiv (2022)
30. Qiao, K., Cheng, J., Ou, C.: A new mixture differential cryptanalysis on round-reduced AES. Mathematics **10**(24), 4736 (2022). https://doi.org/10.3390/math10244736
31. Qiao, K., Zhang, Z., Niu, Z., Zhu, L.: The exchange attack and the mixture differential attack revisited: from the perspective of automatic evaluation. Chin. J. Electron. **33**(1), 19–29 (2024). https://doi.org/10.23919/cje.2023.00.008
32. Rønjom, S., Bardeh, N.G., Helleseth, T.: Yoyo tricks with AES. In: Takagi, T., Peyrin, T. (eds.) ASIACRYPT 2017. LNCS, vol. 10624, pp. 217–243. Springer, Cham (2017). https://doi.org/10.1007/978-3-319-70694-8_8
33. Sakamoto, K., et al.: Tweakable TWINE: building a tweakable block cipher on generalized feistel structure. In: Attrapadung, N., Yagi, T. (eds.) IWSEC 2019. LNCS, vol. 11689, pp. 129–145. Springer, Cham (2019). https://doi.org/10.1007/978-3-030-26834-3_8
34. Tolba, M., Abdelkhalek, A., Youssef, A.M.: A meet in the middle attack on reduced round Kiasu-BC. IEICE Trans. Fundam. Electron. Commun. Comput. Sci. **99-A**(10), 1888–1890 (2016). https://doi.org/10.1587/transfun.E99.A.1888
35. Xie, X., Tian, T.: Structural evaluation of AES-like ciphers against mixture differential cryptanalysis. Des. Codes Crypt. **91**(12), 3881–3899 (2023). https://doi.org/10.1007/S10623-023-01277-7

Weak Keys of the Full MISTY1 Recovered in Practical Time

Bungo Taga[1(✉)], Norimitsu Ito[2], and Takako Okano[1]

[1] National Police Academy, 3-12-1, Asahi-cho, Fuchu-shi, Tokyo 183-8558, Japan
{b.taga.54,t.okano}@nparc.npa.go.jp
[2] National Police Agency, 2-1-2, Kasumigaseki, Chiyoda-ku, Tokyo 100-8974, Japan
n.itou.6r.vp@npa.go.jp
https://www.npa.go.jp/keidai/, https://www.npa.go.jp

Abstract. The MISTY1 is a 64-bit block cipher designed by Matsui in 1997. It is listed on the Japanese CRYPTREC Candidate Recommended Ciphers List. Cryptanalysis against the full MISTY1 has already been known, which is the analysis of weak keys in a related-key setting and the integral attack using the division property in a single-key setting. However, these attacks require large amounts of data and time complexity that are practically infeasible. In this paper, we show the existence of new weak keys for the full MISTY1. The MISTY1 can be distinguished from a random permutation and the keys are recovered with a realistically feasible computational complexity, in a related-key setting. It means that a pair of weak keys, one key of which has a specific differential relationship with the other, is used. The computational complexity of the attacks is 2^5 chosen plaintexts for distinguishing the MISTY1 from a random permutation, and 2^8 chosen plaintexts, 2^{25} bytes of memory and a few seconds computed by a desktop PC for key recovery.

Keywords: MISTY1 · Weak keys · Related-key attack

1 Introduction

The MISTY1 [1] is a symmetric key 64-bit block cipher designed by Matsui in 1997, which is listed on the Japanese CRYPTREC Candidate Recommended Ciphers List [2] and has been standardized in NESSIE [4], ISO/IEC [5] and RFCs [6].

Theoretical attacks on the full-round MISTY1 are already known. We summarize attacks on the full-round MISTY1 in Table 1. In 2013, Lu et al. showed the existence of weak keys in a related-key setting [7], followed by the related work [8]. In 2015, Todo presented the integral attack in a single-key setting using the division property [9], followed by the related work [10,11]. However, these attacks are not yet a realistic threat due to the very large amount of computational complexity (Table 1).

Table 1. Attacks on the full MISTY1

Attack	Keys	Data	Time	Memory
Related-key differential [7]	$2^{103.57}$	2^{61}CC	$2^{90.93}$	$2^{99.2}$Bytes
Related-key amplified boomerang [8]	2^{92}	$2^{60.5}$CP	$2^{87.33}$	$2^{80.07}$Bytes
Related-key differential				
Distinguisher Section 4.1	$3 \cdot 2^{74}$	2^5CP	$2^{9\dagger}$	
Key recovery Section 4.2	$3 \cdot 2^{74}$	2^8CP	$\lesssim 2^{29}$	2^{25}Bytes
Integral [9]	2^{128}	$2^{63.58}$CP	2^{121}	not specified
Integral [10]	2^{128}	$2^{63.994}$CP	$2^{108.3}$	not specified
Integral [11]	2^{128}	$2^{63.9999}$CC	2^{79}	not specified
Integral [11]	2^{128}	$2^{64} - 2^{36}$CPC	$2^{69.5}$	not specified

CP: chosen plaintexts, CC: chosen ciphertexts
CPC: chosen plaintexts and ciphertexts
† The unit of time is the time for comparing two ciphertexts
In the other cases it is the time for encrypting one time.

Weak keys mean the keys whose use would cause some kind of unexpected behavior in this paper. The related-key attacks [14] are attacks under the condition that a ciphertext and the corresponding plaintext encrypted with multiple keys that are related to each other are available.

Our contributions presented in this paper are as follows.

- We found weak keys of the MISTY1, which have not been previously shown.
- We showed that it is possible to distinguish the MISTY1 from random permutations and to recover the keys when the weak keys are used.
- We estimated the computational complexity required for these attacks, and by conducting computer experiments using a desktop PC we demonstrated that the keys are recovered in less than a few seconds.

Note that the attacks are not considered to be a realistic threat for two reasons. Firstly, they are related-key attacks where two weak keys with a differential relationship between them convenient for attackers need to be used. Secondly, the number of weak keys we found is $3 \cdot 2^{74}$. It is not small, but extremely smaller than the total number of keys.

This paper is organized as follows. In Sect. 2 we describe the notation used in this paper, weak keys, related-key attacks and the structure of the MISTY1. In Sect. 3 we analyze the key scheduling part of the MISTY1 to derive the weak keys, and show that there is a differential characteristic in the data randomizing part with a very large differential probability in a related-key setting. In Sect. 4, we construct a related-key distinguisher of the MISTY1 and recover secret key exploiting the differential characteristic shown in Sect. 3. In Sect. 5 we summarize our results.

2 Preliminaries

In this section we describe the notation used in this paper, weak keys, related-key attacks and the structures of the data randomizing and key scheduling parts of the MISTY1.

2.1 Notation

The notation used throughout this paper is as shown in the reference [3] and Table 2.

Table 2. The notation used in this paper

Subscript:$_{\text{in/out}}$	Denotes the input/output data of the function e.g., FO_{in}, FO_{out}
Subscript: $_i$	Denotes the i-th 16-bit data from the left
Subscript: $_{(Rj)}$	The right (lower) j-bit value of 16-bit data
Subscript: $_{(Lj)}$	The left (upper) j-bit value of 16-bit data
e.g.,	$P = P_1\|\|P_2\|\|P_3\|\|P_4$
	$K_1 = K_{1(L9)}\|\|K_{1(R7)} = K_{1(L7)}\|\|K_{1(R9)}$
Prefix: Δ	Denotes a differential between two data
Typewriter style	Hexadecimal notation (e.g., 0a)
$\Delta K := K_{\text{sec}} \oplus K_{\text{rel}}$	The differential between the secret key and the related key
$\Delta K'$	The differential between the two corresponding extended keys

2.2 MISTY1

The MISTY1 is a symmetric key block cipher with a data block length of 64 bits and a secret key length of 128 bits. It consists of two parts: the data randomizing part, which randomizes a 64-bit plaintext and outputs the 64-bit ciphertext, and the key scheduling part, which outputs the 128-bit extended key for an input of 128-bit secret key. Both the secret key and the extended key are used in the data randomizing part. The structures of the data randomizing and the key scheduling parts are explained below.

2.2.1 The Data Randomizing Part The structure of the data randomizing part of the MISTY1 is shown in Fig. 1. It is a Feistel structure in which the input 64-bit plaintext is divided into two 32-bit blocks, and each block is transformed alternately by the function FO. The function FO and its internal function, the function FI, also have Feistel structures. As a whole, the data randomizing part has a three-layer nested structure, and also has a structure in which the transformation is repeated with two function FLs and two function FOs as a unit.

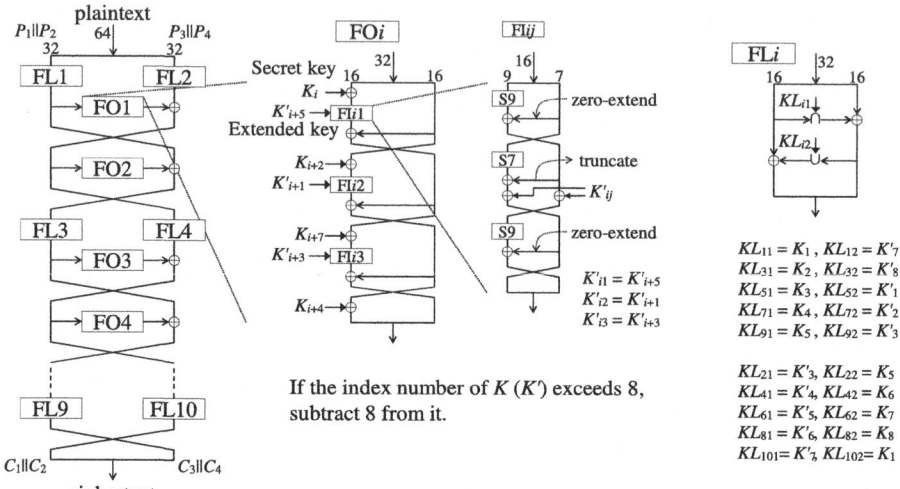

Fig. 1. The Data randomizing part of the MISTY1

The keys used in the data randomizing part are the 16-bit secret keys K_1 to K_8 and the extended keys K'_1 to K'_8, which are described in Sect. 2.2.2. In the function FO, the extended keys are used in its internal functions, the function FIs, and the secret keys are used outside the function FIs. In the function FL, one secret key and one extended key are used.

The non-linear operations with respect to the exclusive-or (XOR) operation are the bitwise AND (∩) and OR (∪) operations in the function FL and are the substitution tables S7 and S9 in the function FI. Within one function FO, the transformations by substitution tables S7 and S9 are performed many times, which is the reason why the differential probability in single-key settings is small. If there are differential characteristics of the function FO with a large differential probability, the differential probability of the entire data randomizing part may be also large.

2.2.2 The Key Scheduling Part The structure of the key scheduling part of the MISTY1 is shown in Fig. 2. In the key scheduling part, the 128-bit secret key is divided into eight 16-bit secret keys K_1 to K_8, each 16-bit key is input to two adjacent function FIs and eight 16-bit extended keys K'_1 to K'_8 are output. Each extended key K'_i is obtained as an output for two secret key inputs, K_i and K_{i+1}, to the function FI. In the function FI, the substitution tables S9 and S7 are used, which are non-linear operations with respect to the XOR operation. The function FI is identical to that in the data randomizing part.

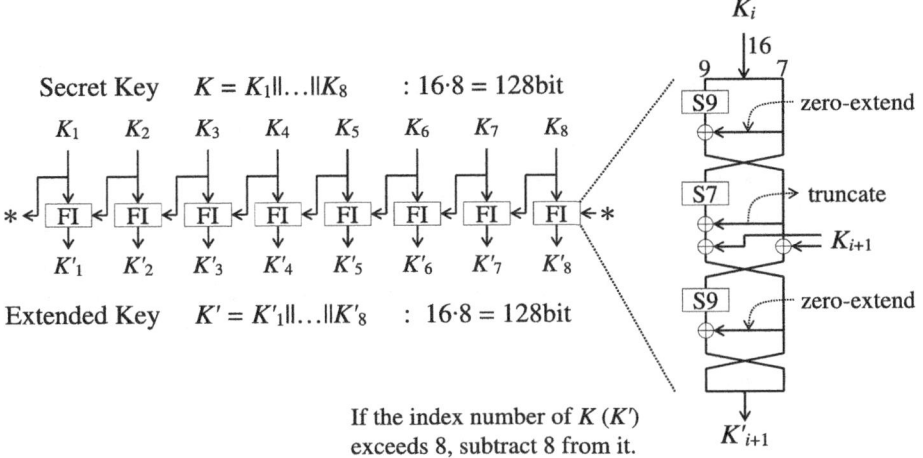

Fig. 2. The Key Scheduling part of the MISTY1

2.3 Weak Keys

In this paper, weak keys are defined as the keys whose use would cause some kind of unexpected behavior as mentioned in Sect. 1. Although, a weak key was initially defined as a key that reverts to the original plaintext in the block cipher DES [12] when encrypted twice with the same key for any plaintext, the former definition is used in the previous works [7,8]. When a pair of weak keys shown in this paper is used, we can distinguish MISTY1 from a random permutation and recover the keys.

2.4 Related-Key Attacks

Related-key attacks were proposed in the early 1990s [14,15]. Biryukov et al. illustrated the first attack on the full-round AES-192 and AES-256 [13] in a related-key setting, which distinguished AES from a random permutation and recovered an AES encryption key more efficiently than a brute force attack [16, 17].

In a related-key setting, attackers can obtain pairs of plaintexts and the corresponding pairs of ciphertexts associated with each other by related keys besides the encryption key. Attackers can also know and control the relationships between the encryption key and related keys, even if they do not know the encryption key itself. Thus, the related-key attack is an attack under very favourable conditions for the attackers, and conversely, the conditions for the attack to be successful are so severe that it is considered to be an attack with a small chance of being realized in normal encryption applications. However, depending on the method of secret key generation and distribution, etc., an attacker may be able to obtain the differential between multiple secret keys, and therefore the related-key attack may be a realistic attack.

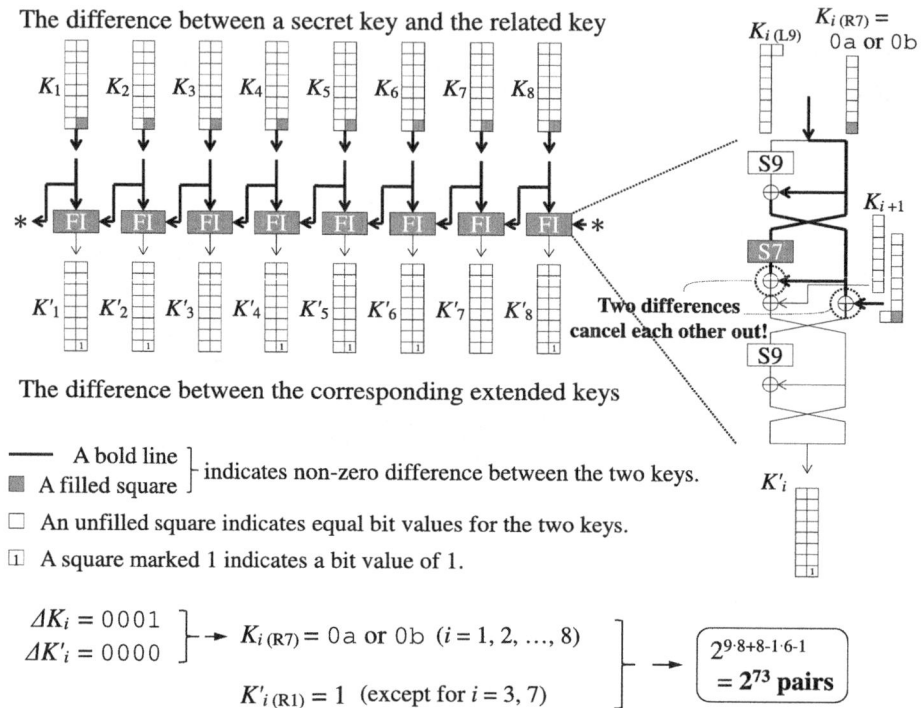

Fig. 3. Differences between weak key pairs

In this paper, we consider the related-key differential attack shown below:

$$P \xrightarrow{K} C$$
$$P \oplus \Delta P \xrightarrow{K \oplus \Delta K} C \oplus \Delta C,$$

where P, C and K denote a plaintext, a ciphertext and a secret key and ΔP, ΔC and ΔK are differences between the two plaintexts, the two ciphertexts and the two secret keys, respectively. When Ps, ΔP, and ΔK are chosen to be convenient to the attacker, the probability of differential characteristic is large enough for the attacker to distinguish MISTY1 from a random permutation and to recover the secret key.

3 Weak Keys of the MISTY1

When the weak key shown in this paper is used together with another weak key with a specific differential relationship as the related key, the MISTY1 can be distinguished from a random permutation and the secret key can be recovered. In this section, we first illustrate what pairs of secret keys and related keys can be weak keys, and then show that when these pairs of weak keys are used, there exists a differential characteristic with very large probability in the data randomizing part.

3.1 Pairs of Weak Keys and the Differentials in Them

Table 3. Tuples of differences between two weak keys, and the lower 7-bit values of the weak keys

h	Tuples of $\Delta K_{i(\mathrm{R7})}$ and $(K_{\mathrm{sec}i(\mathrm{R7})}, K_{\mathrm{rel}i(\mathrm{R7})})$	Number of keys
1	01(0a,0b),20(0c,2c),40(18,58)	$3 \cdot 2^{74}$
2	03(61,62),06(31,37),09(53,5a),0c(30,3c),18(4c,54), 21(45,64),24(5e,7a),28(50,78),30(41,71),41(26,67), 42(35,77),60(2e,4e)	$12 \cdot 2^{68}$
3	07(72,75),0d(21,2c),13(28,3b),1c(2e,32),25(48,6d), 26(19,3f),29(1c,35),38(01,39),43(03,40),46(07,41), 49(08,41),52(0b,59),61(1e,7f),64(36,52),68(06,6e), 70(0d,7d)	$16 \cdot 2^{62}$
4	0f(07,08),1b(2f,34),1d(25,38),1e(45,5b),27(15,32), 2d(0c,21),2e(46,68),3c(1e,22),4b(02,49),4d(39,74), 53(0a,59),71(1a,6b),78(27,5f)	$13 \cdot 2^{56}$
5	1f(00,1f),2f(04,2b),3b(15,2e),3e(58,66),57(09,5e), 5b(15,4e),5d(22,7f),6b(1c,77),73(09,7a),75(01,74), 76(07,71),79(08,71),7c(32,4e)	$13 \cdot 2^{50}$
6	3f(5b,64),7d(2a,57),7e(18,66)	$3 \cdot 2^{44}$
7	N/A	

h: Hamming weight of $\Delta K_{i(\mathrm{R7})}$

The key scheduling part is a function that outputs a 128-bit extended key for an input of 128-bit secret key (Fig. 2). As this function is not bijection, there may be more than one secret key such that the key scheduling part outputs extended keys with the same value. For example, if the conditions $K_{\mathrm{sec}i(\mathrm{R7})} = $ 0a or 0b and $\Delta K_i := K_{\mathrm{sec}i} \oplus K_{\mathrm{rel}i} = $ 01 $(i = 1, \cdots, 8)$ for the secret key and the related key pair $(K_{\mathrm{sec}}, K_{\mathrm{rel}})$ are satisfied, the key scheduling part outputs the extended keys with the same value.

This weak key pair thus satisfies the condition that the lower 7-bit value of a 16-bit secret key, $K_{\mathrm{sec}i(\mathrm{R7})}$, is one of the two values and that the differential between K_{sec} and K_{rel}, ΔK_i, is the same for all i. Furthermore, another condition is imposed on the extended key K' as described in Sect. 3.2.2. The conditions to be satisfied by the weak key pair are as follows:

Conditions on pairs of weak keys

$$\Delta K_{i(\text{L9})} = 0 \ (i = 1, \cdots, 8), \quad \Delta K_{1(\text{R7})} = \Delta K_{2(\text{R7})} = \cdots = \Delta K_{8(\text{R7})} \quad (1)$$

$$\Delta K'_i = 0 \ (i = 1, \cdots, 8) \quad (2)$$

$$K'_{i(\text{R7})} \cap \Delta K_{i(\text{R7})} = \Delta K_{i(\text{R7})} \ (\text{except for } i = 3, 7) \quad (3)$$

Figure 3 shows a differential between a pair of weak keys in case of $\Delta K_{i(\text{R7})} = 01$. To satisfy the condition (2), the input and output differential values of S7 must be equal in the differential path on the right-hand side of Fig. 3, and such tuples of input differentials $\Delta K_{i(\text{R7})}$ and pairs of input values ($K_{\text{sec}i(\text{R7})}$, $K_{\text{rel}i(\text{R7})}$) for S7 are limited to the 60 tuples shown in Table 3. $\Delta K_{i+1(\text{R9})}$ on the right-hand side of Fig. 3 always cancels out with the input differential $\Delta K_{i(\text{R9})}$ according to the condition (1).

The condition (3) is imposed on the extended key that the bit value of the extended key K'_i corresponding to the bit position with a non-zero difference of ΔK_i is 1. This is necessary for the differential characteristic of the function FL described in Sect. 3.2.2 to be possible.

The number of weak keys is estimated as follows. From the conditions (1) and (2), each $K_{\text{sec}i(\text{L9})}$ can take 2^9 values and each $K_{\text{sec}i(\text{R7})}$ can take two values. If the Hamming weight of $\Delta K_{i(\text{R7})}$ is h, from condition (3) h bits of the extended key K'_i must be 1 (except for $i = 3, 7$). Therefore, for each $\Delta K_{i(\text{R7})}$ in Table 3, the number of weak keys is $2^{9 \cdot 8 + 8 - 6h} = 2^{80 - 6h}$ and decreases exponentially as h increases.

The number of weak keys is the largest when $\Delta K_{i(\text{R7})} = 01, 20, 40$ with $h = 1$, which is $2^{9 \cdot 8 + 8 - 6 \cdot 1} = 2^{74}$ each. It is also when h=1 that the differential probability of the data randomizing part is the largest, as described in Sect. 4. In the following, unless otherwise stated, we will discuss the case $\Delta K_{i(\text{R7})} = 01$, but exactly the same argument holds for the cases $\Delta K_{i(\text{R7})} = 20$ and 40.

3.2 Differential Characteristics

It has been shown by the developers that the MISTY1 is based on the theory of provable security against differential cryptanalysis in single-key settings [1]. When the differential path is actually explored, it can be seen that the differential probability is significantly small in the function FOs. If the differential probability is sufficiently large in each function FO, the differential probability of the entire data randomizing part may be large.

In this section, we first show that there exists a differential characteristic for the function FO with a differential probability of 1 when a pair of weak keys satisfying conditions (1) to (3) in Sect. 3.1 is used. Next, it is shown that for the entire data randomizing part, there exists a differential characteristic where the differential probability of all function FOs is 1, and the differential characteristics and differential probabilities of the function FLs in that case are shown.

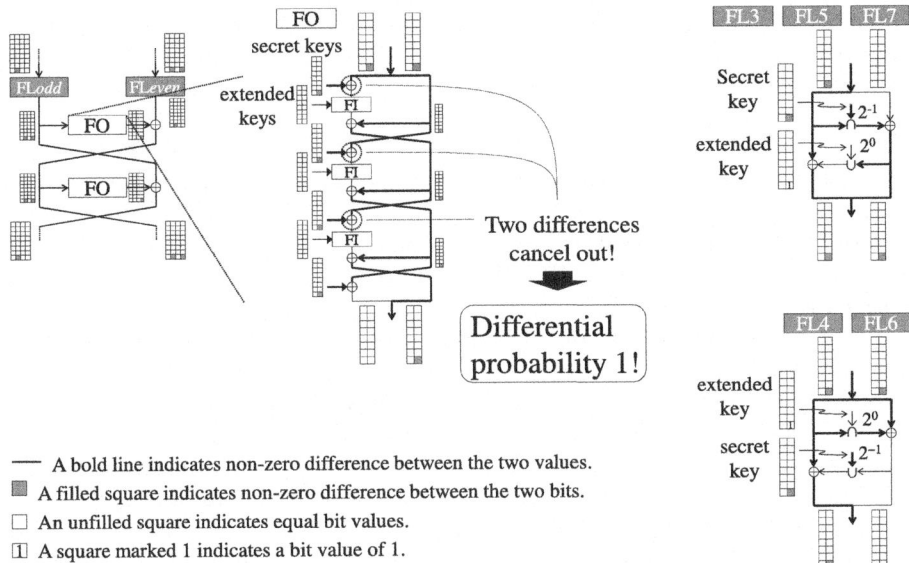

Fig. 4. Differential characteristics of the 2-round function that can be exploited for the attacks

3.2.1 The Function FO For the case $\Delta K_{i(R7)} = 01$, the differential characteristic of the function FO, where the differential probability is 1, is shown in the center of Fig. 4. In this differential characteristic, the input differential values of the function FI are always zero because a difference between two secret keys, ΔK_i, and the difference between two input values cancel just before the function FI. Also, since $\Delta K'_i = 0$ for the extended key, no differences occur in the function FI. This results in an output differential value $\Delta FO_{out} = 0000\ 0001$ with probability 1 for the input differential value $\Delta FO_{in} = 0001\ 0001$ of the function FO.

Note that such differential paths of the function FO exist that the differential probability be 1 not only when the Hamming weight of $\Delta K_{i(R7)}$ is 1, but also for all 60 cases in Table 3.

3.2.2 The Function FL The data randomizing part has a structure in which transformations using two function FLs and two function FOs are repeated as a unit. So, if a differential characteristic exists in which the input differential value and output differential value are equal and the differential probability is sufficiently large in the transformation of this unit, then a differential characteristic with a large differential probability also exists for the entire data randomizing part.

Using the differential characteristic of the function FO with probability 1 described in Sect. 3.2.1 to search for the differential characteristics in the transformation of the unit iteration described above, it can be seen that in order for the input and output differential values to be equal, the input and output differences of the odd-th (FL*odd*) and even-th (FL*even*) of the function FL must be the following values (right-hand of Fig. 4).

$$\begin{aligned} \text{Odd-th}: \Delta \text{FL}odd_{\text{in}} &= 0001\ 0000, & \Delta \text{FL}odd_{\text{out}} &= 0001\ 0001 \\ \text{Even-th}: \Delta \text{FL}even_{\text{in}} &= 0001\ 0001, & \Delta \text{FL}even_{\text{out}} &= 0001\ 0000 \end{aligned} \quad (4)$$

In order for the differential property of the function FL taking such input and output differences to actually exist, condition (3) of Sect. 3.1 is required for the extended key K'_i, as follows.

In the FL*odd*, the condition (3) of Sect. 3.1, where the least significant bit of the extended key K'_i is 1, is required because the output difference of the ∪ operation must be zero. Conversely, if this condition is satisfied, the differential after the ∪ operation is 0 with probability 1. The differential probability is 2^{-1} in the ∩ operation and therefore also 2^{-1} for the whole FL*odd* (top right of Fig. 4).

Since the output difference of the ∩ operation must be 0001 in the FL*even*,, the condition that the least significant bit of the extended key K'_i is 1 is required, as in the FL*odd* case. If this condition is satisfied, the difference of the ∩ operation is 0001 with probability 1. The differential probability is 2^{-1} in the ∪ operation and therefore also 2^{-1} for the whole FL*even* (bottom right of Fig. 4).

In general, the differential probability of the function FL when the Hamming weight of $\Delta K_{i(\text{R7})}$ is h is found to be 2^{-h} by the same argument. In addition, the condition of a bit value of 1 for h bits of the extended key K'_i is required, which means that the number of weak keys decreases exponentially as h increases (Table 3).

3.2.3 The Data Randomizing Part

Figure 6 shows the differential characteristics used in the attacks. The left-hand side is used to distinguish the MISTY1 from a random permutation, while the right-hand side is used for key recovery.

In the function FL1 and FL2, each of the upper 15 bits of the plaintext difference ΔP_1 to ΔP_4 must be 0 and each of the least significant bit of them are not restricted, while the output difference must satisfy the condition (4) in Sect. 3.2.2. In the function FL9 and FL10, even if the output differential value does not satisfy condition (4), the attack is possible because the upper 15 bits of the ciphertext differentials ΔC_1 and ΔC_2 are 0. Therefore, condition (3) in Sect. 3.1 is not necessary for the extended keys K'_3 and K'_7, which are used in the function FL1, 2, 9 and 10 but not in the function FL3 to 8. The function FL8 is discussed later.

In the attacks, plaintext pairs that take the differential values of all patterns with respect to the least significant bits of ΔP_1 to ΔP_4 are used.

The differential values of the ciphertext used in the attack differ between the case of distinguishing from a random permutation and the case of key recovery. For ΔC_1 and ΔC_2, the upper 15-bit values are 0 in both cases, whereas for ΔC_3 and ΔC_4, there is no restriction in the case of distinguishing from a random permutation, but the upper 15-bit value is non-zero for key recovery.

The differential probabilities are as follows. The differential probabilities for the function FL3 to FL7 are 2^{-1} each, as described in Sect. 3.2.2. For the function FL1 and FL2, the differential probability is 2^{-1} for each of the $\cap$ and $\cup$ operations, so the probabilities of the function FL1 and FL2 are both 2^{-2}. For the function FL8, the differential probabilities are different in the case of distinguishing from a random permutation and the case of key recovery. For the input difference $\Delta\text{FL8}_{\text{in}} = 0001\ 0001$, the output difference is either $\Delta\text{FL8}_{\text{out}} = 0001\ 0000$ or $0000\ 0000$, both with a differential probability of 2^{-1}. In the case of distinguishing from a random permutation, the attack succeeds because $\Delta C_{1(\text{L}15)} = \Delta C_{2(\text{L}15)} = 0$, regardless of the value of $\Delta\text{FL8}_{\text{out}}$, so the differential probability of the function FL8 can be regarded as 1. On the other hand, in the case of key recovery, the differential probability of the function FL8 is 2^{-1} because $\Delta\text{FL8}_{\text{out}}$ must be $= 0000\ 0000$. For the function FL9 and FL10, the differential probability can be regarded as 1, as there is no restriction imposed on the output differences. Therefore, the differential probability for the entire data randomizing part is $2^{-(2\cdot 2+1\cdot 5)} = 2^{-9}$ for distinguishing from a random permutation and $2^{-(2\cdot 2+1\cdot 6)} = 2^{-10}$ for key recovery.

4 Attacks on the MISTY1

In this section, we show the attack procedure for distinguishing the MISTY1 from a random permutation and for key recovery by using the differential characteristics of the data randomizing part described in Sect. 3.2.

4.1 Distinguisher

In this attack, plaintext pairs need to be encrypted with a weak key and the related key, respectively, and the corresponding ciphertext pairs be compared with each other, in order to distinguish MISTY1 from a random permutation. The values of the chosen plaintext and the corresponding ciphertext are assumed to be known to the attacker. The attack procedure and computational complexity are shown later.

The Attack Procedure. The attacker chooses plaintexts according to the following procedure.

(i) For an arbitrarily chosen plaintext $P = P_1||P_2||P_3||P_4$, fix the upper 15 bits of each P_i, take the all values for the least significant bit, and a total of $2^4 = 16$ plaintexts make up a set.
(ii) Choose a total of 2^n sets of plaintexts described in (i) that differ from each other (the total number of chosen plaintexts is $2^n \cdot 2^4 = 2^{n+4}$).

Next, the attacker obtains two ciphertexts encrypted with the weak key and the related key, respectively, for each of the $2^4 = 16$ plaintexts, constructs $2^4 \cdot 2^4 = 2^8$ ciphertext pairs for each set of plaintexts, that is, $2^n \cdot 2^8 = 2^{n+8}$ ciphertext pairs for 2^n sets of plaintexts. The paired ciphertexts are compared with each other and if a ciphertext pair is found for which $\Delta C_{1(\text{L}15)} = \Delta C_{2(\text{L}15)} = 0$, the attack is considered successful. $\Delta C_{3(\text{L}15)}$ and $\Delta C_{4(\text{L}15)}$ may or may not be zero and are determined by the output difference of the function FL8.

Complexity. Since the differential probability of the data randomizing part is 2^{-9} as calculated in Sect. 3.2.3, one ciphertext pair per $2^{n+8} = 2^9$ pairs is expected to satisfy the condition $\Delta C_{1(\text{L}15)} = \Delta C_{2(\text{L}15)} = 0$. That is, if the attacker obtains about 2^9 ciphertext pairs, then the attacker can distinguish MISTY1 from a random permutation. The data complexity required is $2^{n+4} = 2^5$ chosen plaintexts and the time complexity is the comparison of 2^9 pairs of ciphertexts.

4.2 Key Recovery

Table 4. Examples of pairs of CPs and the corresponding ciphertexts that are exploited for key recovery

Pairs of CPs	ciphertexts
b707 5efb b524 23a5	9e1c 104c eaac 4784
b706 5efb b525 23a5	9e1c 104d b9a7 285f
1622 a031 4495 b33c	06e8 0d03 2b57 5ae9
1623 a030 4495 b33c	06e9 0d02 a0a6 7273
01b9 8a3f 1b4e 5471	2678 717a 8e1a 9671
01b8 8a3f 1b4f 5471	2678 717b 062f 5fbb
170c 43b5 75e6 01e4	aeaa 0b5c dd53 bc03
170d 43b4 75e6 01e4	aeaa 0b5d 8d91 21f8
499f f3d3 916e 382b	a8bb 1931 b66a 9275
499e f3d3 916f 382b	a8ba 1930 a624 0556
2281 76ff 86c0 1446	b072 ab51 4865 11eb
2280 76ff 86c0 1446	b073 ab50 3978 f941
2280 76ff 86c0 1447	2484 25c8 fcef c910
2281 76fe 86c1 1447	2484 25c9 cd4e 2ac5
366f 51ca b97c e559	b7d0 ea3c 941a 0e58
366e 51ca b97d e559	b7d0 ea3d 7830 3fa0
e724 f9e3 960d ce69	dc99 dd98 7143 8869
e725 f9e2 960c ce69	dc99 dd99 e8dd 133e
$\Delta K_i = 0001$	
K_{sec} = 170b 438a 758b 018b 498b f38a 910a 380b	
K_{rel} = 170a 438b 758a 018a 498a f38b 910b 380a	

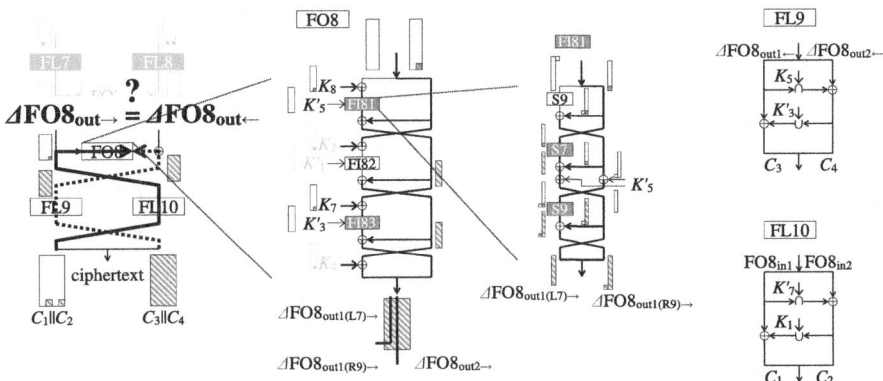

■ When $\Delta FO8_{out\rightarrow} = \Delta FO8_{out\leftarrow}$, the assumed keys are considered to be the correct key.

(a) By comparing $\Delta FO8_{out1(L7)\rightarrow}$ with $\Delta FO8_{out1(L7)\leftarrow}$, $K_{1(R7)}$, $K_{8(R7)}$ and $K'_{3(L7)}$ can be narrowed down (9 bits).

(b) By comparing $\Delta FO8_{out1(R9)\rightarrow}$ with $\Delta FO8_{out1(R9)\leftarrow}$, K_1, K_8, K'_3 and $K'_{5(R9)}$ can be narrowed down (44 bits).

(c) By comparing $\Delta FO8_{out2\rightarrow}$ with $\Delta FO8_{out2\leftarrow}$, K_1, K_5 to K_8 and K'_3 can be narrowed down (63 bits).

Fig. 5. Key recovery for K_1, K_5 to K_8 and K'_3

In this attack, the attacker recovers the weak key by exploiting the ciphertext pairs obtained by encrypting the chosen plaintexts with the weak key and the related key, respectively. The attacker needs to know the values of the ciphertexts and that the ciphertext pairs are obtained by encrypting the chosen plaintexts with a weak key and the related key, but does not need to know the values of the plaintexts.

The Attack Procedure. The attacker chooses 2^n sets of plaintexts to form 2^{n+8} pairs of ciphertexts by the same procedure as for distinguisher, and picks up the ciphertext pairs with $\Delta C_{1(L15)} = \Delta C_{2(L15)} = 0$, $\Delta C_{3(L15)} \neq 0$, $\Delta C_{4(L15)} \neq 0$ among these pairs. Since the differential probability is 2^{-10} as obtained in Sect. 3.2.3, the expected value of the number of the ciphertext pairs to be picked up is 2^{n-2}.

The attacker then calculates $\Delta FO8_{out}$ in two different ways, denoted as $\Delta FO8_{out\rightarrow}$ and $\Delta FO8_{out\leftarrow}$. The subscript $\rightarrow$ shows that $\Delta FO8_{out}$ are obtained by calculating the inverse function of FO10 and the function FO8, and the subscript $\leftarrow$ shows that $\Delta FO8_{out}$ are obtained by the inverse function of FO9. $\Delta FO8_{out\rightarrow}$ depends on C_1s, C_2s, K_1, K_7, K_8, $K'_{3(R9)}$ and K'_5, and $\Delta FO8_{out\leftarrow}$ is obtained depends on C_3s, C_4s, K_5 and K'_3 (see Fig. 5). The correct key candidate is narrowed down using the fact that $\Delta FO8_{out\rightarrow}$ is always equal to $\Delta FO8_{out\leftarrow}$ if the key candidate is correct and that $\Delta FO8_{out\rightarrow} \neq \Delta FO8_{out\leftarrow}$ with a high probability if it is incorrect.

The keys that need to be assumed are K_1, K_5 to K_8 and K'_3, as K'_5 is obtained from K_5 and K_6 by calculating the function FI. According to the conditions (1) to (3) of Sect. 3.1, 6 of the lower 7 bits in each K_i and 1 bit in each of the K'_5, K'_6 and K'_8 are known, so the total number of bits of the key to need to be assumed is $5 \cdot 10 - 3 + 16 = 63$ bits.

The search for the entire 63 bits of the key is very time-consuming using a desktop PC. Therefore, $\Delta FO8_{out}$ was divided into three blocks to reduce the search time in our analysis, which are (a) $\Delta FO8_{out1(L7)}$, (b) $\Delta FO8_{out1(R9)}$ and (c) $\Delta FO8_{out2}$, and then key recovery was performed by calculating (a) to (c) in sequence.

First, in the calculation of (a), $K_{1(R7)}$, $K_{8(R7)}$ and $K'_{3(L7)}$ are narrowed down by comparing $\Delta FO8_{out1(L7)\rightarrow}$ with $FO8_{out1(L7)\leftarrow}$. Next, in the calculation of (b), K_1, K_8, K'_3 and $K'_{5(R7)}$ are narrowed down by comparing $\Delta FO8_{out1(R9)\rightarrow}$ with $FO8_{out1(R9)\leftarrow}$. Then, in the calculation of (c), K_1, K_5 to K_8 and K'_3 are narrowed down by comparing $\Delta FO8_{out2\rightarrow}$ with $FO8_{out2\leftarrow}$. Finally, an exhaustive search of the remaining unknown bits containing K_2 to K_4 completes key recovery for all bits. Note that 6 bits of each of K_2 to K_4 and the least significant bit of K'_1, K'_2 and K'_4 are known, and the 16 bits of K'_3 have been narrowed down in (a) to (c). The time complexity is reduced because it can be expressed as the sum of those required for each procedure, not the product.

In the case of $\Delta K_{i(R7)} = 01$, 6 of the lower 7 bits of each K_i and the least significant bit each of K'_1, K'_2, K'_4 to K'_6 and K'_8 are already known before these procedures are performed, so $8 \cdot (16-6) - 6 \cdot 1 = 74$ bits of the keys are recovered in these procedures.

As the key assumptions required for the $\Delta FO8_{out\rightarrow}$ and $\Delta FO8_{out\leftarrow}$ calculations can be made independently, the number of calculations can be reduced in exchange for requiring memory by expanding the data related to the key assumed in one of them into memory.

Table 5. The number of ciphertext pairs and time required for key recovery

The number of ciphertext pairs: N	3	4	5	6
Average timeseconds	54	1.4	0.81	0.71
Time complexity[†]	$\lesssim 2^{33.7}$	$\lesssim 2^{28.8}$	$\lesssim 2^{27.2}$	$\lesssim 2^{27.0}$
Memory (MiB)	$\lesssim 82$	32	32	32

[†] The unit of time is the time for encrypting one time
($\simeq$ the time for calculating the function FO8 eight times)

Complexity. In the calculation of (a), 9 bits of the keys are searched exhaustively, which are the 1 bit of $K_{1(R7)}$, the 1 bit of $K_{8(R7)}$ and the 7 bits of $K'_{3(L7)}$. In the calculation of (b), 34 bits of the keys, which are the 17 bits of $K_{1(L9)}$ and $K_{8(L9)}$, the 9 bits of $K'_{3(R9)}$ and the 8 bits of $K'_{5(R9)}$, are searched, in addition to the bits that are narrowed down in (a). Note that the condition (3) on

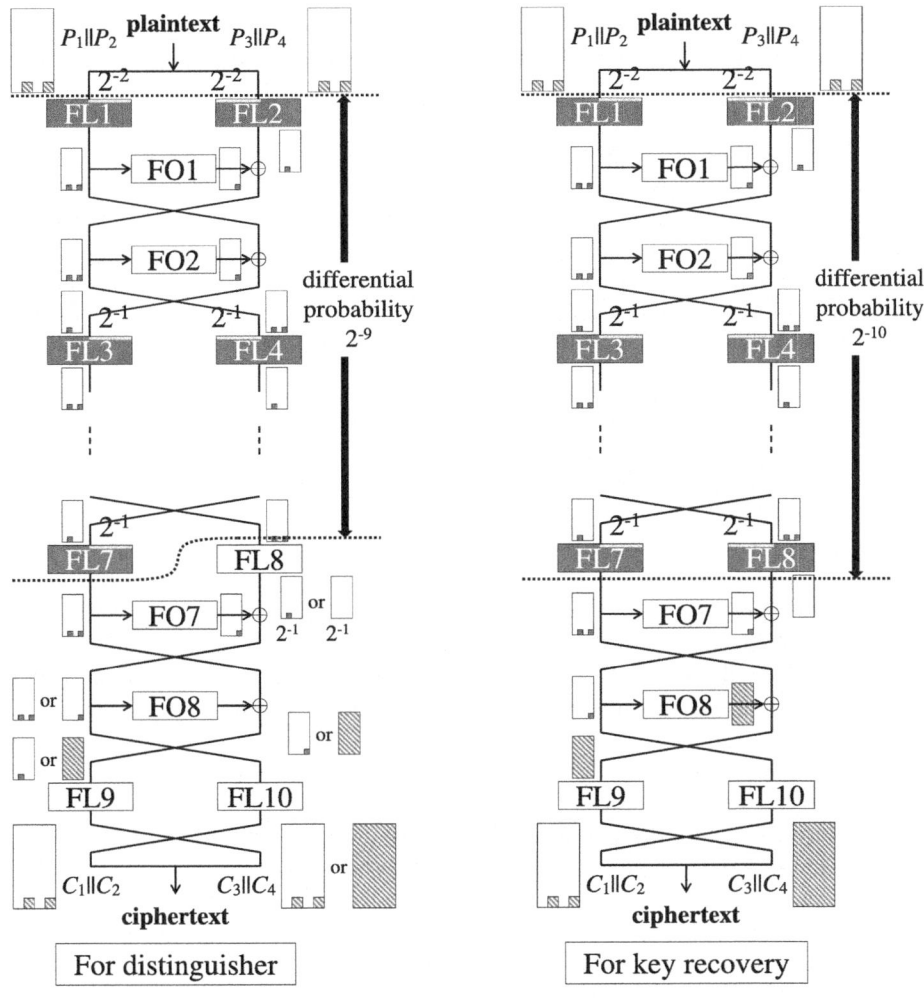

Fig. 6. Differential characteristics of the data randomizing part that can be exploited for the attacks

K_8' reduces the complexity of searching K_1 and K_8 by 1 bit. Furthermore, by narrowing down K_1, K_8 and $K_{5(R9)}'$ prior to narrowing down $K_{3(R9)}'$, though memory complexity is increased, the time complexity is reduced. In the calculation of (c), $10 \cdot 3 - 9 - 1 = 20$ bits of K_5, K_6 and K_7 in addition to the bits that are narrowed down in (a) and (b) are searched exhaustively. Note that the complexity of searching K_5, K_6 and K_7 is reduced by 9 bits because the $K_{5(R9)}'$

are narrowed down in (b) and by 1 bit because of the condition 3 on K_6'. The key to be searched for in the calculations of (a) to (c) is 63 bits in total, as described above.

If the number of ciphertext pairs used for key recovery is small, then the keys cannot be sufficiently narrowed down in each calculation of (a) to (c) as a result the time complexity increases in subsequent calculations. Also, the time/memory complexity varies depending on the value of the ciphertext pairs. Therefore, it is difficult to estimate the time/memory complexity theoretically. So, we measured the time, the number of calculations of the function FO and amount of memory required for the key recovery by computational experiment. The results are shown in Table 4. The desktop PC used was as follows.

> Processor: Intel(R) Core (TM) i9-9900K CPU
> Memory: 32GB
> Development environment: Microsoft Visual C++ 2015

In Table 5, N $(= 2^{n-2})$ is the number of ciphertext pairs used, and Average time is the average of the search time required for all combinations of N pairs from the 9 ciphertext pairs in Table 4. The search time was about 1.4 s when $N = 4$ and less than 1 s when $N = 5$ and 6. It also took less than about 1 min when $N = 3$. When $N = 2$ it took between 15 min and 65 h in the range measured, although this is not shown in the table because only part of it could be measured because it was too time-consuming. The amount of memory required is 82MiB maximum when $N = 3$ and is 32MiB when $N \geq 4$.

As the search time increases rapidly with $N < 4$, the number of ciphertext pairs required in this paper is defined to be N $(= 2^{n-2}) = 4$, though the key recovery is also feasible when $N = 3$ or $N = 2$. When $n = 4$, the required number of chosen plaintexts is $2^{n+4} = 2^8$. We counted the number of the function FO calculations and measured the amount of memory used during the search. The number of the function FO calculations was $\lesssim 2^{32}$, then the time complexity is $\lesssim 2^{29}$ in terms of one encryption which contains $8 = 2^3$ function FOs, and the memory used was about 2^{25} bytes $(= 32\text{MiB})$.

5 Summary

In this paper, we first described how to derive the weak keys by analyzing the key scheduling part and showed that when a weak key and the related key are used, there is a differential characteristic with a very large differential probability in the data randomizing part of the MISTY1 in the related-key setting.

Next, we described the attack procedures of distinguishing MISTY1 from a random permutation and the key recovery using this differential characteristic, and show that the computational complexity for these attacks is realistically feasible. For distinguishing MISTY1 from a random permutation, data and time complexity is 2^5 chosen plaintexts and the time for comparing 2^9 ciphertext pairs. For the key recovery, data, memory and time complexity is 2^8 chosen plaintexts, 2^{25} bytes and the time for encrypting $\lesssim 2^{29}$ times. The actual time measured on a desktop PC was less than or equal about 2 s on average, although it depends on the value of secret keys and ciphertexts.

It should be noted that the set of the weak keys occupies a small fraction of the entire key space and that this attack is the related-key attack, so it is not considered to be a realistic threat in normal encryption applications.

References

1. Matsui, M.: New block encryption algorithm MISTY. In: Biham, E. (ed.) FSE 1997. LNCS, vol. 1267, pp. 54–68. Springer, Heidelberg (1997). https://doi.org/10.1007/BFb0052334
2. CRYPTREC Homepage. http://www.cryptrec.go.jp/en/method.html
3. Specifications in 2001 MISTY1. http://www.cryptrec.go.jp/en/cryptrec_03_spec_cypherlist_files/PDF/05_02espec.pdf
4. NESSIE Homepage. https://www.cosic.esat.kuleuven.be/nessie/
5. ISO/IEC Homepage. JTC1: ISO/IEC 18033: Security techniques - encryption algorithms - part 3: Block ciphers (2005)
6. Ohta, H., Matsui, M.: A description of the MISTY1 encryption algorithm (2000). https://tools.ietf.org/html/rfc2994
7. Lu, J., Yap, W.-S., Wei, Y.: Weak keys of the full MISTY1 block cipher for related-key differential cryptanalysis. In: Dawson, E. (ed.) CT-RSA 2013. LNCS, vol. 7779, pp. 389–404. Springer, Heidelberg (2013). https://doi.org/10.1007/978-3-642-36095-4_25
8. Lu, J., Yap, W.S., Wei, Y.: Weak keys of the full MISTY1 block cipher for related-key amplified boomerang cryptanalysis. IET J. **12**(5), 389–397 (2018)
9. Todo, Y.: Integral cryptanalysis on full MISTY1. In: Gennaro, R., Robshaw, M. (eds.) CRYPTO 2015. LNCS, vol. 9215, pp. 413–432. Springer, Heidelberg (2015). https://doi.org/10.1007/978-3-662-47989-6_20
10. Todo, Y.: Integral cryptanalysis on full MISTY1. J. Cryptology. **30**, 920–959 (2017)
11. Bar-On, A., Keller, N.: A 2^{70} attack on the full MISTY1. In: Robshaw, M., Katz, J. (eds.) CRYPTO 2016. LNCS, vol. 9814, pp. 435–456. Springer, Heidelberg (2016). https://doi.org/10.1007/978-3-662-53018-4_16
12. NIST FIPS PUB 46-3.: Data Encryption Standard (DES). http://csrc.nist.gov/csrs/media/publications/fips/46/3/archive/1990-10-25/documents/fips46-3.pdf
13. NIST FIPS PUB 197.: Advanced Encryption Standard (2001). http://csrc.nist.gov/publications/fips/fips197/fips-197.pdf
14. Biham, E.: New types of cryptanalytic attacks using related keys. J. Cryptology **7**(4), 229–246 (1994)
15. Knudsen, L.R.: Cryptanalysis of LOKI 91. In: Seberry, J., Zheng, Y. (eds.) AUSCRYPT 1992. LNCS, vol. 718, pp. 196–208. Springer, Heidelberg (1993). https://doi.org/10.1007/3-540-57220-1_62
16. Biryukov, A., Khovratovich, D.: Related-key cryptanalysis of the full AES-192 and AES-256. In: Matsui, M. (ed.) ASIACRYPT 2009. LNCS, vol. 5912, pp. 1–18. Springer, Heidelberg (2009). https://doi.org/10.1007/978-3-642-10366-7_1
17. Biryukov, A., Khovratovich, D., Nikolić, I.: Distinguisher and related-key attack on the full AES-256. In: Halevi, S. (ed.) CRYPTO 2009. LNCS, vol. 5677, pp. 231–249. Springer, Heidelberg (2009). https://doi.org/10.1007/978-3-642-03356-8_14

Protocols

Efficient Card-Based Protocols with a Standard Deck of Playing Cards Using Partial Opening

Yoshiaki Honda[1] and Kazumasa Shinagawa[1,2(✉)]

[1] Ibaraki University, Hitachi, Japan
kazumasa.shinagawa.np92@vc.ibaraki.ac.jp
[2] National Institute of Advanced Industrial Science and Technology, Tokyo, Japan

Abstract. Card-based protocols are cryptographic protocols that use a deck of physical cards. In this paper, we deal with card-based protocols using a standard deck of playing cards, which are commonly available commercially. For finite-runtime committed-format protocols, Mizuki (CANS 2016) proposed an eight-card AND protocol with four random bisection cuts and a six-card COPY protocol with one random bisection cut. In this paper, we propose a *partial-open* action, which reveals any position of the face of cards, by generalizing the *half-open* action introduced by Miyahara and Mizuki (IJTCS-FAW 2022). Using the partial-open action, we propose a four-card AND protocol with three random cuts and a four-card COPY protocol with three random cuts. We note that, without partial-open actions, these protocols are known to be impossible to construct. Therefore, the partial-open actions are inherently necessary to obtain our results.

Keywords: Card-based cryptography · Playing cards · Committed-format · Finite-runtime · Random cut · Half-open action · Partial-open action

1 Introduction

1.1 Background

Card-based cryptography studies cryptographic techniques that uses a deck of physical cards to realize cryptographic tasks such as secure multiparty computation and zero-knowledge proof. The historically first studies [1,2] used a *two-color deck* consisting of ♣ and ♡, while Niemi and Renvall [13] used a *standard deck of playing cards*, which is commercially available and easy to prepare. Using the standard deck of playing cards, they constructed a Las Vegas protocol for any function, and later Mizuki [11] constructed a finite-time protocol for any function. Since these studies, efficient protocols have been proposed for various functions: a two-input AND protocol [5], a three-input AND protocol [6], a Millionaire's protocol [9], a Sudoku protocol [14,15], and a three-input majority protocol [3]. There have also been proposed card-based protocols based on private permutations [8,12].

Fig. 1. A card and the cover   **Fig. 2.** Half-open action

Most of the existing protocols have three basic actions on a sequence of cards: permutation, shuffle, and turn. In particular, a turn action for a face-down card reveals the face of the card. Since the face of a playing card has a number (from 1 to 13) and a suit (i.e., ♣, ♡, ♢, or ♠), it is natural to *partially* reveal the face, although this is an extraordinary idea. Miyahara and Mizuki [10] proposed a *half-open* action that reveals only the suit of a face-down card while hiding the number. They designed a four-card AND protocol with a half-open action. One way to implement the half-open action is to use a cover (i.e., a piece of paper with a hole in it). For example, a half-open action for $\boxed{1}$ of the heart suit can be done by overlaying the cover, which is a joker card (as an example) with a hole as in Fugire 1, as shown in Fig. 2. Note that we are using a joker as a cover, but the cover does not have to be a card. Therefore, we do not count the cover as an additional card.

1.2 Our Contribution

In this paper, we introduce a *partial-open* action, which is a generalized version of the half-open action by Miyahara and Mizuki [10]. A partial-open action reveals any part of the face of cards. For example, applying a partial-open action for the center of the face, we can see whether the card has a suit mark in the center of the face. Using the partial-open actions, we propose AND and COPY protocols (see Table 1). Here, our protocols are *committed-format* protocols, in which both input and output follow the encoding rule called a *commitment*, so these protocols can be combined with each other. In addition, our protocols require only the most basic shuffle called a *random cut*, which shifts a sequence of cards cyclically and uniformly at random. In particular, we construct a four-card AND protocol with three random cuts and a four-card COPY protocol with three random cuts. Since our protocols do not use additional cards besides the input and output, they are optimal in terms of the number of cards.

Table 1. Existing committed-format protocols and ours using the standard deck of cards: RC stands for random cut and RBC stands for random bisection cut

	# of Cards	Runtime	# of Shuffles	Shuffle	Partial-Open
○ AND Protocol					
Niemi–Renvall [13]	5	Las Vegas	9.5 (exp.)	RC	
Mizuki [11]	8	finite	4	RBC	
Koch et al. [5]	4	Las Vegas	6 (exp.)	RC	
Ours	4	finite	3	RC	✓
○ COPY Protocol					
Niemi–Renvall [13]	6	Las Vegas	5.5 (exp.)	RC	
Mizuki [11]	6	finite	1	RBC	
Koyama et al. [7]	6	Las Vegas	3 (exp.)	RC	
Ours	4	finite	3	RC	✓
○ Committed-Format XOR Protocols					
Niemi–Renvall [13]	4		7 (exp.)	RC	
Mizuki [11]	4	finite	1	RBC	
Koyama et al. [7]	4	finite	1	RC	

In the setting without partial-open actions, Koch et al. [5] showed the impossibility of a finite-runtime four-card AND protocol and Kastner et al. [4] showed the impossibility of a finite-runtime four-card COPY protocol [5]. Thus, the partial-open actions are inherently necessary to obtain our results.

It should be noted, however, that our protocols cannot choose any one as the *base* (the type of cards that consisting the commitment, see Sect. 2.2) of the input/output commitments, but must choose an appropriate base. For our AND protocol, the base of the input commitments are $\boxed{2}\boxed{4}$ and $\boxed{5}\boxed{6}$ and the base of the output commitment is $\boxed{2}\boxed{4}$. For our COPY protocol, the bases of the input commitment and additional cards are $\boxed{1}\boxed{2}$ and $\boxed{9}\boxed{10}$. Fortunately, there are several existing protocols for base conversion, so when executing our protocols, one can either create commitments using the appropriate bases in advance or convert them to the appropriate bases using base conversion protocols. We also note that there are other bases where our protocols can be executed. In Appendix A, we give a list of other bases for executing our protocols.

2 Preliminaries

In this section, we introduce basic definitions for card-based cryptography and the existing AND and COPY protocols.

2.1 Playing Cards

In this paper, we will use the standard deck of playing cards called *BICYCLE* shown in Fig. 3, which is made by the U.S. Playing Card Company. The backs of

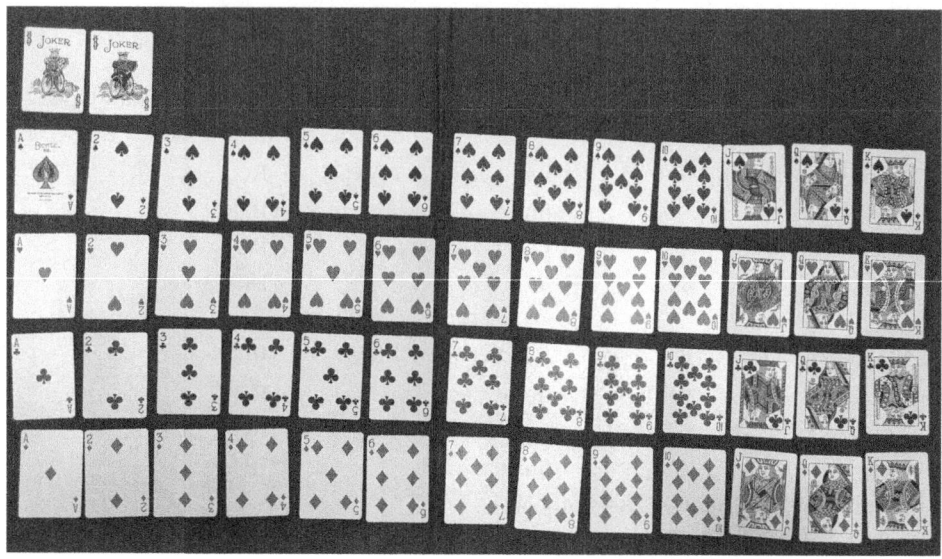

Fig. 3. The standard deck of playing cards called BICYCLE

all cards have the same pattern and are assumed to be indistinguishable. In this paper, we will use cards numbered from 1 to 10 of the same suit in a single protocol, and denote the front sides of these cards as $\boxed{1}\,\boxed{2}\,\boxed{3}\,\boxed{4}\,\boxed{5}\,\boxed{6}\,\boxed{7}\,\boxed{8}\,\boxed{9}\,\boxed{10}$ and the back side as $\boxed{?}$.

Note that although we assume BICYCLE as the deck of playing cards in this paper, our protocols can be implemented with other decks of playing cards. For example, other deck by U.S. Playing Card Company, such as *TALLY-HO* and *Bee*, are similar in design to BICYCLE and can be used for our protocols.

2.2 Commitment

A *commitment* is a pair of face-down cards holding a binary value. For two cards $\boxed{i}\,\boxed{j}$ with $1 \leq i < j \leq 10$, we define the encoding as follows:
$$\boxed{i}\,\boxed{j} = 0,\ \boxed{j}\,\boxed{i} = 1.$$
We denote a commitment holding $x \in \{0, 1\}$ as follows:
$$\underbrace{\boxed{?}\,\boxed{?}}_{[x]^{\{i,j\}}}.$$
Here we call the set $\{i, j\}$ a *base* of the commitment.

2.3 Random Cut

A random cut is a shuffle action that performs a random cyclic shifting on a sequence of cards. For example, applying a random cut to a sequence of face-down cards $\boxed{1}\boxed{2}\boxed{3}\boxed{4}$ yields one of four sequences of face-down cards as follows:

$$\boxed{1}\boxed{2}\boxed{3}\boxed{4},\ \boxed{2}\boxed{3}\boxed{4}\boxed{1},\ \boxed{3}\boxed{4}\boxed{1}\boxed{2},\ \boxed{4}\boxed{1}\boxed{2}\boxed{3}.$$

The probabilities of transition to each sequence are all equal, and in the above example, 1/4 for each. The application of a random cut is denoted as follows:

$$\left\langle \boxed{?}\boxed{?}\boxed{?}\boxed{?} \right\rangle.$$

2.4 Random-Cut-Based Search

The *random-cut-based search* [11,13] is a technique to search for a specific card in a sequence of face-down cards using random cuts. For example, when searching for $\boxed{1}$ from a sequence of face-down cards consisting of $\boxed{1}\boxed{2}\boxed{3}\boxed{4}$, do the following procedure:

1. Apply a random cut to the sequence as follows:

$$\left\langle \boxed{?}\boxed{?}\boxed{?}\boxed{?} \right\rangle.$$

2. Reveal the first card as follows:

$$\boxed{}\boxed{?}\boxed{?}\boxed{?}.$$

3. If the revealed card is $\boxed{1}$, the search is over. Otherwise, turn the revealed card face-down and return to Step 1.

In the random-cut-based search with n cards, the expected number of shuffles until finding the desired card is n. The idea of our protocols is to perform the search in finite runtime by using partial-open actions.

2.5 Koch–Schrempp–Kirsten's AND Protocol

Koch, Schrempp, and Kirsten [5] proposed a four-card Las Vegas AND protocol using the standard deck of playing cards. It uses only random cuts, and the expected number of shuffles is 6.

Here, we give a simplified version of the Koch–Schrempp–Kirsten's protocol. The expected number of shuffles in the protocol below is 11, while the number is 6 in the original protocol. The idea of this protocol is shown in Table 2.

The protocol procedure is as follows.

1. Arrange the input commitments as follows:

$$\underbrace{\boxed{?}\boxed{?}}_{[a]^{\{1,2\}}}\ \underbrace{\boxed{?}\boxed{?}}_{[b]^{\{3,4\}}}.$$

Table 2. The idea of the simplified Koch–Schrempp–Kirsten's AND protocol

	Input	Find 1	After swap	Remove 3	Find 4
(0,0)	1234	1234	1243	124	412
(0,1)	1243	1243	1234	412	412
(1,0)	2134	1342	1324	241	412
(1,1)	2143	1432	1423	142	421

2. Apply the random-cut-based search to find $\boxed{1}$ as follows:

$$\langle \boxed{?}\boxed{?}\boxed{?}\boxed{?} \rangle \rightarrow \boxed{1}\boxed{?}\boxed{?}\boxed{?}.$$

3. Rearrange the sequence as:

$$\boxed{?}\boxed{?}\boxed{?}\boxed{?}$$
$$\boxed{?}\boxed{?}\boxed{?}\boxed{?}.$$

4. Apply the random-cut-based search to find $\boxed{3}$ and remove it as follows:

$$\langle \boxed{?}\boxed{?}\boxed{?}\boxed{?} \rangle \rightarrow \boxed{3}\boxed{?}\boxed{?}\boxed{?} \rightarrow \boxed{?}\boxed{?}\boxed{?}.$$

5. For the sequence of the remaining three cards, apply the random-cut-based search to find $\boxed{4}$ and obtain a commitment to $a \wedge b$ as follows:

$$\langle \boxed{?}\boxed{?}\boxed{?} \rangle \rightarrow \boxed{?}\boxed{?}\boxed{4} \rightarrow \boxed{4}\underbrace{\boxed{?}\boxed{?}}_{[a \wedge b]^{\{1,2\}}}.$$

The expected number of shuffles in the above protocol is $4+4+3 = 11$, while the number of shuffles is 6 in the original protocol.

2.6 Niemi–Renvall's COPY Protocol

Niemi and Renvall [13] proposed a six-card Las Vegas COPY protocol using the standard deck of playing cards. The expected number of shuffles is 5.5, and all of them are random cuts.

The protocol procedure is as follows.

1. Arrange the input commitments as follows:

$$\boxed{5}\underbrace{\boxed{?}\boxed{?}}_{[a]^{\{1,2\}}}\boxed{6}\boxed{3}\boxed{4}.$$

2. Apply the random cut to the right two face-down cards as follows:

$$\boxed{5}\underbrace{\boxed{?}\boxed{?}}_{[a]^{\{1,2\}}}\boxed{6}\langle\boxed{?}\boxed{?}\rangle \rightarrow \boxed{5}\underbrace{\boxed{?}\boxed{?}}_{[a]^{\{1,2\}}}\boxed{6}\underbrace{\boxed{?}\boxed{?}}_{[r]^{\{3,4\}}}.$$

3. Turn over all face-up cards as follows:

$$\boxed{?}\underbrace{\boxed{?}\boxed{?}}_{[a]^{\{1,2\}}}\boxed{?}\underbrace{\boxed{?}\boxed{?}}_{[r]^{\{3,4\}}}.$$

4. Using the random-cut-based search, find one of four cards $\boxed{1}\boxed{2}\boxed{3}\boxed{4}$. Then, reveal the fourth card. For instance, if we found $\boxed{1}$ in the random-cut-based search, we have either two possible cases as follows:

$$\boxed{1}\boxed{?}\boxed{?}\boxed{3}\boxed{?}\boxed{?} \text{ or } \boxed{1}\boxed{?}\boxed{?}\boxed{4}\boxed{?}\boxed{?}.$$

If the opened cards are either $\boxed{1}\boxed{3}$ or $\boxed{2}\boxed{4}$, then $a = r$, and if they are either $\boxed{1}\boxed{4}$ or $\boxed{2}\boxed{3}$, then $a \neq r$.

5. Turn over all face-up cards as follows:

$$\boxed{?}\boxed{?}\boxed{?}\boxed{?}\boxed{?}\boxed{?}.$$

6. Using the random-cut-based search to find one of two cards $\boxed{5}\boxed{6}$ and obtain the commitments to $[a]^{\{1,2\}}$ and $[r]^{\{3,4\}}$ as follows:

$$\boxed{5}\underbrace{\boxed{?}\boxed{?}}_{[a]^{\{1,2\}}}\underbrace{\boxed{?}\boxed{?}}_{[r]^{\{3,4\}}} \text{ or } \boxed{6}\underbrace{\boxed{?}\boxed{?}}_{[r]^{\{3,4\}}}\underbrace{\boxed{?}\boxed{?}}_{[a]^{\{1,2\}}}.$$

Note that from Step 4, we know whether it is either $a = r$ or $a \neq r$. Thus these commitments imply two copies of the commitment to a.

The expected number of shuffles in the above protocol is $1 + 6/4 + 6/2 = 5.5$.

3 Partial-Open Action for Playing Cards

3.1 Partial-Open Action

A *partial-open action* is an action that reveals only a part of the face of cards, rather than the entire face. It is a generalized action of *half-open action* [10], which reveals only the suit of cards. Since the partial-open action reveals any part of the face, the half-open action can be considered a special case of the partial-open action when the revealed position is the suit.

We consider seven positions for partial-open actions (see Fig. 4). Note, however, that these seven positions are representative disclosure positions in terms of ease of operation, and that other disclosure positions may also be useful.

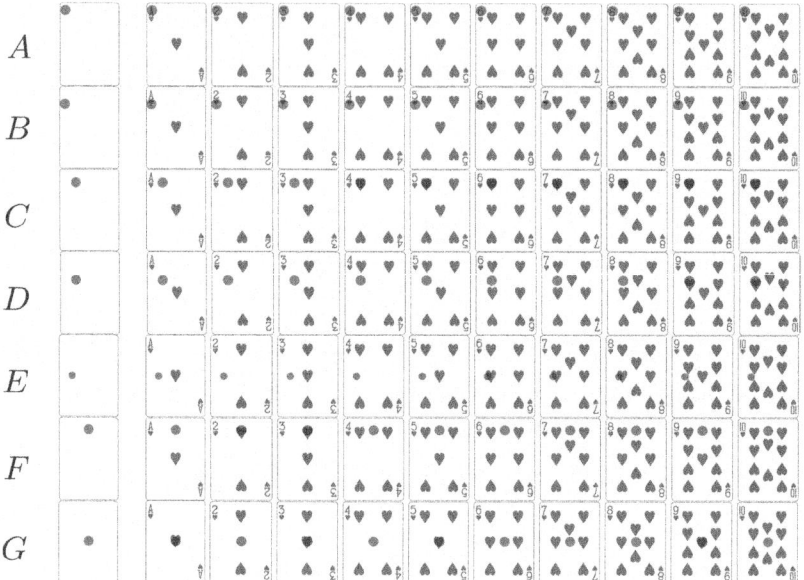

Fig. 4. Seven disclosure positions for partial-open actions

The circle (A) is the position for revealing the number (and the color) of the card. The circle (B) is the position for revealing the suit of the card, which is equivalent to the half-open action by Miyahara and Mizuki [10]. The circles (C), (D), (E), (F), and (G) are positions for revealing the left topmost suit, the left second suit, the left centered suit, the middle topmost suit, and the centered suit, respectively. For example, by applying the partial-open action at the position (G) to a face-down card, we will know whether it is either one of $\boxed{1}\,\boxed{3}\,\boxed{5}\,\boxed{9}$ or one of $\boxed{2}\,\boxed{4}\,\boxed{6}\,\boxed{7}\,\boxed{8}\,\boxed{10}$. For example, if a partial-open action is applied to a sequence of four face-down cards and it reveals $\heartsuit$ for only the second card, we would write it as follows:

$$\boxed{?}\,\boxed{?}\,\boxed{?}\,\boxed{?} \to (\perp, \heartsuit, \perp, \perp).$$

We will use to denote the application of a partial-open action in a similar way. See Table 3 for summary of partial-open actions.

Note that partial-open actions for cards of different suits are also useful, although our protocols use only partial-open actions for cards of the same suit. For example, for cards of the four suits (hearts, diamonds, clubs, and spades), a partial-open action through a small hole in the middle of the suit (under the number) provides one bit information about whether red or black is being revealed. Such partial-open actions seem to be useful in constructing protocols for the standard deck of cards. We left as an future research to construct new protocols using such operations.

Table 3. Summary of the revealed symbols by partial-open actions

Position	1	2	3	4	5	6	7	8	9	10
A	1	2	3	4	5	6	7	8	9	10
B	♡	♡	♡	♡	♡	♡	♡	♡	♡	♡
C				♡	♡	♡	♡	♡	♡	♡
D									♡	♡
E						♡	♡	♡		
F		♡	♡							
G	♡		♡		♡				♡	

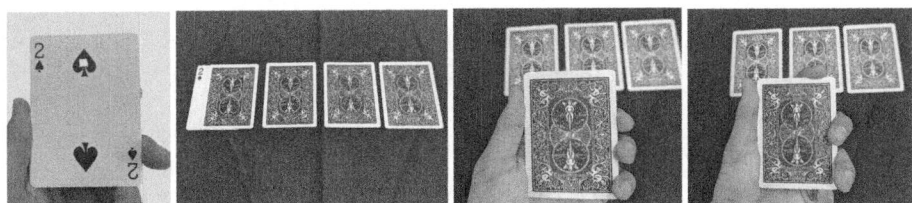

Fig. 5. An implementation of the partial-open action using the cover

3.2 Implementation of Partial-Open Actions

The procedure of the partial-open action is as follows. First, prepare a piece of paper with a hole in the position to be revealed, which we call a *cover*, as in the leftmost in Fig. 5. Next, insert the cover under the card to be applied the partial-open action as in the second from the left in Fig. 5. Next, the card and the cover are lifted together as in the third from the left in Fig. 5. Finally, the card and the cover are turned over as in the rightmost in Fig. 5. In the case of Fig. 5, the red color can be seen through the hole, indicating that the suit is in that position.

4 Our Protocols

4.1 Our AND Protocol

In this section, we propose a finite-runtime committed-format AND protocol that uses four cards $\boxed{2}\boxed{4}\boxed{5}\boxed{6}$ and three random cuts. The protocol is based on a simplified version of Koch et al.'s AND protocol in Sect. 2.5. The idea of the proposed protocol is shown in Table 4. The protocol procedure is as follows.

1. Arrange the input commitments as follows:

$$\underbrace{\boxed{?}\boxed{?}}_{[a]^{\{2,4\}}}\underbrace{\boxed{?}\boxed{?}}_{[b]^{\{5,6\}}}.$$

Table 4. Our AND protocol

	Input	Find 2	After swap	Remove 5	Find 6
(0,0)	2456	2456	2465	246	624
(0,1)	2465	2465	2456	624	624
(1,0)	4256	2564	2546	462	624
(1,1)	4265	2654	2645	264	642

2. Apply a random cut to the sequence as follows:

$$\langle\ ?\ ?\ ?\ ?\ \rangle.$$

3. Apply the partial-open action at (F) in Fig. 4, which reveals $\heartsuit$ for $\boxed{2}$ and nothing for $\boxed{4}\boxed{5}\boxed{6}$, to each card as follows:

$$\boxed{?}\boxed{?}\boxed{?}\boxed{?} \rightarrow \begin{cases}(\heartsuit, \bot, \bot, \bot)\\(\bot, \heartsuit, \bot, \bot)\\(\bot, \bot, \heartsuit, \bot)\\(\bot, \bot, \bot, \heartsuit)\end{cases}.$$

From this, the position of $\boxed{2}$ in the sequence is determined.

4. Cyclically shift the sequence so that $\boxed{2}$ will be the leftmost card. For example, if the third card is $\boxed{2}$, rearrange the sequence as follows:

$$\boxed{?}\boxed{?}\boxed{?}\boxed{?} \rightarrow \boxed{?}\boxed{?}\boxed{?}\boxed{?}.$$
$$\bot\ \bot\ \heartsuit\ \bot \qquad \heartsuit\ \bot\ \bot\ \bot$$

5. Rearrange the sequence as:

$$\boxed{?}\boxed{?}\boxed{?}\boxed{?}$$
$$\times$$
$$\boxed{?}\boxed{?}\boxed{?}\boxed{?}.$$

6. Apply a random cut to the sequence as follows:

$$\langle\ ?\ ?\ ?\ ?\ \rangle.$$

7. Apply the partial-open action at (G) in Fig. 4, which reveals $\heartsuit$ for $\boxed{5}$ and nothing for $\boxed{2}\boxed{4}\boxed{6}$, to each card as follows:

$$\boxed{?}\boxed{?}\boxed{?}\boxed{?} \rightarrow \begin{cases}(\heartsuit, \bot, \bot, \bot)\\(\bot, \heartsuit, \bot, \bot)\\(\bot, \bot, \heartsuit, \bot)\\(\bot, \bot, \bot, \heartsuit)\end{cases}.$$

From this, the position of $\boxed{5}$ in the sequence is determined.

8. Discard $\boxed{5}$ from the sequence. For example, if the second card is $\boxed{5}$, discard the second card as follows:

$$\underset{\bot\;\heartsuit\;\bot\;\bot}{\boxed{?}\boxed{?}\boxed{?}\boxed{?}} \rightarrow \underset{\bot\;\bot\;\bot}{\boxed{?}\boxed{?}\boxed{?}}.$$

9. Apply a random cut to the sequence as follows:

$$\left\langle \boxed{?}\boxed{?}\boxed{?} \right\rangle.$$

10. Apply the partial-open action at (E) in Fig. 4, which reveals $\heartsuit$ for $\boxed{6}$ and nothing for $\boxed{2}\boxed{4}\boxed{5}$, to each card as follows:

$$\boxed{?}\boxed{?}\boxed{?}\boxed{?} \rightarrow \begin{cases} (\heartsuit, \bot, \bot, \bot) \\ (\bot, \heartsuit, \bot, \bot) \\ (\bot, \bot, \heartsuit, \bot) \\ (\bot, \bot, \bot, \heartsuit) \end{cases}.$$

From this, the position of $\boxed{6}$ in the sequence is determined.

11. Cyclically shift the sequence so that $\boxed{6}$ will be the leftmost card; then the remaining cards are the output. For example, if the second card is $\boxed{6}$, the output is obtained as follows:

$$\boxed{?}\boxed{6}\boxed{?} \rightarrow \underset{[a \wedge b]^{\{2,4\}}}{\boxed{6}\boxed{?}\boxed{?}}.$$

Correctness. The correctness of the proposed protocol follows from Table 4.

Security. In the proposed protocol, the front-side symbol information of the card sequence is revealed only in the partial-open action in Steps 3, 7, and 10. In Step 3, the partial-open action at (F) in Fig. 4 is applied to all cards. Due to the random cut in Step 2, the sequence of the opened symbols in Step 3 is chosen uniformly at random from $(\heartsuit, \bot, \bot, \bot)$, $(\bot, \heartsuit, \bot, \bot)$, $(\bot, \bot, \heartsuit, \bot)$, and $(\bot, \bot, \bot, \heartsuit)$, and independent of the inputs. Similarly, the sequences of the opened symbols in Steps 7 and 10 are chosen uniformly at random and independent of the inputs due to the random cut in Steps 6 and 9, respectively. Therefore, the protocol is secure.

4.2 Our COPY Protcol

In this section, we present a finite-runtime COPY protocol that uses four cards and three random cuts. The procedure is as follows.

1. Apply a random cut to the sequence as follows:

$$\underset{[a]^{\{1,2\}}}{\boxed{?}\boxed{?}}\boxed{9}\boxed{10}.$$

2. Turn the face-up cards and apply a random cut to them as follows:

$$\boxed{?}\boxed{?}\langle\boxed{?}\boxed{?}\rangle \rightarrow \underbrace{\boxed{?}\boxed{?}}_{[a]^{\{1,2\}}}\underbrace{\boxed{?}\boxed{?}}_{[b]^{\{9,10\}}},$$

where $b \in \{0,1\}$ is a uniformly random bit.

3. Apply a random cut to the sequence as follows:

$$\langle\boxed{?}\boxed{?}\boxed{?}\boxed{?}\rangle.$$

4. Apply the partial-open action at (G) in Fig. 4, which reveals $\heartsuit$ for $\boxed{1}\boxed{9}$ and nothing for $\boxed{2}\boxed{10}$, to each card as follows:

$$\boxed{?}\boxed{?}\boxed{?}\boxed{?} \rightarrow \begin{cases} (\heartsuit, \heartsuit, \bot, \bot) \\ (\bot, \heartsuit, \heartsuit, \bot) \\ (\bot, \bot, \heartsuit, \heartsuit) \\ (\heartsuit, \bot, \bot, \heartsuit) \end{cases} \text{or} \begin{cases} (\heartsuit, \bot, \heartsuit, \bot) \\ (\bot, \heartsuit, \bot, \heartsuit) \end{cases}.$$

From this, whether $\boxed{1}$ and $\boxed{9}$ are cyclic neighbors or not is determined.

5. Apply a random cut to the sequence as follows:

$$\langle\boxed{?}\boxed{?}\boxed{?}\boxed{?}\rangle.$$

6. Apply the partial-open action at (C) in Fig. 4, which reveals $\heartsuit$ for $\boxed{9}\boxed{10}$ and nothing for $\boxed{1}\boxed{2}$, to each card as follows:

$$\boxed{?}\boxed{?}\boxed{?}\boxed{?} \rightarrow \begin{cases} (\heartsuit, \heartsuit, \bot, \bot) \\ (\bot, \heartsuit, \heartsuit, \bot) \\ (\bot, \bot, \heartsuit, \heartsuit) \\ (\heartsuit, \bot, \bot, \heartsuit) \end{cases}.$$

From this, the position of $\boxed{9}\boxed{10}$ (or $\boxed{10}\boxed{9}$) is determined.

7. Cyclically shift the sequence so that $\boxed{9}\boxed{10}$ will be the leftmost card as follows:

$$\underset{\bot\ \heartsuit\ \heartsuit\ \bot}{\boxed{?}\boxed{?}\boxed{?}\boxed{?}} \rightarrow \underset{\heartsuit\ \heartsuit\ \bot\ \bot}{\boxed{?}\boxed{?}\boxed{?}\boxed{?}}.$$

8. If $\boxed{1}\boxed{9}$ are not cyclic neighbors in Step 4, then we have $a = b$ and the current card sequence consists of two copies of $[a]$.

$$\underbrace{\boxed{?}\boxed{?}}_{[a]^{\{9,10\}}}\underbrace{\boxed{?}\boxed{?}}_{[a]^{\{1,2\}}}.$$

9. If $\boxed{1}\,\boxed{9}$ are cyclic neighbors in Step 4, then we have $a \neq b$ and the current card sequence consists of $[\bar{a}]$ and $[a]$.

$$\underbrace{\boxed{?}\boxed{?}}_{[\bar{a}]\{9,10\}}\ \underbrace{\boxed{?}\boxed{?}}_{[a]\{1,2\}}.$$

Correctness. The suits at position (G) of the Fig. 4 in Step 4 are $\boxed{1}$ and $\boxed{9}$. In the relationship between the numbers $\boxed{1}$ and $\boxed{2}$ and $\boxed{9}$ and $\boxed{10}$, $\boxed{1}$ and $\boxed{9}$ are both the smaller values, so if they are not cyclically adjacent, the values of a and b are identical, and if they are adjacent, the values are not identical. Then, since $\boxed{9}$ and $\boxed{10}$ are the suits in position (C) of the figure in Step 4 in Step 6, we can identify the commitment to which we are copying. Since this commitment can be identified as a or $\bar{a}$ by the result of Step 4, a copy can be obtained by outputting the commitment as is in the case of a and inverting it in the case of $\bar{a}$. This proves the validity.

Security. In the proposed protocol, the front-side symbol information of the card sequence is revealed only in the partial-open action in Steps 4 and 6. In Step 4, the partial-open action at (G) in Fig. 4 is applied to all cards. Due to the random cut in Step 3, the sequence of the opened symbols in Step 4 is chosen uniformly at random from $(\heartsuit, \heartsuit, \bot, \bot)$, $(\bot, \heartsuit, \heartsuit, \bot)$, $(\bot, \bot, \heartsuit, \heartsuit)$, $(\heartsuit, \bot, \bot, \heartsuit), (\heartsuit, \bot, \heartsuit, \bot)$ and $(\bot, \heartsuit, \bot, \heartsuit)$, and independent of the inputs. Similarly, the sequences of the opened symbols in Step 6 is chosen uniformly at random and independent of the inputs due to the random cut in Step 5, respectively. Therefore, the protocol is secure.

5 Conclusion

In this paper, we proposed the partial-open action, which is a generalization of Miyahara–Mizuki's half-open action. Using the partial-open action, we constructed four-card AND and COPY protocols using only random cuts.

A future research direction is to further develop protocols using the partial-open actions and other applications. In particular, many of the Las Vegas protocols using the standard deck of cards may be converted to finite-runtime protocols using our method. Although we have studied secure computation protocols for the elementary functions, the construction of secure computation protocols for other functions and physical zero-knowledge proof protocols for puzzles are also future work.

A Bases for Our Protocols

Tables 6 and 5 show the bases for our protocols, where "Position" indicates the position of the partial-open action. For example, FG for our COPY protocol indicates that the positions of the partial-open action in Steps 4 and 6 are F and G, respectively. The bases of a and b in our COPY protocol can be interchanged.

Table 5. Bases for our COPY protocol

a	b	Position
$\{3,5\}$	$\{2,4\}$	FG
$\{3,5\}$	$\{2,6\}$	FG
$\{3,5\}$	$\{2,7\}$	FG
$\{3,5\}$	$\{2,8\}$	FG
$\{3,5\}$	$\{2,10\}$	FG
$\{3,9\}$	$\{2,4\}$	FG
$\{3,9\}$	$\{2,6\}$	FG
$\{3,9\}$	$\{2,7\}$	FG
$\{3,9\}$	$\{2,8\}$	FG
$\{3,9\}$	$\{2,10\}$	FG
$\{5,6\}$	$\{1,2\}$	GC
$\{5,7\}$	$\{1,2\}$	GC
$\{5,8\}$	$\{1,2\}$	GC
$\{5,10\}$	$\{1,2\}$	GC
$\{9,10\}$	$\{1,2\}$	GC
$\{9,10\}$	$\{1,2\}$	GD
$\{9,10\}$	$\{1,4\}$	GD
$\{9,10\}$	$\{1,6\}$	GD
$\{9,10\}$	$\{1,7\}$	GD
$\{9,10\}$	$\{1,8\}$	GD
$\{9,10\}$	$\{3,4\}$	GD
$\{9,10\}$	$\{3,6\}$	GD
$\{9,10\}$	$\{3,7\}$	GD
$\{9,10\}$	$\{3,8\}$	GD
$\{9,10\}$	$\{5,6\}$	GD
$\{9,10\}$	$\{5,7\}$	GD
$\{9,10\}$	$\{5,8\}$	GD

Table 6. Bases for our AND protocol

a	b	$a \wedge b$	Position	a	b	$a \wedge b$	Position
$\{1,2\}$	$\{6,10\}$	$\{1,2\}$	GEC	$\{2,8\}$	$\{5,10\}$	$\{2,8\}$	FGD
$\{1,2\}$	$\{6,10\}$	$\{1,2\}$	GED	$\{2,8\}$	$\{9,10\}$	$\{2,8\}$	FGD
$\{1,2\}$	$\{7,10\}$	$\{1,2\}$	GEC	$\{2,10\}$	$\{1,6\}$	$\{2,10\}$	FGE
$\{1,2\}$	$\{7,10\}$	$\{1,2\}$	GED	$\{2,10\}$	$\{1,7\}$	$\{2,10\}$	FGE
$\{1,2\}$	$\{8,10\}$	$\{1,2\}$	GEC	$\{2,10\}$	$\{1,8\}$	$\{2,10\}$	FGE
$\{1,2\}$	$\{8,10\}$	$\{1,2\}$	GED	$\{2,10\}$	$\{5,6\}$	$\{2,10\}$	FGE
$\{1,4\}$	$\{2,6\}$	$\{1,4\}$	GFE	$\{2,10\}$	$\{5,7\}$	$\{2,10\}$	FGE
$\{1,4\}$	$\{2,7\}$	$\{1,4\}$	GFE	$\{2,10\}$	$\{5,8\}$	$\{2,10\}$	FGE
$\{1,4\}$	$\{2,8\}$	$\{1,4\}$	GFE	$\{2,10\}$	$\{6,9\}$	$\{2,10\}$	FEG
$\{1,4\}$	$\{2,10\}$	$\{1,4\}$	GFD	$\{2,10\}$	$\{7,9\}$	$\{2,10\}$	FEG
$\{1,4\}$	$\{6,10\}$	$\{1,4\}$	GED	$\{2,10\}$	$\{8,9\}$	$\{2,10\}$	FEG
$\{1,4\}$	$\{7,10\}$	$\{1,4\}$	GED	$\{3,4\}$	$\{6,9\}$	$\{3,4\}$	FED
$\{1,4\}$	$\{8,10\}$	$\{1,4\}$	GED	$\{3,4\}$	$\{6,10\}$	$\{3,4\}$	FED
$\{1,6\}$	$\{2,10\}$	$\{1,6\}$	GFD	$\{3,4\}$	$\{6,10\}$	$\{3,4\}$	GED
$\{1,7\}$	$\{2,10\}$	$\{1,7\}$	GFD	$\{3,4\}$	$\{7,9\}$	$\{3,4\}$	FED
$\{1,8\}$	$\{2,10\}$	$\{1,8\}$	GFD	$\{3,4\}$	$\{7,10\}$	$\{3,4\}$	FED
$\{1,10\}$	$\{2,6\}$	$\{1,10\}$	GFE	$\{3,4\}$	$\{7,10\}$	$\{3,4\}$	GED
$\{1,10\}$	$\{2,7\}$	$\{1,10\}$	GFE	$\{3,4\}$	$\{8,9\}$	$\{3,4\}$	FED
$\{1,10\}$	$\{2,8\}$	$\{1,10\}$	GFE	$\{3,4\}$	$\{8,10\}$	$\{3,4\}$	FED
$\{2,4\}$	$\{1,6\}$	$\{2,4\}$	FGE	$\{3,4\}$	$\{8,10\}$	$\{3,4\}$	GED
$\{2,4\}$	$\{1,7\}$	$\{2,4\}$	FGE	$\{3,5\}$	$\{6,9\}$	$\{3,5\}$	FED
$\{2,4\}$	$\{1,8\}$	$\{2,4\}$	FGE	$\{3,5\}$	$\{6,10\}$	$\{3,5\}$	FED
$\{2,4\}$	$\{1,10\}$	$\{2,4\}$	FGD	$\{3,5\}$	$\{7,9\}$	$\{3,5\}$	FED
$\{2,4\}$	$\{5,6\}$	$\{2,4\}$	FGE	$\{3,5\}$	$\{7,10\}$	$\{3,5\}$	FED
$\{2,4\}$	$\{5,7\}$	$\{2,4\}$	FGE	$\{3,5\}$	$\{8,9\}$	$\{3,5\}$	FED
$\{2,4\}$	$\{5,8\}$	$\{2,4\}$	FGE	$\{3,5\}$	$\{8,10\}$	$\{3,5\}$	FED
$\{2,4\}$	$\{5,10\}$	$\{2,4\}$	FGD	$\{5,6\}$	$\{2,10\}$	$\{5,6\}$	GFD
$\{2,4\}$	$\{6,9\}$	$\{2,4\}$	FED	$\{5,7\}$	$\{2,10\}$	$\{5,7\}$	GFD
$\{2,4\}$	$\{6,9\}$	$\{2,4\}$	FEG	$\{5,8\}$	$\{2,10\}$	$\{5,8\}$	GFD
$\{2,4\}$	$\{6,10\}$	$\{2,4\}$	FED	$\{5,10\}$	$\{2,6\}$	$\{5,10\}$	GFE
$\{2,4\}$	$\{7,9\}$	$\{2,4\}$	FED	$\{5,10\}$	$\{2,7\}$	$\{5,10\}$	GFE
$\{2,4\}$	$\{7,9\}$	$\{2,4\}$	FEG	$\{5,10\}$	$\{2,8\}$	$\{5,10\}$	GFE
$\{2,4\}$	$\{7,10\}$	$\{2,4\}$	FED	$\{6,10\}$	$\{1,2\}$	$\{6,10\}$	EGF
$\{2,4\}$	$\{8,9\}$	$\{2,4\}$	FED	$\{6,10\}$	$\{2,5\}$	$\{6,10\}$	EFG
$\{2,4\}$	$\{8,9\}$	$\{2,4\}$	FEG	$\{6,10\}$	$\{2,9\}$	$\{6,10\}$	EFG
$\{2,4\}$	$\{8,10\}$	$\{2,4\}$	FED	$\{6,10\}$	$\{3,5\}$	$\{6,10\}$	EFG
$\{2,4\}$	$\{9,10\}$	$\{2,4\}$	FGD	$\{6,10\}$	$\{3,9\}$	$\{6,10\}$	EFG
$\{2,5\}$	$\{6,9\}$	$\{2,5\}$	FED	$\{7,10\}$	$\{1,2\}$	$\{7,10\}$	EGF
$\{2,5\}$	$\{6,10\}$	$\{2,5\}$	FED	$\{7,10\}$	$\{2,5\}$	$\{7,10\}$	EFG
$\{2,5\}$	$\{7,9\}$	$\{2,5\}$	FED	$\{7,10\}$	$\{2,9\}$	$\{7,10\}$	EFG
$\{2,5\}$	$\{7,10\}$	$\{2,5\}$	FED	$\{7,10\}$	$\{3,5\}$	$\{7,10\}$	EFG
$\{2,5\}$	$\{8,9\}$	$\{2,5\}$	FED	$\{7,10\}$	$\{3,9\}$	$\{7,10\}$	EFG
$\{2,5\}$	$\{8,10\}$	$\{2,5\}$	FED	$\{8,10\}$	$\{1,2\}$	$\{8,10\}$	EGF
$\{2,6\}$	$\{1,10\}$	$\{2,6\}$	FGD	$\{8,10\}$	$\{2,5\}$	$\{8,10\}$	EFG
$\{2,6\}$	$\{5,10\}$	$\{2,6\}$	FGD	$\{8,10\}$	$\{2,9\}$	$\{8,10\}$	EFG
$\{2,6\}$	$\{9,10\}$	$\{2,6\}$	FGD	$\{8,10\}$	$\{3,5\}$	$\{8,10\}$	EFG
$\{2,7\}$	$\{1,10\}$	$\{2,7\}$	FGD	$\{8,10\}$	$\{3,9\}$	$\{8,10\}$	EFG
$\{2,7\}$	$\{5,10\}$	$\{2,7\}$	FGD	$\{9,10\}$	$\{2,6\}$	$\{9,10\}$	GFE
$\{2,7\}$	$\{9,10\}$	$\{2,7\}$	FGD	$\{9,10\}$	$\{2,7\}$	$\{9,10\}$	GFE
$\{2,8\}$	$\{1,10\}$	$\{2,8\}$	FGD	$\{9,10\}$	$\{2,8\}$	$\{9,10\}$	GFE

References

1. Boer, B.D.: More efficient match-making and satisfiability the five card trick. In: Quisquater, J.-J., Vandewalle, J. (eds.) EUROCRYPT 1989. LNCS, vol. 434, pp. 208–217. Springer, Heidelberg (1990). https://doi.org/10.1007/3-540-46885-4_23
2. Crépeau, C., Kilian, J.: Discreet solitary games. In: Stinson, D.R. (ed.) Advances in Cryptology–CRYPTO' 93. LNCS, vol. 773, pp. 319–330. Springer, Heidelberg (1994). https://doi.org/10.1007/3-540-48329-2_27
3. Haga, R., Hayashi, Y., Miyahara, D., Mizuki, T.: Card-minimal protocols for three-input functions with standard playing cards. In: Batina, L., Daemen, J. (eds.) AFRICACRYPT 2022. LNCS, vol. 13503, pp. 448–468. Springer, Cham (2022). https://doi.org/10.1007/978-3-031-17433-9_19
4. Kastner, J., Koch, A., Walzer, S., Miyahara, D., Hayashi, Y., Mizuki, T., Sone, H.: The minimum number of cards in practical card-based protocols. In: Takagi, T., Peyrin, T. (eds.) Advances in Cryptology–ASIACRYPT 2017. LNCS, vol. 10626, pp. 126–155. Springer, Cham (2017). https://doi.org/10.1007/978-3-319-70700-6_5
5. Koch, A., Schrempp, M., Kirsten, M.: Card-based cryptography meets formal verification. In: Galbraith, S.D., Moriai, S. (eds.) Advances in Cryptology-ASIACRYPT 2019. LNCS, vol. 11921, pp. 488–517. Springer, Cham (2019). https://doi.org/10.1007/s00354-020-00120-0
6. Koyama, H., Miyahara, D., Mizuki, T., Sone, H.: A secure three-input AND protocol with a standard deck of minimal cards. In: Santhanam, R., Musatov, D. (eds.) Computer Science - Theory and Applications. LNCS, vol. 12730, pp. 242–256. Springer, Cham (2021). https://doi.org/10.1007/978-3-030-79416-3_14
7. Koyama, H., Toyoda, K., Miyahara, D., Mizuki, T.: New card-based copy protocols using only random cuts. In: ASIA Public-Key Cryptography Workshop, pp. 13–22. ACM (2021)
8. Manabe, Y., Ono, H.: Card-based cryptographic protocols with a standard deck of cards using private operations. In: Cerone, A., Ölveczky, P.C. (eds.) Theoretical Aspects of Computing - ICTAC 2021. LNCS, vol. 12819, pp. 256–274. Springer, Cham (2021). https://doi.org/10.1007/s00354-024-00257-2
9. Miyahara, D., Hayashi, Y., Mizuki, T., Sone, H.: Practical card-based implementations of Yao's millionaire protocol. Theor. Comput. Sci. **803**, 207–221 (2020)
10. Miyahara, D., Mizuki, T.: Secure computations through checking suits of playing cards. In: Li, M., Sun, X. (eds.) Frontiers in Algorithmics. LNCS, vol. 13461, pp. 110–128. Springer, Cham (2023). https://doi.org/10.1007/978-3-031-20796-9_9
11. Mizuki, T.: Efficient and secure multiparty computations using a standard deck of playing cards. In: Foresti, S., Persiano, G. (eds.) Cryptology and Network Security. LNCS, vol. 10052, pp. 484–499. Springer, Cham (2016). https://doi.org/10.1007/978-3-319-48965-0_29
12. Morooka, T., Manabe, Y., Shinagawa, K.: Malicious player card-based cryptographic protocols with a standard deck of cards using private operations. In: Meng, W., Yan, Z., Piuri, V. (eds.) ISPEC 2023. LNCS, vol. 14341, pp. 332–346. Springer, Heidelberg (2023). https://doi.org/10.1007/978-981-99-7032-2_20
13. Niemi, V., Renvall, A.: Solitaire zero-knowledge. Fund. Inf. **38**(1,2), 181–188 (1999)
14. Ruangwises, S.: Two standard decks of playing cards are sufficient for a ZKP for Sudoku. In: Chen, C.-Y., Hon, W.-K., Hung, L.-J., Lee, C.-W. (eds.) Computing and Combinatorics. LNCS, vol. 13025, pp. 631–642. Springer, Cham (2021). https://doi.org/10.1007/s00354-021-00146-y
15. Ruangwises, S.: Two standard decks of playing cards are sufficient for a ZKP for Sudoku. New Gener. Comput. **40**, 49–65 (2022)

Attribute-Based Inner Product Functional Encryption in Key-Policy Setting from Pairing

Anushree Belel[✉] and Ratna Dutta

Indian Institute of Technology Kharagpur, Kharagpur 721302, West Bengal, India
anushreebelel1@iitkgp.ac.in, ratna@maths.iitkgp.ac.in

Abstract. Cloud computing is becoming more and more popular among enterprises for high performance, accessibility from any device, removing hardware and software dependencies and cost savings. However, shifting sensitive information and infrastructure from trusted domain to public cloud often leads to privacy concerns and security threats in sectors like medical and finance. *Functional encryption* (FE) with access control is a promising cryptographic technique playing an important role in fine-grained handling of encrypted data as well as preventing unauthorized access to encrypted data. *Key-policy attribute based inner product functional encryption* (KP-ABIPFE) is a specific technique that enables sender to encrypt message with respect to attributes and embeds access policy into secret-keys with the aim that only a specific class of recipients would be able to obtain inner product on encrypted data they need for their designated tasks. In this work, we provide an instantiation of KP-ABIPFE based on simple and well-studied pairing based subgroup decisional assumptions in composite order bilinear groups. Our design uses *dual system encryption* technique of Waters from Crypto 2009. Our scheme performs significantly better in terms of communication overhead compared to the previous similar schemes in bilinear setting.

Keywords: Attribute based encryption · Key-policy setting · Inner product functional encryption · Adaptive security

1 Introduction

With the advancement of modern technology, a growing tendency among system users is to shift the load of storage as well as complicated computing tasks to the cloud servers to save space, power and time. Consequently, there has been a rise in industrial services hosted by cloud service providers, particularly from large corporations like Microsoft, Google, and Amazon. However, fine-grained access control on encrypted data is a major concern in cloud services provided to the users by third party producers through Internet. To fulfill this demand, traditional public key encryption has been sophisticated over the years into *identity-based encryption, attribute-based encryption, searchable encryption, predicate encryption*, and many more. All these techniques can be generalized as a single novel notion called *functional encryption* (FE) [6] where decryption keys are associated with functions. Particularly, given a ciphertext $\mathsf{Enc}(m)$ and a secret key SK_F corresponding to a function F, the user with secret key SK_F learns only $F(m)$ and no other information related to message m. For example, decrypting an encrypted picture with cropping key exposes only the cropped version of the picture and no other information about the picture. This property of FE is extremely useful in practical applications such as spam filtering on encrypted mail, targeted advertising, data mining on encrypted medical record, and privacy-preserving computations.

Inner product functional encryption (IPFE) [1] is a special case of FE that enables computation of inner product on encrypted data. IPFE generates secret keys $\mathsf{SK}_\mathbf{y}$ for randomly selected vectors $\mathbf{y}$ that can be utilized to decrypt ciphertext $\mathsf{CT}_\mathbf{x}$ corresponding to vector $\mathbf{x}$ and retrive the inner product $\langle \mathbf{x}, \mathbf{y} \rangle$. As inner product measures the weighted mean, IPFE can be directly applied in privacy preserving statistical analysis. However, inherent issues in IPFE are that each secret key leaks information and while encrypting a vector of length n, owning n number of different secret keys enables the owner to fully retrieve the plaintext vector. To prevent this inherent leakage, IPFE with more advanced functionalities should be applied. IPFE with access control is one technique that embeds access policy in secret key or encrypted data and allows decryptor to compute the desired inner product only if access policy is satisfied. In particular, *ciphertext-policy attribute based inner product functional encryption* (CP-ABIPFE) [9] embeds access policy into ciphertext and issues secret keys to users corresponding to attribute set so that one user with a particular attribute set can compute the inner product on encrypted data if the attribute set satisfies the access structure mentioned in the ciphertext. On the other hand, *key-policy attribute based inner product functional encryption* (KP-ABIPFE) [16] embeds access policy into secret keys and allows sender to encrypt message corresponding to an attribute set so that one user can compute the inner product on encrypted data if the attribute set satisfies the access structure mentioned in the secret key of the user. We describe below two real life applications of KP-ABIPFE in medical and financial sector.

Suppose that a medicine company maintains some encrypted cancer patient data, including some features of those who are going through trials of a new discovered cancer medicine. The head of company wants to release a decryption key that can be utilized by particular employees of the company such as a particular team of cancer scientists and oncology researchers. The key can only reveal a particular statistical analysis of patient variables that could be used to assess the applicability of the medicine on a broader basis. But these statistics should not be made public to all the employees and the secret key should not decrypt the entire data collection for protecting privacy of the company. So, it is required to embed a policy (specifying which employees are supposed to learn) and a particular vector (that will be applied to the data collection in order to calculate a particular statistic) into a single key which can be issued to the desired employees. We consider another example of financial data access within a bank. The bank manages encrypted customer data, including some informations of those who have alleged against sensitive infomation leakage. The head of the bank wants to produce a decryption key that can be utilized by particular employees of bank such as officers in Risk Management department and staffs in Cyber Security department. The key can only disclose a specific statistical analysis of customer variables that could be used to prevent these type of attacks in future to guarantee safety of all customers. But these statistics should not be published to all employees and the secret key should not decrypt entire data set for welfare of the bank. Therefore, we need to embed a policy and a specific vector into a single key that can be provided to the intended employees.

A Naive Approach Towards Building KP-ABIPFE. Given the extensive research on *key-policy attribute based encryption* (KP-ABE) and *inner product functional encryption* (IPFE), the initial query that naturally comes into mind is if it is possible to compose an existing KP-ABE scheme with an IPFE scheme in a black box way to achieve the desired functionality. In the resulting scheme, each ciphertext is associated with a set of attributes S and encrypts a vector $\mathbf{x}$. Each secret key $\mathsf{SK}_{\mathsf{P},\mathbf{y}}$ corresponds to an access policy P and a vector $\mathbf{y}$. Decryption recovers the inner product $\langle \mathbf{x}, \mathbf{y} \rangle$ if S satisfies the access policy P (say, $\mathsf{P}(S) = 1$). Otherwise, there should be no leakage regarding information about $\mathbf{x}$. Now, let us consider the technique of encrypting $\mathbf{x}$ via an IPFE and then the produced ciphertext using KP-ABE. This naive solution is clearly vulnerable to collusion attacks because if the outer ciphertext is decrypted, the inner one does not depend anymore on ABE. For the sake of clarity, assume that we have secret keys $\mathsf{SK}_{\mathsf{P}_0,\mathbf{y}_0}$, $\mathsf{SK}_{\mathsf{P}_1,\mathbf{y}_1}$ and a ciphertext $\mathsf{CT}_{S,\mathbf{x}}$ encrypted under attribute set S and vector $\mathbf{x}$ such that S satisfies the access policy P_0 (i.e. $\mathsf{P}_0(S) = 1$) and S does not satisfy the access policy P_1 (i.e. $\mathsf{P}_1(S) = 0$). The naive solution enables us to utilize $\mathsf{SK}_{\mathsf{P}_0,\mathbf{y}_0}$ to recover the original IPFE ciphertext which can then be used with $\mathsf{SK}_{\mathsf{P}_1,\mathbf{y}_1}$ to obtain $\langle \mathbf{x}, \mathbf{y}_1 \rangle$. Note that the inner product $\langle \mathbf{x}, \mathbf{y}_1 \rangle$ can be recovered although $\mathsf{P}_1(S) = 0$. Hence, this naive approach is not secure at all.

Related Work. In 2019, Chen et al. [9] first introduced the notion of CP-ABIPFE and provided an instantiation based on the subgroup decisional problems [12] in composite order bilinear group. Their proposed construction was proved to be secure against adaptive adversary. In 2020, Abdalla et al. [2] provided two instantiations of CP-ABIPFE based on the hardness of the *decisional Diffie- Hellman* (DDH) problem in prime order bilinear group. Technically, one of their constructions integrates the DDH-based IPFE of Agrawal et al. [3] with any predicate encoding [18] and achieves security against selective adversary. They introduced the notion of function encoding and combined it with the DDH-based IPFE [3] to obtain their second construction that achieves security against adaptive adversary. However, these constructions are quite generic. In 2021, Pal et al. [16] introduced the notion of KP-ABIPFE and provided an instantiation based on the hardness of the *learning with errors* (LWE) problem. They combined the

LWE-based IPFE of Agrawal et al. [3] with the LWE-based attribute based encryption of Boneh et al. [5] and achieved security against coselective adversary. In 2022, Luo et al. [13] came up with another LWE-based KP-ABIPFE that achieves selective security. Technically, their construction integrates an existing matrix embedding technique by Brakerski et al. [7] with the LWE-based IPFE of [3]. Concurrently, Nguyen et al. [14] proposed selective and adaptive secure KP-ABIPFE schemes based on the hardness of the *symmetric external Diffie-Hellman* (SXDH) problem and further extended their techniques in multi-client setting. Technically, their instantiations exploit *Dual Pairing Vector Spaces* (DPVS) by Okamoto-Takashima [15]. In 2023, Datta et al. [10] introduced the notion of registered CP-ABIPFE that resolves the key-escrow issues in IPFE setting.

Technical Overview. Our KP-ABIPFE scheme constitutes a tuple of algorithms (Setup, Encrypt, KeyGen, Decrypt). A trusted authority takes input the attribute universe U_{att} along with the vector length n (an integer) to produce the master public key MPK and master secret key MSK. Utilizing MSK, the trusted authority produces secret keys $\text{SK}_{\varGamma, \mathbf{y}}$ corresponding to a pair $(\varGamma, \mathbf{y})$ where $\varGamma$ is an access structure and $\mathbf{y}$ is a vector in $\mathbb{Z}_N^n$ for a composite integer N ($N = p_1 p_2 p_3$, product of three distinct primes). The encryptor employs MPK to encrypt a plaintext vector $\mathbf{x} \in \mathbb{Z}_N^n$ with respect to an attribute set $S \subseteq U_{\text{att}}$ and generates the corresponding ciphertext $\text{CT}_{\mathbf{x}, S}$. A recipient possessing secret key $\text{SK}_{\varGamma, \mathbf{y}}$ can retrieve $\langle \mathbf{x}, \mathbf{y} \rangle$ from ciphertext $\text{CT}_{\mathbf{x}, S}$ if S satifies the access structure $\varGamma$. Our approach is to start with the *key-policy attribute based encryption* (KP-ABE) scheme developed by Lewko et al. [11] for our KP-ABIPFE construction, and show how to leverage it's intrinsic algebraic structure to add an inner product functionality. To be precise, the setup algorithm samples a n-length masking vector $\boldsymbol{\beta} = (\beta_1, \beta_2, \ldots, \beta_n)$ instead of a single element β and publishes its encoding $[\boldsymbol{\beta}]_t$ in the target group as part of master public key MPK $= (N, g_1, g_t = e(g_1, g_1), \{Q_j = [\beta_j]_t = g_t^{\beta_j}\}, \{R_i = g_1^{r_i}\}_{\text{att}_i \in U_{\text{att}}})$ where g_1 is an element of $\mathbb{G}_{p_1}$. The encryption algorithm encrypts message vector $\mathbf{x} = (x_1, x_2, \ldots, x_n)$ as $[\mathbf{x} + \boldsymbol{\beta} s]_t$ where $s \in \mathbb{Z}_N$ randomly chosen and outputs ciphertext CT $= (\{C_j = [x_j + \beta_j s]_t\}_{j \in [n]}, C_0, \{\widehat{C}_i\}_{\text{att}_i \in S})$. The key-generation algorithm splits each β_j into shares $\lambda_{z,j}$ and puts the term $g_1^{y_j \lambda_{z,j}}$ as a part of $\mathbb{G}_{p_1}$ component of $K_{z,j}^{(1)}$ and outputs secret key SK $= (\{K_{z,j}^{(1)}\}_{z \in [l], j \in [n]}, \{K_{z,j}^{(2)}\}_{z \in [l], j \in [n]})$ where l is number of attributes associated with policy in secret key. The decryption algorithm performs $\prod_{j \in [n]} e(C_0, K_{z,j}^{(1)}) / \prod_{j \in [n]} e(\widehat{C}_{\eta(z)}, K_{z,j}^{(2)})$ and outputs $\prod_{j \in [n]} [s y_j \lambda_{z,j}]_t$ for each $z \in I = \{z : \eta(z) \in S\}$. Also note that $\prod_{j \in [n]} C_j^{y_j} = [x_j y_j + \beta_j s y_j]_t$. If S is an authorized set, a set of constants $\{w_z\}_{z \in I}$ can be obtained so that $\prod_{z \in I} \prod_{j \in [n]} [s y_j w_z \lambda_{z,j}]_t$ outputs $[\beta_j s y_j]_t$. Thus, the additional term can be cancelled from $\prod_{j \in [n]} C_j^{y_j}$ to recover $[x_j y_j]_t$. We prove the *adaptive indistinguishability* (Adp-IND) security of our KP-ABIPFE protocol following the *dual system encryption* technique of Waters [17] in a setting where the adversary is not allowed to get secret keys that can decrypt the challenge ciphertext. Ciphertexts and secret keys of our scheme each are in two forms – *normal* and *semi-functional*. The semi-functional keys are further divided into two types – type-1 and type-2. Normal keys and normal ciphertexts are used in the scheme as well as in the security proof whereas semi-functional keys and semi-functional ciphertexts are used only in the security proof. We analyze the security of our construction following a sequence of games. The first game G_{Real} is the original Adp-IND security game and the next game G_0 is exactly the same as the game G_{Real} except the fact that the challenge ciphertext is semi-functional. Assuming that the number of secret key queries asked by the adversary is q, the game G_0 is followed by $2q$ number of games namely $G_{k,1}$ and $G_{k,2}$ for $k \in \{1, 2, \ldots, q\}$. In the game $G_{k,1}$, the challenge ciphertext is semi-functional, the first $k-1$ queried keys are semi-functional of type-2, the k-th queried key is semi-functional of type-1 and the later keys are normal. In the game $G_{k,2}$, the challenge ciphertext is semi-functional, the first k queried keys are semi-functional of type-2, and the later queried keys are normal. Thus in the game $G_{q,2}$, the challenge ciphertext is semi-functional and all the secret keys are semi-functional of type-2. The last game G_{Final} is the same as the game $G_{q,2}$ except the fact that the challenge ciphertext is encryption of a random message and hence advantage of adversary in this game is 0. We prove via Lemmas that these consecutive games ($G_{\mathsf{Real}}, G_0, G_{1,1}, G_{1,2}, G_{2,1}, G_{2,2}, \ldots, G_{q,1}, G_{q,2}, G_{\mathsf{Final}}$) are indistinguishable from each other based on three subgroup decisional assumptions in bilinear group of composite order.

Our Contribution. In this work, we provide construction of KP-ABIPFE with short ciphertext in pairing based setting based on three simple and well-studied subgroup decisional assumptions in composite order bilinear groups. We take inspiration from the *key-policy attribute based encryption* (KP-ABE) scheme developed by Lewko et al. [11] for our construction. Our work exploits dual system encryption technique of Waters [17]. Although our technique uses composite order bilinear groups, it could be adapted to prime-order groups using the framework of Chen et al. [8] from the standard k-linear assumption. We point out an issue in the security proof of existing adaptive CP-ABIPFE scheme of Chen et al. [9] that also utilizes dual system encryption technique and subgroup decision assumptions. They take n (n: vector length) many instances of the underlying subgroup decision assumptions while proving security which makes their assumption stronger and security of scheme weaker. We fix this by using single instance of the underlying hardness assumption while analysing security and achieves stronger security. We establish the following result.

Theorem 1. *Assuming the subgroup decisional assumptions [12], our scheme* KP-ABIPFE = (Setup, Encrypt, KeyGen, Decrypt) *is secure against adaptive adversary.*

We summarize below the comparison of our construction with the existing similar schemes.

Table 1. Comparison of predicate / function class, group elements in ciphertext and security

Scheme	$\mathcal{P}$	$\mathcal{F}$	|ct|	Security
[2], Sect. 3.1	MSP; CP	$\mathcal{F}^{\text{IP,poly}}_{n,p,\text{MSP}}$	$n + 2d + 2$	Selective
[2], Sect. 3.2	roMSP; CP	$\mathcal{F}^{\text{IP,poly}}_{n,p,\text{roMSP}}$	$3nd + 3d + 2$	Adaptive
[14]	LSSS; KP	$\mathcal{F}^{\text{IP,poly}}_{n,p,\text{LSSS}}$	$n + 8d + 4$	Selective
[14]	LSSS; KP	$\mathcal{F}^{\text{IP,poly}}_{n,p,\text{LSSS}}$	$nd + 2n + 7d + 3$	Adaptive
[9]	roMSP; CP	$\mathcal{F}^{\text{IP,poly}}_{n,N,\text{roMSP}}$	$2nd + 2n$	Adaptive
Our work	roMSP; KP	$\mathcal{F}^{\text{IP,poly}}_{n,N,\text{roMSP}}$	$n + d + 1$	Adaptive

$\mathcal{P}$: largest predicate class, $\mathcal{F}$: function class, \|ct\|: number of group elements in ciphertext, CP: ciphertext-policy, KP: key-policy, d: number of attributes (needed by access structure in ciphertext for CP case/associated with ciphertext for KP case), $\mathcal{F}^{\text{IP,poly}}_{n,N,\text{roMSP}} = \mathcal{F}^{\text{IP}} \times$ roMSP formed by $\mathcal{F}^{\text{IP}} = \{F_\mathbf{y} : \mathbb{Z}_N^n \rightarrow \mathbb{Z}_N : \mathbf{x} \rightarrow \langle \mathbf{x}, \mathbf{y} \rangle \in \mathcal{R}(\mathbb{Z}_N)\}$ and roMSP of read once monotone span programs over attribute universe, where $n, N \in \mathbb{N}$, N is composite and $|\mathcal{R}(\mathbb{Z}_N)| = \text{poly}(\log N)$, $\mathcal{F}^{\text{IP,poly}}_{n,p,\text{MSP}} = \mathcal{F}^{\text{IP}} \times \text{MSP}$ formed by $\mathcal{F}^{\text{IP}} = \{F_\mathbf{y} : \mathbb{Z}_p^n \rightarrow \mathbb{Z}_p : \mathbf{x} \rightarrow \langle \mathbf{x}, \mathbf{y} \rangle \in \mathcal{R}(\mathbb{Z}_p)\}$ and MSP of read once monotone span programs over attribute universe, where $n, p \in \mathbb{N}$, p is prime and $|\mathcal{R}(\mathbb{Z}_p)| = \text{poly}(\log p)$, $\mathcal{F}^{\text{IP,poly}}_{n,p,\text{LSSS}} = \mathcal{F}^{\text{IP}} \times \text{LSSS}$ where LSSS are linear secret sharing schemes over attribute universe

- As exhibited in Table 1, we observe that selective-secure instantiation of [14] is almost as efficient as the selective-secure instantiation of [2], the adaptive-secure instantiation of [14] is nearly three times as efficient as the adaptive-secure instantiation of [2] and nearly two times as efficient the adaptive-secure instantiation. We emphasize that our proposed adaptive-secure version outperforms the adaptive-secure version of [14] in terms of \|ct\|. Even, our scheme is more efficient than the existing selective secure versions of [2,14].
- As exhibited in Table 2, we achieve better storage compared to [9]. The master public key size (\|MPK\|) of our design is $\mathcal{O}(n + |U_{\text{att}}|)$ which is less than that of [9] where $|\text{MPK}| = \mathcal{O}(n|U_{\text{att}}|)$. The master secret key size (\|MSK\|) of [9] as well as our design is $\mathcal{O}(n)$. In terms of the secret key size (\|SK\|), our scheme is comparable to the work of [9] as $|S| \leq |U_{\text{att}}|$ and $l \leq |U_{\text{att}}|$.
- As exhibited in Table 2, our adaptive-secure construction is as efficient as the adaptive-secure version of [14] in terms of master secret key size \|MSK\| and secret key size \|SK\|. However, master public key size (\|MPK\|) are more in our design compared to that of [14].
- The scheme of Pal et al. [16], Luo et al. [13] achieves security against co-selective and selective adversary respectively. On the other hand, our design achieves security against adaptive adversary. Although these lattice based schemes provide post-quantum security, the public key contains large matrix and the secret key and ciphertext contain large vectors. In contrast, our pair-

Table 2. Comparison of storage overhead

Scheme	Storage		
	|MPK|	|MSK|	|SK|
[9]	$\mathcal{O}(n|U_{\text{att}}|)$	$\mathcal{O}(n)$	$\mathcal{O}(n|S|)$
[14], Selective	$\mathcal{O}(n)$	$\mathcal{O}(n)$	$\mathcal{O}(n+l)$
[14], Adaptive	$\mathcal{O}(n)$	$\mathcal{O}(n)$	$\mathcal{O}(ln)$
Our work	$\mathcal{O}(n+|U_{\text{att}}|)$	$\mathcal{O}(n)$	$\mathcal{O}(ln)$

\|MPK\| = master public key size, \|MSK\| = master secret key size, \|CT\| = ciphertext size, \|SK\| = secret key size, l = number of attributes in the access structure, n = length of the vector, $|U_{\text{att}}|$ = cardinality of attribute universe U_{att}, $|S|$ = cardinality of attribute set S

ing based design offers better storage, communication overhead and computation.
- The scheme of Datta et al. [10] is designed in the common reference string model, uses key aggregation technique and issues helper decryption key. The underlying setting is asymmetric prime order bilinear group and security proof is in the generic group model. Our scheme, on the other hand, achieves the security proof in the standard model under standard subgroup decision assumptions.

2 Preliminaries

2.1 Notation

Let λ represents the security parameter and $[n]$ stands for the set $\{1, 2, \ldots, n\}$. The notation $x \xleftarrow{u} S$ is used to indicate that x is arbitrarily selected from the set S. A function $f : \mathbb{N} \to \mathbb{R}$ is said to be *negligible* in n if it is $\mathcal{O}(n^{-c})$ for each $c > 0$ and it is written as $\mathsf{negl}(n)$. We use the symbol $\bot$ to represent null value and $\langle \cdot, \cdot \rangle$ to represent inner product of two vectors.

2.2 Access Structure and Linear Secret Sharing Scheme [4]

Definition 1. *(Access Structure) Let $\mathcal{P} = \{P_1, P_2, \ldots, P_{n'}\}$ represents a group of parties. A collection $\Gamma \subseteq 2^{\mathcal{P}}$ is called monotone if for all sets $B, C \in 2^{\mathcal{P}}$ fulfilling $B \in \Gamma, B \subseteq C$, we have $C \in \Gamma$. A monotone collection $\Gamma \subseteq 2^{\mathcal{P}} \setminus \varnothing$ of non-empty subsets of $\mathcal{P}$ is a monotone access structure on $\mathcal{P}$. The sets in Γ are said to be authorized sets and the sets not in Γ are said to be unauthorized sets. A set S is said to satisfy the access structure if $S \in \Gamma$.*

Definition 2. *(Linear Secret Sharing Scheme) Let p be a prime. A secret sharing scheme Λ for a monotone access structure Γ over a group of parties $\mathcal{P}$ is said to be linear over $\mathbb{Z}_p$ if*

1. The shares of every party form a vector over $\mathbb{Z}_p$.
2. *(Share generation)*. *There exists a share generating matrix A for Λ with l rows and n columns called the share generating matrix and a mapping η that links each row of the matrix A to a party. For $i \in [l]$, the i-th row A_i of A is marked by a party $\eta(i)$ where $\eta : [l] \to \mathcal{P}$. For the column vector $\mathbf{u} = (s, r_2, \ldots, r_n)$ where $s \in \mathbb{Z}_p$ is the secret to be shared and $r_2, r_3, \ldots, r_n$ are arbitrarily chosen from $\mathbb{Z}_p$, $A\mathbf{u}$ is the vector of l shares of the secret s corresponding to Λ. The share $\lambda_i = (A\mathbf{u})_i = \langle A_i, \mathbf{u}^T \rangle = A_i \cdot \mathbf{u}$ belongs to party $\eta(i)$.*

Reconstruction of Secret. As demonstrated in [4], any *linear secret sharing scheme* (LSSS) enjoys the linear reconstruction property described as follows: Let (A, η) be an LSSS for access structure Γ and $S \in \Gamma$ be an authorized set. Let $I \subset [l]$ be a subset given by $I = \{i : \eta(i) \in S\}$. Then there are constants $\{w_i \in \mathbb{Z}_p\}_{i \in I}$ fulfilling $\sum_{i \in I} w_i A_i = (1, 0, \ldots, 0)$. These constants $\{w_i \in \mathbb{Z}_p\}_{i \in I}$ can be found in time polynomial in the size of the share generating matrix A. Thus if $\{\lambda_i\}_{i \in I}$ are valid shares of a secret s according to Γ, then we have $\sum_{i \in I} w_i \lambda_i = \sum_{i \in I} w_i A_i \cdot \mathbf{u} = (1, 0, \ldots, 0) \cdot \mathbf{u} = s$. An access structure Γ is called LSSS-realizable if there exists an LSSS $\Lambda = (A, \eta)$ implementing Γ where A is an $l \times n$ matrix, $\eta : [l] \to \mathcal{P}$, $\mathcal{P}$ is the set of parties and $\Gamma \subseteq 2^{\mathcal{P}}$. For an authorized set $S \in \Gamma$ where Γ is LSSS-realizable, the rows of the matrix A marked by the attributes in S hold the n-length vector $(1, 0, \ldots, 0)$ in their span modulo p. We say that $S \in \Gamma$ satisfies LSSS-realizable access structure Γ. On the contrary, for an unauthorized set $S \notin \Gamma$, the corresponding rows of A do not contain the n-length vector $(1, 0, \ldots, 0)$ in their span modulo p.

2.3 Key-Policy Attribute-Based Inner Product Functional Encryption (KP-ABIPFE)

A key-policy attribute-based inner product functional encryption (KP-ABIPFE) for an attribute universe U_{att} consists of the polynomial time algorithms KP-ABIPFE = (Setup, Encrypt, KeyGen, Decrypt) satisfying the following requirements.

- Setup $(1^\lambda, U_{\text{att}}, n) \to (\text{MPK}, \text{MSK})$: A trusted authority runs this algorithm on input the security parameter λ, attribute universe U_{att}, vector length n and outputs a master public key MPK together with a master secret key MSK. It publishes MPK and holds MSK secret to itself.
- Encrypt (MPK, S, $\mathbf{x}$) $\to \text{CT}_{S, \mathbf{x}}$: An encryptor on input the master public key MPK, a collection of attributes $S \subseteq U_{\text{att}}$, a plaintext vector $\mathbf{x}$ of length n, generates the corresponding ciphertext $\text{CT}_{S, \mathbf{x}}$ and publishes it.
- KeyGen (MPK, MSK, $\Gamma, \mathbf{y}$) $\to \text{SK}_{\Gamma, \mathbf{y}}$: The trusted authority runs this algorithm taking input the master public key MPK, the master secret key MSK, an LSSS-realizable monotone access structure Γ that is assigned by the trusted authority to the user, a vector $\mathbf{y}$ of length n and generates the corresponding secret key $\text{SK}_{\Gamma, \mathbf{y}}$.

- **Decrypt** $(\mathsf{MPK}, \mathsf{SK}_{\Gamma,\mathbf{y}}, \mathsf{CT}_{S,\mathbf{x}}) \to \langle \mathbf{x}, \mathbf{y} \rangle / \bot$: On input the master public key MPK, a ciphertext $\mathsf{CT}_{S,\mathbf{x}}$ encrypted under a collection of attributes $S \subseteq U_{\mathsf{att}}$, the secret key $\mathsf{SK}_{\Gamma,\mathbf{y}}$ associated with LSSS- realizable monotone access structure Γ and a vector $\mathbf{y}$ of length n, a decryptor recovers the inner product $\langle \mathbf{x}, \mathbf{y} \rangle$ or outputs $\bot$.

Correctness. A KP-ABIPFE scheme is said to be correct if for $(\mathsf{MPK}, \mathsf{MSK}) \leftarrow \mathsf{Setup}(1^\lambda, U_{\mathsf{att}}, n)$, $\mathsf{CT}_{S,\mathbf{x}} \leftarrow \mathsf{Encrypt}(\mathsf{MPK}, S, \mathbf{x})$, $\mathsf{SK}_{\Gamma,\mathbf{y}} \leftarrow \mathsf{KeyGen}(\mathsf{MPK}, \mathsf{MSK}, \Gamma, \mathbf{y})$, it holds that

$$\mathsf{Decrypt}(\mathsf{MPK}, \mathsf{SK}_{\Gamma,\mathbf{y}}, \mathsf{CT}_{S,\mathbf{x}}) = \begin{cases} \langle \mathbf{x}, \mathbf{y} \rangle & \text{if } S \text{ satisfies } \Gamma \\ \bot & \text{Otherwise} \end{cases}$$

Security. We describe below the *adaptive indistinguishability* (Adp-IND) security notion [9] of KP-ABIPFE which is modelled as a game played between a challenger $\mathcal{C}$ and an adversary $\mathcal{B}$.

- **Setup**: The challenger $\mathcal{C}$ executes the algorithm Setup to produce (MPK, MSK) pair and provides MPK to the adversary $\mathcal{B}$.
- **Query phase 1**: The adversary $\mathcal{B}$ asks for secret keys corresponding to the access structure and vector pairs $(\Gamma_1, \mathbf{y}_1), (\Gamma_2, \mathbf{y}_2), \ldots, (\Gamma_{q_1}, \mathbf{y}_{q_1})$ and $\mathcal{C}$ returns the corresponding secret key $\mathsf{SK}_{\Gamma_i, \mathbf{y}_i} \leftarrow \mathsf{KeyGen}(\mathsf{MPK}, \mathsf{MSK}, \Gamma_i, \mathbf{y}_i)$ for $i \in [q_1]$.
- **Challenge**: The adversary $\mathcal{B}$ sends two message vectors $\mathbf{x}_0^\star, \mathbf{x}_1^\star$ and a collection of attributes $S^\star$ subjected to the condition that for each $i \in [q_1]$, $S^\star$ does not satisfy access structure Γ_i. The challenger $\mathcal{C}$ arbitrarily chooses $b \in \{0, 1\}$, computes $\mathsf{CT}_{S^\star, \mathbf{x}_b^\star} \leftarrow \mathsf{Encrypt}(\mathsf{MPK}, S^\star, \mathbf{x}_b^\star)$ and sends the challenge ciphertext $\mathsf{CT}_{S^\star, \mathbf{x}_b^\star}$ to $\mathcal{B}$.
- **Query phase 2**: The adversary $\mathcal{B}$ asks for secret key queries corresponding to the access structure and vector pairs $(\Gamma_{q_1+1}, \mathbf{y}_{q_1+1}), (\Gamma_{q_1+2}, \mathbf{y}_{q_1+2}), \ldots, (\Gamma_q, \mathbf{y}_q)$ under the condition that for each $i \in \{q_1+1, \ldots, q\}$, $S^\star$ does not satisfy the access structure Γ_i. Then, challenger $\mathcal{C}$ in turn returns the corresponding secret key $\mathsf{SK}_{\Gamma_i, \mathbf{y}_i} \leftarrow \mathsf{KeyGen}(\mathsf{MPK}, \mathsf{MSK}, \Gamma_i, \mathbf{y}_i)$ for $i \in \{q_1+1, \ldots, q\}$.
- **Guess**: Finally, $\mathcal{C}$ outputs a guess b' for b and wins the game if $b' = b$.

The advantage of $\mathcal{B}$ in this game is defined as $\mathsf{Adv}_{\mathsf{KP\text{-}ABIPFE}, \mathcal{B}}^{\mathsf{Adp\text{-}IND}}(\lambda) = \left| \Pr[b' = b] - \frac{1}{2} \right|$

A KP-ABIPFE scheme is said to be secure if $\mathsf{Adv}_{\mathsf{KP\text{-}ABIPFE}, \mathcal{B}}^{\mathsf{Adp\text{-}IND}}(\lambda) \leq \mathsf{negl}(\lambda)$.

2.4 Symmetric Bilinear Map and Subgroup Decision Assumptions

Definition 3. *(Symmetric Bilinear Map) Suppose that $\mathbb{G}$, $\mathbb{G}_t$ are multiplicative cyclic groups of composite order $N = p_1 p_2 p_3$ where p_1, p_2, p_3 are distinct primes. Let $1_{\mathbb{G}}$ and $1_{\mathbb{G}_t}$ be the identity elements of $\mathbb{G}$ and $\mathbb{G}_t$ respectively. A symmetric bilinear map $e : \mathbb{G} \times \mathbb{G} \to \mathbb{G}_t$ is a function such that the following conditions hold.*

1. $e(g^a, h^b) = e(g, h)^{ab}$ for all $g, h \in \mathbb{G}$ and $a, b \in \mathbb{Z}_N$.
2. There exists $g \in \mathbb{G}$ such that $e(g, g)$ is a generator of $\mathbb{G}_t$.
3. Each group operation in $\mathbb{G}$ and $\mathbb{G}_t$ together with the bilinear map e can be computed efficiently.

We assume that $\mathbb{G}_{p_i}$ stands for the subgroup of order p_i in $\mathbb{G}$ for $i \in [3]$ and $\mathbb{G}_{p_i p_j}$ denotes the subgroup of order $p_i p_j$ in $\mathbb{G}$ for $i \neq j$, $i, j \in [3]$. Observe that if $h_i \in \mathbb{G}_{p_i}$ and $h_j \in \mathbb{G}_{p_j}$ for $i \neq j$, then $e(h_i, h_j)$ is the identity of $\mathbb{G}_t$ as shown below. Let g be a generator of $\mathbb{G}$. Then $g^{p_1 p_2}$ generates $\mathbb{G}_{p_3}$, $g^{p_2 p_3}$ generates $\mathbb{G}_{p_1}$ and $g^{p_1 p_3}$ generates $\mathbb{G}_{p_2}$. Hence, $h_1 \in \mathbb{G}_{p_1}$ can be written as $h_1 = (g^{p_2 p_3})^{\beta_1}$ for some $\beta_1 \in \mathbb{Z}_N$ and $h_2 \in \mathbb{G}_{p_2}$ can be written as $h_2 = (g^{p_1 p_3})^{\beta_2}$ for some $\beta_2 \in \mathbb{Z}_N$. This in turn implies that $e(h_1, h_2) = e(g^{p_2 p_3 \beta_1}, g^{p_1 p_3 \beta_2}) = e(g^{\beta_1}, g^{p_3 \beta_2})^{p_1 p_2 p_3} = e(g^{\beta_1}, g^{p_3 \beta_2})^N = 1_{\mathbb{G}_t}$ as $\mathbb{G}_t$ is a group of order N.

We state below three assumptions that we will rely on to prove security of our construction. Lewko et al. [12] first introduced these subgroup decision assumptions and showed that these hold in the generic group model if finding a nontrivial factor of the group order is hard. They constructed adaptively secure hierarchical identity-based encryption [12] and adaptively secure attribute-based encryption [11] under these assumptions.

Assumption 1 [12]: Let $\mathcal{G}$ be a bilinear group generator that outputs the tuple $\mathcal{BG} = (N = p_1 p_2 p_3, \mathbb{G}, \mathbb{G}_t, e)$. Let $g_1 \xleftarrow{u} \mathbb{G}_{p_1}, Y_3 \xleftarrow{u} \mathbb{G}_{p_3}, D = \left(\mathcal{BG}, g_1, Y_3\right), \mu_1 \xleftarrow{u} \mathbb{G}_{p_1 p_2}, \mu_2 \xleftarrow{u} \mathbb{G}_{p_1}$. Define distributions $D_b = (D, \mu_b)$ for $b \in \{1, 2\}$ containing common component D and a challenge element μ_b. We say that Assumption 1 holds corresponding to the group generator $\mathcal{G}$ if no probabilistic polynomial time adversary $\mathcal{B}$ can distinguish between the distributions D_1 and D_2. In other words, there exists a negligible function $\mathsf{negl}(\cdot)$ such that the advantage of any adversary $\mathcal{B}$ in breaking Assumption 1 is $\mathsf{negl}(\lambda)$ where $\lambda \in \mathbb{N}$ is the security parameter. That is, $\mathsf{Adv}_{\mathsf{Assumption1}, \mathcal{G}, \mathcal{B}}(\lambda) = \left|\Pr[\mathcal{B}(D, \mu_1) \to 1] - \Pr[\mathcal{B}(D, \mu_2) \to 1]\right| = \mathsf{negl}(\lambda)$.

Assumption 2 [12]: Let $\mathcal{G}$ be a bilinear group generator that outputs the tuple $\mathcal{BG} = (N = p_1 p_2 p_3, \mathbb{G}, \mathbb{G}_t, e)$. Let $g_1, Y_1 \xleftarrow{u} \mathbb{G}_{p_1}$, $Y_2, Z_2 \xleftarrow{u} \mathbb{G}_{p_2}$, $Y_3, Z_3 \xleftarrow{u} \mathbb{G}_{p_3}$, $D = \left(\mathcal{BG}, g_1, Y_1 Y_2, Y_3, Z_2 Z_3\right), \mu_1 \xleftarrow{u} \mathbb{G}, \mu_2 \xleftarrow{u} \mathbb{G}_{p_1 p_3}$. $\mathsf{Adv}_{\mathsf{Assumption2}, \mathcal{G}, \mathcal{B}}(\lambda) = \left|\Pr[\mathcal{B}(D, \mu_1) \to 1] - \Pr[\mathcal{B}(D, \mu_2) \to 1]\right| = \mathsf{negl}(\lambda)$.

Assumption 3 [12]: Let $\mathcal{G}$ be a bilinear group generator that outputs the tuple $\mathcal{BG} = (N = p_1 p_2 p_3, \mathbb{G}, \mathbb{G}_t, e)$. Let

$$g_1 \xleftarrow{u} \mathbb{G}_{p_1}, \ Y_2, Z_2, X_2 \xleftarrow{u} \mathbb{G}_{p_2}, \ Y_3 \xleftarrow{u} \mathbb{G}_{p_3}, \ \beta, s \xleftarrow{u} \mathbb{Z}_N,$$

$$D = \left(\mathcal{BG}, g_1^\beta Y_2, Y_3, g_1^s Z_2, X_2\right), \mu_1 = e(g_1, g_1)^{\beta s}, \mu_2 \xleftarrow{u} \mathbb{G}_t.$$

$\mathsf{Adv}_{\mathsf{Assumption3}, \mathcal{G}, \mathcal{B}}(\lambda) = \left|\Pr[\mathcal{B}(D, \mu_1) \to 1] - \Pr[\mathcal{B}(D, \mu_2) \to 1]\right| = \mathsf{negl}(\lambda)$.

3 Our Construction

Our key-policy attribute-based inner product functional encryption KP-ABIPFE = (Setup, Encrypt, KeyGen, Decrypt) for an attribute universe $U_{\text{att}} = \{\text{att}_1, \text{att}_2, \ldots, \text{att}_m\}$ and a set of LSSS-realizable monotone access structures on U_{att} works as follows.

- Setup($1^\lambda, U_{\text{att}}, n$) → (MPK, MSK): A trusted authority takes as input the security parameter λ, attribute universe $U_{\text{att}} = \{\text{att}_1, \text{att}_2, \ldots, \text{att}_m\}$, vector length n and proceeds as follows.
    - Runs bilinear group generator $\mathcal{G}$ to generate a symmetric bilinear map $e : \mathbb{G} \times \mathbb{G} \to \mathbb{G}_t$ where $\mathbb{G}, \mathbb{G}_t$ are multiplicative cyclic groups of composite order $N = p_1 p_2 p_3$ with $1_\mathbb{G}$ and $1_{\mathbb{G}_t}$ the identity elements of $\mathbb{G}$ and $\mathbb{G}_t$ respectively (Here p_1, p_2, p_3 are distinct primes). Let $\mathbb{G}_{p_i}$ be the subgroup of order p_i for $i \in [3]$ and $\mathcal{T}$ denote a subset of $\mathbb{Z}_N$ defining polynomial range for inner product value to be obtained after the decryption.
    - Selects a random $r_i \in \mathbb{Z}_N$ for each attribute $\text{att}_i \in U_{\text{att}}$ and chooses arbitrarily $g_1 \in \mathbb{G}_{p_1}$ and $\beta_j \in \mathbb{Z}_N$ for each $j \in [n]$.
    - Sets the master public key MPK and the master secret key MSK as MPK = $(N, g_1, g_t = e(g_1, g_1), \{Q_j = g_t^{\beta_j}\}_{j \in [n]}, \{R_i = g_1^{r_i}\}_{\text{att}_i \in U_{\text{att}}})$, MSK = $(\{\beta_j\}_{j \in [n]}, Y_3)$ where Y_3 is a generator of $\mathbb{G}_{p_3}$.
    - Publishes MPK and holds MSK secret to itself.
- Encrypt(MPK, $S, \mathbf{x}$) → $\text{CT}_{S, \mathbf{x}}$: Taking input the master public key MPK = $(N, g_1, g_t = e(g_1, g_1), \{Q_j = g_t^{\beta_j}\}_{j \in [n]}, \{R_i = g_1^{r_i}\}_{\text{att}_i \in U_{\text{att}}})$, an attribute set $S \subseteq U_{\text{att}}$ and a message vector $\mathbf{x} = (x_1, x_2, \ldots, x_n) \in \mathbb{Z}_N^n$, an encryptor does the following.
    - Selects random $s \in \mathbb{Z}_N$ for $j \in [n]$ and computes $C_j = g_t^{x_j} Q_j^s = g_t^{x_j} g_t^{\beta_j s}, j \in [n], C_0 = g_1^s, \widehat{C}_i = R_i^s = g_1^{r_i s}, \text{att}_i \in S$ extracting $g_1, g_t, \{Q_j\}_{j \in [n]}$ and $\{R_i\}_{\text{att}_i \in S}$ from MPK.
    - Sets $\text{CT}_{S, \mathbf{x}} = (\{C_j\}_{j \in [n]}, C_0, \{\widehat{C}_i\}_{\text{att}_i \in S})$ and makes it public.
- KeyGen(MPK, MSK, $\Gamma, \mathbf{y}$) → $\text{SK}_{\Gamma, \mathbf{y}}$: The trusted authority takes as input the master public key MPK = $(N, g_1, g_t = e(g_1, g_1), \{Q_j = g_t^{\beta_j}\}_{j \in [n]}, \{R_i = g_1^{r_i}\}_{\text{att}_i \in U_{\text{att}}})$, the master secret key MSK = $(\{\beta_j\}_{j \in [n]}, Y_3)$, an attribute vector $\mathbf{y} = (y_1, y_2, \ldots, y_n) \in \mathbb{Z}_N^n$ and a monotone access structure Γ realizable by LSSS $\Lambda = (A, \eta)$ where A is an $l \times n$ matrix and η associates every row z of A to attribute $\eta(z) \in U_{\text{att}}$. Let $I_{\eta(z)}$ be the index of $\eta(z)$, i.e. $I_{\eta(z)} = k$ if $\eta(z) = \text{att}_k \in U_{\text{att}}$. The trusted authority proceeds in the following manner.
    - For each $j \in [n]$, selects randomly $(n-1)$ elements $\beta_{2,j}, \beta_{3,j}, \ldots, \beta_{n,j} \in \mathbb{Z}_N$ and sets the n-length column vector $\mathbf{u}_j = (\beta_j, \beta_{2,j}, \beta_{3,j}, \ldots, \beta_{n,j}) \in \mathbb{Z}_N^n, j \in [n]$ where β_j is extracted from MSK.
    - For each row A_z of A, $z \in [l]$, arbitrarily chooses $V_{z,j} \in \mathbb{G}_{p_3}, \widehat{r}_{z,j} \in \mathbb{Z}_N$, $W_{z,j} \in \mathbb{G}_{p_3}$ for $j \in [n]$ and computes $K_{z,j}^{(1)} = g_1^{y_j (A_z \cdot \mathbf{u}_j)} R_{I_{\eta(z)}}^{\widehat{r}_{z,j}} W_{z,j}$, $K_{z,j}^{(2)} = g_1^{\widehat{r}_{z,j}} V_{z,j}$.
    - Sets $\text{SK}_{\Gamma, \mathbf{y}} = (\{K_{z,j}^{(1)}\}_{z \in [l], j \in [n]}, \{K_{z,j}^{(2)}\}_{z \in [l], j \in [n]})$.

- Decrypt $(\mathsf{MPK}, \mathsf{SK}_{\Gamma, \mathbf{y}}, \mathsf{CT}_{S, \mathbf{x}}) \to \langle \mathbf{x}, \mathbf{y} \rangle / \perp$: The decryptor takes as input the master public key $\mathsf{MPK} = (N, g_1, g_t = e(g_1, g_1), \{g_t^{\beta_j}\}_{j \in [n]}, \{R_i = g_1^{r_i}\}_{\mathsf{att}_i \in U_{\mathsf{att}}})$, a secret key $\mathsf{SK}_{\Gamma, \mathbf{y}} = (\{K_{z,j}^{(1)}\}_{z \in [l], j \in [n]}, \{K_{z,j}^{(2)}\}_{z \in [l], j \in [n]})$, and a ciphertext $\mathsf{CT}_{S, \mathbf{x}} = (\{C_j\}_{j \in [n]}, C_0, \{\widehat{C}_i\}_{\mathsf{att}_i \in S})$ where $\mathbf{y} = (y_1, y_2, \ldots, y_n) \in \mathbb{Z}_N^n$, $S \subseteq U_{\mathsf{att}}$ is the set of attributes associated with $\mathsf{CT}_{S, \mathbf{x}}$ and $\Lambda = (A_{l \times n}, \eta)$ is the LSSS corresponding to a monotone access structure Γ associated with $\mathsf{SK}_{\Gamma, \mathbf{y}}$. Let $I = \{z | \eta(z) \in S\}$. The decryptor executes the following steps.
  - Verify whether S satisfies the access structure Γ (realizable by LSSS $\Lambda = (A, \eta)$) by checking whether the n-length vector $(1, 0, \ldots, 0) \in \mathsf{Span}\{A_z \mid \eta(z) \in S\}$, the span of the rows of the share generating matrix A marked by the attributes in S. If not, outputs $\perp$.
  - Otherwise, finds constants $w_z \in \mathbb{Z}_N$ satisfying $\sum_{z \in I} w_z A_z = (1, 0, \ldots, 0)$.
  - For each $z \in I = \{z | \eta(z) \in S\}$, computes $B_z = \dfrac{\prod_{j \in [n]} e(C_0, K_{z,j}^{(1)})}{\prod_{j \in [n]} e(\widehat{C}_{I_{\eta(z)}}, K_{z,j}^{(2)})}$
  - Recovers $e(g_1, g_1)^{\langle \mathbf{x}, \mathbf{y} \rangle} = \dfrac{\prod_{j \in [n]} C_j^{y_j}}{\prod_{z \in I} B_z^{w_z}}$
  - Determines $m \in \mathcal{T}$ so that $e(g_1, g_1)^{\langle \mathbf{x}, \mathbf{y} \rangle} = e(g_1, g_1)^m$ and outputs m.

Correctness. Note that
$$\prod_{j \in [n]} e(C_0, K_{z,j}^{(1)}) = e(C_0, \prod_{j \in [n]} K_{z,j}^{(1)}) = \{\prod_{j \in [n]} e(g_1^s, g_1^{y_j (A_z \cdot \mathbf{u}_j)})\} \prod_{j \in [n]} e(g_1^s, R_{I_{\eta(z)}}^{\widehat{r}_{z,j}})$$
$$\prod_{j \in [n]} e(\widehat{C}_{I_{\eta(z)}}, K_{z,j}^{(2)}) = \prod_{j \in [n]} e(R_{I_{\eta(z)}}^s, g_1^{\widehat{r}_{z,j}}), \; B_z = \prod_{j \in [n]} e(g_1, g_1)^{s y_j (A_z \cdot \mathbf{u}_j)}$$
$$\prod_{j \in [n]} C_j^{y_j} = g_t^{\langle \mathbf{x}, \mathbf{y} \rangle} \prod_{j \in [n]} g_t^{\beta_j s y_j}, \; \prod_{z \in I} B_z^{w_z} = \prod_{z \in I} \{\prod_{j \in [n]} e(g_1, g_1)^{s y_j w_z (A_z \cdot \mathbf{u}_j)}\} = \prod_{j \in [n]} g_t^{s y_j \beta_j}$$

$$\dfrac{\prod_{j \in [n]} C_j^{y_j}}{\prod_{z | \eta(z) \in S} B_z^{w_z}} = \dfrac{g_t^{\langle \mathbf{x}, \mathbf{y} \rangle} \prod_{j \in [n]} g_t^{\beta_j s y_j}}{\prod_{j \in [n]} g_t^{s y_j \beta_j}} = g_t^{\langle \mathbf{x}, \mathbf{y} \rangle}$$

4 Security Analysis

Theorem 2. *The key-policy attribute based inner product functional encryption* KP-ABIPFE = (Setup, Encrypt, KeyGen, Decrypt) *presented in Sect. 3 is secure as per the adaptive indistinguishable* (Adp-IND) *security model described in Sect. 2.3 provided Assumption 1, Assumption 2 and Assumption 3 on subgroup decision problem holds.*

Proof. We refer the ciphertext $\mathsf{CT}_{S,\mathbf{x}} = (\{C_j\}_{j\in[n]}, C_0, \{\widehat{C}_i\}_{\mathsf{att}_i\in S})$ generated by KP-ABIPFE.Encrypt() and the secret key $\mathsf{SK}_{\Gamma,\mathbf{y}} = (\{K_{z,j}^{(1)}\}_{z\in[l],j\in[n]}, \{K_{z,j}^{(2)}\}_{z\in[l],j\in[n]})$ generated by KP-ABIPFE.KeyGen() as normal ciphertext and normal secret key respectively where

$$\{C_j = g_t^{x_j} Q_j^s = g_t^{x_j} g_t^{\beta_j s}\}_{j\in[n]}, C_0 = g_1^s, \{\widehat{C}_i = R_i^s = g_1^{r_i s}\}_{\mathsf{att}_i\in S} \qquad (1)$$

$$\{K_{z,j}^{(1)} = g_1^{y_j(A_z\cdot\mathbf{u}_j)} R_{I_{\eta(z)}}^{\widehat{r}_{z,j}} W_{z,j}\}_{z\in[l],j\in[n]}, \{K_{z,j}^{(2)} = g_1^{\widehat{r}_{z,j}} V_{z,j}\}_{z\in[l],j\in[n]} \qquad (2)$$

We define below semi-functional ciphertexts and semi-functional keys which will be used in our security proof.

Semi-functional Ciphertext: Let us assume that h be a generator of $\mathbb{G}_{p_2}$, $c \in \mathbb{Z}_N$ be a random element and $\delta_i \in \mathbb{Z}_N$ be an arbitrary element for each attribute $\mathsf{att}_i \in S$. Then the semi-functional ciphertext is defined as follows.

$$\{C_j = g_t^{x_j} g_t^{\beta_j s}\}_{j\in[n]}, C_0 = g_1^s h^c, \{\widehat{C}_i = R_i^s h^{c\delta_i} = g_1^{r_i s} h^{c\delta_i}\}_{\mathsf{att}_i\in S} \qquad (3)$$

Semi-functional Key: Semi-functional keys are defined into two forms - type-1 and type-2. Let $\mathbf{v}_j \in \mathbb{Z}_N^n$ be arbitrary vectors for $j \in [n]$ so that $\mathbf{v}_j \cdot (1,0,\ldots,0) = \widetilde{r}_j$ (say) is random and $\rho_{z,j} = A_z \cdot \mathbf{v}_j$, $z \in [l], j \in [n]$. Also suppose that $\gamma_{z,j} \in \mathbb{Z}_N$ is randomly chosen for each $z \in [l], j \in [n]$ and h is a generator of $\mathbb{G}_{p_2}$. Then the semi-functional key of type-1 is defined as

$$\{K_{z,j}^{(1)} = g_1^{y_j(A_z\cdot\mathbf{u}_j)} R_{I_{\eta(z)}}^{\widehat{r}_{z,j}} W_{z,j} h^{\rho_{z,j}+\gamma_{z,j}\delta I_{\eta(z)}}\}_{z\in[l],j\in[n]}, \{K_{z,j}^{(2)} = g_1^{\widehat{r}_{z,j}} V_{z,j} h^{\gamma_{z,j}}\}_{z\in[l],j\in[n]} \qquad (4)$$

and the semi-functional key of type-2 is defined as

$$\{K_{z,j}^{(1)} = g_1^{y_j(A_z\cdot\mathbf{u}_j)} R_{I_{\eta(z)}}^{\widehat{r}_{z,j}} W_{z,j} h^{\rho_{z,j}}\}_{z\in[l],j\in[n]}, \{K_{z,j}^{(2)} = g_1^{\widehat{r}_{z,j}} V_{z,j}\}_{z\in[l],j\in[n]} \qquad (5)$$

When we use a type-1/type-2 semi-functional key to decrypt a semi-functional ciphertext, we get

$$\frac{\prod_{j\in[n]} C_j^{y_j}}{\prod_{z\in I} B_z^{w_z}} = \frac{e(g,g)^{\langle\mathbf{x},\mathbf{y}\rangle}}{\prod_{j\in[n]} e(h,h)^{c\widetilde{r}_j}}$$

Thus in both cases we get an extra term $\prod_{j\in[n]} e(h,h)^{c\widetilde{r}_j}$.

A semi-functional key (Eq. 4 and 5) is said to be *nominally* semi functional if $\mathbf{v}_j \cdot (1,0,\ldots,0) = \widetilde{r}_j = 0$ (where $\rho_{z,j} = A_z \cdot \mathbf{v}_j$) for each $j \in [n]$. Thus a nominally semi-functional key of type-1 is

$$\{K_{z,j}^{(1)} = g_1^{y_j(A_z\cdot\mathbf{u}_j)} R_{I_{\eta(z)}}^{\widehat{r}_{z,j}} W_{z,j} h^{\rho_{z,j}+\gamma_{z,j}\delta I_{\eta(z)}}\}_{z\in[l],j\in[n]}, \{K_{z,j}^{(2)} = g_1^{\widehat{r}_{z,j}} V_{z,j} h^{\gamma_{z,j}}\}_{z\in[l],j\in[n]} \qquad (6)$$

and a nominally semi-functional key of type-2 is defined as

$$\{K_{z,j}^{(1)} = g_1^{y_j(A_z \cdot \mathbf{u}_j)} R_{I_{\eta(z)}}^{\widehat{r}_{z,j}} W_{z,j} h^{\rho_{z,j}}\}_{z \in [l], j \in [n]}, \{K_{z,j}^{(2)} = g_1^{\widehat{r}_{z,j}} V_{z,j}\}_{z \in [l], j \in [n]} \quad (7)$$

where $\rho_{z,j} = A_z \cdot \mathbf{v}_j$ with $\mathbf{v}_j \cdot (1, 0, \ldots, 0) = \widetilde{r}_j = 0$ for each $j \in [n]$. Note that Eq. 6 and 7 are identical to Eq. 4 and 5 and the decryption is successful even if we use a *nominally* semi-functional key to decrypt a semi-functional ciphertext.

To prove security of our construction, we utilize a sequence of games. Let us suppose that q is the number of secret key queries asked by the adversary. The game G_{Real} is the original Adp-IND security game where the challenge ciphertext and all queried secret keys are normal. The next game is G_0 where all keys happen to be normal, but the challenge ciphertext is semi-functional. In game $G_{k,1}$, $k \in [q]$, the challenge ciphertext happens to be semi-functional, the first $(k-1)$ keys happen to be semi-functional of type-2, the k-th key is semi functional of type-1 and the later keys are normal. In game $G_{k,2}$, $k \in [q]$, the challenge ciphertext happens to be semi-functional, the first k keys happen to be semi-functional of type-2 and the later keys are normal. (Note that, G_0 is same as $G_{0,2}$ in terms of notation.) In game $G_{q,2}$, the challenge ciphertext happens to be semi-functional and all keys are semi-functional of type-2. The final game is G_{Final} where the challenge ciphertext happens to be encryption of an arbitrary message which is not related to any of the two messages sent by the adversary and all keys are semi-functional of type-2.

Note that the advantage of the adversary in the game G_{Final} is 0 as the challenge ciphertext is encryption of a random message. Let $\mathsf{Adv}_{G,\mathcal{B}}^{\mathsf{Adp\text{-}IND}}(\lambda)$ be the advantage of a probabilistic polynomial time (PPT) adversary $\mathcal{B}$ in game G. Then, the Theorem follows from Lemma 1–Lemma 4 below which prove that these series of games are indistinguishable.

Lemma 1. *Suppose Assumption 1 on subgroup decision problem holds corresponding to the group generator $\mathcal{G}$. Then, for any PPT adversary $\mathcal{B}$, there exists a negligible function $\mathsf{negl}(\cdot)$ such that for all $\lambda \in \mathbb{N}$, $\mathsf{Adv}_{G_{\mathsf{Real}},\mathcal{B}}^{\mathsf{Adp\text{-}IND}}(\lambda) - \mathsf{Adv}_{G_0,\mathcal{B}}^{\mathsf{Adp\text{-}IND}}(\lambda) = \mathsf{negl}(\lambda)$.*

Lemma 2. *Suppose Assumption 2 on subgroup decision problem holds corresponding to the group generator $\mathcal{G}$. Then, for any PPT adversary $\mathcal{B}$, there exists a negligible function $\mathsf{negl}(\cdot)$ such that for all $\lambda \in \mathbb{N}$, $\mathsf{Adv}_{G_{k-1,2},\mathcal{B}}^{\mathsf{Adp\text{-}IND}}(\lambda) - \mathsf{Adv}_{G_{k,1},\mathcal{B}}^{\mathsf{Adp\text{-}IND}}(\lambda) = \mathsf{negl}(\lambda)$.*

Lemma 3. *Suppose Assumption 2 on subgroup decision problem holds corresponding to the group generator $\mathcal{G}$. Then, for any PPT adversary $\mathcal{B}$, there exists a negligible function $\mathsf{negl}(\cdot)$ such that for all $\lambda \in \mathbb{N}$, $\mathsf{Adv}_{G_{k,1},\mathcal{B}}^{\mathsf{Adp\text{-}IND}}(\lambda) - \mathsf{Adv}_{G_{k,2},\mathcal{B}}^{\mathsf{Adp\text{-}IND}}(\lambda) = \mathsf{negl}(\lambda)$.*

Lemma 4. *Suppose Assumption 3 on subhroup decision problem holds corresponding to the group generator $\mathcal{G}$. Then, for any PPT adversary $\mathcal{B}$, there exists a negligible function $\mathsf{negl}(\cdot)$ such that for all $\lambda \in \mathbb{N}$, $\mathsf{Adv}_{G_{q,2},\mathcal{B}}^{\mathsf{Adp\text{-}IND}}(\lambda) - \mathsf{Adv}_{G_{\mathsf{Final}},\mathcal{B}}^{\mathsf{Adp\text{-}IND}}(\lambda) = \mathsf{negl}(\lambda)$.*

4.1 Proof of Lemmas

Proof of Lemma 1. Let $\mathcal{B}$ be a PPT adversary such that $\mathsf{Adv}^{\mathsf{Adp\text{-}IND}}_{G_{\mathsf{Real}},\mathcal{B}}(\lambda) - \mathsf{Adv}^{\mathsf{Adp\text{-}IND}}_{G_0,\mathcal{B}}(\lambda) = \epsilon$ where ϵ is non-negligible. We show below that it is possible to construct a PPT adversary $\mathcal{A}$ that breaks Assumption 1 with non-negligible advantage ϵ.

On input an instance $(\mathcal{BG} = (N, \mathbb{G}, \mathbb{G}_t, e), g_1, Y_3, \mu)$ of Assumption 1, the adversary $\mathcal{A}$ simulates either G_{Real} or G_0 using $\mathcal{B}$ as subroutine as follows. The adversary $\mathcal{A}$ chooses arbitrary element $\beta_j \in \mathbb{Z}_N$ for $j \in [n]$ and selects random $r_i \in \mathbb{Z}_N$ for each $\mathsf{att}_i \in U_{\mathsf{att}}$. It sets the master public key $\mathsf{MPK} = (N, g_1, g_t = e(g_1, g_1), \{g_t^{\beta_j}\}_{j \in [n]}, \{R_i = g_1^{r_i}\}_{\mathsf{att}_i \in U_{\mathsf{att}}})$ and provides MPK to the adversary $\mathcal{B}$. It sets the master secret key $\mathsf{MSK} = (\{\beta_j\}_{j \in [n]}, Y_3)$ and replies to normal key queries asked by $\mathcal{A}$ using MSK as described in the security model.

The adversary $\mathcal{B}$ provides two challenge vectors $\mathbf{x}_0^\star = (x_{0,1}^\star, x_{0,2}^\star, \ldots, x_{0,n}^\star)$, $\mathbf{x}_1^\star = (x_{1,1}^\star, x_{1,2}^\star, \ldots, x_{1,n}^\star)$, and challenge attribute set $S^\star$. To create the challenge ciphertext, the adversary $\mathcal{A}$ implicitly sets s so that g_1^s is the $\mathbb{G}_{p_1}$ part of μ. The adversary $\mathcal{A}$ randomly selects $b \in \{0,1\}$ and forms the challenge ciphertext $\mathsf{CT}_{S^\star, \mathbf{x}_b^\star} = (\{C_j\}_{j \in [n]}, C_0, \{\widehat{C}_i\}_{\mathsf{att}_i \in S^\star})$ by setting $\{C_j = g_t^{x_{b,j}^\star} e(g_1, \mu)^{\beta_j}\}_{j \in [n]}, C_0 = \mu, \{\widehat{C}_i = \mu^{r_i}\}_{\mathsf{att}_i \in S^\star}$. It can be verified that if $\mu \in \mathbb{G}_{p_1}$, the ciphertext is a properly generated normal ciphertext given in eqn 1 and hence $\mathcal{A}$ simulates G_{Real}. Else, if $\mu \in \mathbb{G}_{p_1 p_2}$, the ciphertext is a properly generated semi-functional ciphertext given in eqn 3 and hence $\mathcal{A}$ simulates G_0. Thus, $\mathcal{A}$ can use the output of $\mathcal{B}$ to break Assumption 1 with non-negligible advantage and the Lemma follows.

Proof of Lemma 2. Let $\mathcal{B}$ be a PPT adversary such that $\mathsf{Adv}^{\mathsf{Adp\text{-}IND}}_{G_{k-1,2},\mathcal{B}}(\lambda) - \mathsf{Adv}^{\mathsf{Adp\text{-}IND}}_{G_{k,1},\mathcal{B}}(\lambda) = \epsilon$ where ϵ is non-negligible. We show below how to construct a PPT adversary $\mathcal{A}$ that breaks Assumption 2 with non-negligible advantage ϵ.

On receiving an instance $\Big((N, \mathbb{G}, \mathbb{G}_t, e), g_1, g_1^s Y_2, Y_3, Z_2 Z_3, \mu\Big)$ of Assumption 2, the adversary $\mathcal{A}$ simulates either $G_{k-1,2}$ or $G_{k,1}$ using $\mathcal{B}$ as a subroutine in the following manner. The adversary $\mathcal{A}$ selects random element $\beta_j \in \mathbb{Z}_N$ for each $j \in [n]$, random $r_i \in \mathbb{Z}_N$ for each $\mathsf{att}_i \in U_{\mathsf{att}}$, computes the master public key as $\mathsf{MPK} = (N, g_1, g_t = e(g_1, g_1), \{g_t^{\beta_j}\}_{j \in [n]}, \{R_i = g_1^{r_i}\}_{\mathsf{att}_i \in U_{\mathsf{att}}})$ and sets the master secret key $\mathsf{MSK} = (\{\beta_j\}_{j \in [n]}, Y_3)$. It provides MPK to the adversary $\mathcal{B}$ and keeps MSK secret to itself. It also records r_i for each $\mathsf{att}_i \in U_{\mathsf{att}}$ in list Rand for the simulation of $\widehat{C}$ components of the challenge ciphertext.

On receiving two challenge vectors $\mathbf{x}_0^\star = (x_{0,1}^\star, x_{0,2}^\star, \ldots, x_{0,n}^\star)$, $\mathbf{x}_1^\star = (x_{1,1}^\star, x_{1,2}^\star, \ldots, x_{1,n}^\star)$ and challenge attribute set $S^\star$, the adversary $\mathcal{A}$ randomly selects $b \in \{0,1\}$ and forms the challenge ciphertext $\mathsf{CT}_{S^\star, \mathbf{x}_b^\star} = (\{C_j\}_{j \in [n]}, C_0, \{\widehat{C}_i\}_{\mathsf{att}_i \in S^\star})$ by setting $\{C_j = g_t^{x_{b,j}^\star} e(g_1, g_1^s Y_2)^{\beta_j}\}_{j \in [n]}, C_0 = g_1^s Y_2, \{\widehat{C}_i = (g_1^s Y_2)^{r_i}\}_{\mathsf{att}_i \in S^\star}$. This has the same distribution as a semi-functional ciphertext given in Eq. 3 where we implicitly set $\delta_i = r_i$ modulo N. It follows from the fact that the value of r_i

modulo p_1 is uncorrelated to the value of δ_i modulo p_2 by the Chinese Remainder Theorem, making distribution of $\widehat{C}_i$ identical to that in Eq. 3.

For generating key query on access structure $\Gamma = (A_{l \times n}, \eta)$ and vector $\mathbf{y}$, $S^\star$ should not satisfy Γ as described in the security model. The key queries of the adversary $\mathcal{B}$ are simulated as follows by the adversary $\mathcal{A}$.

- To answer the l-th normal key query where $l > k$ made by $\mathcal{B}$ on an access structure $\Gamma = (A_{l \times n}, \eta)$ and a vector $\mathbf{y} = (y_1, y_2, \ldots, y_n)$, the adversary $\mathcal{A}$ uses MSK and employs the algorithm KP-ABIPFE.KeyGen.
- For responding the l-th semi-functional key of type-2 query where $l < k$, the adversary $\mathcal{A}$ selects arbitrary column vector $\mathbf{u}_j \in \mathbb{Z}_N^n$ for each $j \in [n]$ such that $(1, 0, \ldots, 0) \cdot \mathbf{u}_j = \beta_j$, arbitrary column vectors $\mathbf{v}'_j \in \mathbb{Z}_N^n$, random values $\widehat{r}_{z,j}$ and arbitrary group members $W_{z,j}, V_{z,j} \in \mathbb{G}_{p_3}$ and computes $\{K_{z,j}^{(1)} = g_1^{y_j(A_z \cdot \mathbf{u}_j)} R_{I_{\eta(z)}}^{\widehat{r}_{z,j}} W_{z,j} (Z_2 Z_3)^{A_z \cdot \mathbf{v}'_j}\}_{z \in [l], j \in [n]}, \{K_{z,j}^{(2)} = g_1^{\widehat{r}_{z,j}} V_{z,j}\}_{z \in [l], j \in [n]}$. If we take $Z_2 = h^c$ where h is a generator of $\mathbb{G}_{p_2}$, we see that $\mathbf{v}_j$ in our description of semi-functional key corresponds to $\mathbf{v}_j = c\mathbf{v}'_j$ (hence $\rho_{z,j} = A_z \cdot \mathbf{v}_j = A_z \cdot (c\mathbf{v}'_j)$).
- In response to the k-th key query of $\mathcal{B}$ on access structure $\Gamma = (A_{l \times n}, \eta)$ and vector $\mathbf{y} = (y_1, y_2, \ldots, y_n)$, the adversary $\mathcal{A}$ generates a key which is either normal (as in Eq. 2) or nominally semi-functional of type-1 (as in Eq. 6 with $\widetilde{r}_j = 0$ for each $j \in [n]$) subjected to the value of μ. It will be discussed later that although this is a nominally semi-functional key of type-1, its distribution is the same as that of a regular semi-functional key of type-1 given in eqn 4 from adversary's point of view since this key cannot decrypt the challenge ciphertext.

To answer the k-th key query, $\mathcal{A}$ selects arbitrary column vector $\mathbf{v}_j \in \mathbb{Z}_N^n$ for $j \in [n]$ such that $(1, 0, \ldots, 0) \cdot \mathbf{v}_j = 0$ and arbitrary vectors $\mathbf{u}'_j$ for $j \in [n]$ such that $(1, 0, \ldots, 0) \cdot \mathbf{u}'_j = \beta_j$. Let us implicitly set $\mathbf{u}_j = y_j^{-1} t \mathbf{v}_j + \mathbf{u}'_j$ for $j \in [n]$ where g_1^t is the $\mathbb{G}_{p_1}$ part of μ. The adversary $\mathcal{A}$ chooses random values $\gamma_{z,j} \in \mathbb{Z}_N, V_{z,j}, W_{z,j} \in \mathbb{G}_{p_3}$ and computes $\{K_{z,j}^{(1)} = g_1^{y_j(A_z \cdot \mathbf{u}'_j)} \mu^{A_z \cdot \mathbf{v}_j} \mu^{\gamma_{z,j} r_{I_{\eta(z)}}} W_{z,j}\}_{z \in [l], j \in [n]}, \{K_{z,j}^{(2)} = \mu^{\gamma_{z,j}} V_{z,j}\}_{z \in [l], j \in [n]}$ by extracting $r_{I_{\eta(z)}} \, \forall \text{att}_{I_{\eta(z)}} \in U_{\text{att}}$ from the list Rand maintained by $\mathcal{A}$. Let us set $\widehat{r}_{z,j} = t \gamma_{z,j}$ and use $\widehat{r}_{z,j}$ as modulo p_1 value and $\gamma_{z,j}$ as modulo p_2 value.

- If $\mu \in \mathbb{G}$, then it can be verified that the k-th queried key $\mathsf{SK}_{\Gamma, \mathbf{y}} = (\{K_{z,j}^{(1)}\}_{z \in [l], j \in [n]}, \{K_{z,j}^{(2)}\}_{z \in [l], j \in [n]})$ is a properly generated nominally semi-functional key of type-1 (see Eq. 6). On the other hand, if $\mu \in \mathbb{G}_{p_1 p_3}$, it can be similarly verified that the k-th queried key $\mathsf{SK}_{\Gamma, \mathbf{y}} = (\{K_{z,j}^{(1)}\}_{z \in [l], j \in [n]}, \{K_{z,j}^{(2)}\}_{z \in [l]})$ is properly generated normal key as in Eq. 2.

Claim: The distribution of k-th nominally semi-functional key of type-1 has identical distribution to that of a regular semi-functional key of type-1.

Proof of Claim. Note that attributes are used only once in the mapping η of the matrix rows in each key. Let att_i be an attribute that is not a member of the challenge attribute set $S^\star$. We observe that $\delta_i = r_i$ modulo N is not needed anywhere except the k-th secret key simulation because other semi-functional keys are of type-2.

As the k-th key fails to decrypt the challenge ciphertext, the vector $(1, 0, \ldots, 0)$ does not beong to the span of the rows of the corresponding matrix A when restricted to rows z such that $\eta(z) \in S^\star$. It may be thought that this holds modulo p_2, otherwise N can be factored easily which is contrary to our assumption. Hence, a vector $\mathbf{w} \in \mathbb{Z}_N^n$ can be found which is orthogonal to the above specified rowspace, but not orthogonal to $(1, 0, \ldots, 0)$ (modulo p_2). We fix a basis containing $\mathbf{w}$. So, we can write $\mathbf{v}_j = f_j \mathbf{w} + \mathbf{v}_j''$ modulo p_2 where $f_j \in \mathbb{Z}_{p_2}$ and $\mathbf{v}_j''$ belongs to the span of other basis elements. Observe that $\mathbf{v}_j''$ does not leak any information about f_j. As $\mathbf{w}$ is orthogonal to the above specified rowspace, $A_z \cdot \mathbf{w} = 0$. Thus the shares for rows z (that is $A_z \cdot \mathbf{v}_j$) with $\eta(z) \in S^\star$ leaks information only about $\mathbf{v}_j''$. As $\mathbf{w}$ is not orthogonal to $(1, 0, \ldots, 0)$, $(1, 0, \ldots, 0) \cdot \mathbf{w} \neq 0$. Hence, $(1, 0, \ldots, 0) \cdot \mathbf{v}_j$ cannot be obtained from $\mathbf{v}_j''$ only and requires some knowledge about f_j.

We now argue that information about f_j cannot be obtained. The term $f_j \mathbf{w}$ can only occur in the equations of the form $A_z \cdot \mathbf{v}_j + \gamma_{z,j} \delta_{I_{\eta(z)}}$ ($\delta_{I_{\eta(z)}} = r_{I_{\eta(z)}}$ modulo N) where $\eta(z)$'s are each unique attributes not present in the challenge ciphertext. On the assumption that each $\gamma_{z,j}$ is not congruent to 0 modulo p_2, each of these equations presents a new unknown $\delta_{I_{\eta(z)}}$ that does not occur anywhere else. Hence, the attacker cannot obtain any information about f_j.

Thus, the value of $(1, 0, \ldots, 0) \cdot \mathbf{v}_j = \tilde{r}_j$ is information-theoretically hidden provided none of $\gamma_{z,j}$ values are 0 modulo p_2. The probability that any of $\gamma_{z,j}$ values are 0 modulo p_2 is negligible. Hence, the claim follows.

We see that if $\mu \in \mathbb{G}_{p_1 p_3}$, then the adversary $\mathcal{A}$ has generated $G_{k-1,2}$ perfectly. On the contrary, if $\mu \in \mathbb{G}$ then $\mathcal{A}$ has generated $G_{k,1}$ perfectly. Thus, $\mathcal{A}$ can use the output of $\mathcal{B}$ to break Assumption 2 with non-negligible advantage ϵ and the Lemma follows.

Proof of Lemma 3. Let $\mathcal{B}$ be a PPT adversary such that $\mathsf{Adv}^{\mathsf{Adp\text{-}IND}}_{G_{k,1},\mathcal{B}}(\lambda) - \mathsf{Adv}^{\mathsf{Adp\text{-}IND}}_{G_{k,2},\mathcal{B}}(\lambda) = \epsilon$ where ϵ is non-negligible. We construct below a PPT adversary $\mathcal{A}$ that breaks Assumption 2 with non-negligible advantage ϵ.

Given an instance $((N, \mathbb{G}, \mathbb{G}_t, e), g_1, Y_3, g_1^s Y_2, Z_2 Z_3, \mu)$ of Assumption 2, the adversary $\mathcal{A}$ uses $\mathcal{B}$ as a subroutine and simulates either $G_{k,1}$ or $G_{k,2}$ as follows. The adversary $\mathcal{A}$ selects random element $\beta_j \in \mathbb{Z}_N$ for each $j \in [n]$, random $r_i \in \mathbb{Z}_N$ for each $\mathsf{att}_i \in U_{\mathsf{att}}$, computes the master public key as $\mathsf{MPK} = (N, g_1, g_t = e(g_1, g_1), \{g_t^{\beta_j}\}_{j \in [n]}, \{R_i = g_1^{r_i}\}_{\mathsf{att}_i \in U_{\mathsf{att}}})$, sets the master secret key $\mathsf{MSK} = (\{\beta_j\}_{j \in [n]}, Y_3)$. It provides MPK to the adversary $\mathcal{B}$ and keeps MSK secret to itself. It also records r_i for each $\mathsf{att}_i \in U_{\mathsf{att}}$ in a list Rand for the simulation of $\widehat{C}$ components of the challenge ciphertext.

On receiving two challenge vectors $\mathbf{x}_0^\star = (x_{0,1}^\star, x_{0,2}^\star, \ldots, x_{0,n}^\star)$, $\mathbf{x}_1^\star = (x_{1,1}^\star, x_{1,2}^\star, \ldots, x_{1,n}^\star)$ and challenge attribute set $S^\star$, the adversary $\mathcal{A}$ randomly selects $b \in \{0, 1\}$ and forms the challenge ciphertext $\mathsf{CT}_{S^\star, \mathbf{x}_b^\star} = (\{C_j\}_{j \in [n]}, C_0, \{\widehat{C}_i\}_{\mathsf{att}_i \in S^\star})$ by setting $\{C_j = g_t^{x_{b,j}^\star} e(g_1, g_1^s Y_2)^{\beta_j}\}_{j \in [n]}, C_0 = $

$g_1^s Y_2, \{\widehat{C}_i = (g_1^s Y_2)^{r_i}\}_{\text{att}_i \in S^\star}$. Implicitly setting $r_i = \delta_i$ modulo N and observing the fact that the value of r_i modulo p_1 is uncorrelated to the value of δ_i modulo p_2 by the Chinese Remainder Theorem, the distribution of this challenge ciphertext is identical to that of a semi-functional ciphertext in Eq. 3.

The adversary $\mathcal{B}$ can make key query on access structure $\Gamma = (A_{l \times n}, \eta)$ and vector $\mathbf{y}$ subject to the fact that $S^\star$ does not satisfy Γ (see the security model of Sect. 2.3). The adversary $\mathcal{A}$ simulates the key queries as follows.

- In response to the l-th normal key query where $l > k$ made by $\mathcal{B}$ on an access structure $\Gamma = (A_{l \times n}, \eta)$ and a vector $\mathbf{y} = (y_1, y_2, \ldots, y_n)$, the adversary $\mathcal{A}$ uses MSK and employs the algorithm KP-ABIPFE.KeyGen.
- For answering the l-th semi-functional key of type-2 query (see eqn 5) where $l < k$, the adversary $\mathcal{A}$ selects an arbitrary column vector $\mathbf{u}_j \in \mathbb{Z}_N^n$ for each $j \in [n]$ such that $(1, 0, \ldots, 0) \cdot \mathbf{u}_j = \beta_j$, arbitrary column vectors $\mathbf{v}_j' \in \mathbb{Z}_N^n$, random values $\widehat{r}_{z,j}$ and arbitrary group members $W_{z,j}, V_{z,j} \in \mathbb{G}_{p_3}$ and computes $\{K_{z,j}^{(1)} = g_1^{y_j(A_z \cdot \mathbf{u}_j)} R_{I_{\eta(z)}}^{\widehat{r}_{z,j}} W_{z,j} (Z_2 Z_3)^{A_z \cdot \mathbf{v}_j'}\}_{z \in [l], j \in [n]}, \{K_{z,j}^{(2)} = g_1^{\widehat{r}_{z,j}} V_{z,j}\}_{z \in [l], j \in [n]}$. If $Z_2 = h^{c'}$ where h is a generator of $\mathbb{G}_{p_2}$, then $\mathbf{v}_j$ in our description of semi-functional key in eqn 5 corresponds to $\mathbf{v}_j = c' \mathbf{v}_j'$ and $\rho_{z,j} = A_z \cdot \mathbf{v}_j = A_z \cdot (c' \mathbf{v}_j')$. Then the distribution of this key is the same as that of a semi-functional key of type-2 given in eqn 5.
- For simulating the k-th key query of $\mathcal{B}$ on an access structure $\Gamma = (A_{l \times n}, \eta)$ and a vector $\mathbf{y} = (y_1, y_2, \ldots, y_n)$, the adversary $\mathcal{A}$ will generate a key which is either semi-functional of type-1 as in eqn 4 or semi-functional of type 2 as in eqn 5 subject to the values of μ. The adversary $\mathcal{A}$ selects an arbitrary column vector $\mathbf{u}_j \in \mathbb{Z}_N^n$ such that $(1, 0, \ldots, 0) \cdot \mathbf{u}_j = \beta_j$ for each $j \in [n]$, arbitrary column vector $\mathbf{v}_j \in \mathbb{Z}_N^n$ for each $j \in [n]$. The adversary $\mathcal{A}$ also chooses arbitrary $\gamma_{z,j} \in \mathbb{Z}_N$, random $W_{z,j}, V_{z,j} \in \mathbb{G}_{p_3}$ for each $z \in [l], j \in [n]$, implicitly sets $\widehat{r}_{z,j} = t \gamma_{z,j}$ where g_1^t is the $\mathbb{G}_{p_1}$ part of μ and computes $\{K_{z,j}^{(1)} = g_1^{y_j(A_z \cdot \mathbf{u}_j)} (Z_2 Z_3)^{A_z \cdot \mathbf{v}_j} \mu^{\gamma_{z,j} r I_{\eta(z)}} W_{z,j}\}_{z \in [l], j \in [n]}, \{K_{z,j}^{(2)} = \mu^{\gamma_{z,j}} V_{z,j}\}_{z \in [l], j \in [n]}$.

We observe the following.

- If $\mu \in \mathbb{G}$, the k-th queried secret key $\mathsf{SK}_{\Gamma, \mathbf{y}} = (\{K_{z,j}^{(1)}\}_{z \in [l], j \in [n]}, \{K_{z,j}^{(2)}\}_{z \in [l], j \in [n]})$ is a properly generated semi-functional key of type-1 as in Eq. 4 and hence $\mathcal{A}$ simulates $G_{k,1}$.
- If $\mu \in \mathbb{G}_{p_1 p_3}$, it can be similarly verified that the k-th queried key $\mathsf{SK}_{\Gamma, \mathbf{y}} = (\{K_{z,j}^{(1)}\}_{z \in [l], j \in [n]}, \{K_{z,j}^{(2)}\}_{z \in [l], j \in [n]})$ is a properly generated semi-functional key of type-2 as in eqn 5 and hence $\mathcal{A}$ simulates $G_{k,2}$. Thus, $\mathcal{A}$ can use the output of $\mathcal{B}$ to break Assumption 2 with non-negligible advantage and the Lemma follows.

Proof of Lemma 4. Let $\mathcal{B}$ be a PPT adversary such that

$$\mathsf{Adv}_{G_{q,2}, \mathcal{B}}^{\mathsf{Adp\text{-}IND}}(\lambda) - \mathsf{Adv}_{G_{\mathsf{Final}}, \mathcal{B}}^{\mathsf{Adp\text{-}IND}}(\lambda) = \epsilon$$

where ϵ is non-negligible. We describe below how to construct a PPT adversary $\mathcal{A}$ that breaks Assumption 3 with non-negligible advantage ϵ.

On collecting an instance $((N, \mathbb{G}, \mathbb{G}_t, e), g_1, g_1^\beta Y_2, Y_3, g_1^s Z_2, X_2, \mu)$ of Assumption 3, the adversary $\mathcal{A}$ simulates either $G_{q,2}$ or G_{Final} using $\mathcal{B}$ as a subroutine in the following manner. The adversary $\mathcal{A}$ selects random $\alpha_j \in \mathbb{Z}_N$ for each $j \in [n]$, random $r_i \in \mathbb{Z}_N$ for each $\mathsf{att}_i \in U_{\mathsf{att}}$, implicitly sets $\beta_j = \beta\alpha_j$. The master public key is set as $\mathsf{MPK} = (N, g_1, g_t = e(g_1, g_1), \{e(g_1, g_1^\beta Y_2)^{\alpha_j} = e(g_1, g_1)^{\beta\alpha_j} = e(g_1, g_1)^{\beta_j}\}_{j \in [n]}, \{R_i = g_1^{r_i}\}_{\mathsf{att}_i \in U_{\mathsf{att}}})$ and the master secret key is set as $\mathsf{MSK} = (\{\beta_j\}_{j \in [n]}, Y_3)$. It provides MPK to the adversary $\mathcal{B}$ and keeps MSK secret to itself. It also records r_i for each $\mathsf{att}_i \in U_{\mathsf{att}}$ in a list Rand_1 and α_j for each $j \in [n]$ in a list Rand_2 for the simulation of C and $\widehat{C}$ components of the challenge ciphertext.

On receiving two challenge vectors $\mathbf{x}_0^\star = (x_{0,1}^\star, x_{0,2}^\star, \ldots, x_{0,n}^\star)$, $\mathbf{x}_1^\star = (x_{1,1}^\star, x_{1,2}^\star, \ldots, x_{1,n}^\star)$ and challenge attribute set $S^\star$, the adversary $\mathcal{A}$ randomly selects $b \in \{0, 1\}$ and forms the challenge ciphertext $\mathsf{CT}_{S^\star, \mathbf{x}_b^\star} = (\{C_j\}_{j \in [n]}, C_0, \{\widehat{C}_i\}_{\mathsf{att}_i \in S^\star})$ by setting $\{C_j = g_t^{x_{b,j}^\star} \mu^{\alpha_j}\}_{j \in [n]}, C_0 = g_1^s Z_2, \{\widehat{C}_i = (g_1^s Z_2)^{r_i}\}_{\mathsf{att}_i \in S^\star}$. This implicitly sets $r_i = \delta_i$ modulo N. Note that the value of r_i modulo p_1 is uncorrelated to the value of δ_i modulo p_2 by the Chinese Remainder Theorem. Therefore, if $\mu = e(g_1, g_1)^{\beta s}$, then the challenge ciphertext $\mathsf{CT}_{S^\star, \mathbf{x}_b^\star}$ becomes $\{C_j = g_t^{x_{b,j}^\star} e(g_1, g_1)^{\beta\alpha_j s}\}_{j \in [n]}, C_0 = g_1^s Z_2, \{\widehat{C}_i = (g_1^s Z_2)^{r_i}\}_{\mathsf{att}_i \in S^\star}$ which is a semi-functional encryption of $\mathbf{x}_b^\star$ (see Eq. 3). On the contrary, if μ is an arbitrary element of $\mathbb{G}_t$, the challenge ciphertext $\mathsf{CT}_{S^\star, \mathbf{x}_b^\star}$ is a semi-functional encryption of an arbitrary message and b will be information theoretically hidden from the attacker.

The adversary $\mathcal{B}$ can make key query on access structure $\Gamma = (A_{l \times n}, \eta)$ and vector $\mathbf{y}$ where $S^\star$ does not satisfy Γ as per the requirement of the described security model. The simulation of $\mathcal{B}$'s key query by adversary $\mathcal{A}$ are carried out as follows.

– To generate semi-functional type-2 key for the queried access structure $\Gamma = (A_{l \times n}, \eta)$ and vector $\mathbf{y} = (y_1, y_2, \ldots, y_n)$, the adversary $\mathcal{A}$ chooses arbitrary column vectors $\mathbf{v}_j \in \mathbb{Z}_N^n$, random values $\widehat{r}_{z,j} \in \mathbb{Z}_N$ and arbitrary members $W_{z,j}, V_{z,j} \in \mathbb{G}_{p_3}$. For each $j \in [n]$, the adversary $\mathcal{A}$ also selects the components $u_{2,j}, u_{3,j}, \ldots, u_{n,j}$ of $\mathbf{u}_j = (u_{1,j}, u_{2,j}, \ldots, u_{n,j})$ randomly and implicitly sets $u_{1,j} = \beta_j = \beta\alpha_j$ so that $(1, 0, \ldots, 0) \cdot \mathbf{u}_j = \beta_j$ by setting
$$\{K_{z,j}^{(1)} = g_1^{y_j (\sum_{i=2}^n A_{z,i} u_{i,j})} (g_1^\beta Y_2)^{\alpha_j y_j A_{z,1}} g_1^{r_{I_{\eta(z)}} \widehat{r}_{z,j}} X_2^{A_z \cdot \mathbf{v}_j} W_{z,j}\}_{z \in [l], j \in [n]}, K_{z,j}^{(2)} = g_1^{\widehat{r}_{z,j}} V_{z,j}$$
, $z \in [l], j \in [n]$ where $r_{I_{\eta(z)}}$ and α_j are extracted from the lists Rand_1 and Rand_2 respectively and $A_z = (A_{z,1}, A_{z,2}, \ldots, A_{z,n})$ is the z-th row of A.

It can be verified that the above generated key is a properly generated semi-functional key of type-2 given in Eq. 5. Hence, $\mathcal{A}$ can use the output of $\mathcal{B}$ to break Assumption 3 with non-negligible advantage and the Lemma follows.

5 Conclusion

In this work, we have provided a construction of an *adaptively* secure KP-ABIPFE protocol based on simple subgroup decisional pairing based assumptions in composite order bilinear groups. We analyze the security of our scheme in the standard model using dual system encryption technique. Our design outperforms previous similar schemes in terms of communication overhead.

References

1. Abdalla, M., Bourse, F., De Caro, A., Pointcheval, D.: Simple functional encryption schemes for inner products. In: Katz, J. (ed.) PKC 2015. LNCS, vol. 9020, pp. 733–751. Springer, Heidelberg (2015). https://doi.org/10.1007/978-3-662-46447-2_33
2. Abdalla, M., Catalano, D., Gay, R., Ursu, B.: Inner-product functional encryption with fine-grained access control. In: Moriai, S., Wang, H. (eds.) ASIACRYPT 2020. LNCS, vol. 12493, pp. 467–497. Springer, Cham (2020). https://doi.org/10.1007/978-3-030-64840-4_16
3. Agrawal, S., Libert, B., Stehlé, D.: Fully secure functional encryption for inner products, from standard assumptions. In: Robshaw, M., Katz, J. (eds.) CRYPTO 2016. LNCS, vol. 9816, pp. 333–362. Springer, Heidelberg (2016). https://doi.org/10.1007/978-3-662-53015-3_12
4. Beimel, A., et al.: Secure schemes for secret sharing and key distribution (1996)
5. Boneh, D., et al.: Fully key-homomorphic encryption, arithmetic circuit ABE and compact garbled circuits. In: Nguyen, P.Q., Oswald, E. (eds.) EUROCRYPT 2014. LNCS, vol. 8441, pp. 533–556. Springer, Heidelberg (2014). https://doi.org/10.1007/978-3-642-55220-5_30
6. Boneh, D., Sahai, A., Waters, B.: Functional encryption: definitions and challenges. In: Ishai, Y. (ed.) TCC 2011. LNCS, vol. 6597, pp. 253–273. Springer, Heidelberg (2011). https://doi.org/10.1007/978-3-642-19571-6_16
7. Brakerski, Z., Vaikuntanathan, V.: Constrained key-homomorphic PRFs from standard lattice assumptions. In: Dodis, Y., Nielsen, J.B. (eds.) TCC 2015. LNCS, vol. 9015, pp. 1–30. Springer, Heidelberg (2015). https://doi.org/10.1007/978-3-662-46497-7_1
8. Chen, J., Gong, J., Kowalczyk, L., Wee, H.: Unbounded ABE via bilinear entropy expansion, revisited. In: Nielsen, J.B., Rijmen, V. (eds.) EUROCRYPT 2018. LNCS, vol. 10820, pp. 503–534. Springer, Cham (2018). https://doi.org/10.1007/978-3-319-78381-9_19
9. Chen, Y., Zhang, L., Yiu, S.M.: Practical attribute based inner product functional encryption from simple assumptions. Cryptology ePrint Archive (2019)
10. Datta, P., Pal, T., Yamada, S.: Registered fe beyond predicates:(attribute-based) linear functions and more. Cryptology ePrint Archive (2023)
11. Lewko, A., Okamoto, T., Sahai, A., Takashima, K., Waters, B.: Fully secure functional encryption: attribute-based encryption and (hierarchical) inner product encryption. In: Gilbert, H. (ed.) EUROCRYPT 2010. LNCS, vol. 6110, pp. 62–91. Springer, Heidelberg (2010). https://doi.org/10.1007/978-3-642-13190-5_4
12. Lewko, A., Waters, B.: New techniques for dual system encryption and fully secure HIBE with short ciphertexts. In: Micciancio, D. (ed.) TCC 2010. LNCS, vol. 5978, pp. 455–479. Springer, Heidelberg (2010). https://doi.org/10.1007/978-3-642-11799-2_27
13. Luo, F., Al-Kuwari, S., Wang, F., Chen, K.: Attribute-based inner-product functional encryption from standard lattices. SSRN 4051552 (2022)

14. Nguyen, K., Phan, D.H., Pointcheval, D.: Multi-client functional encryption with fine-grained access control. In: Agrawal, S., Lin, D. (eds.) ASIACRYPT 2022. LNCS, vol. 13791, pp. 95–125. Springer, Heidelberg (2022). https://doi.org/10.1007/978-3-031-22963-3_4
15. Okamoto, T., Takashima, K.: Adaptively attribute-hiding (hierarchical) inner product encryption. In: Pointcheval, D., Johansson, T. (eds.) EUROCRYPT 2012. LNCS, vol. 7237, pp. 591–608. Springer, Heidelberg (2012). https://doi.org/10.1007/978-3-642-29011-4_35
16. Pal, T., Dutta, R.: Attribute-based access control for inner product functional encryption from LWE. In: Longa, P., Ràfols, C. (eds.) LATINCRYPT 2021. LNCS, vol. 12912, pp. 127–148. Springer, Cham (2021). https://doi.org/10.1007/978-3-030-88238-9_7
17. Waters, B.: Dual system encryption: realizing fully secure IBE and HIBE under simple assumptions. In: Halevi, S. (ed.) CRYPTO 2009. LNCS, vol. 5677, pp. 619–636. Springer, Heidelberg (2009). https://doi.org/10.1007/978-3-642-03356-8_36
18. Wee, H.: Dual system encryption via predicate encodings. In: Lindell, Y. (ed.) TCC 2014. LNCS, vol. 8349, pp. 616–637. Springer, Heidelberg (2014). https://doi.org/10.1007/978-3-642-54242-8_26

Analysis of Public-key Cryptosystems

Formal Verification of Emulated Floating-Point Arithmetic in Falcon

Vincent Hwang[✉]

Max Planck Institute for Security and Privacy, Bochum, Germany
vincentvbh7@gmail.com

Abstract. We show that there is a discrepancy between the emulated floating-point multiplication in the submission package of the digital signature Falcon and the claimed behavior. In particular, we show that some floating-point products with absolute values the smallest normal positive floating-point number are incorrectly zeroized. However, we show that the discrepancy doesn't affect the complex fast Fourier transform in the signature generation of Falcon by modeling the floating-point addition, subtraction, and multiplication in CryptoLine. We later implement our own floating-point multiplications in Armv7-M assembly and Jasmin and prove their equivalence with our model, demonstrating the possibility of transferring the challenging verification task (verifying highly-optimized assembly) to the presumably more readable code base (Jasmin).

Keywords: Falcon · Floating-point arithmetic · Formal verification · CryptoLine

1 Introduction

Falcon [Pre+20] is one of the recently selected digital signatures for standardization by the National Institute of Standards and Technology. Essentially the signature is sampled with a probability approximated by floating-point numbers. Since floating-point arithmetic is not always constant-time, [Por19] implemented a series of constant-time floating-point arithmetic with software emulation. We show that

- the emulated floating-point multiplication does not honor its behavior claimed by [Por19];
- the discrepancy does not affect the complex fast Fourier transform in the signature generation of Falcon; and
- how to prove the equivalence between emulated floating-point addition/subtraction/multiplication implementations.

Our source code is publicly available at
https://github.com/vincentvbh/Float_formal.

2 Preliminaries

2.1 Falcon

Falcon is a lattice-based hash-and-sign digital signature based on fast Fourier sampling over an NTRU lattice [Pre+20]. The NTRU lattice is determined by four integer polynomials f, g, F, G satisfying

$$fG - gF = q \bmod (x^n + 1)$$

where $q = 12289$ and $n = 512, 1024$. The lattice is generated by the basis $\mathbf{B} := \begin{pmatrix} g & -f \\ G & -F \end{pmatrix}$.

For the key generation, the four polynomials f, g, F, G form the secret key sk and hence must have small coefficients, and the public key pk is the polynomial $h := gf^{-1} \bmod (x^n + 1, q)$. See Algorithm 1 for an illustration.

For the signature generation, we generate a nonce r and hash it with the message m. We then start sampling two small polynomials s_1 and s_2 satisfying $s_1 + s_2 h = c \bmod (x^n + 1, q)$ where c is the hash. The signature is defined as (r, s_2). Falcon adopts the so-called fast Fourier sampling based on a randomized variant of fast Fourier nearest plane [DP16, Pre+20]. The idea essentially goes as follows: We compute $\hat{\mathbf{B}} = \mathsf{FFT}(\mathbf{B})$ and $\hat{c} = \mathsf{FFT}(c)$ with complex fast Fourier transform, compute $\mathbf{t} = \left(-\frac{\hat{c}\hat{F}}{q}, \frac{\hat{c}\hat{f}}{q}\right)$, construct the corresponding Falcon tree $\mathbf{T}$ from the LDL decomposition of $\hat{\mathbf{B}}\hat{\mathbf{B}}^*$, and apply fast Fourier nearest plane where the nearest plane part at the leaf level is replaced by a discrete Gaussian sampling with secret center constructed serially from $\mathbf{t}$ and prior samples and secret deviation constructed from $\mathbf{T}$. We refer to Algorithm 2 for an overview of the signature generation and [Pre+20, Algorithm 11] for a more detailed explanation of the fast Fourier sampling.

For the signature verification, we compute $s_1 = c - s_2 h \bmod (x^n + 1, q)$ and accept the signature if $\|(s_1, s_2)\|^2$ is small enough (reject otherwise). See Algorithm 3 for an illustration.

Algorithm 1: Falcon key generation from the reference implementation.

Outputs: a public key pk and a secret key sk

1: $(f, g) = \mathtt{mkgauss}()$ ▷ Generate f, g from a discrete gaussian distribution.
2: $(F, G) = \mathtt{solve\_NTRU}(f, g, x^n + 1, q)$ ▷ $fG - gF = q \bmod (x^n + 1)$
3: $h = gf^{-1} \bmod (x^n + 1, q)$
4: $\mathtt{sk} = (f, g, F, G)$
5: $\mathtt{pk} = h$
6: **return** pk, sk

Algorithm 2: Falcon signature generation from the reference implementation.

Inputs: A message m and a secret key sk.
Outputs: A signature sig.
1: $r \leftarrow \{0,1\}^{320}$ uniformly   ▷ Salt.
2: $c = \text{HashToPoint}(r\|m)$
3: $\hat{c} = \text{FFT}(c)$
4: $\mathbf{B} = \begin{pmatrix} g & -f \\ G & -F \end{pmatrix}$
5: $\hat{\mathbf{B}} = \begin{pmatrix} \hat{g} & -\hat{f} \\ \hat{G} & -\hat{F} \end{pmatrix} = \text{FFT}(\mathbf{B})$
6: $\mathbf{T} = \text{ffLDL}^*\left(\hat{\mathbf{B}}\hat{\mathbf{B}}^*\right)$
7: $\mathbf{T} = \text{Normalize}(\mathbf{T})$
8: $\mathbf{t} = \left(\frac{-\hat{c}\hat{F}}{q}, \frac{\hat{c}\hat{f}}{q}\right)$ ▷ $\mathbf{t} = (\hat{c},0)\,\hat{\mathbf{B}}^{-1}$
9: **do**
10:     **do**
11:         $\mathbf{z} = \text{ffSampling}(\mathbf{t},\mathbf{T})$
12:         $\mathbf{s} = (\mathbf{t}-\mathbf{z})\,\hat{\mathbf{B}}$
13:     **while** $\|\mathbf{s}\|^2 > \lfloor \beta^2 \rfloor$
14:     $(s_1, s_2) = \text{iFFT}(\mathbf{s})$
15:     $s = \text{Compress}(s_2, 8\cdot\text{sbytelen} - 328)$
16: **while** $s == \bot$
17: $\text{sig} = (r, s)$
18: **return** sig

2.2 Fast Fourier Transform

Fast Fourier transform (FFT) is a popular approach in signal processing, polynomial multiplication, and sampling. For a power of two n and the primitive $2n$-th root of unity $\omega_{2n} \in \mathbb{C}$, the negacyclic Cooley–Tukey FFT transforms the polynomial ring $\mathbb{C}[x]/\langle x^n + 1\rangle$ into $\prod_{i=0,\ldots,n-1} \mathbb{C}[x]/\langle x - \omega_{2n}^{1+2i}\rangle$ in $O(n\log_2 n)$ operations in $\mathbb{C}$ up to the bitreversal permutation. In Falcon, since the input coefficients are integers, [Por19] implemented an optimized variant of the complex Cooley–Tukey FFT with $\mathbb{C} = \mathbb{R}[z]/\langle z^2 + 1\rangle$. They also approximated the real number arithmetic by floating-point arithmetic in the signature generation.

2.3 Emulated Floating-Point Arithmetic

In Falcon, the real arithmetic in the signature generation is implemented as floating-point arithmetic. We briefly review the IEEE 754 double-precision floating-point specification.

A double-precision floating-point number is a 64-bit element consists of three parts (most significant bits first): a 1-bit s for the sign, an 11-bit e for the biased exponent, and a 52-bit m for the mantissa. We denote a floating-point number as s|e|m with the sign s, the biased exponent e, and the mantissa m. When the biased exponent satisfies $0 < e < 2047$, the floating-point number corresponds to the following real number:

Algorithm 3: Falcon signature verification.
___
Inputs: a message m, a signature $\mathtt{sig}$, and a public key $\mathtt{pk} = h$
1: $c = \mathtt{HashToPoint}\,(r\|m)$
2: $s_2 = \mathtt{Decompress}\,(s, 8 \cdot \mathtt{sbytelen} - 328)$
3: **if** $s_2 == \bot$ **then**
4: $\quad$ reject
5: $s_1 = c - s_2 h$
6: **if** $\|(s_1, s_2)\|^2 > \lfloor \beta^2 \rfloor$ **then**
7: $\quad$ reject
8: accept
___

$$(-1)^{\mathtt{s}}\, 2^{\mathtt{e}-1075} \left(2^{52} + \mathtt{m}\right).$$

We call such a floating-point number normal. In addition to the normal values, we also have the following special values:

- $\mathtt{e} = 0, \mathtt{m} = 0$: This corresponds to a zero value. Notice that there are two zeros ± 0 distinguished by the sign $\mathtt{s}$.
- $\mathtt{e} = 0, \mathtt{m} \ne 0$: This corresponds to the denormalized number $(-1)^{\mathtt{s}}\, 2^{\mathtt{e}-1074}\mathtt{m}$.
- $\mathtt{e} = 2047, \mathtt{m} = 0$: This corresponds to an infinity. Notice that there are also two infinities $\pm \infty$ distinguished by the sign $\mathtt{s}$.
- $\mathtt{e} = 2047, \mathtt{m} \ne 0$: This corresponds to a NaN (not-a-number) value.

In IEEE 754, "rounding to the nearest even" is adopted by default for rounding the real number result to a floating-point number. In Falcon, the authors claimed that infinites, NaNs, and denormalized numbers are not used and implemented a set of functions emulating the elementary floating-point arithmetic where the results are, according to their claim, correctly rounded for all normal values and zeros with "rounding to the nearest even" rule [Por19, Section 3.3]. We show that the latter doesn't hold, but it doesn't impact the complex fast Fourier transform in the signature generation of Falcon.

2.4 CryptoLine

CryptoLine is a domain specific language for modeling straightline cryptographic programs. It was introduced by [TWY17, PTWY18] for verifying elliptic-curve arithmetic with assembly programs optimized "in the wild." In other words, assembly optimized programs were first delivered by experts in assembly programming without considerations on verification, and verification effort was later devoted to verifying the resulting programs. CryptoLine was extended by [LSTWY19] for verifying elliptic-curve C implementations, and by [FLSTWY19] for signed arithmetic. Recently, [Hwa+22] extended CryptoLine with compositional reasoning for verifying large dimensional number-theoretic transforms, and [LLSTWY23] extended CryptoLine with logical equivalence checking for the stream cipher ChaCha20 [Ber08] and the cryptographic hash functions SHA-2 and SHA-3.

In CryptoLine, there are various instructions implementing basic arithmetic, including signed/unsigned addition/subtraction/multiplication, logical/arithmetic shift, bit-wise or/exclusive-or/and/not, bit-field splitting/concatenation, signed/unsigned extension, and conditional move. These instructions effectively capture the commonly used assembly instructions in cryptographic programs. We translate the target assembly programs into strings of CryptoLine instructions, and argue the properties of the strings of CryptoLine instructions.

There are two classes of predicates in CryptoLine for modeling the properties of strings of CryptoLine instructions: the algebraic predicates and the range predicates. An algebraic predicate is a conjunction of equations and modular equations, and a range predicate is a boolean formula with comparisons, equations, and modular equations. We have the assertion `assert` and the assumption `assume` annotations for imposing properties on the predicates. For an algebraic predicate P and a range predicate Q, `assert P && Q` asks the backend to verify P with the associated computer algebra system and Q with the associated SMT solver, and `assume P && Q` adds P and Q to the corresponding backend tools.

Assertions are used alone for verifying properties, and assumptions are commonly used in conjunction with assertions for transferring predicates between the backend tools. For example, we first verify an algebraic predicate P by imposing `assert P && true` and pass it to the SMT solver by imposing `assume true && P`.

For verifying a program as a whole, we specify pre-conditions on the variables, insert the string of CryptoLine instructions translated from the target program, annotate it with assertions and assumptions at proper locations, and finally specify the post-conditions. The most difficult part is the insertions of annotations, which, if ignored, results in non-responseness of the verification process in our context.

2.5 Jasmin

Jasmin is a programming language serving as a vehicle correlating assembly programs and their high-level abstractions. It was introduced by [Alm+17] for verifying the memory safety and constant-timeness of elliptic-curve arithmetic implementations. Jasmin was extended by [Alm+19] for verifying implementation correctness and the security of SHA3 implementations with EasyCrypt, and [Alm+20] revisited the compiler, memory model, and EasyCrypt embedding for verifying the ChaCha20 stream cipher, the Poly1305 message-authentication code [Ber05], and the Gimli permutation [Ber+17]. Recently, [Alm+23] extended Jasmin with function calls, pointers to the stack memory, and the system call `randombytes`, and proved the implementation correctness of the key encapsulation mechanism Kyber recently selected by the National Institute of Standards and Technology as one of the to-be-standardized algorithms for post-quantum cryptography.

Programmers write Jasmin programs with similar control of the computational flow as in assembly, and compile the programs into assembly programs with the certified compiler `jasminc`. For verification purpose, we extract the

Jasmin programs to EasyCrypt according to the Jasmin model in EasyCrypt, and verify the desired properties with EasyCrypt. Compared to CryptoLine, verification in EasyCrypt requires much more effort by explicitly applying various lemmas instead of simply imposing properties in a declarative fashion in CryptoLine, but one can argue more properties in Easycrypt, for example, the indifferentiability of SHA3 from random oracle as shown in [Alm+19].

3 Incorrect Zeroization

3.1 The Problem of Floating-Point Multiplication

We point out an incorrect zeroization in the emulated floating-point multiplications in Falcon. We illustrate the issue in the C reference implementation, and our finding also applies to the Armv7-M assembly optimized implementation.

We briefly review the C reference implementation of the emulated floating-point multiplication in the submission package of Falcon as follows:

1. The inputs are two 64-bit integers with each representing a double-precision floating-point number.
2. Extract the mantissas and add them with 2^{52} as if the floating-point inputs are non-zero.
3. Compute the product of mantissas with radix-25 arithmetic.
4. Normalize the product to a 55-bit value.
5. Compute the exponent field as the sum of input exponent fields with a corrective subtraction.
6. Compute the sign field as the exclusive-or of the input sign fields.
7. Zeroize the product if any of the input exponent fields is zero.
8. Zeroize the product if the resulting exponent is too small.
9. Zeroize the exponent field if the product is zero.
10. Assemble the sign field, exponent field, and the upper 53 bits of the 55-bit product.
11. Increment the resulting floating-point as an unsigned 64-bit integer if the 55-bit product should be rounded.

The issue is that the zeroization due to the smallness of the exponent field should be the last operation since the increment from rounding may results in an exponent field that is slightly above the zeroization threshold. We refer to Algorithm 4 for a more detailed illustration where the line in red (blue) corresponds to the line in red(blue) of the above.

3.2 Extracting Witnesses

We show how to find inputs triggering the incorrect zeroization. For a floating-point number with exponent field e and mantissa m, we find that if $1 \leq e \leq 1022$, $1 \leq m \leq 2^{52} - 2$, and $\left\lfloor \frac{2^{105}}{2^{52}+m} \right\rfloor (2^{52} + m) \geq 2^{105} - 2^{51}$, then a floating-point with exponent field $1023 - e$ and mantissa $\left\lfloor \frac{2^{105}}{2^{52}+m} \right\rfloor$ leads to incorrect zeroization in

Formal Verification of Emulated Floating-Point Arithmetic in Falcon   131

Algorithm 4: Emulated C implementation (with some high-level syntax for the irrelevant parts for readability) of floating-point multiplication in Falcon.

```
1: uint64_t xu, yu, zu, z;
2: uint32_t z0, z1, sticky, round;
3: int ex, ey, e, d, s;
```
4: xu = 2^{52} | x & $(2^{52} - 1)$;
5: yu = 2^{52} | y & $(2^{52} - 1)$;
6: z0 + z1 * 2^{25} + zu * 2^{50} = xu * yu;
7: sticky = ((z0 | z1) + $2^{25} - 1$) » 25;   ▷ sticky $= 0$ if z0 $=$ z1 $= 0$, otherwise 1.
```
8: zu = zu | (uint64_t)sticky;
```
9: ex = (int)((x » 52) & $(2^{11} - 1)$);
10: ey = (int)((y » 52) & $(2^{11} - 1)$);
```
11: e = ex + ey - 2100;
```
12: (zu, e) $=$ normalize(zu, e, 55, sticky);
13: s = (int)((x ^ y) » 63);
14: d = ((ex + $2^{11} - 1$) & (ey + $2^{11} - 1$)) » 11;   ▷ d $= 0$ if ex $= 0$ or ey $= 0$, otherwise 1.
15: zu = zu & (uint64_t)-d;   ▷ zu $= 0$ if d $= 0$, otherwise unchanged.
16: m = zu & (((uint32_t)(e + 1076) » 31) - 1);   ▷ m $= 0$ if e < -1076, otherwise unchanged.
```
17: e = e + 1076;
```
18: e = e & -((int)(uint32_t)(m » 54)); ▷ e $= 0$ if m $= 0$, otherwise unchanged.
19: z = (((uint64_t)s « 63) | (m » 2)) + ((uint64_t)(uint32_t) e) « 52;
20: round = (0xc8 » ((uint32_t)m & 7)) & 1;   ▷ round $= 1$ if m & 7 $= 3, 6, 7$, otherwise 0.
```
21: z = z + (uint64_t)round;
22: return (fpr)z;                            ▷ fpr is defined as uint64_t.
```

Algorithm 4 where the correct result is a floating-point number with absolute value the smallest normal positive floating-point number.

Recall that the issue of Algorithm 4 is that the product is zeroized due to the smallness of the sum of exponents prior to the rounding at the end. We seek for conditions triggering both lines (if-conditions are taken) while the floating-point product is large enough after the rounding.

For simplicity, we first assume that the product of mantissas is an unsigned 105-bit integer (we will explain how this condition is satisfied shortly) so Line 12 changes nothing. We then choose e as the largest value, -1077, triggering Line 16 in Algorithm 4:

$$m = \text{zu \& (((uint32\_t)(e + 1076) » 31) - 1)}.$$

This leads to the exponent fields ex $= e$ and ey $= 1023 - e$ after tracing the code (cf. Line 11). It remains to choose mantissas with a 105-bit product triggering Line 20:

$$\text{round} = \text{(0xc8 » ((uint32\_t)m \& 7)) \& 1}.$$

This leads to the mantissas $\text{xu} = 2^{52}+m$ and $\text{yu} = \left\lfloor \frac{2^{105}}{2^{52}+m} \right\rfloor$ with an m satisfying

- $1 \leq m \leq 2^{52} - 2$, and
- $\left\lfloor \frac{2^{105}}{2^{52}+m} \right\rfloor (2^{52} + m) \geq 2^{105} - 2^{51}$.

This implies that we have $2^{55} - 2$ or $2^{55} - 1$ after normalizing to a 55-bit value (cf. Line 12), whose rounded value is 2^{55} if we round it prior to the zeroization in Line 16. Since the correct mantissa is 2^{55}, we have to increment the exponent by 1, removing the need of zeroization from the smallness of the exponent.

Listing 1.2 is our program testing if we can find a floating-point number b from the input floating-point number a whose floating-point product leads to an incorrect zeroization in Algorithm 4, and Listing 1.1 is an auxiliary function.

Listing 1.1: Our C program testing if the input is small enough. We return 1 if x is small enough, and 0 otherwise.

```
int test_smallness(fpr x){

    fpr e = (x >> 52) & 0x7ff;
    fpr m = x & 0xfffffffffffff;

    if( (1 <= e) && (e <= 1022) )
        if( (1 <= m) && (m <= 0xffffffffffffe) )
            return 1;

    return 0;

}
```

Listing 1.2: Our C program testing if there is an input leading to incorrect zeroization. If we find a floating-point value such that its floating-point product with a leads to incorrect zeroization, the floating-point value is stored in *b and 1 is returned. Otherwise, −1 is returned.

```
int retrieve_zeroization(fpr *b, fpr a){

    uint64_t t;

    __uint128_t a128, b128, t128;

    if(test_smallness(a) == 0)
        return -1;

    a128 = (1ULL << 52) + (a & 0xfffffffffffff);
    t128 = 1; t128 <<= 105;
    b128 = t128 / a128;

    if( a128 * b128 + (1ULL << 51) < t128)
```

```
            return -1;

    t = ( 1023 - ((a >> 52) & 0x7ff) ) << 52;
    t |= b128 - (1ULL << 52);
    *b = t;

    return 1;
}
```

3.3 An Example in Falcon

In Falcon, we need to approximate the real number $\frac{1}{\sqrt{2}}$ for representing the complex number $e^{\frac{\pi i}{4}} = \frac{1}{\sqrt{2}} + \frac{i}{\sqrt{2}}$. The real number $\frac{1}{\sqrt{2}}$ is approximated by the floating-point number s|e|m = 0|1022|1865452045155277. Since $1 \leq$ e ≤ 1022, $1 \leq$ m $\leq 2^{52} - 2$, and $\left\lfloor \frac{2^{105}}{2^{52}+\text{m}} \right\rfloor (2^{52} + \text{m}) = 6369051672525772\,(2^{52} + \text{m}) \geq 2^{105} - 2^{51}$, we know that if the other operand is the floating-point number 0|1|6369051672525772, the result is incorrectly zeroized. One can pass the pair $\left(1022 \cdot 2^{52} + 1865452045155277, 2^{52} + 6369051672525772\right)$ as arguments of the emulated floating-point multiplication in Falcon and compare the result with the native floating-point multiplication to see the difference.

4 Is it Relevant to Falcon?

In previous section, we demonstrate that the emulated floating-point multiplication doesn't honor its claim where some non-zero floating-point numbers are zeroized. An immediate question is its impact to Falcon implementations. Among the functions in Falcon, we are interested in the complex FFT in the signature generation where the inputs are polynomials with integer coefficients in $\left[-2^{15}, 2^{15}\right)$. After going through the tests for all the floating-point constants in the complex FFT, we find that 692 out of 2048 floating-point constants admit floating-point operands leading to incorrect zeroization. Nevertheless, we model the floating-point addition, subtraction, and multiplication in CryptoLine, and show that all non-zero intermediate floating-point numbers have absolute values lie in
$$\left[2^{-476}, 2^{27}(2^{52} + 605182448294568)\right],$$
far away from triggering incorrect zeroizations.

4.1 Modeling with CryptoLine Instructions

We first model our own strings of CryptoLine instructions and start annotating CryptoLine programs with assertions and assumptions to transfer predicates between backend tools. The main difficulties are as follows:

- When to declare statements that should be proved by the backend proof systems?
- Which statements should be transferred between proof systems at a given point?

We do not know of any systematic approaches resolving the two difficulties. Nevertheless, we find the following constructions of intermediate symbols and annotations sufficient for verifying the range:

1. Construct the 128-bit product r of mantissas with the long multiplication.
2. Split the input into radix-25 representation with bitfield arithmetic, verify the correctness of the spliting with the SMT solver, and add the corresponding algebraic identities to the computer algebra system.
3. Compute the multi-limb product, verify its algebraic correctness with r in the computer algebra system, and add the corresponding boolean identities to the SMT solver.
4. Verify the remaining operations (zeroization, rounding, assembling) entirely with the SMT solver.

If we remove Steps 2. and 3., the SMT solver doesn't return a result (it doesn't find an instance disproving the properties, but it doesn't finish verifying over all the possible inputs).

4.2 Range-Checking

We develop our own range arithmetic in C++ computing the pre- and post-conditions to be verified. Once the pre- and post-conditions are computed for all the possible floating-point additions/subtractions/multiplications, we verify the correctness with CryptoLine. Typically, range-checking of floating-point arithmetic focus on upper-bounding the floating-point errors[1]. However, we need to derive non-trivial lower bounds of floating-point numbers for proving the non-smallness of the absolute values of non-zero floating-point numbers.

For two non-negative floating-point numbers $a.l \leq a.u$, we represent the subset $\{0\} \cup [a.l, a.u] \cup [-a.u, -a.l]$ as a structure with lower bound $a.l$ and upper bound $a.u$. Since the definition is symmetric for the positive and negative sides, we only store the positive bounds, and update the positive bounds throughout the entire computation. The zero values are included implicitly and we do not store its existence (it always exists in all the ranges). The range arithmetic of floating-point multiplication is straightforward as shown in Algorithm 5. For the floating-point addition/subtraction with the ranges a and b, we distinguish between two cases:

---

[1] For example, Frama-C [CKKPSY12] only shows that the floating-point number is upper-bounded by a floating-point number and lower-bounded by 0, which is useless for proving the non-smallness of the absolute values of non-zero floating-point numbers.

1. Case $a \cap b = \{0\}$: The upper bound is computed as the sum of upper bounds, and the lower bound is defined as the minimum of the absolute values of the differences between an upper bound and a lower bound from different ranges. In other words, the lower bound is defined as $\min(|a.u - b.l|, |b.u - a.l|)$.
2. Case $a \cap b = t \neq \{0\}$: The upper bound is also computed as the sum of upper bounds, and the lower bound is defined as the floating-point value with mantissa 0 and exponent field 52 smaller than the exponent field of $t.l$, since the smallest value occurs when subtracting two values with the real value difference 2^{e-1075} where e is the smallest exponent field of the two and choosing e as the exponent field of $t.l$ results in a worse case analysis. Since we have to shift the leading bit of mantissa to the 52-th bit position, the exponent field is subtracted by 52 and the mantissa becomes 2^{52}. By the definition of floating-point numbers, the leading bit of mantissa is stored implicity. This is why we set the mantissa to 0 in the floating-point number representation.

Algorithm 6 is an illustration of the range arithmetic of floating-point addition/subtraction. After replacing all the floating-point arithmetic with the range arithmetic in the FFT of Falcon, we transform all the input-output tuples into pre- and post-conditions for the corresponding CryptoLine model. We then run CryptoLine to verify the conditions. Our CryptoLine verification shows that

- All the range arithmetic are correct within our modeling of floating-point addition, subtraction, and multiplication.
- All non-zero intermediate floating-point numbers have absolute values lie in

$$\left[2^{-476}, 2^{27}(2^{52} + 605182448294568)\right]$$

when the input coefficients of FFT are integers in $\left[-2^{15}, 2^{15}\right)$.

Table 1 summarizes the verification time of the range conditions of floating-point additions and multiplications in Falcon's size-1024 complex FFT.

Algorithm 5: Range arithmetic of floating-point multiplication.

Inputs: $a = (a.l, a.u), b = (b.l, b.u)$
Output: $c = (c.l, c.u)$
1: $c.l = a.l \cdot b.l$
2: $c.u = a.u \cdot b.u$
3: **return** c

Algorithm 6: Range arithmetic of floating-point addition/subtraction.

Inputs: $a = (a.l, a.u), b = (b.l, b.u)$
Output: $c = (c.l, c.u)$
 1: $t = a \cap b$.
 2: **if** $t = \{0\}$ **then**
 3: $\quad (d_0, d_1) = (|a.u - b.l|, |b.u - a.l|)$
 4: $\quad c.l = \min(d_0, d_1)$
 5: $\quad c.u = a.u + b.u$
 6: $\quad$ **return** c
 7: $c.u = a.u + b.u$
 8: s|e|m = $t.l$
 9: $c.l$ = s|(e − 52)|0
10: **return** c

Table 1. Verification time of range conditions for a size-1024 complex FFT with $\mathbb{C} \cong \mathbb{R}[z]/\langle z^2 + 1\rangle$ and input polynomials drawn from $\mathbb{Z} \cap \left[-2^{15}, 2^{15}\right]$. Floating-point subtractions are regarded as floating-point additions in our interval arithmetic. FP stands for "floating-point."

Operation	Number of instances	Verification time (avr./total in seconds)
FP addition	767	0.297 886/228.478 732
FP multiplication	511	2.589 009/1 322.983 371

5 Equivalence Proofs

In this section, we briefly describe our implementations of floating-point multiplication and their equivalence proofs.

5.1 Our Implementations and The Claimed Behavior

Since there is a discrepancy between the emulated floating-point multiplications in Falcon and the claimed behavior, we implement our own assembly implementation honoring the following rules:

– It rounds the values correctly by experiment.
– Its output range is always zeros or normal floating-point values by formal verification. If the real number product is too small in absolute value, it returns a zero. If the real number product is too large in absolute value, the largest possible normal value is returned when the result is positive (smallest possible normal value is returned in the negative case).

We start with the assembly implementation in Falcon, which is much more optimized compared to the C reference implementation, and implement the above rules. This ensures that the output range is always a zero or a normal floating-point value when the inputs are zeros or normal floating-point values.

Comparisons to [Por19]. In the emulated floating-point multiplications in Falcon by [Por19], since the program does not handle infinities, one has to verify the correctness within a certain input range avoiding infinity outputs. The former forbids us to argue the correctness of the full range of zeros and normal floating-point values.

In addition, we also implement an emulated floating-point multiplication in Jasmin essentially following the more readable (but slower) C reference implementation. In the follow-up section, we explain how to verify the equivalences of emulated floating-point multiplication implementations.

5.2 Equivalence Proofs in CryptoLine

We start with our CryptoLine model used for range-checking and add more annotations. Essentially, the majority of the effort is still about verifying the multi-limb arithmetic and transferring its correctness to the SMT solver. In principle, whenever we issue a multiplication, we prove its correctness in the computer algebra system, and add the corresponding boolean identities to the SMT solver. We apply the idea to proving the equivalence of our CryptoLine model and our assembly implementation, and the equivalence of our CryptoLine model and our Jasmin implementation. See Table 2 for an overview of verification time of the equivalences. Since equivalence is transitive, we have an equivalence between our assembly optimized implementation and our Jasmin implementation where the former is more optimized and the latter is more readable.

Table 2. Verification time of equivalence proofs between Armv7-M implementations and our CryptoLine model.

Programming langauge	Verification time (in seconds)
Floating-point addition	
Jasmin	53.946 560
Assembly	59.863 976
Floating-point multiplication	
Jasmin	57.108 668
Assembly	5.333 913

6 Discussions

6.1 How the Discrepancy Was Found?

The core of this paper is about modeling floating-point addition, subtraction, and multiplication with the domain specific language CryptoLine, and its application in proving the lower bound and upper bound of non-zero intermediate floating-point numbers and the equivalences between implementations via software emulation. The whole paper is written in a way with concise logical reasoning so readers can follow more easily. However, the true story of the discovery is more disorganized than the story told in the paper.

The true story is that, we first wrote a model in CryptoLine and proved its equivalence with the emulated floating-point multiplication by [Por19]. With a much more readable model at hand, we were confounded by its correctness since it was inconsistent with our understanding of floating-point arithmetic. Our careful examinations eventually led to the C program extracting witnesses with incorrect zeroization, in the sense that the results were different from the native floating-point multiplication on our laptop and the emulated floating-point multiplication by the Arm's toolchain for Cortex-M4. After contacting the author of [Por19], we knew that experimentally, there were no such floating-point numbers but there was no formal proof. We later fixed our model, simplified it for range-checking, and verified the absence of non-zero floating-point numbers with absolute values the smallest normal positive floating-point number throughout the complex FFT in the signature generation of Falcon. The model was finally used for verifying the equivalence of implementations. We hope the true story will give more insights on how to use the tools.

6.2 The Validity of This Paper After Recent Uses of Fixed-Point Arithmetic

Recently, a fixed-point implementation for the complex FFT in the key generation was proposed by [Por23]. An immediate question is the validity of our findings in the emulated floating-point arithmetic. We would like to stress that, the roles of the complex FFTs are quite different in key generation and signature generation.

Key Generation. We review the uses of complex FFT in the key generation of Falcon as follows. We first generate short integer polynomials f and g, and solve for integer polynomials F and G satisfying

$$fG - gF = q \bmod (x^n + 1).$$

Since the coefficients of F and G could be too large for efficient computation for the follow-up computation, we need to reduce the bit-size of the pair (F, G) with respect to the pair (f, g). This can be achieved by the Babai's reduction: we compute $k = \left\lfloor \frac{Ff^* + Gg^*}{ff^* + gg^*} \right\rceil$ and subtract (kf, kg) from (F, G) where $f^* := f_0 - \sum_{i=1}^{n-1} f_i x^{n-i}$ is the adjoint of $f = \sum_{i=0}^{n-1} f_i x^i$. Obviously, if $fG - gF = q \bmod (x^n + 1)$, then $f(G - kg) - g(F - kf) = fG - gF = q \bmod (x^n + 1)$ and $(F - kf, G - kg)$ is a valid solution for the NTRU equation. For the quotient $\frac{Ff^* + Gg^*}{ff^* + gg^*}$ in $\mathbb{Q}[x]/\langle x^n + 1 \rangle$, we instead compute them with the aid of complex FFT in $\mathbb{C}[x]/\langle x^n + 1 \rangle$. In [Por23], the author implemented the complex FFT with scaled 64-bit fixed-point arithmetic and reduced the pair (F, G) several times instead of reducing it once with high-precision complex FFT.

Signature Generation. In the signature generation, the role of the complex FFT is quite different. Essentially, the sampler in Falcon converts the sampling task over the NTRU lattice into several one-dimensional sampling task and the complex FFT is involed in this conversion. If one wants to replace the floating-point FFT with scaled fixed-point arithmetic, one has to thoroughly revise the range analysis of the scaling, potentially use a much higher precision, and revise the security analysis from the implementational perspective. We have not seen effort from the community deploying the scaled fixed-point arithmetic and analyzing the accompanied security impact.

6.3 Possible Future Extensions

We briefly outline several possible future extensions of this paper.

Verifying Additional Constant-Time Emulations of Floating-Point Arithmetic. This paper demonstrates the formal verification of the software emulation of floating-point addition, subtraction, and multiplication with respect to our CryptoLine model. Our approach extends to several interesting floating-point arithmetic, including negation, halving and fused multiply-add/sub. Our approach also applies to other rounding rules. As for the floating-point division, it will be interesting to explore the formal verification of the bit-by-bit division by [Por19].

Applications to ffLDL* and ffSampling. In this paper, we verify the range of the complex FFT computation with input integer polynomials. An immediate question is the applicability of our verification approach to the operations ffLDL* and ffSampling in the signature generation. For ffLDL*, it is a straightline program with floating-point divisions so we can only verify the computation once floating-point division is verified. For ffSampling, it is built upon the one-dimensional discrete Gaussian sampler with a rejection loop. Therefore, CryptoLine along cannot verify this operation. We believe CryptoLine should be used as a plug-in of formal verification tools handling the rejection loop.

6.4 Applications to Other Lattice-Based Schemes

Our formal verification approach applies to several digital signature schemes. For ModFalcon [CPSWX20], since it also relies on the fast Fourier sampling from [DP16], one needs to apply FFT in a similar fashion as in Falcon's signature generation. For Mitaka [Esp+22], there are two samplers proposed by [Esp+22]: the hybrid sampler built upon the Gram-Schmidt orthogonalization with the aid of complex FFT and the integer arithmetic friendly sampler built upon the integral Gram decomposition by [DGPY20]. For the former, our verification approach applies since one needs to apply complex FFT. For the latter, integral Gram decomposition reduces to writing a positive integer as a sum of four squared integers and the fastest know algorithms are the randomized ones [PT18]. It seems difficult to find an unconditional deterministic algorithm for the problem [PT18, Section 5]. Therefore, it is unclear to us whether the integral version of Mitaka can be implemented securely and efficiently.

Acknowledgements. The author would like to thank Tiago Oliveira for a tutorial of Jasmin, Thomas Pornin for providing the experimental range of the intermediate floating-point numbers, eventually motivating the author to develope the range-checking, and Academia Sinica for the hospitality under grant AS-GCS-113-M07.

References

[Alm+17] Almeida, J.B., et al.: Jasmin: high-assurance and high-speed cryptography. In: Proceedings of the 2017 ACM SIGSAC Conference on Computer and Communications Security, pp. 1807–1823 (2017). https://dl.acm.org/doi/10.1145/3133956.3134078

[Alm+19] Almeida, J.B., et al.: Machine-checked proofs for cryptographic standards: indifferentiability of sponge and secure high-assurance implementations of SHA-3. In: Proceedings of the 2019 ACM SIGSAC Conference on Computer and Communications Security, pp. 1607–1622 (2019). https://dl.acm.org/doi/10.1145/3319535.3363211

[Alm+20] Almeida, J.B., et al.: The last mile: high-assurance and highspeed cryptographic implementations. In: 2020 IEEE Symposium on Security and Privacy (SP), pp. 965–982. IEEE (2020)

[Alm+23] Almeida, J.B., et al.: Formally verifying Kyber episode IV: implementation correctness. IACR Trans. Cryptogr. Hardw. Embed. Syst. **2023**(3), 164–193 (2023). https://tches.iacr.org/index.php/TCHES/article/view/10960

[Ber+17] Bernstein, D.J., et al.: GIMLI: a cross-platform permutation. In: Fischer, W., Homma, N. (eds.) CHES 2017. LNCS, vol. 10529, pp. 299–320. Springer, Cham (2017). https://doi.org/10.1007/978-3-319-66787-4_15

[Ber05] Bernstein, D.J.: The Poly1305-AES message-authentication code. In: Gilbert, H., Handschuh, H. (eds.) FSE 2005. LNCS, vol. 3557, pp. 32–49. Springer, Heidelberg (2005). https://doi.org/10.1007/11502760_3

[Ber08] Bernstein, D.J.: ChaCha, a variant of Salsa20. In: Workshop record of The State of the Art of Stream Ciphers, pp. 273–278 (2008). https://www.ecrypt.eu.org/stvl/sasc2008/SASCRecord.zip.Citeseer

[CKKPSY12] Cuoq, P., Kirchner, F., Kosmatov, N., Prevosto, V., Signoles, J., Yakobowski, B.: Frama-C: a software analysis perspective. In: Eleftherakis, G., Hinchey, M., Holcombe, M. (eds.) SEFM 2012. LNCS, vol. 7504, pp. 233–247. Springer, Heidelberg (2012). https://doi.org/10.1007/978-3-642-33826-7_16

[CPSWX20] Chuengsatiansup, C., Prest, T., Stehlé, D., Wallet, A., Xagawa, K.: ModFalcon: compact signatures based on module-NTRU lattices. In: Proceedings of the 15th ACM Asia Conference on Computer and Communications Security, pp. 853–866 (2020)

[DGPY20] Ducas, L., Galbraith, S., Prest, T., Yu, Y.: Integral matrix gram root and lattice gaussian sampling without floats. In: Canteaut, A., Ishai, Y. (eds.) EUROCRYPT 2020. LNCS, vol. 12106, pp. 608–637. Springer, Cham (2020). https://doi.org/10.1007/978-3-030-45724-2_21

[DP16] Ducas, L., Prest, T.: Fast Fourier Orthogonalization. In: Proceedings of the ACM on International Symposium on Symbolic and Algebraic Computation, pp. 191–198 (2016). https://doi.org/10.1007/978-3-031-15777-6_7

[Esp+22] Espitau, T., et al.: Mitaka: a simpler, parallelizable, maskable variant of falcon. In: Dunkelman, O., Dziembowski, S. (eds.) EUROCRYPT 2022. LNCS, vol. 13277, pp. 222–253. Springer, Cham (2022). https://doi.org/10.1007/978-3-031-07082-2_9

[FLSTWY19] Fu, Y.F., Liu, J., Shi, X., Tsai, M.-H., Wang, B.-Y., Yang, B.-Y.: Signed cryptographic program verification with typed cryptoline. In: Proceedings of the 2019 ACM SIGSAC Conference on Computer and Communications Security, pp. 1591–1606 (2019). https://dl.acm.org/doi/abs/10.1145/3319535.3354199

[Hwa+22] Hwang, V., et al.: Verified NTT multiplications for NISTPQC KEM lattice finalists: Kyber, SABER, and NTRU. IACR Trans. Cryptogr. Hardw. Embed. Syst. 718–750 (2022). https://tches.iacr.org/index.php/TCHES/article/view/9838

[LLSTWY23] Lai, L.-C., Liu, J., Shi, X., Tsai, M.-H., Wang, B.-Y., Yang, B.-Y.: Automatic verification of cryptographic block function implementations with logical equivalence checking. Cryptology ePrint Archive, Paper 2023/1861 (2023). https://eprint.iacr.org/2023/1861

[LSTWY19] Liu, J., Shi, X., Tsai, M.-H., Wang, B.-Y., Yang, B.-Y.: Verifying arithmetic in cryptographic C programs. In: 2019 34th IEEE/ACM International Conference on Automated Software Engineering (ASE), pp. 552–564. IEEE (2019). https://ieeexplore.ieee.org/document/8952256

[Por19] Pornin, T.: New efficient, constant-time implementations of falcon (2019). https://eprint.iacr.org/2019/893

[Por23] Pornin, T.: Improved key pair generation for falcon, BAT and Hawk (2023). https://eprint.iacr.org/2023/290

[Pre+20] Prest, T., et al.: Falcon. Submission to the NIST Post-Quantum Cryptography Standardization Project [NISTPQC] (2020). https://falcon-sign.info/

[PT18] Pollack, P., Treviño, E.: Finding the four squares in Lagrange's theorem. Integers **18A**, A15 (2018). https://api.semanticscholar.org/CorpusID:203588112

[PTWY18] Polyakov, A., Tsai, M.-H., Wang, B.-Y., Yang, B.-Y.: Verifying arithmetic assembly programs in cryptographic primitives (invited talk). In: 29th International Conference on Concurrency Theory (CONCUR 2018). Schloss Dagstuhl-Leibniz-Zentrum fuer Informatik (2018). https://drops.dagstuhl.de/entities/document/10.4230/LIPIcs.CONCUR.2018.4

[TWY17] Tsai, M.-H., Wang, B.-Y., Yang, B.-Y.; Certified verification of algebraic properties on low-level mathematical constructs in cryptographic programs. In: Proceedings of the 2017 ACM SIGSAC Conference on Computer and Communications Security, pp. 1973–1987 (2017). https://dl.acm.org/doi/abs/10.1145/3133956.3134076

Experimental Analysis of Integer Factorization Methods Using Lattices

Arata Sato[1], Aurélien Auzemery[2], Akira Katayama[1], and Masaya Yasuda[1(✉)]

[1] Rikkyo University, Tokyo, Japan
{231c002y,22rc001a,myasuda}@rikkyo.ac.jp
[2] University of Limoges, Limoges, France
aurelien.auzemery@etu.unilim.fr

Abstract. Since 1991, Schnorr has proposed methods using lattices for solving the integer factorization problem whose hardness supports the security of the RSA cryptosystem. In 2022, Yan *et al.* proposed a modification of Schnorr's lattices and reported numerical experiments by an optimization method using quantum computation. After that, Yamaguchi *et al.* reported that they succeeded in factoring RSA-type composite numbers of at most 55 bits based on Yan *et al.*'s modification, using classical annealing calculation. In this paper, we report experimental results of integer factorization methods using lattices in classical computing. Specifically, we analyze the structure of Schnorr's lattices to select suitable parameters and apply existing lattice algorithms for finding smooth relations in the difference-of-squares method. We report the running time of integer factorization using lattices for RSA-type composite numbers of at most 90 bits and the success probability of finding a smooth relation from a lattice. We also discuss the time complexity of integer factorization methods using lattices based on experimental results.

Keywords: integer factorization · lattice problems · lattice algorithms

1 Introduction

The RSA cryptosystem [15] is widely used as a public key cryptography, and its security relies on the computational hardness of factoring a huge composite number. Since the publication of Shor's quantum polynomial-time algorithm [21] for the integer factorization problem, many works have been carried out to estimate quantum resources required for factoring a composite number of cryptographic size (see [6,7,12,13,23,25]). On the other hand, since 1991, Schnorr has proposed methods in [16–19] that reduce the problem of finding smooth relations in the difference-of-squares method, one of the classical integer factorization methods, to the problem of finding approximate solutions of the closest vector problem (CVP) in a certain lattice. In 1997, it was reported in [14] that it took about 3 hours to factor a composite number of 58-bit using lattices by block-reduction and pruned enumeration algorithms. Long after that, a trial experiment for Schnorr's methods using lattices by Ducas [3] suggests that the success probability of finding a smooth relation in a lattice decreases as the size of the composite number to be factorized increases, and thus such methods are less effective than the quadratic sieve and the number field sieve methods for factoring a composite number of cryptographic size (see also [4]). In contrast, Yan et al. [26] modified Schnorr methods and applied the Quantum Approximate Optimization Algorithm (QAOA), one of the optimization methods using quantum computation, to search approximate solutions of CVP in modified lattices. They also claimed that it is possible to search smooth relations using modified lattices with a small number of $O(m/\log m)$ qubits for the bit-size m of a composite number to be factorized. Furthermore, for some composite numbers of at most 48 bits, they succeeded in finding several relational expressions in the difference-of-squares method using a quantum computer and QAOA. After that, Yamaguchi et al. [24] verified the feasibility of Yan et al.'s method by experiments to estimate that more qubits than $O(m/\log m)$ are required for factoring a composite number of m bits. It is also reported in [24] that they succeeded in factoring RSA-type composite numbers of at most 55 bits using classical annealing calculation instead of QAOA.

In this paper, we report experimental results of integer factorization methods using lattices in classical computing. In particular, we use Yan et al..'s modified lattices for experiments. We first analyze the structure of Schnorr's lattices to select suitable parameters of Yan et al..'s lattices for factoring a composite number. For experiments, we apply Kannan's embedding method [8] for Yan et al..'s lattices to transform approximate CVP into approximate SVP. For implementation, we reduce a basis of a lattice by the LLL algorithm [9] and then collect smooth relations by enumeration of short vectors in the lattice. We report experimental results for factoring RSA-type composite numbers of at most 90 bits (cf., implementation results in [14,18,24,26] for factoring composite numbers of at most 58 bits). In particular, we show experimental results on the success probability of finding a smooth relation extracted from a short vector in a lattice. Furthermore, we discuss the time complexity of integer factorization methods using lattices based on experimental results.

Notation. Let $\mathbb{N}, \mathbb{Z}, \mathbb{Q}, \mathbb{R}$ denote the set of natural numbers, the ring of integers, the fields of rational numbers and real numbers, respectively. For $z \in \mathbb{R}$, let $\lfloor z \rceil$ denote its rounded value to the nearest integer. We write row vectors (resp., matrices) in bold lower-case (resp., capital) letters as $\boldsymbol{u}$ (resp., $\boldsymbol{A}$). We denote by $\boldsymbol{u}^\top$ (resp., $\boldsymbol{A}^\top$) the transpose of $\boldsymbol{u}$ (resp., $\boldsymbol{A}$). For $\boldsymbol{u} = (u_1, \ldots, u_m)$, $\boldsymbol{v} = (v_1, \ldots, v_m) \in \mathbb{R}^m$, let $\langle \boldsymbol{u}, \boldsymbol{v} \rangle$ denote the inner product defined by $\sum_{i=1}^m u_i v_i$. Let $\|\boldsymbol{u}\|$ denote the Euclidean length defined by $\|\boldsymbol{u}\| = \sqrt{\langle \boldsymbol{u}, \boldsymbol{u} \rangle}$.

2 Preliminaries: Lattices and Lattice Algorithms

In this section, we summarize the basics of lattices and typical lattice algorithms, which shall be used later (see [2,11,27] for details).

2.1 Lattices and Their Bases

For two positive integers d, m with $d \leq m$, the set of all integral linear combinations of d linearly independent vectors $\boldsymbol{b}_1, \ldots, \boldsymbol{b}_d \in \mathbb{R}^m$

$$L = \mathcal{L}(\boldsymbol{b}_1, \ldots, \boldsymbol{b}_d) := \left\{ \sum_{i=1}^{d} x_i \boldsymbol{b}_i : x_i \in \mathbb{Z},\ 1 \leq i \leq d \right\}$$

is called a *lattice* in $\mathbb{R}^m$. The set (resp., number) of linearly independent vectors spanning L is called a *basis* (resp., the *rank*) of L. We call that L is of *full-rank* when $d = m$. For a matrix $\boldsymbol{B}$, we call it a *basis matrix* of L if the rows of $\boldsymbol{B}$ gives a basis of L. For such $\boldsymbol{B}$, we simply write $L = \mathcal{L}(\boldsymbol{B})$. There are infinitely many bases of a lattice of rank $d \geq 2$. For two matrices $\boldsymbol{B}, \boldsymbol{C}$, they are basis matrices of the same lattice if and only if there exists a unimodular matrix $\boldsymbol{T}$ satisfying $\boldsymbol{C} = \boldsymbol{T}\boldsymbol{B}$. The *volume* of a lattice L is defined by

$$\mathrm{vol}(L) := \sqrt{\det(\boldsymbol{B}\boldsymbol{B}^\top)}$$

for a basis matrix $\boldsymbol{B}$ of L, independent of the choice of basis matrices. In particular, it holds $\mathrm{vol}(L) = |\det(\boldsymbol{B})|$ when L is of full-rank. The length of the shortest non-zero vector in L is denoted by $\lambda_1(L)$. Minkowski's first theorem shows that it holds $\lambda_1(L) < \sqrt{d}\,\mathrm{vol}(L)^{\frac{1}{d}}$ for any lattice L of rank d.

2.2 Lattice Problems

Lattice problems are algorithmic problems involving lattices. Below we introduce two famous lattice problems; the *shortest vector problem (SVP)* and *closest vector problem (CVP)*:

Definition 1 (SVP). *Given a basis of a lattice L, it asks us to find the shortest non-zero vector in L, that is, a lattice vector $\boldsymbol{s}$ in L such that $\|\boldsymbol{s}\| = \lambda_1(L)$.*

Definition 2 (CVP). *Given a basis of a lattice L and a target vector $\boldsymbol{t}$, it asks us to find a lattice vector $\boldsymbol{v}$ in L closest to $\boldsymbol{t}$.*

It is proven that CVP is at least as hard as SVP (e.g., see [10] for a proof). However, from a practical point of view, both problems are considered equally hard due to Kannan's embedding method [8] that can transforms CVP into SVP.

2.3 Lattice Algorithms

Here we summarize algorithms solving lattice problems, which shall be used in our experiments. Before presenting them, we recall the *Gram-Schmidt orthogonalization* of a lattice basis. The Gram-Schmidt vectors of a basis $\{\boldsymbol{b}_1, \ldots, \boldsymbol{b}_d\}$ of a lattice L in $\mathbb{R}^m$ are defined recursively by

$$\boldsymbol{b}_1^* := \boldsymbol{b}_1, \quad \boldsymbol{b}_i^* := \boldsymbol{b}_i - \sum_{j=1}^{i-1} \mu_{ij} \boldsymbol{b}_j^*, \quad \mu_{ij} := \frac{\langle \boldsymbol{b}_i, \boldsymbol{b}_j^* \rangle}{\|\boldsymbol{b}_j^*\|^2} \quad (i > j)$$

for $2 \leq i \leq d$. Then we have $\langle \boldsymbol{b}_i^*, \boldsymbol{b}_j^* \rangle = 0$ for any $i \neq j$. For each $1 \leq k \leq d$, we also define the orthogonal projection map

$$\pi_k : \mathbb{R}^m \longrightarrow \langle \boldsymbol{b}_k^*, \ldots, \boldsymbol{b}_d^* \rangle_\mathbb{R}, \quad \pi_k(\boldsymbol{v}) := \sum_{i=k}^{d} \frac{\langle \boldsymbol{v}, \boldsymbol{b}_i^* \rangle}{\|\boldsymbol{b}_i^*\|^2} \boldsymbol{b}_i^* \quad (\boldsymbol{v} \in \mathbb{R}^m),$$

where $\langle \boldsymbol{b}_k^*, \ldots, \boldsymbol{b}_d^* \rangle_\mathbb{R}$ is the $\mathbb{R}$-vector space spanned by $\boldsymbol{b}_k^*, \ldots, \boldsymbol{b}_d^*$. The lattice spanned by projected vectors $\pi_k(\boldsymbol{b}_k), \ldots, \pi_k(\boldsymbol{b}_d)$ is called a *projected lattice* of L, denoted by $\pi_k(L)$, whose rank is equal to $d - k + 1$.

Enumeration. It is a deterministic algorithm solving SVP exactly, whose time complexity is exponential in the rank of a lattice. Given a basis $\{\boldsymbol{b}_1, \ldots, \boldsymbol{b}_d\}$ of L, an enumeration algorithm (e.g., Schnorr-Euchner's algorithm [20]) is based on a depth-first tree search for an integer combination $(v_1, \ldots, v_d)$ such that $\boldsymbol{s} = v_1 \boldsymbol{b}_1 + \cdots + v_d \boldsymbol{b}_d$ is the shortest in $L \setminus \{\boldsymbol{0}\}$, where $\boldsymbol{0}$ denotes the zero vector. With the Gram-Schmidt information of the basis, it can be written as

$$\boldsymbol{s} = \sum_{i=1}^{d} v_i \left(\boldsymbol{b}_i^* + \sum_{j=1}^{i-1} \mu_{ij} \boldsymbol{b}_j^* \right) = \sum_{j=1}^{d} \left(v_j + \sum_{i=j+1}^{d} \mu_{ij} v_i \right) \boldsymbol{b}_j^*.$$

It follows by the orthogonality of Gram-Schmidt vectors that for every $1 \leq k \leq d$, the projected vector $\pi_k(\boldsymbol{s})$ has length

$$\|\pi_k(\boldsymbol{s})\|^2 = \sum_{j=k}^{d} \left(v_j + \sum_{i=j+1}^{d} \mu_{ij} v_i \right)^2 \|\boldsymbol{b}_j^*\|^2.$$

Given a search radius $R > 0$, from d inequalities $\|\pi_k(\boldsymbol{s})\|^2 \leq R^2$ for $1 \leq k \leq d$, we can construct an enumeration tree of depth d, whose nodes at depth $d - k + 1$ correspond to the set of all vectors in $\pi_k(L)$ of length less than R.

The LLL Algorithm. It is currently known as the most famous lattice basis reduction, which finds a basis of a lattice with short and nearly-orthogonal basis vectors. Such a basis is said *good* or *reduced*, and most lattice problems are easier to be solved with a more reduced basis. For example, an enumeration algorithm runs more efficiently on a more reduced basis. Let $\{\boldsymbol{b}_1, \ldots, \boldsymbol{b}_d\}$ be a basis of a lattice L with Gram-Schmidt coefficients μ_{ij}'s and vectors $\boldsymbol{b}_k^*$'s. We say the basis *LLL-reduced* for a constant $\frac{1}{4} < \delta < 1$ if it satisfies the following two conditions:

(i) (Size-reduced) $|\mu_{ij}| \leq \frac{1}{2}$ for any $j < i$.
(ii) (Lovász' condition) $\delta \|\boldsymbol{b}_{k-1}^*\|^2 \leq \|\pi_{k-1}(\boldsymbol{b}_k)\|^2$ for all $2 \leq k \leq d$.

The first basis vector of an LLL-reduced basis satisfies both $\|\boldsymbol{b}_1\| \leq \alpha^{\frac{d-1}{2}} \lambda_1(L)$ and $\|\boldsymbol{b}_1\| \leq \alpha^{\frac{d-1}{4}} \mathrm{vol}(L)^{\frac{1}{d}}$ with $\alpha = \frac{4}{4\delta - 1}$. Given any basis $\{\boldsymbol{b}_1, \ldots, \boldsymbol{b}_d\}$ of L, the LLL algorithm [9] repeatedly performs size-reduction as $\boldsymbol{b}_i \leftarrow \boldsymbol{b}_i - \lfloor \mu_{ij} \rceil \boldsymbol{b}_j$ and swaps adjacent basis vectors $\boldsymbol{b}_{k-1}, \boldsymbol{b}_k$ that do not satisfy Lovász' condition until it finds an LLL-reduced basis of L. Its time complexity is polynomial in d.

Babai's Nearest Plane Algorithm. It is an algorithm to find an approximate solution of CVP, whose time complexity is polynomial in the rank of a lattice. Specifically, given a basis $\{\boldsymbol{b}_1, \ldots, \boldsymbol{b}_d\}$ of a full-rank lattice L and a target vector $\boldsymbol{t}$, it finds a unique lattice vector $\boldsymbol{v}$ in L such that the difference vector $\boldsymbol{v} - \boldsymbol{t}$ has the form $\sum_{i=1}^{d} x_i \boldsymbol{b}_i^*$ ($x_i \in \mathbb{R}$) with $|x_i| \le \frac{1}{2}$ for all $1 \le i \le d$ (see [1]). This implies that it can find a lattice vector in L closer to $\boldsymbol{t}$ on a more reduced basis. For example, on an LLL-reduced basis with $\delta = \frac{3}{4}$, it outputs a lattice vector $\boldsymbol{v}$ in L satisfying

$$\|\boldsymbol{v} - \boldsymbol{t}\|^2 \le 2^d \text{dist}(L, \boldsymbol{t})^2, \tag{1}$$

where $\text{dist}(L, \boldsymbol{t}) = \min_{\boldsymbol{u} \in L} \|\boldsymbol{u} - \boldsymbol{t}\|$ denotes the minimum distance between $\boldsymbol{t}$ and any lattice vector $\boldsymbol{u}$ in L.

3 Integer Factorization Methods Using Lattices

In this section, we summarize integer factorization methods using lattices. For an integer N to be factorized, their basic framework is to build a congruence of squares modulo N by collecting smooth relations, as in the quadratic sieve and the number field sieve methods. Below we recall the basic framework and then present Schnorr's method (referencing [19] mainly) for finding smooth relations using lattices and its modification by Yan *et al.* [26].

3.1 Basic Framework: Difference-of-Squares Method

Here we describe the difference-of-squares method to factorize a composite number N. Below we define several notions used in the method.

Definition 3 (factor base). *For every $k \in \mathbb{N}$, let p_k denote the k-th smallest prime (for example, $p_1 = 2, p_2 = 3, p_3 = 5$). We also let $p_0 = -1$ for convenience. For each $\ell \in \mathbb{N}$, we call the set $P_\ell := \{p_0, p_1, p_2, \ldots, p_\ell\}$ a **factor base**.*

Definition 4 (p_ℓ-smooth). *For a factor base P_ℓ, an integer M is p_ℓ-**smooth** if any prime factor of M does not exceed p_ℓ. Such an integer can be factorized in the form $M = \prod_{j=0}^{\ell} p_j^{e_j}$ with $e_j \in \mathbb{Z}_{\ge 0}$.*

Definition 5 (p_ℓ-smooth relation pair). *For a factor base P_ℓ and an integer N to be factorized, a pair of integers (u, v) is called a p_ℓ-**smooth relation pair** if u and $u - vN$ are both p_ℓ-smooth. In this case, we can write*

$$u = \prod_{j=0}^{\ell} p_j^{e_j}, \quad u - vN = \prod_{j=0}^{\ell} p_j^{e_j'} \quad (e_j, e_j' \in \mathbb{Z}_{\ge 0}). \tag{2}$$

Furthermore, if $\gcd(u, N) = 1$, then it holds

$$\prod_{j=0}^{\ell} p_j^{e_j' - e_j} = \frac{u - vN}{u} \equiv 1 \pmod{N}. \tag{3}$$

After this, we assume that any p_ℓ-smooth relation pair satisfies $\gcd(u, N) = 1$.

Let N be a composite number (of RSA type). To factorize N, the difference-of-squares method attempts to find a pair (X, Y) of two different integers satisfying $X^2 \equiv Y^2 \pmod{N}$. Since the square difference $X^2 - Y^2 = (X+Y)(X-Y)$ is a multiple of N, prime factors of N may be distributed into $X+Y$ and $X-Y$. Then we can find prime factors of N from values of $\gcd(X \pm Y, N)$. Below we show the overall procedure of the difference-of-squares method for factoring N:

1. (Finding smooth relations) We fix a factor base P_ℓ and find $\#P_\ell + 1 = \ell + 2$ different p_ℓ-smooth relation pairs (u_i, v_i) with $1 \leq i \leq \ell + 2$. (In the next subsection, we will present methods for finding smooth relation pairs using lattices.) Similarly to Eq. (2), we express each (u_i, v_i) in the form

$$u_i = \prod_{j=0}^{\ell} p_j^{e_{i,j}}, \quad u_i - v_i N = \prod_{j=0}^{\ell} p_j^{e'_{i,j}} \quad (e_{i,j}, e'_{i,j} \in \mathbb{Z}_{\geq 0}).$$

2. (Linear algebra) From the p_ℓ-smooth relation pairs (u_i, v_i) for $1 \leq i \leq \ell + 2$, we construct the matrix $\boldsymbol{A} = \left(e'_{i,j} - e_{i,j}\right)_{1 \leq i \leq \ell+2,\, 0 \leq j \leq \ell}$ of size $(\ell+2) \times (\ell+1)$. We consider the $\mathbb{F}_2$-linear mapping

$$\varphi: \mathbb{F}_2^{\ell+2} \longrightarrow \mathbb{F}_2^{\ell+1}, \quad \boldsymbol{t} \longmapsto \boldsymbol{t} \boldsymbol{A} \bmod 2,$$

whose kernel has dimension $\dim \ker \varphi = \ell + 2 - \dim \operatorname{im} \varphi \geq 1$. Therefore there exists a non-trivial vector $\boldsymbol{t} = (t_1, t_2, \ldots, t_{\ell+2})$ in $\ker \varphi$. This means that we have $\sum_{i=1}^{\ell+2} t_i(e'_{i,j} - e_{i,j}) \equiv 0 \pmod{2}$ for all $0 \leq j \leq \ell$. Then we set

$$X := \prod_{j=0}^{\ell} p_j^{m_j} \quad \text{with} \quad m_j = \frac{1}{2} \sum_{i=1}^{\ell+2} t_i(e'_{i,j} - e_{i,j}) \in \mathbb{Z}.$$

It follows by Eq. (3) that we have

$$X^2 = \prod_{j=0}^{\ell} p_j^{\sum_{i=1}^{\ell+2} t_i(e'_{i,j} - e_{i,j})} = \prod_{j=0}^{\ell} \prod_{i=1}^{\ell+2} \left(p_j^{e'_{i,j} - e_{i,j}}\right)^{t_i}$$

$$= \prod_{i=1}^{\ell+2} \left(\prod_{j=0}^{\ell} p_j^{e'_{i,j} - e_{i,j}}\right)^{t_i} \equiv 1 \pmod{N}.$$

In other words, when we set $Y = 1$, we have $X^2 \equiv Y^2 \pmod{N}$. If $X \not\equiv \pm 1 \pmod{N}$, then $p = \gcd(X \pm 1, N)$ may be a prime factor of N.

3.2 Finding Smooth Relation Pairs Using Lattices

In [16–19], Schnorr proposed methods to find smooth relation pairs using lattices Here we show Schnorr's lattices and their modification by Yan et al. [26].

Schnorr's Lattices. Let $N > 0$ be a composite number to be factorized. With the first n primes $p_1, p_2, \ldots, p_n$ and a precision parameter $c \in \mathbb{R}_{>0}$, we consider the $n \times (n+1)$-matrix

$$\boldsymbol{B}_{n,c} = \begin{pmatrix} \boldsymbol{b}_1 \\ \boldsymbol{b}_2 \\ \vdots \\ \boldsymbol{b}_n \end{pmatrix} := \begin{pmatrix} f(1) & 0 & \cdots & 0 & N^c \ln p_1 \\ 0 & f(2) & \cdots & 0 & N^c \ln p_2 \\ \vdots & \vdots & \ddots & \vdots & \vdots \\ 0 & 0 & \cdots & f(n) & N^c \ln p_n \end{pmatrix}, \quad (4)$$

where f is a permutation of the set $\{\sqrt{\ln p_1}, \sqrt{\ln p_2}, \ldots, \sqrt{\ln p_n}\}$. (Here 'ln x' is the logarithm of a positive number x with base of Napier's constant e. In contrast, we shall use 'log x' with base of 2 later.) We also set the vector

$$\boldsymbol{t} := \begin{pmatrix} 0 & 0 & \cdots & 0 & N^c \ln N \end{pmatrix} \in \mathbb{R}^{n+1} \quad (5)$$

of length $n+1$. We write $\boldsymbol{b}_1, \ldots, \boldsymbol{b}_n$ for the n rows of $\boldsymbol{B}_{n,c}$ as in Eq. (4), and let $L_{n,c} := \mathcal{L}(\boldsymbol{b}_1, \ldots, \boldsymbol{b}_n)$ denote the lattice spanned by them, that is, $L_{n,c} = \mathcal{L}(\boldsymbol{B}_{n,c})$. We correspond each lattice vector $\boldsymbol{b} = \sum_{i=1}^n e_i \boldsymbol{b}_i$ in $L_{n,c}$ with $e_1, \ldots, e_n \in \mathbb{Z}$ to the pair (u, v) of relatively prime p_n-smooth integers defined by

$$u := \prod_{e_i > 0} p_i^{e_i} \quad \text{and} \quad v := \prod_{e_i < 0} p_i^{-e_i}. \quad (6)$$

We denote $\boldsymbol{b} \sim (u, v)$, which satisfies the inequality

$$\|\boldsymbol{b}\|^2 = \sum_{i=1}^n e_i^2 f(i)^2 + N^{2c} \ln^2\left(\frac{u}{v}\right)$$

$$\geq \sum_{i=1}^n |e_i| \ln p_i + N^{2c} \ln^2\left(\frac{u}{v}\right) = \ln(uv) + N^{2c} \ln^2\left(\frac{u}{v}\right).$$

In particular, the equality holds if and only if $e_i \in \{0, \pm 1\}$ for all $1 \leq i \leq n$, namely, uv is square-free. Similarly, for the distance between $\boldsymbol{b}$ and $\boldsymbol{t}$, we have

$$\|\boldsymbol{b} - \boldsymbol{t}\|^2 = \sum_{i=1}^n e_i^2 f(i)^2 + N^{2c} \ln^2\left(\frac{u}{vN}\right) \geq \ln(uv) + N^{2c} \ln^2\left(\frac{u}{vN}\right). \quad (7)$$

We let $z = \frac{u-vN}{vN} \in \mathbb{Q}$. Since u, v are both p_n-smooth integers and thus their sizes are at most $O(p_n) = \widetilde{O}(n)$, we expect $|z| < 1$ with high probability when $n \ll N$ such as $n = O(\log N)$. Then we apply the Taylor form $\ln(1+x) = \sum_{i=1}^\infty \frac{(-1)^{i-1}}{i} x^i$ for $-1 < x \leq 1$ to roughly estimate

$$\ln^2\left(\frac{u}{vN}\right) = \ln^2(1+z) \approx \left|\frac{u-vN}{vN}\right|^2 \quad (8)$$

by ignoring the terms of z^i for $i \geq 2$ in $\ln(1+z)$. When we take $c > 0$ such that $\ln(uv) \ll N^{2c}$, we have

$$\|\boldsymbol{b} - \boldsymbol{t}\|^2 \gtrsim N^{2c} \ln^2\left(\frac{u}{vN}\right) \approx N^{2c} \left|\frac{u-vN}{vN}\right|^2 \quad (9)$$

from Eqs. (7) and (8). (In other words, c is a parameter that adjusts the weight of the right-hand equation of (7). Schnorr sets $c = \frac{1}{n+1}$ in [19].) Therefore, if the distance between $\boldsymbol{b}$ and $\boldsymbol{t}$ is sufficiently small, the absolute value of $u - vN$ should be sufficiently small and it might be p_n-smooth. This implies that the problem of finding a p_n-smooth pair (u, v) such that $|u - vN|$ is also p_n-smooth can be reduced to the problem of finding an approximate solution of CVP on the lattice $L_{n,c}$ with the target vector $\boldsymbol{t}$. Furthermore, we can generate many different lattices $L_{n,c}$ by replacing the diagonal elements of the left-part square matrix of $\boldsymbol{B}_{n,c}$ to find many p_n-smooth relation pairs.

Yan et al.'s Modification. For Schnorr's lattice basis (4), Yan et al. [26] replaced $\sqrt{\ln p_i}$ and $N^c \ln p_i$ by $\lfloor i/2 \rfloor$ and $\lfloor 10^c \ln p_i \rfloor$, respectively, to generate the integer matrix

$$\boldsymbol{B}'_{n,c} := \begin{pmatrix} g(1) & 0 & \cdots & 0 & \lfloor 10^c \ln p_1 \rfloor \\ 0 & g(2) & \cdots & 0 & \lfloor 10^c \ln p_2 \rfloor \\ \vdots & \vdots & \ddots & \vdots & \vdots \\ 0 & 0 & \cdots & g(n) & \lfloor 10^c \ln p_n \rfloor \end{pmatrix}, \qquad (10)$$

where g is a permutation of the set $\{\lfloor i/2 \rfloor \ (i = 1, 2, \ldots, n)\}$. With the modification, they also set the target vector

$$\boldsymbol{t}' := \begin{pmatrix} 0 & 0 & \cdots & 0 & \lfloor 10^c \ln N \rfloor \end{pmatrix} \in \mathbb{Z}^{n+1} \qquad (11)$$

alternative to Eq. (5). We let $L'_{n,c} := \mathcal{L}(\boldsymbol{B}'_{n,c})$. Similarly to Eq. (6), we correspond each lattice vector in $L'_{n,c}$ to the pair of relatively prime p_n-smooth integers. Then for every $\boldsymbol{b}' \in L'_{n,c}$ with $\boldsymbol{b}' \sim (u, v)$, we roughly have

$$\|\boldsymbol{b}' - \boldsymbol{t}'\|^2 \gtrsim 10^{2c} \left| \frac{u - vN}{vN} \right|^2$$

like Eq. (7) when we take $c > 0$ such that $\ln(uv) \ll 10^{2c}$. Therefore the value $|u - vN|$ is sufficiently small if $\|\boldsymbol{b}' - \boldsymbol{t}'\|$ is sufficiently small. Different from Schnorr's methods, Yan et al. relaxed the condition of finding smooth relations. Specifically, they searched lattice vectors $\boldsymbol{b}'$ in $L'_{n,c}$ with $\boldsymbol{b}' \sim (u, v)$ such that $|u - vN|$ is p_ℓ-smooth for some large ℓ such as $\ell = O(n^2)$. This relaxation enables us to increase the success probability of finding smooth relations. On the other hand, it requires us to collect $\#P_\ell + 1 = \ell + 2$ smooth relations for factoring N.

4 Analysis of the Structure of Schnorr's Lattices

In this section, we shall analyze the structure of Schnorr's lattices $L_{n,c} = \mathcal{L}(\boldsymbol{B}_{n,c})$. To analyze $L_{n,c}$, we expand its basis matrix $\boldsymbol{B}_{n,c}$ using the target vector $\boldsymbol{t}$ to construct a square matrix of size $n + 1$ as

$$\bar{\boldsymbol{B}}_{n,c} := \begin{pmatrix} \boldsymbol{B}_{n,c} \\ \boldsymbol{t} \end{pmatrix} = \begin{pmatrix} f(1) & 0 & \cdots & 0 & N^c \ln p_1 \\ 0 & f(2) & \cdots & 0 & N^c \ln p_2 \\ \vdots & \vdots & \ddots & \vdots & \vdots \\ 0 & 0 & \cdots & f(n) & N^c \ln p_n \\ 0 & 0 & \cdots & 0 & N^c \ln N \end{pmatrix}. \qquad (12)$$

We let $\bar{L}_{n,c} := \mathcal{L}(\bar{B}_{n,c})$ denote the expanded lattice, spanned by the rows of $\bar{B}_{n,c}$. It is a full-rank lattice of rank $n+1$. We give the following result on the distance between $L_{n,c}$ and t. (It is a generalization of [26, Proposition 1 in Appendix B]. See also [26, Proposition 2].)

Proposition 1. *Let N be a positive integer for generating Schnorr's lattice $L_{n,c}$, and $m = \lceil \log N \rceil$ its bit-size. Let b denote the closest vector in $L_{n,c}$ to the target vector t. We assume that the difference between b and t is the shortest non-zero vector in the expanded lattice $\bar{L}_{n,c}$. Then we have the followings:*

(1) In case of $n+1 \approx 2c \ln N = O(m)$, we have $\|b-t\|^2 = O(m)$.
(2) In case of $n+1 \approx \frac{2c \ln N}{\ln(\ln N)} = O(m/\ln m)$, we have $\|b-t\|^2 = O(m^2)$.

Proof. Set $\lambda = \lambda_1(\bar{L}_{n,c})$. Then we have $\lambda = \|b-t\|$ by assumption, and thus it is sufficient to show $\lambda^2 = O(m)$ and $O(m^2)$ in two cases (1) and (2), respectively. We apply Minkowski's first theorem for $\bar{L}_{n,c}$ to obtain the inequality

$$\lambda^2 < (n+1)\text{vol}(\bar{L}_{n,c})^{\frac{2}{n+1}}.$$

It follows from the construction of $\bar{B}_{n,c}$ (see Eq. (12)) that we have

$$\text{vol}(\bar{L}_{n,c})^2 = N^{2c} \ln^2 N \prod_{i=1}^{n} f(i)^2 = N^{2c} \ln^2 N \left(\prod_{i=1}^{n} \ln p_i \right).$$

We may assume $\prod_{i=1}^{n} \ln p_i = O(1)$ from settings of n (that is, we consider two cases of $n = O(m)$ and $O(m/\log m)$), and thus we may have

$$\lambda^2 = O\left((n+1)\left(N^{2c} \ln^2 N\right)^{\frac{1}{n+1}}\right).$$

In case of $n+1 \approx 2c \ln N$, since $N^{\frac{2c}{n+1}} \approx N^{\frac{1}{\ln N}} = O(1)$, we have

$$\lambda^2 = O(\ln N) = O(m).$$

Similarly, in case of $n+1 \approx \frac{2c \ln N}{\ln(\ln N)}$, since $N^{\frac{2c}{n+1}} \approx N^{\frac{\ln(\ln N)}{\ln N}} = \ln N$, we have

$$\lambda^2 = O\left(\frac{\ln^2 N}{\ln(\ln N)}\right) = O(m^2).$$

This completes the proof. □

Remark 1. With the same notation as in Proposition 1, when $n+1 \approx \frac{2c \ln N}{k \ln(\ln N)}$ for an integer $k \geq 1$, we have $\|b-t\|^2 = O(m^{k+1})$ since $N^{\frac{2c}{n+1}} \approx N^{\frac{\ln(\ln^k N)}{\ln N}} = \ln^k N$.

We give the following lemma on the size of $|u - vN|$ for a lattice vector b in $L_{n,c}$ with $b \sim (u,v)$. (If $|u-vN| = O(p_\ell)$ for some positive integer ℓ, then $|u-vN|$ can be p_ℓ-smooth with some probability.)

Lemma 1. *With the same notation as in Proposition 1, if $\|\boldsymbol{b} - \boldsymbol{t}\|^2 = O(m^k)$ and $1 \leq v \leq \frac{N^{c-1} p_\ell}{m^{k/2}}$ with $\boldsymbol{b} \sim (u, v)$ for two positive integers k, ℓ, then we likely have $|u - vN| = O(p_\ell)$.*

Proof. It follows by Eq. (9) that we roughly have

$$O(m^k) = \|\boldsymbol{b} - \boldsymbol{t}\|^2 \gtrsim N^{2c} \left| \frac{u - vN}{vN} \right|^2$$

$$\geq \frac{N^{2c-2} m^k}{N^{2c-2} p_\ell^2} |u - vN|^2 = \frac{m^k}{p_\ell^2} |u - vN|^2.$$

Therefore we likely have $|u - vN| = O(p_\ell)$. □

5 Experiments for Integer Factorization Using Lattices

In this section, we report implementation results for integer factorization using lattices on classical computing. Since it is easy to handle integer lattices for implementation, we use Yan et al.'s modified lattices $L'_{n,c}$ to collect smooth relations for factoring a composite number N. We also select appropriate parameters (n, c, ℓ) based on the analysis of Schnorr's lattices in the previous section.

5.1 Strategy and Implementation

Let N be a composite number of RSA-type to be factorized. In our experiments, we apply Kannan's embedding method [8] to find approximate solutions of the closest lattice vector in $L'_{n,c} = \mathcal{L}(\boldsymbol{B}'_{n,c})$ to the target vector $\boldsymbol{t}'$ (see Eqs. (10) and (11) for $\boldsymbol{B}'_{n,c}$ and $\boldsymbol{t}'$, respectively). Specifically, we build the $(n+1) \times (n+2)$-matrix

$$\bar{\boldsymbol{B}}'_{n,c} := \begin{pmatrix} \boldsymbol{B}'_{n,c} & \boldsymbol{0}^\top \\ \boldsymbol{t}' & 1 \end{pmatrix}$$

to consider the lattice $\bar{L}'_{n,c} := \mathcal{L}(\bar{\boldsymbol{B}}'_{n,c})$ spanned by the rows of the matrix. Then every lattice vector $\boldsymbol{b}'$ in $L'_{n,c}$ close to $\boldsymbol{t}'$ is embedded in the form

$$(\boldsymbol{t}', 1) - (\boldsymbol{b}', 0) = (\boldsymbol{t}' - \boldsymbol{b}', 1)$$

as a short vector in the expanded lattice $\bar{L}'_{n,c}$. Therefore we search approximate solutions of the non-zero shortest lattice vector in $\bar{L}'_{n,c}$ of the above form. To do so, we first reduce the basis matrix $\bar{\boldsymbol{B}}'_{n,c}$ of $\bar{L}'_{n,c}$ by the LLL algorithm. (We did not use the BKZ algorithm [20] since we handled lattices of ranks less than 40 in our experiments. See the parameter n in Table 1.) After that, we apply a variant of the enumeration algorithm [5, Algorithm 2]. To determine an enumeration radius, we apply Babai's nearest plane algorithm for $\boldsymbol{t}'$ over an LLL-reduced basis of $L'_{n,c}$ to obtain an approximate solution $\boldsymbol{v}'$ of the closest lattice vector in $L'_{n,c}$ to $\boldsymbol{t}'$. Then we set $R = \|\boldsymbol{t}' - \boldsymbol{v}'\|$ as an enumeration radius. In other words, we search all lattice vectors $\boldsymbol{b}'$ in $L'_{n,c}$ satisfying $\|\boldsymbol{t}' - \boldsymbol{b}'\|^2 + 1 \leq R^2$. For such every b', we compute the p_n-smooth relation pair (u,v) with $b' \sim (u,v)$ (see Eq. (6) for construction of (u,v)) to check whether $|u - vN|$ is p_ℓ-smooth or not for a fixed positive integer ℓ. We collect more than $\ell + 2$ pairs of (u,v) such that $|u - vN|$ is p_ℓ-smooth by shuffling the diagonal elements of the left-part square matrix of $\bar{B}'_{n,c}$ until we factorize N.

We implemented the method described above in C++ programs with the NTL library [22]. (We used g++ compiler with -O3 option.) Specifically, we used the NTL library function for the LLL algorithm with the default reduction parameter $\delta = 0.99$. In our implementation, we used the ZZ class in the NTL library for integral entries of any lattice basis B and the RR class for floating point numbers on Gram-Schmidt information of B. In particular, we used the default setting of RR for high precision (150-bit precision). For enumeration, we did not use any pruning since we wanted as many short lattice vectors as possible, and not just the non-zero shortest one. In contrast, we aborted the enumeration process after we collected an amount of short lattice vectors (e.g., 30 million vectors). Such abort could occur in an unlucky case where an enumeration radius is extremely big. (It is most likely to happen on high-rank lattices, as Babai's bounding inequality is exponential. See Eq. (1).) This empirical threshold made the enumeration process terminate in a shorter time even in unlucky cases, with a significant speed-up of up to 33% for factoring a composite number of 65-bit (untested on bigger numbers).

5.2 Selection of Parameters

Here we set three parameters (n, c, ℓ) for experiments. (Recall that two parameters n, c are for the lattice $L'_{n,c}$ or $\bar{L}'_{n,c}$, and ℓ for a factor base P_ℓ.) From the analysis of Proposition 1, we consider two cases of $n = O(m)$ and $O(m/\ln m)$ for the bit-size m of a composite number N to be factorized. (Note that the analysis in the previous section is applicable for Yan et al.'s lattice $L'_{n,c}$ since it is just a modification of Schnorr's lattice $L_{n,c}$.)

Case of $n = O(m)$. This case is similar to Schnorr's original setting in [19]. We estimate from the case (1) of Proposition 1 that there exists a lattice vector b' in $L'_{n,c}$ satisfying $\|b' - t'\|^2 = O(m)$. From the same discussion as in Lemma 1 for Yan et al.'s lattices $L'_{n,c}$, we should take c and ℓ so that $10^{c-1} p_\ell \gg \sqrt{m}$ to obtain a p_ℓ-smooth relation pair (u,v) from $b' \in L'_{n,c}$. For our experiments, we set $c = 5.0$ and $\ell = 2n$ with an enough margin. (Cf., Schnorr took $c = \frac{1}{n+1}$ and $\ell = n$ in [19] for his lattices $L_{n,c}$ with $N^{c-1} p_n \gg \sqrt{m}$ from Lemma 1.) In addition, we write n in the form $\lfloor am \rfloor$, and choose a suitable constant $a > 0$ from our preliminary experiments for several N of around $m = 40, 45$, and 50 bits. Specifically, we set $a = 0.55$, which determines $n = 22$ (resp., 24 and 27) for $m = 40$ (resp., 45 and 50).

Case of $n = O(m/\ln m)$. This case was handled by Yan et al. in [26]. In this case, we estimate from the case (2) of Proposition 1 that there exists a lattice vector b' in $L'_{n,c}$ satisfying $\|b' - t'\|^2 = O(m^2)$. Similarly to the above case, we need to set c and ℓ so that $10^{c-1}p_\ell \gg m$ to obtain a p_ℓ-smooth relation pair from $\boldsymbol{b}' \in L'_{n,c}$. We set $c = 5.0$ and $\ell = 2n^2$ like in [26]. (Yan et al. [26] set the same ℓ, but took c between 1.5 and 10.) We also write n in the form $\lfloor bm/\ln m \rfloor$, and choose a suitable constant $b > 0$ from our preliminary experiments for several N of around $m = 45, 50,$ and 55 bits. Specifically, we set $b = 2.3$, which determines $n = 18$ (resp., 20 and 21) for $m = 45$ (resp., 50 and 55).

Remark 2. For factoring a composite number of m-bit, an optimal rank parameter n depends on lattice algorithms. From preliminary experiments with LLL and full enumeration, an appropriate value of n is quite limited for each m, and an optimal n is likely to be around the above setting in both cases of $n = O(m)$ and $n = O(m/\log m)$ for our experiments. In contrast, when using pruned enumeration or sieving, we could find short vectors efficiently in a high-rank lattice and thus a higher n could be optimal like implementation reports in [14, 18].

5.3 Experimental Results

In Table 1, we summarize experimental results on the average running times of factoring composite numbers N of RSA-type using lattices $\bar{L}'_{n,c}$ with parameters (n, c, ℓ) selected in the previous subsection. (We conducted experiments on a single core of Intel Xeon Gold 5222 CPU @ 3.80 GHz with 32 GByte memory.) For each m in Table 1, we randomly selected 5 composite numbers N of RSA-type with bit-size m and conducted experiments for factoring those numbers N. For each instance, we show the success probability of finding a p_ℓ-smooth relation pair extracted from a short vector in a lattice $\bar{L}'_{n,c}$ in Table 1. (As described in Subsect. 3.2, we shuffle the diagonal elements of the left-part square matrix of $\boldsymbol{B}'_{n,c}$, defined in Eq. (10), to generate different lattices $\bar{L}'_{n,c} = \mathcal{L}\left(\bar{\boldsymbol{B}}'_{n,c}\right)$, in which some short vectors can generate p_ℓ-smooth relation pairs.) In Fig. 1, we plot the success probabilities of finding a p_ℓ-smooth relation pair in Table 1, along with approximation curves by exponential regression in each case of $O(m)$ and $O(m/\ln m)$.

Discussion. According to Table 1, the case of $n = O(m/\ln m)$ is more efficient than the case of $n = O(m)$. In particular, in the case of $n = O(m/\ln m)$, we succeeded in factoring RSA-type composite numbers N of $m = 90$ bits using lattices $\bar{L}'_{n,c}$ of rank $n + 1 = 32$ within 83.3 h $\approx$3.5 d in average. (Cf., implementation results in [14, 18, 24, 26] for factoring composite numbers of at most 58 bits. In particular, Schnorr [18] used his lattices $L_{n,c}$ of rank $n = 90$ for a composite number of 47-bit. It was also reported in [14] that it took about 3 h to succeed in factoring a composite number of 58-bit using lattices of rank 160 by block-reduction and pruned enumeration algorithms.) It is related to the success probability of finding a p_ℓ-smooth relation pair from a lattice. Specifically, in the case of $n = O(m)$ with $\ell = O(n)$, only vectors in $\bar{L}'_{n,c}$ close to the shortest can generate p_ℓ-smooth relation pairs, and thus the success probability is very low, seen from Table 1. In contrast, the case of $n = O(m/\ln m)$ with $\ell = O(n^2)$

Table 1. Experimental results on the average running times of factoring composite numbers N of RSA-type using lattices $\bar{L}'_{n,c}$ with parameters (n, c, ℓ) selected in Subsect. 5.2 ("Probability" means the success probability of finding a p_ℓ-smooth relation pair extracted from a short vector in a lattice $\bar{L}'_{n,c}$)

Bit-size m of N ($m = \lceil \log N \rceil$)	Case of $n = O(m)$			Case of $n = O(m/\ln m)$		
	$n = \lfloor 0.55m \rfloor$, $c = 5.0$, $\ell = 2n$			$n = \lfloor 2.3m/\ln m \rfloor$, $c = 5.0$, $\ell = 2n^2$		
	n	Probability	Total Time	n	Probability	Total Time
45	24	1.1%	2.8 min	18	23.7%	6.5 s
50	27	0.35%	25.2 min	20	17.3%	32.2 s
55	30	0.13%	1.7 h	21	11.5%	1.4 min
60	33	0.028%	9.2 h	23	6.6%	5.1 min
65	35	0.006%	58.3 h	24	4.8%	14.2 min
70	38	< 0.001%	> 3 days	26	2.2%	57.5 min
75	–	–	–	27	1.6%	2.2 h
80	–	–	–	29	0.75%	8.3 h
85	–	–	–	30	0.43%	23.5 h
90	–	–	–	31	0.17%	83.3 h

relaxes the condition of finding p_ℓ-smooth relation pairs from short lattice vectors. It is the main factor that we succeeded in factoring composite numbers of at most 90 bits using lattices. (In experiments, we only used the LLL algorithm to reduce lattice bases. For high lattice ranks such as $n \geq 30$, the BKZ algorithm [20] might be available for reducing lattice bases more to speed up the total processing.) On the other hand, we see from Fig. 1 that in both cases of $n = O(m)$ and $n = O(m/\ln m)$, the success probability p of finding a smooth relation pair from a lattice decreases *exponentially* in the bit-size m of N. Note that the probability p depends only on the form of lattices, regardless of lattice algorithms. It implies that an exponential number of lattices $\bar{L}'_{n,c}$ are required to collect smooth relation pairs for factoring N, and thus the time complexity of integer factorization using lattices $\bar{L}'_{n,c}$ is exponential in the size of N. In fact, average running times in Table 1 increase exponentially with the bit-size m of N for large m in both cases of $O(m)$ and $O(m/\ln m)$.

Remark 3. For factoring a composite number N of bit-size m, we might be able to use other parameter settings such as $n = O\left(m/\ln^k m\right)$ for integers $k \geq 2$. Then we need to roughly set $\ell = O(m^{k+1})$ since the minimum squared distance of a vector in Schnorr's lattice to the target vector $\boldsymbol{t}$ is estimated as $O(m^{k+1})$ from Remark 1. In other words, we need to prepare $O(m^{k+1})$ primes in the difference-of-squares method for factoring an m-bit composite number N. It could be very costly to generate such a large amount of primes for large m.

Remark 4. In the above experiments, we used an enumeration algorithm to investigate the success probability p of finding a smooth relation from a lat-

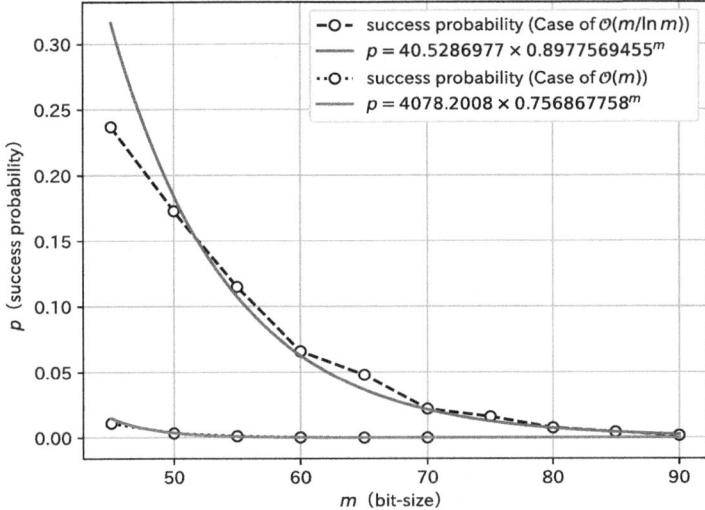

Fig. 1. Plots of the success probabilities of finding a p_ℓ-smooth relation pair in Table 1 for factoring m-bit composite numbers, along with approximation curves by exponential regression in each case of $O(m)$ and $O(m/\ln m)$

tice. In contrast, sieving is useful to generate a huge number of short lattice vectors and is asymptotically faster than enumeration. Hence sieving is more efficient than enumeration to collect smooth relations for factoring a large composite number N using lattices. However, the probability p depends only on a lattice, not lattice algorithms. Therefore, even when using a sieve algorithm, the time complexity of factoring N using lattices would behave exponentially in the size of N like in Table 1.

6 Conclusion

We reported experimental results of integer factorization methods using lattices proposed by Schnorr in [16–19]. Specifically, we implemented Yan et al.'s modification [26] for experiments by LLL and full enumeration on classical computing. We selected suitable parameters based on analysis of the structure of lattices to succeed in factoring RSA-type composite numbers of at most 90 bits using lattices (cf., implementation results in [14,18,24,26] for factoring composite numbers of at most 58 bits). On the other hand, in Fig. 1, we showed experimental results on the success probability p of finding a smooth relation extracted from a short vector in a lattice. Figure 1 shows that the success probability p decreases exponentially in the bit-size of a composite number N to be factorized. It implies that it requires an exponential number of lattices to collect smooth relations for factoring N. Therefore the complexity of integer factorization methods using lattices must be exponential in the size of N, since the success probability p depends on the form of lattices, regardless of lattice algorithms in classical and quantum computing. Hence, as suggested by Ducas [3] in his trial experiment, for a composite number N of cryptographic size, lattice-based integer factorization methods cannot outperform existing methods such as the quadratic sieve and the number field sieve methods, whose time complexities are sub-exponential in the size of N.

Acknowledgements. This work was supported by JST CREST Grant Number JPMJCR2113, Japan.

References

1. Babai, L.: On Lovász' lattice reduction and the nearest lattice point problem. Combinatorica **6**, 1–13 (1986)
2. Bremner, M.R.: Lattice Basis Reduction: An Introduction to the LLL Algorithm and its Applications. CRC Press, Boca Raton (2011)
3. Ducas, L.: Testing Schnorr's factoring claim in SageMath. https://github.com/lducas/SchnorrGate
4. Ducas, L.: Schnorr's approach to factoring via lattices. RISC seminar (2021). https://projects.cwi.nl/crypto/risc_materials/2021_05_20_ducas_slides.pdf
5. Gama, N., Nguyen, P.Q., Regev, O.: Lattice enumeration using extreme pruning. In: Gilbert, H. (ed.) EUROCRYPT 2010. LNCS, vol. 6110, pp. 257–278. Springer, Heidelberg (2010). https://doi.org/10.1007/978-3-642-13190-5_13
6. Gidney, C., Ekerå, M.: How to factor 2048 bit RSA integers in 8 hours using 20 million noisy qubits. Quantum **5**, 433 (2021)
7. Gouzien, É., Sangouard, N.: Factoring 2048-bit RSA integers in 177 days with 13436 qubits and a multimode memory. Phys. Rev. Lett. **127**(14), 140503 (2021)
8. Kannan, R.: Minkowski's convex body theorem and integer programming. Math. Oper. Res. **12**(3), 415–440 (1987)
9. Lenstra, A.K., Lenstra, H.W., Lovász, L.: Factoring polynomials with rational coefficients. Math. Ann. **261**, 515–534 (1982)
10. Micciancio, D., Goldwasser, S.: Complexity of Lattice Problems: A Cryptographic Perspective, vol. 671. Springer, Heidelberg (2012). https://doi.org/10.1007/978-1-4615-0897-7
11. Nguyen, P.Q.: Hermite's constant and lattice algorithms. In: Nguyen, P., Vallee, B. (eds.) The LLL Algorithm, pp. 19–69. Springer, Heidelberg (2009). https://doi.org/10.1007/978-3-642-02295-1_2
12. Ragavan, S., Vaikuntanathan, V.: Optimizing space in Regev's factoring algorithm. arXiv preprint arXiv:2310.00899 (2023)
13. Regev, O.: An efficient quantum factoring algorithm. arXiv preprint arXiv:2308.06572 (2023)
14. Ritter, H., Rössner, C.: Factoring via strong lattice reduction algorithms. IACR Cryptology ePrint Archive 1997/008 (1997). https://eprint.iacr.org/1997/008
15. Rivest, R.L., Shamir, A., Adleman, L.: A method for obtaining digital signatures and public-key cryptosystems. Commun. ACM **21**(2), 120–126 (1978)
16. Schnorr, C.P.: Factoring integers and computing discrete logarithms via Diophantine approximation. In: Advances in Computational Complexity Theory, pp. 171–181 (1991)
17. Schnorr, C.P.: Average time fast SVP and CVP algorithms: factoring integers in polynomial time. Rump session at EUROCRYPT 2009 (2009). https://eurocrypt2009rump.cr.yp.to/e074d37e10ad1ad227200ea7ba36cf73.pdf

18. Schnorr, C.P.: Factoring integers by CVP algorithms. In: Number Theory and Cryptography: Papers in Honor of Johannes Buchmann on the Occasion of His 60th Birthday, pp. 73–93 (2013)
19. Schnorr, C.P.: Fast factoring integers by SVP algorithms, corrected. IACR Cryptology ePrint Archive 2021/933 (2021). https://eprint.iacr.org/2021/933
20. Schnorr, C.P., Euchner, M.: Lattice basis reduction: improved practical algorithms and solving subset sum problems. Math. Program. **66**, 181–199 (1994)
21. Shor, P.W.: Algorithms for quantum computation: discrete logarithms and factoring. In: Proceedings 35th Annual Symposium on Foundations of Computer Science, pp. 124–134. IEEE (1994)
22. Shoup, V.: NTL: a library for doing Number Theory. http://www.shoup.net/ntl/
23. Takahashi, Y., Kunihiro, N.: A quantum circuit for Shor's factoring algorithm using $2n + 2$ qubits. Quant. Inf. Comput. **6**(2), 184–192 (2006)
24. Yamaguchi, J., Izu, T., Kunihiro, N.: Experimental report on integer factorization methods using lattice and optimization methods (in Japanese). In: IPSJ Technical Report, vol. 2023-IOT-61, no. 22, pp. 1–8 (2023)
25. Yamaguchi, J., Yamazaki, M., Tabuchi, A., Honda, T., Izu, T., Kunihiro, N.: Estimation of Shor's circuit for 2048-bit integers based on quantum simulator. IACR Cryptology ePrint Archive 2023/092 (2023). https://eprint.iacr.org/2023/092
26. Yan, B., et al.: Factoring integers with sublinear resources on a superconducting quantum processor. arXiv preprint arXiv:2212.12372 (2022)
27. Yasuda, M.: A survey of solving SVP algorithms and recent strategies for solving the SVP challenge. In: Takagi, T., Wakayama, M., Tanaka, K., Kunihiro, N., Kimoto, K., Ikematsu, Y. (eds.) International Symposium on Mathematics, Quantum Theory, and Cryptography. MI, vol. 33, pp. 189–207. Springer, Singapore (2021). https://doi.org/10.1007/978-981-15-5191-8_15

Sieving Method for SDP with the Zero Window: An Improvement in Low Memory Environments

Naoki Yoshiguchi[✉], Yusuke Aikawa, and Tsuyoshi Takagi

Department of Mathematical Informatics, Graduate School of Information Science and Technology, The University of Tokyo, 7-3-1 Hongo, Bunkyo-ku, Tokyo, Japan
yoshiguchi@g.ecc.u-tokyo.ac.jp

Abstract. Code-based cryptography is a type of post-quantum cryptography, relying on the complexity of the syndrome decoding problem for its security. Information set decoding (ISD) is a well-known method for solving the syndrome decoding problem, based on an algorithm proposed by Prange in 1962. In 1989, Stern introduced a partitioning called zero window to Prange's method and realized a faster ISD. In 2023, Guo-Johansson-Nguyen proposed a method to apply the sieving method to ISD, which is known as a fast method for solving shortest vector problems. In this study, we propose a method that introduces the zero window for ISD using the sieving method and evaluate its computational complexity. The proposed method reduces the time complexity by up to approximately 10 bits compared to the original sieving method for 128-bit secure parameters of the Classic McEliece cipher under memory-saving conditions.

Keywords: Code-based cryptography · Syndrome decoding problem · Information Set Decoding · The sieving method

1 Introduction

RSA cryptography and elliptic curve cryptography, widely used today, can be broken by a quantum computer. Therefore, post-quantum cryptography has been studied extensively. Code-based cryptography relies on the difficulty of computing vectors with specific weights of linear codes, and various schemes have been proposed, including the McEliece [13], Niederreiter [15], and Alekhnovich's [2] Cryptosystems. Among them, the code-based cryptographs BIKE [3], HQC [14], and Classic McEliece [9] are finalists in NIST's post-quantum cryptography standardization project [1]. For more information on code-based cryptography, please refer to [18].

The security of code-based cryptography relies on the computational complexity of the syndrome decoding problem (SDP). Information set decoding (ISD) is a method for solving SDP. ISD solves SDP by partitioning the parity check matrix, followed by permutation and Gaussian elimination, thereby constraining the search space. ISD is characterized by its approach to partitioning the parity check matrix and subsequent solving methods.

Initially proposed by Prange [16], ISD exhibits an asymptotic time complexity of $\tilde{O}(2^{0.121n})$ and polynomial spatial complexity. Stern further enhanced ISD by introducing the *zero window* to Prange's partitioning method, achieving an asymptotic time complexity of $\tilde{O}(2^{0.117n})$. Subsequently, May-Meurer-Thomae [12], developed a method with an asymptotic time complexity of $\tilde{O}(2^{0.112n})$ and Becker, Joux, May, and Meurer [6] introduced a method achieving $\tilde{O}(2^{0.102n})$ complexity, Both-May [8] developed a method with a complexity of $\tilde{O}(2^{0.095n})$. In 2023, Guo-Johansson-Nguyen [11] introduced the sieving method to ISD. According to Ducas-Esser-Etinski-Kirshanova [10], the asymptotic complexity of the sieving method is $\tilde{O}(2^{0.117n})$, surpassing that of Both-May's algorithm. However, for the 128-bit security parameter of the aforementioned code-based cryptography, the actual computational complexity of the sieving method is evaluated to be smaller than that of Both-May's method in a memory-constrained environment.

Contribution. In this paper, we apply the sieving method to other ISD. Specifically, we integrate the sieving method into Stern's algorithm, which shares the same equation form after partitioning. The most memory-consuming part of the sieving method is the storage of vectors in a list, which is called the memory size in this paper. By combining this approach with Stern's method and shortening the vector length, the list size is reduced, leading to more efficient spatial computation. However, Stern's method requires more iterations due to its imposition of stronger assumptions on the weights of the vectors to be solved compared to the original sieving method. Consequently, our proposed method reduces time complexity by up to 10 bits in memory-constrained environments.

Notations. The n-dimensional vector space on $\mathbb{F}_2$ is denoted by $\mathbb{F}_2^n$. The vector $\boldsymbol{x} \in \mathbb{F}_2^n$ is denoted as $\boldsymbol{x} = (x_1, \ldots, x_n)$. $\mathbb{F}_2^{n \times m}$ denotes the set of $n \times m$ matrices on $\mathbb{F}_2$. For a vector $\boldsymbol{x} \in \mathbb{F}_2^n$ and $i = 1, \ldots, n$, $\boldsymbol{x}_{[i]} := (x_1, \ldots, x_i)$. The symbol $\boldsymbol{0}_k$ denotes a k-dimensional vector in which all elements are 0. For $\boldsymbol{A} \in \mathbb{F}_2^{n \times m}$, let $\boldsymbol{A}_{[i]}$ be a submatrix formed by taking the first through the ith columns of $\boldsymbol{A}$. $\mathrm{GL}_n(\mathbb{F}_2)$ represents the set of n-th invertible matrices over $\mathbb{F}_2$. $\mathcal{P}_n$ is the set of $n \times n$ permutation matrices. We endow $\mathbb{F}_2^n$ with the standard bilinear form: $\langle \boldsymbol{x}, \boldsymbol{y} \rangle := \sum_{i=1}^n x_i y_i (\boldsymbol{x}, \boldsymbol{y} \in \mathbb{F}_2^n)$. Binomial coefficients are denoted as $\binom{n}{k}$.

2 Syndrome Decoding Problem (SDP)

In this section, we explain the SDP, which forms the basis for the security of code-based cryptography.

First, we introduce the concept of a linear code. An $[n, k]$ linear code $\mathcal{C}$ over $\mathbb{F}_2$ is a k-dimensional linear subspace of an n-dimensional vector space over $\mathbb{F}_2$. A linear code $\mathcal{C}$ can be expressed by a generator matrix $\boldsymbol{G}$ defined as follows. Let $\mathcal{C}$ be an $[n, k]$ linear code, and let $\boldsymbol{G}$ be a generator matrix of $\mathcal{C}$. A linear code $\mathcal{C}$ can also be represented by a parity check matrix $\boldsymbol{H}$ defined as follows.

Let $\mathcal{C}$ be an $[n, k]$ linear code. The parity check matrix of $\mathcal{C}$, $\boldsymbol{H} \in \mathbb{F}_2^{(n-k) \times n}$, is defined as a matrix that satisfies the following equation:

$$\mathcal{C} = \mathrm{Ker}(\boldsymbol{H}) = \{\boldsymbol{x} : \boldsymbol{H}\boldsymbol{x} = \boldsymbol{0}\}.$$

Then, we explain how to construct the McEliece cryptosystem [13], a public key encryption scheme based on linear codes. In the McEliece cryptosystem, the secret key consists of three matrices: the generator matrix $\boldsymbol{G}$ of the $[n, k]$ linear code, a permutation matrix $\boldsymbol{P} \in \mathcal{P}_n$, and a invertible matrix $\boldsymbol{S} \in \mathrm{GL}_k(\mathbb{F}_2)$. We set $\boldsymbol{G}' := \boldsymbol{SGP}$ as the public key. To encrypt a message $\boldsymbol{m} \in \mathbb{F}_2^k$ the sender computes $\boldsymbol{c} := \boldsymbol{m}\boldsymbol{G}' + \boldsymbol{e}$, where $\boldsymbol{e} \in \mathbb{F}_2^n$ is a randomly chosen vector, known as the error vector, with Hamming weight $\mathrm{wt}_H(\boldsymbol{e}) = t$. Therefore, in the McEliece cryptosystem, the decryptor needs to find $\boldsymbol{e} \in \mathbb{F}_2^n$, $\boldsymbol{x} \in \mathbb{F}_2^k$ such that $\mathrm{wt}_H(\boldsymbol{e}) = t$ and $\boldsymbol{c} = \boldsymbol{x}\boldsymbol{G}' + \boldsymbol{e}$ from the received ciphertext $\boldsymbol{c}$ and the public key $\boldsymbol{G}'$.

The decryption process involves solving $\boldsymbol{e} \in \mathbb{F}_2^n$ and $\boldsymbol{x} \in \mathbb{F}_2^k$ such that $\mathrm{wt}_H(\boldsymbol{e}) = t$ and $\boldsymbol{c} = \boldsymbol{x}\boldsymbol{G}' + \boldsymbol{e}$ from $\boldsymbol{c}$ and $\boldsymbol{G}'$. Here, we define $\boldsymbol{H}'$ as the parity-check matrix corresponding to $\boldsymbol{G}'$. Then, $\boldsymbol{c} = \boldsymbol{x}\boldsymbol{G}' + \boldsymbol{e} \Leftrightarrow \boldsymbol{c}\boldsymbol{H}'^T = \boldsymbol{e}\boldsymbol{H}'^T$. From this observation, we define the SDP as follows.

Problem 1 (Syndrome Decoding Problem (SDP)). Let $k \leq n$ be positive integers. Given $\boldsymbol{H} \in \mathbb{F}_2^{(n-k) \times n}$, $\boldsymbol{s} \in \mathbb{F}_2^{n-k}$, and $t \in \mathbb{N}$, the problem of finding $\boldsymbol{e} \in \mathbb{F}_2^n$ such that $\mathrm{wt}_H(\boldsymbol{e}) = t$ and $\boldsymbol{e}\boldsymbol{H}^T = \boldsymbol{s}$ is called the Syndrome Decoding Problem.

If SDP is solved, McEliece cryptosystem is no longer secure, so the security of cryptosystems is based on the hardness of SDP. SDP has been proven to be NP-complete by Berlekamp, McEliece, and Van Tilborg [7], on which the security of code-based cryptography relies. Therefore, improving the techniques for solving the computational hardness of SDP is a fundamental research question.

3 Information Set Decoding (ISD)

ISD is a method that solves the SDP more efficiently than the exhaustive search. In this section, we explain ISD by Prange [16] and by Stern [17].

3.1 Prange's Algorithm

Prange [16] proposed the first ISD algorithm in 1962. Let us explain the principle. From $\mathrm{wt}_H(\boldsymbol{e}) = t$, there exists $\boldsymbol{P} \in \mathcal{P}_n$ such that

$$\boldsymbol{e}\boldsymbol{P} = (\boldsymbol{0}_k \ \boldsymbol{e}_1) \qquad (1)$$

where $\boldsymbol{e}_1 \in \mathbb{F}_2^{n-k}$. By using Gaussian elimination, we can compute $\boldsymbol{U} \in \mathrm{GL}_{n-k}(\mathbb{F}_2)$ and $\boldsymbol{H}' \in \mathbb{F}_2^{(n-k) \times k}$ such that $\boldsymbol{UHP} = (\boldsymbol{H}' \ \boldsymbol{I}_{n-k})$. Then, we can transform $\boldsymbol{e}\boldsymbol{H}^T = \boldsymbol{s}$ as follows: $\boldsymbol{s}\boldsymbol{U}^T = (\boldsymbol{e}\boldsymbol{P})(\boldsymbol{UHP})^T = (\boldsymbol{0}_k \ \boldsymbol{e}_1)(\boldsymbol{H}' \ \boldsymbol{I}_{n-k})^T = \boldsymbol{e}_1$. Here, $\mathrm{wt}_H(\boldsymbol{s}\boldsymbol{U}^T) = t$ is a necessary and sufficient condition for Eq. (1) to be satisfied. Prange's algorithm searches for $\boldsymbol{P}$ that satisfies Eq. (1) by trial and error. The algorithm proceeds as in Algorithm 1.

Algorithm 1: Prange's algorithm

Input: $H \in \mathbb{F}_2^{(n-k) \times n}$, $s \in \mathbb{F}_2^{n-k}$, $t \in \mathbb{N}$
Output: $e \in \mathbb{F}_2^n$ s.t. $\text{wt}_H(e) = t$, $eH^T = s$

1 **while** true **do**
2   Randomly pick a matrix $P \in \mathcal{P}_n$;
3   Calculate U, H' s.t. $UHP = (H' \; I_k)$;
4     $s' \leftarrow sU^T$;
5   **if** $\text{wt}_H(s') = t$ **then**
6   **return** $(\mathbf{0}_k \; s')P^{-1}$;
7   **end if**
8 **end while**

3.2 Stern's Algorithm

Stern's algorithm improves Prange's algorithm by introducing a new partition of matrices, known as the zero window [17]. In this paper, we follow the definition of Stern's algorithm in [18]. It solves an SDP by transforming it into an SDP with smaller Hamming weights, making it faster than Prange's algorithm. Stern's algorithm takes parameters $\ell, p \in \mathbb{N}$, where $0 \leq \ell \leq n - k$ and $0 \leq 2p \leq t$. Given $\text{wt}_H(e) = t$, there exists a matrix $P \in \mathcal{P}_n$ such that for some $e_1 \in \mathbb{F}_2^k$ and $e_2 \in \mathbb{F}_2^{n-k-\ell}$:

$$(\mathbf{0}_\ell \; e_1 \; e_2) = eP,$$

where $\text{wt}_H(e_1) = 2p, \text{wt}_H(e_2) = t - 2p$. For arbitrary $P \in \mathcal{P}_n$, by using Gaussian elimination, we can compute $U \in \text{GL}_{n-k}(\mathbb{F}_2)$, $H' \in \mathbb{F}_2^{\ell \times (k+\ell)}$, $H'' \in \mathbb{F}_2^{(n-k-\ell) \times (k+\ell)}$ such that

$$UHP = \begin{pmatrix} * & H' & O \\ * & H'' & I_{n-k-\ell} \end{pmatrix}.$$

Then, $(eP)(UHP)^T = sU^T$ holds. By defining

$$(s_1 \; s_2) := sU^T = (\mathbf{0}_\ell \; e_1 \; e_2) \begin{pmatrix} * & * \\ H'^T & H''^T \\ \mathbf{0} & I_{n-k-\ell} \end{pmatrix} \in \mathbb{F}_2^\ell \times \mathbb{F}_2^{n-k-\ell},$$

we can represent s_1, s_2 as

$$e_1 H'^T = s_1, \quad (2)$$

$$e_1 H''^T + e_2 = s_2. \quad (3)$$

Subsequently, by solving for e_1 satisfying Eq. (2) and $\text{wt}_H(e_1) = 2p$, we can obtain $e_2 = e_1 H''^T + s_2$. If $\text{wt}_H(e_1 H''^T + s_2) = t - 2p$, then $(\mathbf{0}_\ell \; e_1 \; e_1 H''^T + s_2)P^{-1}$ becomes the solution to the original SDP. The algorithm proceeds as in Algorithm 2.

Algorithm 2: Stern's Algorithm

Input: $H \in \mathbb{F}_2^{(n-k) \times n}$, $s \in \mathbb{F}_2^{n-k}$, $t \in \mathbb{N}$
Output: $e \in \mathbb{F}_2^n$ s.t. $\mathrm{wt}_H(e) = t$, $eH^T = s$

1. **while** true **do**
2.   Take a random matrix $P \in \mathcal{P}_n$;
3.   Let $(0_\ell\ e_1\ e_2) := eP$ $(e_1 \in \mathbb{F}_2^k, e_2 \in \mathbb{F}_2^{n-k-\ell})$;
4.   Calculate $U \in \mathrm{GL}_{n-k}(\mathbb{F}_2)$ s.t. $UHP = \begin{pmatrix} * & H' & O \\ * & H'' & I_{n-k-\ell} \end{pmatrix}$;
5.   **for** e_1 s.t. $e_1 H'^T = s_1$ **do**
6. $e_2 \leftarrow e_1 H''^T + s_2$;
7.   **if** $\mathrm{wt}_H(s_2 - e_1 H''^T) = t - 2p$ **then**
8.   **return** $(0_\ell\ e_1\ e_2)P^{-1}$;
9.   **end if**
10.   **end for**
11. **end while**

4 Sieving Method

Guo-Johansson-Nguyen [11] proposed a sieving style ISD [11], which we call the sieving method. In this section, we provide a brief review of this method. In this section, we use the following notation. To represent a Hamming sphere, we use the notation $\mathcal{S}_r^n$, where $\mathcal{S}_r^n := \{e \in \mathbb{F}_2^n \mid \mathrm{wt}_H(e) = r\}$.

4.1 Algorithm

First, we outline the general approach. The sieving method takes parameters $\ell, p \in \mathbb{N}$. While Stern's algorithm solved the problem by transforming SDP into SDP for smaller Hamming weight through matrix partitioning, the idea of the sieving method is to speed up solving SDP for small Hamming weights by repeatedly updating a list of candidate solutions. The sieving method first partitions e and H as follows. Let $P \in \mathcal{P}_n$. Then, using $U \in \mathrm{GL}_{n-k}(\mathbb{F}_2)$, $H' \in \mathbb{F}_2^{\ell \times (k+\ell)}$, $H'' \in \mathbb{F}_2^{(n-k-\ell) \times (k+\ell)}$, $e_1 \in \mathbb{F}_2^{k+\ell}$, $e_2 \in \mathbb{F}_2^{n-k-\ell}$, we can express:

$$(e_1\ e_2) = eP,$$
$$\begin{pmatrix} H'^T & H''^T \\ O & I_{n-k-\ell} \end{pmatrix} = UHP.$$

Under this partition, similar relations to Eq. (2) and Eq. (3) hold.

Let us explain the principle of the sieving method. In an SDP with a parity-check matrix $H \in \mathbb{F}_2^{\ell \times (k+\ell)}$, $eH^T = s$ represents a collection of ℓ linear equations over $\mathbb{F}_2$. The principle idea is to recursively construct a list of vectors that satisfy the first i equations for $i = 0, 1, \ldots, \ell$.

Here, let us assume the existence of a list $\mathcal{L}_i \subset \{e \in \mathcal{S}_{2p}^{k+\ell} \mid e(H^T)_{[i]} \in \{s_{[i]}, 0_i\}\}$. Our aim is to construct a list $\mathcal{L}_{i+1} \subset \{e \in \mathcal{S}_{2p}^{k+\ell} \mid e(H^T)_{[i+1]} \in$

$\{s_{[i+1]}, 0_{i+1}\}\}$ from $\mathcal{L}_i$. In essence, we need to generate sufficient vectors in $\mathcal{L}_{i+1}$ from those in $\mathcal{L}_i$.

In the sieving method, $\mathcal{L}_{i+1}$ is constructed in two ways:

- For each $e \in \mathcal{L}_i$, if $e(H^T)_{[i]} \in \{s_{[i]}, 0_i\}$, then $e(H^T)_{[i+1]} \in \{s_{[i+1]}, 0_{i+1}\}$ can be considered to hold with a probability of $1/2$ because an additional condition based on one equation over $\mathbb{F}_2$ is imposed on e. In this case, e is added to $\mathcal{L}_{i+1}$.
- For each combination of two vectors $u, v \in \mathcal{L}_i$ satisfying $\text{wt}_H(u+v) = 2p$, if $(u+v)(H^T)_{[i]} \in \{s_{[i]}, 0_i\}$, then $(u+v)(H^T)_{[i+1]} \in \{s_{[i+1]}, 0_{i+1}\}$ can be considered to hold with a probability of $1/2$. In this case, $u+v$ is added to $\mathcal{L}_{i+1}$.

In these two ways, $\mathcal{L}_{i+1}$ can be constructed from $\mathcal{L}_i$. By randomly selecting several vectors from $\mathcal{S}_{2p}^{k+\ell}$ and denoting them as $\mathcal{L}_0$, repeating the operations described above allows us to construct $\mathcal{L}_\ell$ from $\mathcal{L}_0$, thereby solving the SDP with a smaller Hamming weight.

In the original paper [11], the algorithm for constructing $\mathcal{L}_\ell$, which is a list containing some $e \in \mathbb{F}_2^{k+\ell}$ satisfying $eH'^T = s$, is called Sieve_Syndrome_Dec (Algorithm 4). Also, the entire algorithm that transforms the original SDP into a SDP with smaller Hamming weight and solves it using Sieve_Syndrome_Dec is called Full_ISD (Algorithm 3).

To implement Merge_Set, Guo, Johannson, and Nguyen [11] used a function named Find_Collision that enumerates the combinations of vectors $v, u \in \mathcal{L}$ such that $v + u \in \mathcal{S}_{2p}^{k+\ell}$.

4.2 Parameter Selection

Following, we explain the constraints on the parameters M, ℓ, and z. The size M of $\mathcal{L}_0$ is chosen such that when constructing $\mathcal{L}_i$ from $\mathcal{L}_{i-1}$, $|\mathcal{L}_{i-1}| \approx |\mathcal{L}_i|$. Among the vectors contained in $\mathcal{L}_{i-1}$, we can assume that half of them satisfy $eH_{[i]}^T \in \{0, s_{[i]}\}$. Therefore, it is sufficient if $\left|\{v + u \mid v, u \in \mathcal{L}_{i-1}, v + u \in \mathcal{S}_{2p}^{k+\ell}\}\right| \approx M/2$. Let q be the probability that the sum of the two randomly chosen vectors from $\mathcal{L}_{i-1}$ has a Hamming weight of $2p$. Assuming that the vectors in $\mathcal{L}_{i-1}$ are independently and uniformly distributed, we have:

$$q = \binom{2p}{p}\binom{k+\ell-2p}{p}\binom{k+\ell}{2p}^{-1}$$

Furthermore, the number of pairs of vectors contained in $\mathcal{L}_{i-1}$ is approximately $M^2/2$. However, the vectors in $\mathcal{L}_{i-1}$ are not independent, which may result in overlapping sum vectors. To evaluate this overlapping on the formula, let δ be the probability of obtaining a new vector, then $\dfrac{\delta \cdot M^2 \cdot q}{2 \cdot 2} \approx \dfrac{M}{2}$, where the left-hand side is the number of elements of $\mathcal{L}_i$ obtained from the sum of the two vectors in $\mathcal{L}_{i-1}$. Thus, we have

$$M \approx \frac{2}{\delta \cdot q}. \tag{4}$$

Algorithm 3: Full_ISD

Input: $H \in \mathbb{F}_2^{(n-k)\times n}$, $s \in \mathbb{F}_2^{n-k}$, $t \in \mathbb{N}$, parameters $\ell, p \in \mathbb{N}$
Output: Vector $e \in \mathcal{S}_t^n$ s.t. $eH^T = s$

1 **while** true **do**
2   Take a random $P \in \mathcal{P}_n$;
3   Calculate $U \in \mathrm{GL}_{n-k}(\mathbb{F}_2), H', H''$ s.t. $UHP = \begin{pmatrix} H' & O \\ H'' & I_{n-k-\ell} \end{pmatrix}$;
4     $(s_1\ s_2) \leftarrow sU^T$ ($s_1 \in \mathbb{F}_2^\ell$, $s_2 \in \mathbb{F}_2^{n-k-\ell}$);
5     $\mathcal{L} \leftarrow$ Sieve_Syndrome_Dec($H', s_1, 2p$);
6   **for** $e_1 \in \mathcal{L}$ **do**
7   **if** $\mathrm{wt}_H(e_1 H''^T + s_2) = t - 2p$ **then**
8   **return** $(e_1\ e_1 H''^T + s_2)P^{-1}$;
9   **end if**
10   **end for**
11 **end while**

Algorithm 4: Sieve_Syndrome_Dec

Input: $H \in \mathbb{F}_2^{\ell \times (k+\ell)}$, $s \in \mathbb{F}_2^\ell$, $2p \in \mathbb{N}$, $M \in \mathbb{N}$
Output: $\mathcal{L} \subset \{e \mid e \in \mathcal{S}_{2p}^{k+\ell}, eH^T = s\}$

1 Make a list $\mathcal{L}_0 \subset \mathcal{S}_{2p}^{k+\ell}$ such that $|\mathcal{L}_0| = M$;
2 **for** $i = 1, \ldots, \ell$ **do**
3     $\mathcal{L}_i \leftarrow \{e \in \mathcal{L}_{i-1} \mid e(H^T)_{[i]} \in \{s_{[i]}, 0_i\}\}$;
4     $\mathcal{L}_i \leftarrow \mathcal{L}_i \cup$ Merge_Set($\mathcal{L}_{i-1}$);
5 **end for**
6 **return** $\{e \in \mathcal{L}_\ell \mid e(H^T)_{[\ell]} = s_{[\ell]}\}$;

Algorithm 5: Merge_Set

Input: $H \in \mathbb{F}_2^{(k+\ell) \times \ell}$, $s \in \mathbb{F}_2^\ell$, $i \in \mathbb{N}$,
       $\mathcal{L} \subset \{e \in \mathbb{F}_2^n \mid e(H^T)_{[i-1]} \in \{s_{[i-1]}, 0_{i-1}\}\}$, $p', p'' \in \mathbb{N}$
Output: $\{x + y \mid x, y \in \mathcal{L}, \mathrm{wt}_H(x+y) = 2p, (x+y)(H^T)_{[i]} \in \{s_{[i]}, 0_i\}\}$

1 $\mathcal{M} \leftarrow \varnothing$;
2 **for** $v \in$ Find_Collision$(\mathcal{L}, p, p', p'')$ **do**
3   **if** $v(H^T)_{[i]} \in \{s_{[i]}, 0\}$ **then**
4        $\mathcal{M} \leftarrow \mathcal{M} \cup \{v\}$;
5   **end if**
6 **end for**
7 **return** $\mathcal{M}$;

Here, let N be the set of e satisfying $eH^T = s$. Since N is the set of vectors satisfying ℓ equations out of $k + \ell$, we can estimate:

$$|N| \approx \binom{k+\ell}{2p} 2^{-\ell}.$$

Since $\mathcal{L}_\ell$ is a set of vectors satisfying $eH \in \{0, s\}$, the number of vectors satisfying $eH = s$ can be considered to be $M/2$. Additionally, it is desirable for $\mathcal{L}_\ell$ to contain almost all vectors in N. Therefore, the condition is $\dfrac{M}{2} \geq \binom{k+\ell}{2p} 2^{-\ell}$, which implies

$$M \geq \binom{k+\ell}{2p} 2^{-(\ell-1)}. \tag{5}$$

Based on Eqs. (4) and (5), M and ℓ can be determined. In particular, M is the size of the list used in the sieving method, representing the space complexity of the sieving method.

4.3 Complexity

Guo, Johansson, Nguyen [11] also calculated the time complexity of the entire algorithm as follows. The probability that $\text{wt}_H(e_1) = 2p$ holds for a single $P \in \mathcal{P}_n$ is given by:

$$\text{Pr}_{\text{success}} := \binom{k+\ell}{2p} \binom{n-k-\ell}{t-2p} \binom{n}{t}^{-1}$$

After selecting P, the following three calculations are performed: (i) We try to find U such that UHP for given H and P. (ii) Syndrome_Dec is performed to create a list of candidate solutions. (iii) Checks for the existence of a solution to the list by calculating, for all vectors in the list, whether each satisfies the conditions for a solution. The time complexity of (i), (ii), (iii) is denoted by C_{Gauss}, $C_{\text{Syndrome\_Dec}}$, $C_{\text{solution\_check}}$, respectively. Given that the expected value of the number of iterations is $1/\text{Pr}_{\text{success}}$, the following proposition holds.

Proposition 1 *The time complexity of Full_ISD (Algorithm 3) is given by* $\dfrac{1}{\text{Pr}_{\text{success}}}(C_{\text{Gauss}} + C_{\text{Syndrome\_Dec}} + C_{\text{solution\_check}}).$

According to the original paper [11], $C_{\text{Syndrome\_Dec}}$ is estimated using the following preposition with parameter $p', p'' \in \mathbb{N}$ which satisfy $p' + p'' = p$ (6).

Proposition 2 *We have*

$$C_{\text{Syndrome\_Dec}} = \ell \cdot M \cdot \left(2p + \binom{2p}{p} c_{\text{label}} + \binom{2p - p''}{p'} + 4(p + \log M)\right). \tag{6}$$

Here, the first term in the parentheses is the time complexity for Step 3 of Algorithm 4, the second and third terms are the time complexity of Find_Collision, and the fourth term is the time complexity for checking for duplicates of the obtained vectors.

Next, $C_{\text{solution\_check}}$ is estimated as follows. The time complexity for computing $\text{wt}_H(s_2 - v(H'')^T)$ is $2p(n-k-\ell)$. Additionally, there exist $\binom{k+\ell}{2p} 2^{-\ell}$ vectors e_1 satisfying $e_1 H'^T = s_1$. Hence, we obtain the following proposition.

Proposition 3 *We have* $C_{\text{solution\_check}} = 2p(n-k-\ell) \binom{k+\ell}{2p} 2^{-\ell}.$

5 Proposed Method

The proposed method combines the advantages of both Stern's algorithm and the sieving method, noting that both methods solve the SDP by transforming it into one for smaller Hamming weights. This section introduces the proposed method, which integrates the zero window into the sieving method. Furthermore, we explain the algorithm while comparing it with the sieving method and conduct computational complexity evaluation.

5.1 Observation

In Stern's algorithm and the sieving method, the expressions after partitioning the matrix (Eq. (2), (3)) have the same form. Therefore, the partitioning used in Stern's ISD can be applied to the sieving method. In this study, we propose introducing zero window Stern used into the partitioning of $\boldsymbol{H}$ and $\boldsymbol{e}$ used in the sieving method, as shown in Fig. 1. This reduces the number of vectors held in the list and thus reduces the space complexity. In particular, in memory-constrained environments, it is possible to reduce the time complexity compared to the original sieving method while utilizing the same amount of memory.

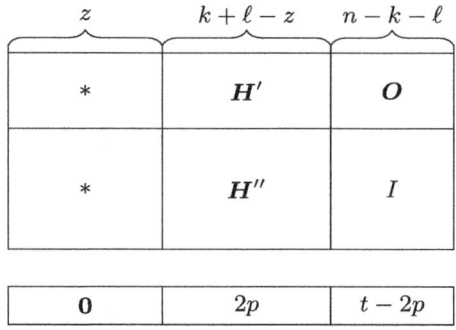

Fig. 1. Introducing zero window

5.2 Algorithm

The algorithm of the proposed method is outlined below. The main difference from the algorithm of the sieving method, as explained in Sect. 4, lies in the introduction of the zero window during the partitioning of the matrix in Step 2.

1. Choose a matrix $\boldsymbol{P} \in \mathcal{P}_n$ randomly.
2. Calculate $\boldsymbol{U} \in \mathrm{GL}_{n-k}(\mathbb{F}_2), \boldsymbol{H}' \in \mathbb{F}_2^{\ell \times (k+\ell-z)}, \boldsymbol{H}'' \in \mathbb{F}_2^{(n-k-\ell) \times (k+\ell-z)}$ such that $\boldsymbol{UHP} = \begin{pmatrix} * & \boldsymbol{H}' & \boldsymbol{O} \\ * & \boldsymbol{H}'' & \boldsymbol{I}_{n-k-\ell} \end{pmatrix}$.
3. Let $(\boldsymbol{s}_1\ \boldsymbol{s}_2) \leftarrow \boldsymbol{s}\boldsymbol{U}^T$ ($\boldsymbol{s}_1 \in \mathbb{F}_2^{\ell}, \boldsymbol{s}_2 \in \mathbb{F}_2^{n-k-\ell}$).

4. Set $\mathcal{L} \leftarrow$ Sieve_Syndrome_Dec($\boldsymbol{H}', \boldsymbol{s}_1, 2p$).
5. For each $\boldsymbol{e}_1 \in \mathcal{L}$, if $\text{wt}_H(\boldsymbol{e}_1 \boldsymbol{H}''^T + \boldsymbol{s}_2) = t - 2p$, output
   $(\boldsymbol{0}_\ell\ \boldsymbol{e}_1\ \boldsymbol{e}_1 \boldsymbol{H}''^T + \boldsymbol{s}_2) \boldsymbol{P}^{-1}$.
6. If no solution is found, return to Step 1.

Here is a detailed explanation of each step of the overview: First, in Step 1, begin by selecting the n-th permutation matrix P randomly, similar to the sieving method. Next, in Step 2, using Gaussian elimination, find $\boldsymbol{U} \in \text{GL}_{n-k}(\mathbb{F}_2)$, $\boldsymbol{H}' \in \mathbb{F}_2^{\ell \times (k+\ell-z)}$, $\boldsymbol{H}'' \in \mathbb{F}_2^{(n-k-\ell) \times (k+\ell-z)}$ such that $\boldsymbol{UHP} = \begin{pmatrix} * & \boldsymbol{H}' & \boldsymbol{O} \\ * & \boldsymbol{H}'' & \boldsymbol{I}_{n-k-\ell} \end{pmatrix}$. In Step 3, apply the same elimination performed on $\boldsymbol{H}$ to $\boldsymbol{s}$. In Step 4, using Sieve_Syndrome_Dec, obtain a list $\mathcal{L}$ of $\boldsymbol{e}_1 \in \mathbb{F}_2^\ell$ such that $\boldsymbol{e}_1 \boldsymbol{H}'^T = \boldsymbol{s}_1$ and $\text{wt}_H(\boldsymbol{e}_1) = t$. Finally, in Step 5, for each element of $\mathcal{L}$, compute the corresponding $\boldsymbol{e}_2$ and check if there exists $\boldsymbol{e}$ that completes $\boldsymbol{e}$. If not, return to the beginning and repeat the calculation in Step 6.

The main difference from the sieving method relies the introduction of the zero window during matrix partitioning in Step 2, resulting in changes to the column numbers of $\boldsymbol{H}'$ and $\boldsymbol{H}''$, as well the change from $\ell + k$ to $\ell + k - z$. In particular, for $z = 0$, proposed method is consistent with original method. The subsequent flow is similar to the sieving method in Sect. 4, but the length of the vectors saved in the list in Sieve_Syndrome_Dec changes to $k + \ell - z$. Therefore, it can be expected that the space complexity of the sieving method will be significantly improved due to the reduction in list size. When represented in pseudocode, the algorithm becomes like Algorithm 6. The difference from the original sieving algorithm (Sect. 4) is that the size of J changes from $k + \ell$ to $k + \ell - z$ in the second line. Consequently, the number of columns of $\boldsymbol{H}'$ and $\boldsymbol{H}''$ changes to $k + \ell - z$. Also, in the sixth line of Sieve_Syndrome_Dec, the length of vectors saved in the list changes from $k + \ell$ to $k + \ell - z$.

5.3 Computational Complexity Evaluation

In this subsection, similar to the complexity estimation of the sieving method in Sect. 4, we estimate the computational complexity of the proposed method and compare it to the original sieving method.

First, we examine the change in space complexity. With the introduction of the zero window, the size of $\mathcal{L}_0$ in Algorithm 6 is estimated by

$$M = \frac{2}{\delta q} = \frac{2}{\delta} \binom{k + \ell - z}{2p} \binom{2p}{p}^{-1} \binom{k + \ell - 2p - z}{p}^{-1}, \tag{7}$$

where q is the probability that the sum of the two randomly chosen vectors from $\mathcal{L}_{i-1}$ in Algorithm 6 is of Hamming weight $2p$. As demonstrated in Sect. 6, when $z > 0$, the proposed method's space complexity derived here is smaller than that of the original sieving method.

Next, we consider the change in time complexity from Proposition 1.

In the proposed method, the function Sieve_Syndrome_Dec is executed similarly, so the above equation also holds true for the proposed method. However,

---
Algorithm 6: Full_ISD with zero window

Input : $H \in \mathbb{F}_2^{(n-k) \times n}$, $s \in \mathbb{F}_2^{n-k}$, $t \in \mathbb{N}$, parameters $\ell, p, z \in \mathbb{N}$
Output: Vector $e \in \mathbb{F}_2^n$ such that $\text{wt}_H(e) = t$, $eH^T = s$

1 **while** true **do**
2   Take a random $P \in \mathcal{P}_n$;
3   Calculate $U \in \text{GL}_{n-k}(\mathbb{F}_2)$, $H' \in \mathbb{F}_2^{\ell \times (k+\ell-z)}$, $H'' \in \mathbb{F}_2^{(n-k-\ell) \times (k+\ell-z)}$ such that $UHP = \begin{pmatrix} * & H' & O \\ * & H'' & I_{n-k-\ell} \end{pmatrix}$;
4     $(s_1 \; s_2) \leftarrow sU^T$ $(s_1 \in \mathbb{F}_2^{\ell}, s_2 \in \mathbb{F}_2^{n-k-\ell})$;
5     $\mathcal{L} \leftarrow$ Sieve_Syndrome_Dec$(H', s_1, 2p)$;
6   **for** $e_1 \in \mathcal{L}$ **do**
7   **if** $\text{wt}_H(e_1 H''^T + s_2) = t - 2p$ **then**
8   **return** $(0_z \; e_1 \; e_1 H''^T + s_2) P^{-1}$;
9   **end if**
10   **end for**
11 **end while**

---

with the change in M, $C_{\text{Syndrome\_Dec}}$ varies. Additionally, the success rate of matrix partitioning $\text{Pr}_{\text{success}}$ is given by:

$$\text{Pr}_{\text{success}} = \binom{k+\ell-z}{2p}\binom{n-k-\ell}{t-2p}\binom{n}{t}^{-1}. \tag{8}$$

Furthermore, we have

$$C_{\text{solution\_check}} = 2p(n-k-\ell)\binom{k+\ell-z}{2p} \cdot 2^{-\ell}.$$

Note that C_{Gauss} is the same in both the proposed method and the original method, since the size of n, k, ℓ is fixed as input. With this, we have calculated M, $\text{Pr}_{\text{success}}$, $C_{\text{Syndrome\_Dec}}$, and $C_{\text{solution\_check}}$ in the proposed method. Let $\text{time}(\ell, p, z)$ denote the time complexity corresponding to parameters ℓ, p, and z, and $\text{space}(\ell, p, z)$ denote the space complexity. Here, $\text{space}(\ell, p, z)$ is equal to M in Eq. (7). Then, we have the following proposition:

Proposition 4 *The space and time complexity of the proposed method (Algorithm 6) are given by*

$$\text{space}(\ell, p, z) = \frac{2}{\delta}\binom{k+\ell-z}{2p}\binom{2p}{p}^{-1}\binom{k+\ell-2p-z}{p}^{-1}$$

$$\text{time}(\ell, p, z) = \frac{1}{\text{Pr}_{\text{success}}} \cdot (C_{\text{Gauss}} + C_{\text{Syndrome\_Dec}} + C_{\text{solution\_check}}).$$

6 Experiment

In this section, based on the computational complexity evaluation results from the previous section, we numerically compare the computational complexity of [11] and the proposed method.

6.1 Parameters

We conducted decryption experiments on three schemes of Classic McEliece, HQC, and BIKE. Their specific values of 128-bit secure parameters are $(n, k, t) = (3488, 2720, 64), (35338, 17669, 132), (24646, 12323, 134)$, respectively [4,11].

Following Guo-Johansson-Nguyen [11], we set $c_{\text{label}} = 2$ and $\delta = 2/3$. We set $p' = 0$ in Eq. 6 as $C_{\text{Syndrome\_Dec}}$ is minimized when $p' = 0$ in the model evaluating space complexity as M.

6.2 Experimental Results

First, we present the results of experiments on Classic McEliece in the top plots of Figs. 2 and 3. For the computational complexity of the original sieving method [11], we plot space(ℓ, p, z) and time(ℓ, p, z) while varying ℓ, p, and z within the ranges $0 \leq \ell \leq n - k$, $0 \leq p \leq \lfloor t/2 \rfloor$, and $z = 0$. For the computational complexity evaluation of the proposed method, we plot space(ℓ, p, z) and time(ℓ, p, z) while varying ℓ, p, and z within the ranges $0 \leq \ell \leq n - k$, $0 \leq p \leq \lfloor t/2 \rfloor$, and $0 \leq z \leq k + \ell - 3p$, respectively. Points plotted in this manner are shown in Fig. 2.

Furthermore, based on these results, we plot the minimum achievable time complexity at a fixed space complexity. The results are shown in Fig. 3. Note that for the computation of C_{Gauss}, we use the Method of Four Russians. According to Bard [5], when the number of rows is greater than the number of columns, the time complexity for Gaussian elimination of a matrix with a rows and b columns ($a > b$) is $O\left(\frac{18ab^2 - 8b^3}{4 \log b}\right)$. The Gaussian elimination used in this method is performed up to the $(n-k-\ell)$-th row instead of the $(n-k)$-th row. Substituting $a = n$ and $b = n - k$ into the equation and multiplying by $\frac{n-k-\ell}{n-k}$ to account for the early termination of computation, we obtain:

$$C_{\text{Gauss}} = \frac{(n - k - \ell)(n - k)(5n + 4k)}{2 \log(n - k)}.$$

This formula is used in the numerical experiments. Subsequently, similar experiments were conducted for BIKE (in the middle plots of Figs. 2 and 3) and HQC (in the bottom plots of Figs. 2 and 3). Since the values of n, k, and t differ from those of Classic McEliece, the ranges of parameters ℓ, p, and z also differ. Figures 2 and 3 use logarithmic scales for both the horizontal (space complexity) and vertical axis (time complexity), ranging from $[0, 52.5]$ and $[140, 180]$, respectively.

Table 1 compares the time computations of the conventional and proposed methods in tabular form for several memory quantities.

Table 1. Comparison of time complexity between original and proposed method (Classic McEliece: $(n, k, t) = (3488, 2720, 64)$, BIKE: $(n, k, t) = (35338, 17669, 132)$, HQC: $(n, k, t) = (24646, 12323, 134)$)

		2^{10} vectors	2^{15} vectors	2^{20} vectors
Classic McEliece	original [11]	173.0	160.0	149.7
	proposed §5	161.5	155.0	149.7
BIKE	original [11]	174.9	162.0	162.0
	proposed §5	168.4	162.0	156.8
HQC	original [11]	174.2	161.3	161.3
	proposed §5	168.7	161.3	158.2

6.3 Discussion

In Fig. 2, the achievable computational complexity using the original sieving method is represented by black dots, while that with the proposed method is represented by red dots. The black dots are aligned along several lines, each corresponding to different values of p. Additionally, the columns of red dots extending from each black dot toward the upper left indicate that increasing z results in a decrease in space complexity and an increase in time complexity. The space complexity of the original sieving method varies significantly with the value of p, but the introduction of the zero window increased the degree of freedom, filling in the gaps. As a result, time complexity was improved by up to 10 bits.

We aim to identify the region where the introduction of the zero window improves the time complexity. For example, when $p = 2$, consider points A $(\text{space}(\ell_A, 1, 0), \text{time}(\ell_A, 1, 0))$, B $(\text{space}(\ell_B, 2, 0), \text{time}(\ell_B, 2, 0))$, and C $(\text{space}(\ell_C, 2, z_C), \text{time}(\ell_C, 2, z_C))$, where ℓ_A, ℓ_B, ℓ_C, and z_C are parameters. If the value of p is the same, smaller values of ℓ result in smaller time and space complexities. Therefore, ℓ_A, ℓ_B, and ℓ_C are the smallest ℓ values at each point that satisfy $M \geq \binom{k+\ell-z}{2p} \cdot 2^{-(\ell-1)}$. Furthermore, as the time complexities of points A and C are equal, $\text{time}(\ell_C, 2, z_C) = \text{time}(\ell_A, 1, 0)$ holds true. From Fig. 3, it can be observed that in the interval $[\text{space}(\ell_C, 2, z_C), \text{space}(\ell_B, 2, 0)]$, the introduction of the zero window improves the time complexity. Similar considerations can be made for other values of p.

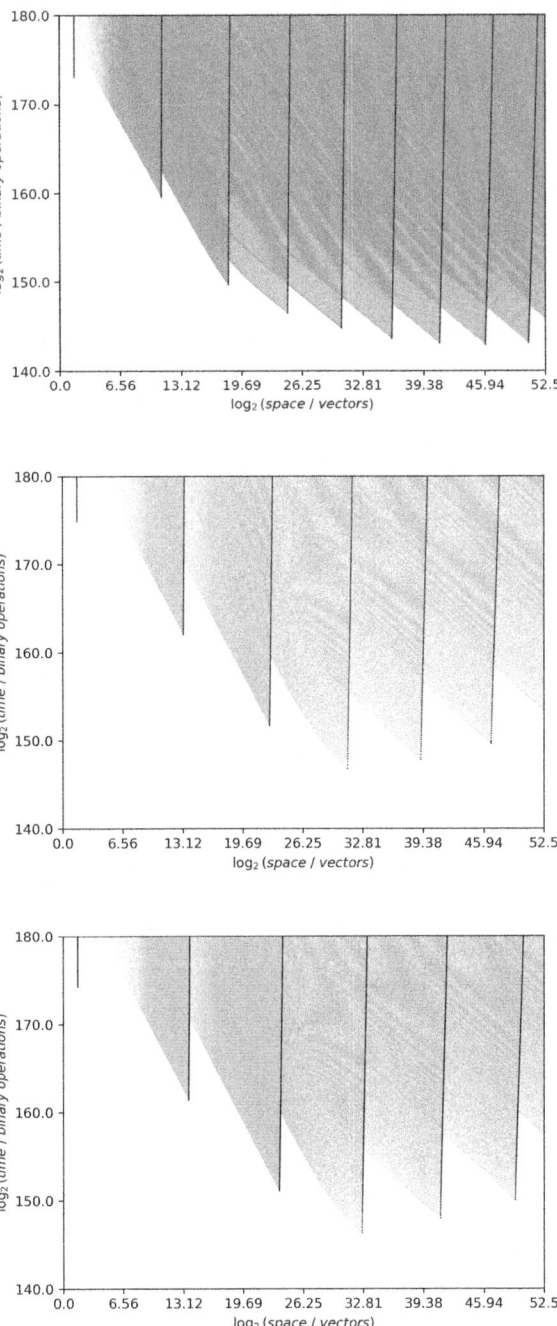

Fig. 2. Possible ranges of time (vertical axis) and space (horizontal axis) computational quantities for parameter (k, ℓ, z). (Top plot: Classic McEliece, Middle plot: BIKE, Bottom plot: HQC)

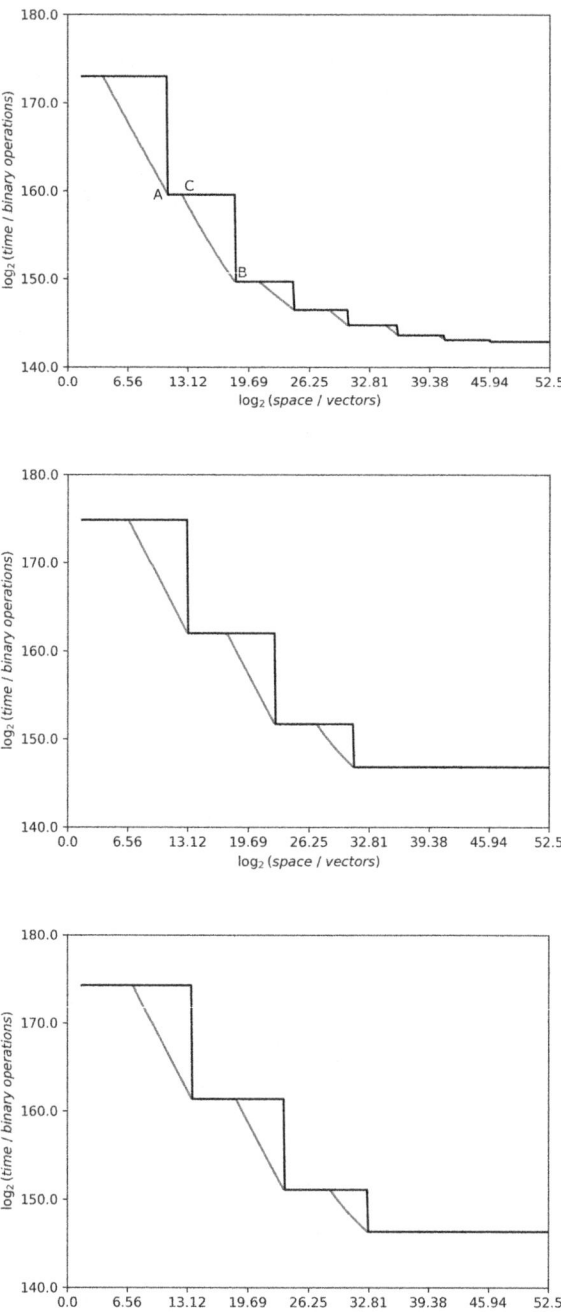

Fig. 3. Comparison of time with and without zero window (red: proposed method, black: original method) [11]) (Top plot: Classic McEliece, Middle plot: BIKE, Bottom plot: HQC) (Color figure online)

6.4 Decryption Experiment

To investigate and compare the distribution of time complexity associated with actual decoding, we implemented both the original (Algorithm 3) and proposed (Algorithm 6) methods using Python 3.10 and conducted decoding experiments. In this section, we provide an overview of the experiments and the results.

Parameters. We set the code word length n, the dimension of the linear code k, and the Hamming weight of the solution t to $(n, k, t) = (120, 60, 17)$ as the SDP parameters defined in Problem 1. In this paper, the memory size M is defined by the number of vectors to be included in the list to be used in Sieve_Sindrome_Dec (Algorithm 4), was set to $2^{7.5}$.

Experimental Settings and Results. The original method requires (ℓ, p) and the proposed method requires (ℓ, p, z) as parameters. We used the algorithm parameters that minimize the expected time complexity for (n, k, t) set above. For the original method, the parameter (ℓ, p) that minimizes the time complexity was determined to be $(\ell, p) = (7, 1)$ by estimating the parameter using the Proposition 1. The parameters (ℓ, p, z) that minimize the time complexity for the proposed method were also determined using Proposition 4, and $(\ell, p, z) = (13, 2, 9)$ was obtained.

Under this setup, we randomly generated SDP instances H and s and performed experiments. The problem instances were generated using the code from the code-based challenges (https://decodingchallenge.org/). The experiment was conducted 1000 times. We plotted the relationship between the number of iterations of the main loop of Algorithm 3, 6 and the time required, shown in Fig. 4. We also illustrated the distribution of actual time required in Fig. 5.

Discussion. For both the original (Algorithm 3) and the proposed (Algorithm 6) methods, Fig. 4 shows the results of plotting the relationship between the number of iterations of the main loop (Step 1 of Algorithm 3, 6) and the time required. As can be seen from Fig. 4, the dots representing both the original and the proposed methods appear to lie on a straight line passing through the origin. These points on the same line maintain a consistent ratio between the time taken and the number of iterations, i.e., the number of loops in the Step 1 of Algorithm 3 and 6. This alignment suggests that the time required per iteration remains constant across the experiments. Comparing the gradient of the straight lines, it can be seen that the time required per iteration is longer for the proposed method. This is because we used a larger parameter p for the experiment of the proposed method. Consequently, this increases the computational complexity of the Merge_Set operation (Step 4 of Algorithm 4), leading to a larger $C_{\text{Syndrome\_dec}}$ as defined in Eq. (6).

We also illustrate the distribution of actual time required in Fig. 5. It can be seen that both the original and proposed methods appear to follow a distribution similar to the geometric distribution. In the sieving method, the computation

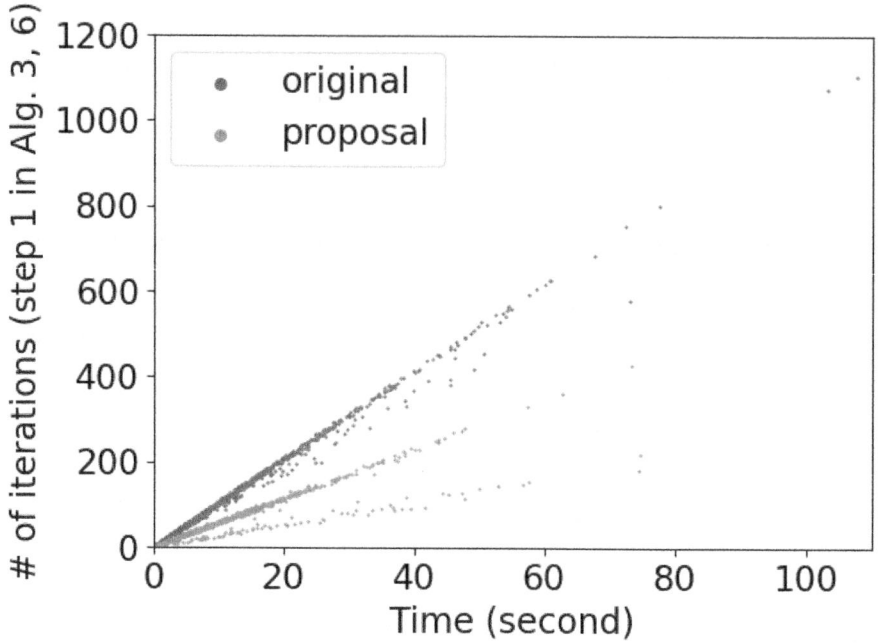

Fig. 4. Relationship between time and the number of iterations in Step 1 of Algorithms 3 and 6 with $(n, k, t = 120, 60, 17)$.

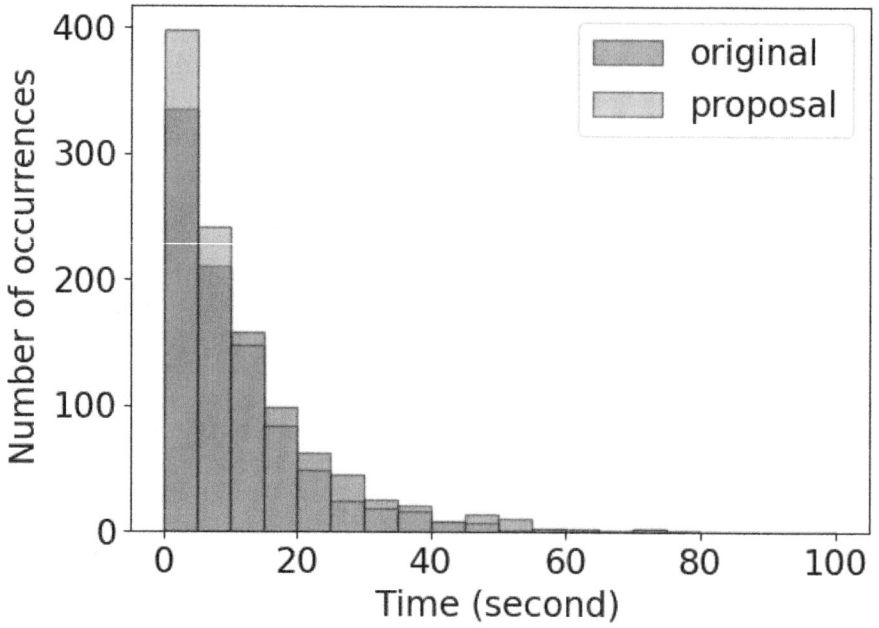

Fig. 5. Time distribution for Algorithms 3 and 6 with $(n, k, t = 120, 60, 17)$.

in Step 2 of Algorithm 3 and 6 is repeated by randomly choosing the permutation matrix $\boldsymbol{P}$. Consequently, the distribution of the number of iterations is considered to follow a geometric distribution. Specifically, the probability that the number of iterations is i is $\Pr_{\text{success}}(1-\Pr_{\text{success}})^{i-1}$, so as mentioned in Subsect. 4.3, the expected number of iterations is $1/\Pr_{\text{success}}$. Figure 5 also shows that the proposed method solves the SDP in less time. With the introduction of the zero window, the spatial computational complexity M given by Eq. (7) decreases, allowing for a larger p selection. This larger p value increases $\Pr_{\text{success}}$ as given in Eq. (8) leading to fewer iterations required for solving the SDP.

7 Conclusion

In this paper, we studied the difficulty of the sieving method for solving the SDP used in code-based cryptography. Specifically, we introduced an algorithm aimed at enhancing the efficiency of the sieving method by incorporating the zero window approach used in Stern's ISD. We provided several formulas to estimate the time and space complexity of our method and compared them to those of the sieving method. Additionally, we conducted numerical comparisons to demonstrate that our proposed method can achieve up to a 10-bit reduction in time complexity, particularly in memory-constrained environments, compared to original methods with similar memory usage. Furthermore, we implemented our proposed sieving method and observed that, under fixed parameters, the time required to solve the SDP was faster and exhibited a similar geometric distribution as the original method.

Future challenges include further accelerating the sieving method. For example, exploring partitioning methods for the parity-check matrix and error vector other than those used in this study, and introducing the LSH/F method [10], known to accelerate the sieving method, are some of the tasks. Another future task is to conduct experiments in a larger memory environment than what was done in this study. Furthermore, a comparison of time complexity with other ISD methods in a memory-constrained environment is also an issue to be addressed in the future.

Acknowledgements. This work was supported by JST CREST Grant Number JPMJCR2113 and JSPS KAKENHI 24K20771, Japan.

References

1. Alagic, G., et al.: Status report on the third round of the NIST post-quantum cryptography standardization process. US Department of Commerce, NIST (2022)
2. Alekhnovich, M.: More on average case vs approximation complexity. In: 2003 Proceedings of the 44th Annual IEEE Symposium on Foundations of Computer Science, pp. 298–307 (2003). https://doi.org/10.1109/SFCS.2003.1238204
3. Aragon, N., et al.: BIKE: bit flipping key encapsulation (2022)
4. Aragon, N., et al.: Round 3 submission

5. Bard, G.V.: Accelerating cryptanalysis with the method of four Russians. Cryptology ePrint Archive (2006)
6. Becker, A., Joux, A., May, A., Meurer, A.: Decoding random binary linear codes in $2^{n/20}$: how 1+1=0 improves information set decoding. In: Pointcheval, D., Johansson, T. (eds.) EUROCRYPT 2012. LNCS, vol. 7237, pp. 520–536. Springer, Heidelberg (2012). https://doi.org/10.1007/978-3-642-29011-4_31
7. Berlekamp, E., McEliece, R., Van Tilborg, H.: On the inherent intractability of certain coding problems (corresp.). IEEE Trans. Inf. Theory **24**(3), 384–386 (1978)
8. Both, L., May, A.: Optimizing BJMM with nearest neighbors: full decoding in 22/21n and McEliece security. In: WCC Workshop on Coding and Cryptography, vol. 214 (2017)
9. Chou, T., et al.: Classic McEliece: conservative code-based cryptography, 10 October 2020 (2020)
10. Ducas, L., Esser, A., Etinski, S., Kirshanova, E.: Asymptotics and improvements of sieving for codes. Cryptology ePrint Archive (2023)
11. Guo, Q., Johansson, T., Nguyen, V.: A new sieving-style information-set decoding algorithm. Cryptology ePrint Archive (2023)
12. May, A., Meurer, A., Thomae, E.: Decoding random linear codes in $\tilde{\mathcal{O}}(2^{0.054n})$. In: Lee, D.H., Wang, X. (eds.) ASIACRYPT 2011. LNCS, vol. 7073, pp. 107–124. Springer, Heidelberg (2011). https://doi.org/10.1007/978-3-642-25385-0_6
13. McEliece, R.J.: A public-key cryptosystem based on algebraic. Coding Thv **4244**, 114–116 (1978)
14. Melchor, C.A., et al.: Hamming quasi-cyclic (HQC). NIST PQC Round **2**(4), 13 (2018)
15. Niederreiter, H.: Knapsack-type cryptosystems and algebraic coding theory. Prob. Contr. Inform. Theory **15**(2), 157–166 (1986)
16. Prange, E.: The use of information sets in decoding cyclic codes. IRE Trans. Inf. Theory **8**(5), 5–9 (1962)
17. Stern, J.: A method for finding codewords of small weight. In: Cohen, G., Wolfmann, J. (eds.) Coding Theory 1988. LNCS, vol. 388, pp. 106–113. Springer, Heidelberg (1989). https://doi.org/10.1007/BFb0019850
18. Weger, V., Gassner, N., Rosenthal, J.: A survey on code-based cryptography. arXiv preprint arXiv:2201.07119 (2022)

Vulnerability

Race Condition Vulnerabilities in WordPress Plug-ins

Rin Miyachi[✉][iD], Konan Nagashima, and Taiichi Saito

Tokyo Denki University, Senju Asahicho, Adachiku 120-8551, Japan
`24kmc23@ms.dendai.ac.jp`

Abstract. WordPress is the world's most popular content management system, developed as an open-source software with many plugins. However, since these plugins are developed and released by anyone, they may have security problems. Web applications need to be designed and developed in consideration of possible race conditions that may occur when multiple processes access shared resources at the same time, but race conditions aren't paid much attention by developers and may result in vulnerability. This vulnerability is known to cause problems such as unauthorized data access, database inconsistency, and file content corruption by an attacker who intentionally creates a race condition. It is also considered that this vulnerability is not as well-known as XSS and SQLi. In this paper, we investigate the race condition vulnerabilities in WordPress plugins. Based on the results of this survey, we discuss the trends and causes of these vulnerabilities, as well as countermeasures for them.

Keywords: Race Condition · TOCTOU · WordPress · Web Security

1 Introduction

WordPress is the most popular content management system in the world [1]. It uses PHP and MySQL and was developed as an open-source software. WordPress.org provide many themes and plugins to change the exterior and add some functionality to the website. The extensibility and flexibility of these themes and plugins are a feature of WordPress. However, plug-ins can be developed by anyone, and sometimes have security problems.

In 2022 and 2023 years, race condition vulnerabilities were ranked in the CWE Top 25 Most Dangerous Software Weaknesses, an annual ranking of dangerous vulnerabilities published by MITRE [2, 3]. Recently, the Japan Security Operations Group (ISOG-J), a security organization, and PortSwigger, a security vendor, have published documents and learning content on how to investigate race condition vulnerabilities in web applications, and the vulnerabilities has been drawing increasing attention [4, 5].

Race condition vulnerability is a problem in which multiple processes access the same resource, causing unexpected processing. This vulnerability causes problems such as unauthorized data access, database inconsistencies, and file corruption.

© The Author(s), under exclusive license to Springer Nature Singapore Pte Ltd. 2024
K. Minematsu and M. Mimura (Eds.): IWSEC 2024, LNCS 14977, pp. 179–194, 2024.
https://doi.org/10.1007/978-981-97-7737-2_10

There is a type of race condition vulnerability called TOCTOU (Time-Of-Use Time-Of-Check). TOCTOU is a problem in which unexpected processing is caused by the difference between the state of data at the time of validation and at the time of use. It is attracting increasing attention, with the release of OWASP's TimeGap Theory about TOCTOU [6].

The vulnerabilities caused by these race conditions are difficult to investigate due to the nature of the business logic, and the actual situation is not yet clear. It is considered that when compared to well-known vulnerabilities in web applications such as XSS (Cross-Site-Scripting) and SQLi (SQL injection), race condition vulnerabilities have not been widely acknowledged by developers and have not received sufficient attention. The same can be said for WordPress plug-ins. Based on this, we conduct a survey on race condition vulnerabilities in WordPress plug-ins. To the best of our knowledge, this is the first survey on race condition vulnerabilities in WordPress plug-ins. In this paper, we report the survey results and describe the results of our analysis. We also discuss the causes of the vulnerabilities and countermeasures against them based on the trends of the vulnerabilities revealed by the analysis.

2 Race Condition Vulnerabilities

Race condition vulnerabilities result from situations in which multiple independent processes or threads can simultaneously access a shared resource and modify its state to produce inappropriate results. An example of a race condition vulnerability is CVE-2016-7098. This is a race condition vulnerability in `wget` that allows other processes to access files downloaded by `wget` while `wget` is making an HTTP connection, bypassing access list restrictions. In this vulnerability, independent processes include the process executing `wget` and other processes, shared resources include those downloaded by `wget`, and state changes include references to files that should not be accessible. As described above, since race condition vulnerabilities are deeply related to the logic of the program, it is difficult to conduct an exhaustive investigation and detect them [7, 8]. Besides, compared to other well-known vulnerabilities such as XSS and SQLi, race condition vulnerabilities are not well known to developers, and it is considered that sufficient countermeasures against race condition vulnerabilities have not been widely adopted.

This vulnerability is classified as "Concurrent Execution using Shared Resource with Improper Synchronization ('Race Condition')" (CWE-362) in the CWE classification published by MITRE [9].

2.1 Race Conditions in Web Applications

Race Condition vulnerabilities are also known to occur in web applications. Often web applications are conceived as a set of scripts that query and update an underlying database. However, even though multi-process execution is common in web applications, developers often design and develop without considering this. It is also often ignored that the DBMS (Data Base Management System) that manages data on the server is a shared resource that can be accessed by multiple script instances simultaneously [10]. Based on these facts, an attacker can induce a race condition by sending multiple simultaneous requests to access the shared resource.

In web applications, there is a case in which an unauthorized use of a coupon exceeded its limit as an event caused by a race condition vulnerability [11]. There are also other cases of over-booking due to the concentration of reservations on accommodation sites [12].

2.2 TOCTOU

TOCTOU (Time-Of-Check Time-Of-Use) is a specific kind of race condition vulnerability described above, in which unexpected processing is caused by the difference between the data state at the time of validation and the time of use. The TOCTOU vulnerability is a specific type of race condition vulnerability with more restrictive conditions. This vulnerability is classified as "Time-of-check Time-of-use (TOCTOU) Race condition" (CWE-367) in the CWE classification published by MITER [13].

As the name suggests, this is a vulnerability that causes problems due to the difference between the state at the time of check and the state at the time of use, and it is known that it tends to be introduced in the following types of processes –

- Processing related to remittance
- Processing related to coupons
- rocesses related to login
- Processes related to reservations

All of the race condition vulnerabilities mentioned in this paper belong to TOCTOU.

In this section, we give an overview of TOCTOU using the case of hotel reservations as an example. Figure 1a shows the process flow in the case of a normal system, and Fig. 1b shows the process flow in the case of TOCTOU. As a precondition, assume that only one hotel room is left to be reserved. Normally, a user makes a hotel reservation through a reservation site. If the room is available and can be reserved, the reservation is made. On the other hand, when TOCTOU exists, the flow is as shown in Fig. 1b. As a condition for the problem to occur, consider the case where multiple users make hotel reservations at almost the same time. User A and user B send their reservation requests almost simultaneously. As the next process, the server checks whether the reservation is available or not, but since the process takes place in a short period of time, both users satisfy the condition that the reservation is available. Then, user A and user B make their reservations. However, since both users satisfy the availability conditions in the last availability check, the reservations are made in duplicate.

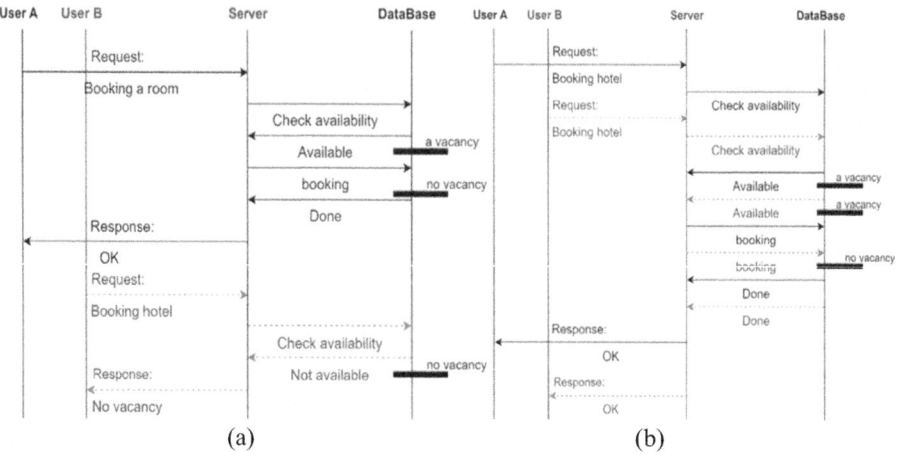

Fig. 1. Processing of a hotel booking system. (a) The process as expected by the developer. (b) The behavior in the presence of insufficient synchronization. There is a possibility of duplicate reservations that are not intended by the developer.

3 Survey on Race Condition Vulnerabilities in WordPress Plug-ins

3.1 Target WordPress Plug-ins

In this section, we describe the survey targets. Plug-ins that satisfy the following conditions were selected for this study. First, the plug-ins must be downloadable from the official WordPress page. Second, the number of active installations must be more than 10,000, because the plug-ins are still maintained, and we consider the impact if vulnerabilities are found. Third, the functionality is available free of charge. Fourth, the plug-ins should provide limiting functions, such as a limit on the number of attempts. Based on these conditions, we searched for plug-ins by using keywords such as "login", "shopping" and "eCommerce" on the official WordPress page and conducted a survey of the applicable plug-ins.

In this paper, we surveyed 76 plug-ins and categorized them according to their functionality. Plug-ins with few similar functions are placed in the "others" category. The following six categories were used.

- Login plug-ins
- Reservation plug-ins
- Voting/Rating plug-ins
- eCommerce plug-ins
- Membership plug-ins
- Others

3.2 Survey Method

In this survey, in order to investigate whether vulnerabilities actually exist and whether they can have adverse effects, we install the target plug-ins in our hosted WordPress and test them before analyzing the code. The application's behavior is then checked to determine whether a vulnerability exists. Since race condition vulnerabilities in web applications require sending requests coordinated in milliseconds and sending multiple HTTP requests in a single HTTP pipeline, we use tools specialized for diagnosis to investigate [14]. As tools for conducting the investigation, we used the web proxy *Burp Suite Community Edition* and its extension *Turbo Intruder*. *Turbo Intruder* is a tool developed to investigate race condition vulnerabilities [15]. By writing a dedicated script in Python, Turbo Intruder provides the functions necessary to investigate race condition vulnerabilities that send multiple requests in a short period of time.

We used docker to host WordPress to build the investigation environment. The software versions used are WordPress 6.4.1, PHP 8.0, and MySQL 8.0.

In our survey, to identify vulnerabilities, we analyzed the differences between successful responses to normal requests and responses to requests that failed due to exceeding the limit. In the case that when a site receives duplicate requests, it normally returns a response with a status of 200 for one request and responses in the 400s for the other requests. Also in this case, if multiple requests are sent to this site in a short time period, one might observe that two or more responses with a status of 200 are returned. This means that two or more requests were successfully completed, indicating the presence of the vulnerability. In the other case that the length of the response varies depending on the success or failure of the request, this characteristic may be used to identify the vulnerability. Furthermore, when the presence or absence of a vulnerability cannot be determined from the response alone, one can directly check the database to see if any values have been exceeded due to duplicate requests.

An overview of the investigation is shown in Fig. 2.

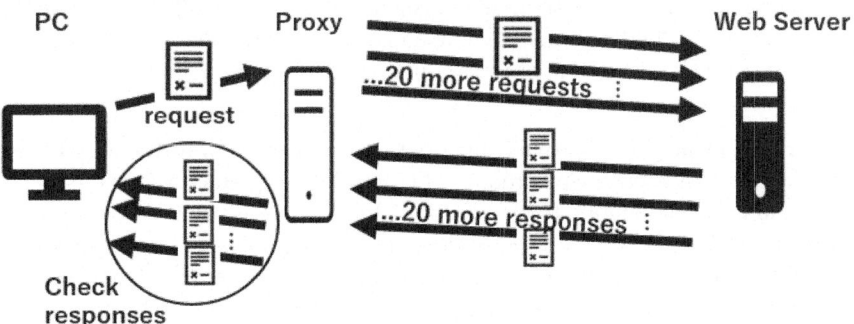

Fig. 2. Survey Overview

3.3 Analysis Results

We present the results of this survey. As mentioned above, the plug-ins that were found to be vulnerable are categorized according to their functions.

Login Plug-ins. They provide functions to prohibit access to the login page after a certain number of failed login attempts in order to prevent login attacks. Of the 17 plug-ins surveyed in this category, 10 were found to be vulnerable. Due to a race condition vulnerability in the login plug-in, if multiple login attempt requests are sent once, the plug-in fails to count the number of attempts and multiple requests are counted as one attempt. We have confirmed that multiple login attempts are possible in this survey. As for the impact, it is considered that the attacker may gain an advantage by disabling or relaxing some restrictions on login attempts, which may lead to brute-force attacks.

Booking Plug-ins. They provide functions for making hotel and event bookings. Of the 16 plug-ins surveyed in this category, 6 were found to be vulnerable. The vulnerabilities were found in functions such as reservation limits and coupons that provide discounts. The race condition vulnerabilities were found to cause the reservation limit to be exceeded or the maximum number of coupons to be used to be exceeded. The impact of the race condition vulnerability is that the maximum number of reservations can be bypassed, and coupons can be used beyond the maximum number of coupons. Also, when the access to the reservation is concentrated, it may lead to unexpected behaviors such as double booking.

Voting/Rating Plug-ins. They provide functions for rating products and voting. Of the 21 plug-ins surveyed in this category, 6 were found to be vulnerable. Many of the plug-ins in this category provide a function that limits the number of votes and ratings to one per user. We have confirmed the existence of a race condition vulnerability in these functions, which allows users to vote and rate multiple times. The impact of this vulnerability is that it may lead to process tampering such as exceeding voting and rating limits.

eCommerce Plug-ins. They provide functions for building e-commerce sites, inventory management, and payment to sell products. Of the 14 plug-ins surveyed in this category, 2 were found to be vulnerable. In many cases, plug-ins in this category were not found to be vulnerable. This is because most of the plug-ins are provided as an extension of the plug-ins with sufficient countermeasures. The functions that were found to be vulnerable include inventory management and coupons that provide discounts. The race condition vulnerability causes the purchase of more products than the number of items in stock or the maximum number of coupons to be used to be exceeded. The impact of the race condition vulnerabilities is the purchase of products that exceed the number of items in stock and the unauthorized use of coupons that exceed the maximum number of coupons. In addition, the concentration of access at the time of purchase may lead to unexpected behavior, such as inconsistencies in inventory processing (Table 1).

Membership Plug-ins. They provide functions for building membership registration, subscriptions to blogs, and coupons for discounts on subscriptions. Of the 4 plug-ins surveyed in this category, 3 were found to be vulnerable. We have confirmed that the Race condition vulnerability allows the coupon usage limit to be exceeded. The impact

Table 1. Result of this survey

Category	Number of survey subjects	Number of bugs
Login	17	10
Booking	16	6
Voting/Rating	21	6
eCommerce	14	2
Membership	4	3
Others	4	2
Total	**76**	**29**

of the race condition vulnerabilities is that coupons may be used beyond the maximum number of times they can be used at the time of subscription to the membership.

Others. In this category, we mention plug-ins that could not be classified into the aforementioned categories. The race condition vulnerabilities found in plug-ins other than those in the categories mentioned above include plug-ins that issue invitation codes and plug-ins that give out points. In these plug-ins, we confirmed that the race condition vulnerabilities cause bypassing of the number of times the invitation code can be used and bypass the coupon limit.

4 Analysis on Race Condition Vulnerabilities in WordPress Plug-ins

In this section, we discuss the characteristics of the code of plug-ins in which vulnerabilities have been discovered. Through the analysis of code containing race condition vulnerabilities, we can classify them into two patterns: the case that code utilizes API functions provided by WordPress, and the case that code directly manipulates SQL statements using wpdb.

4.1 Case: Use of WordPress Functions

We discuss the case where API functions provided by WordPress are utilized. This was particularly found in login plug-ins and in the implementation of coupon functionality. These functions are paired with one that retrieves stored data and another that updates it.

We illustrate this case with an example where the get_user_meta and update_user_meta functions are used, which are particularly found in many implementations. According to the WordPress developer documentation, get_user_meta is a function to retrieve the value set in a user's meta field and update_user_meta is a function to update the value set in the user's meta field [16, 17]. Both functions are used to retrieve and update meta field values by manipulating SQL in the internal

Table 2. The functions related to retrieval and update data provided by WordPress.

Name	Function
get_user_meta	Retrieves user meta field for a user
update_user_meta	Updates user meta field based on user ID
get_option	Retrieves an option value based on an option name
update_option	Updates the value of an option that was already added
get_post_meta	Retrieves a post meta field for the given post ID
update_post_meta	Updates a post meta field based on the given post ID

process. The other functions shown in Table 2 also provide the same functionality, only the target data is different.

Figure 3 shows an example of code with a race condition vulnerability caused by the function related to retrieval and update data provided by WordPress. In this code, the value obtained by get_user_meta is stored in $val, and the executability is determined based on this value. If the value of $val is less than 1, the executable condition is satisfied, so the value is updated by update_user_meta and the number of attempts is counted. If this process is performed multiple times with a very short interval, the value stored in $val may overlap. In this situation, there are more cases than expected where multiple sessions satisfy the condition in the conditional branching process. This is caused by a time lag, called a race window, between the acquisition of the value by get_user_meta and the update of the value by update_user_meta.

Figure 5a shows the process flow when the race condition vulnerability is triggered in the code in Fig. 3. In Fig. 5a (1), multiple sessions execute get_user_meta for a short period of time to obtain values and store them in $val. At this time, the value stored in the variable is a duplicate value. Next, in (2), based on the acquired values in (1), check whether they satisfy the conditions of executability. Since the same value is stored in $val in multiple sessions, both Session A and Session B satisfy the condition of executability. Finally, in (3), the value is updated by update_user_meta. However, this function does not update the value if the value after the update is the same as the value before the update. As a result, only the first processed update_user_meta updates the value. This behavior causes problems such as incorrect counting in processes that limit the number of attempts.

One reason this pattern of vulnerability is frequently observed is the ease of using API functions provided by WordPress for creating plug-ins. Additionally, it is possible that the potential for race conditions was not adequately considered when these functions were employed.

4.2 Case: Use of SQL Statements

We discuss the case where wpdb functions are utilized to manipulate SQL. This was often found in the implementation of voting/rating plug-ins. Wpdb is an API provided by WordPress for database operations that has a function for the direct execution of SQL

```
1:   $val = get_user_meta(1,"total");
2:
3:   if($val < 1){
4:          update_user_meta(1,"total",$val+1);
5:}
```

Fig. 3. Example of a vulnerable code used the functions by WordPress

```
1:   $val = $wpdb->query("SELECT vote FROM wp_total WHERE
     id = 1");
2:
3:   if ($val < 1) {
4:      $wpdb->query("UPDATE wp_total SET vote = vote + 1
WHERE id = 1");
5:   }
```

Fig. 4. Example of a vulnerable code used wpdb.

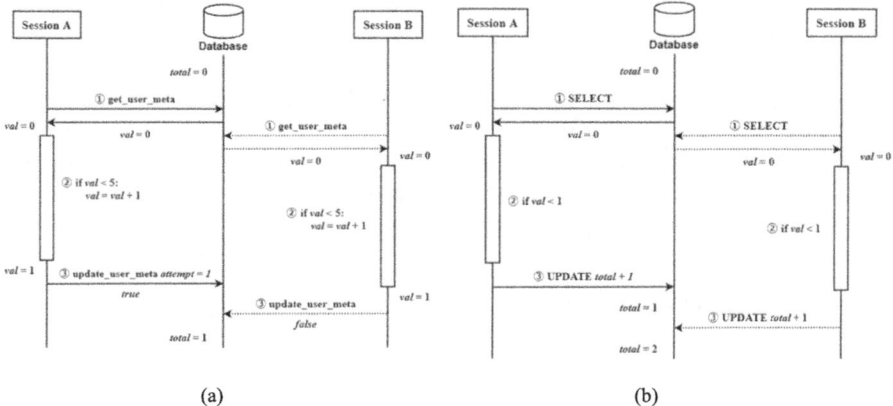

Fig. 5. (a) A process flow used the functions provided by WordPress. (b) A process flow used wpdb.

[18]. By using it, SQL can be directly executed. The plug-ins were implemented in such a way that SQL is executed with SELECT statements to retrieve values, and UPDATE statements to update values. In the case of this pattern, as in the previous section, the vulnerability is caused by the difference in timing between the acquisition and use of values. Figure 4 shows an example of code with a race condition vulnerability caused by wpdb function. In this code, the value obtained by executing a SELECT statement using wpdb is stored in $val, and the executability is determined based on this value. If the executable condition is met, an UPDATE statement is executed using wpdb to update the value, and the number of attempts is counted. Figure 5b shows the process flow when the race condition vulnerability is triggered in the code in Fig. 4. In (1), multiple sessions execute SELECT statements in a short period of time to obtain values and store them in $val. Currently, the value stored in the variable is a duplicate value. Next, in (2), based on the acquired values in (1), checks whether the executable condition is satisfied. Since

the same value is stored in $val in multiple sessions, both Session A and Session B satisfy the condition. Finally, in (3), the UPDATE statement is used to update the value, and the value is added the number of times it passes the condition because it is an update using only the SQL statement. This is different from the pattern in which the WordPress function described above is used. The reason why many implementations of this pattern were observed is considered to be that the development was not conducted with consideration of the occurrence of a race condition.

5 Countermeasures

We discuss effective countermeasures against the two patterns that cause the vulnerabilities described in the previous section. Since the race condition vulnerability is caused by a time gap between read and update operations when multiple operations access a shared resource simultaneously, and the integrity of the shared resource fails to be maintained during the sequence of operations. This can be solved by ensuring that the Web server processes only one client request at a time. However, this method significantly degrades the performance of the web application. Therefore, it is necessary to consider a countermeasure that allows concurrent execution while still maintaining security.

As mentioned before, vulnerabilities arise due to the time difference between the read and update processes. To solve this problem, it is necessary to maintain the integrity of the shared resources by prohibiting other processes from accessing the shared resources when one process is reading and updating values to the shared resources. We propose countermeasures at both the database and application levels.

5.1 Database-Level Countermeasures

We propose a database-level countermeasure using exclusive lock with the FOR UPDATE clause of SQL. Exclusive lock allows us to restrict concurrent access to specified columns. This method can be used by adding a FOR UPDATE clause to the SQL statement used to retrieve the value. However, we confirm that the countermeasure is not sufficient when only the FOR UPDATE clause is added. MySQL is commonly used as a database in WordPress. The default specification of MySQL is to enable the autocommit function, which executes a single SQL statement as a single transaction [19]. This causes read and update to be processed as separate transactions. Therefore, even if exclusive lock is performed using the FOR UPDATE clause, the locking time is not sufficient and the same value may be obtained before the database is updated. To solve this problem, it is necessary to perform get and update operations in the same transaction. As mentioned above, the autocommit function is enabled by default in MySQL. Therefore, in order to process multiple SQLs in a transaction, it is necessary to explicitly write START TRANSACTION at the start transaction and COMMIT at the end of the transaction.

Figure 6 and Fig. 7 show code that implements an exclusive lock using the FOR UPDATE clause. In this code, after starting a transaction, this code performs read and write operations in a transaction. Note that it is impossible to modify only using the API

```
1:  $wpdb->query("START TRANSACTION");
2:  $val = $wpdb->get_var("SELECT meta_value FROM wp_us
    ermeta WHERE metakey = 'total' AND user_id = 1 LIMIT
    1 FOR UPDATE");
3:
4:  if ($val < 1) {
5:      $val = $val + 1
6:  }
7:  update_user_meta(1, 'total', $val);
8:  $wpdb->query("COMMIT");
```

Fig. 6. Example of a fix using FOR UPDATE for vulnerable code that is used the functions provided by WordPress

```
1:  $wpdb->query("START TRANSACTION");
2:  $val = $wpdb->get_var("SELECT * FROM wp_total WHERE
    id = 1 FOR UPDATE");
3:
4:  if ($val < 1) {
5:      $wpdb->query("UPDATE wp_total SET total = total + 1
        WHERE id = 1");
6:  }
7:
8:  $wpdb->query("COMMIT");
```

Fig. 7. Example of fixing vulnerable code that is used wpdb using FOR UPDATE

functions provided by WordPress shown in Table 2. Therefore, API functions such as get_user_meta to retrieve values are replaced with wpdb function to modify.

Figure 8 shows the process flow of the codes in Fig. 6 and Fig. 7. In the process (1), Session A and Session B try to retrieve values at the same time, but Session B does not retrieve values at this time because of the transaction in Session A, and a wait occurs. After the update process of Session A is completed, the requested value

is returned in Session B, and then Session B is processed. This ensures consistency in the shared resources of each session processing and allows the race condition vulnerability to be fixed.

5.2 Application-Level Countermeasures

We propose an application-level countermeasure using PHP's flock function [20]. Since this method does not use transactions, it can be used for database-independent processing. We have confirmed that this method is widely used to fix WordPress plug-ins with race condition vulnerabilities.

Figure 9 shows the code modified with the flock function. By using the flock function to file lock before and after read and update operations on a shared resource, it is possible to prevent multiple sessions from accessing the shared resource simultaneously.

Figure 10 shows the flow of the codes in for Fig. 9. The file is opened in process (1) and the file lock is acquired in process (2), but because Session A locks the file, Session B cannot lock the file and a wait occurs. Session A reads and updates the shared

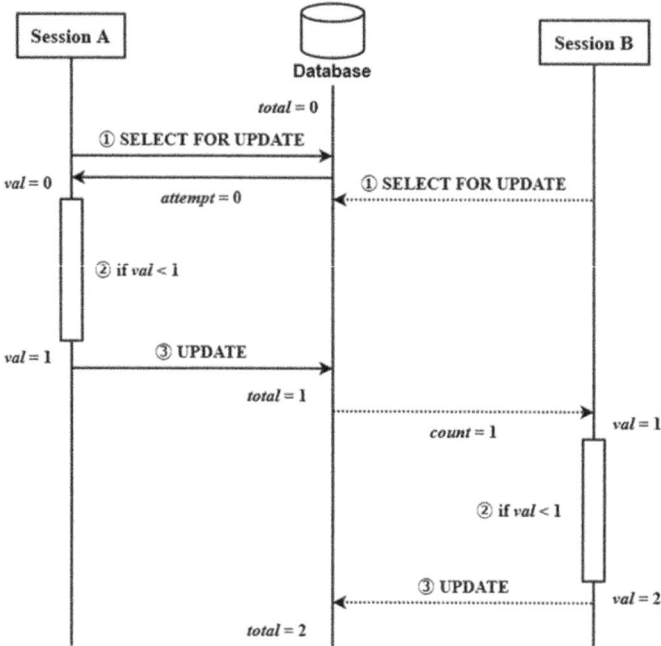

Fig. 8. A process flow modified by FOR UPDATE

resource, and then releases the file lock. Session B then releases the waiting state and performs subsequent processing.

```
1:   $fp = fopen("/tmp/flock.lock", "r");
2:
3:   if (!flock($fp, LOCK_EX) {
4:      exit;
5:   }
6:
7:   $val = $wpdb->get_var("SELECT * FROM wp_total WHERE id = 1");
8:
9:   if ($val < 1) {
10:     $wpdb->query("UPDATE wp_total SET total = total + 1 WHERE id = 1");
11:  }
12:
13:  fclose($fp);
```

Fig. 9. Example of fixing vulnerable code using flock function.

We also have confirmed that the countermeasure using the flock function does not work correctly when you use some functions provided by WordPress to retrieve values, such as get_user_meta function. This is due to the cache feature provided by those functions. These functions internally use cache-related functions such as

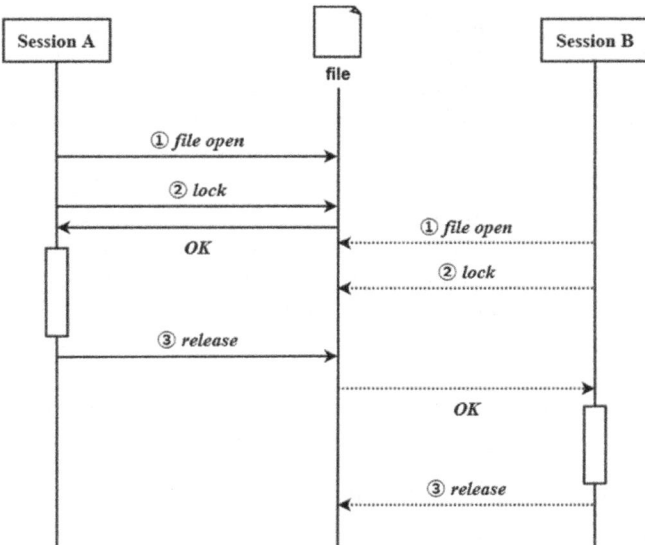

Fig. 10. A process flow modified by `flock` function

`wp_cache_get` function [21]. Under conditions where a race condition vulnerability exists, the code that uses the `flock` function to fix the vulnerability has a cache lifetime that is long enough to allow retrieval of the stored value from the cache with multiple accesses within a short period of time. To solve this problem, it is necessary to change to retrieving values by `wpdb`.

5.3 Note

We discussed the database-level modification method using the FOR UPDATE clause and the application-level modification method using the `flock` function. It is important to select those corrective measures according to the situation. Note that when we reported the vulnerabilities, we observed some cases where full database locks were used, but it is important to note that other functions may be affected. Therefore, when using an exclusive lock of shared resources by SQL and file lock by `flock` function, excessive locking should be avoided so that other processes are not affected. As a side note, we have not mentioned semaphore and mutex as countermeasures in this paper because they require the installation of extension modules.

6 Related Work

While there is a growing interest in race condition vulnerabilities, detailed studies have not been conducted because they are difficult to detect due to their nature and the business logic involved. We show two highly relevant studies to our research: one proposes a new attack method for race condition vulnerabilities, and the other proposes a dynamic framework for detecting server-side request race conditions.

Single-Packet Attack. James [22] proposed a single-packet attack against the race condition vulnerability in web applications that can be attacked with higher accuracy. The proposed method combines multiple requests into a single packet for simultaneous transmission and minimizes the time delay between requests. Comparing the single-packet attack method with the conventional attack method, the former method causes requests to arrive at the server side almost simultaneously, while the latter method only sends a sequence of requests within a short period of time, and the timing of arrival of requests at the server side is random due to delays and other reasons. Therefore, the single packet attack is a more reproducible attack against the race condition vulnerability. This method is implemented in Turbo Intruder, an extension of the Burp Suite used in this study.

RaqRacer. Zhengyi et al. [23] proposed a dynamic detection framework called ReqRacer for various web applications, including WordPress, which was the subject of our research in this study, and conducted a study to collect and analyze 157 server-side request races. ReqRacer is a dynamic framework designed to detect atomicity violations. Specifically, ReqRacer first monitors HTTP requests when a web application is executed on a server, and collects data such as access to shared resources and dependencies among requests. Then, based on the collected data, a dependency graph is constructed to model the "happens-before" relationship between HTTP requests, and by identifying concurrency among requests, requests that may cause a race condition are identified. It then verifies whether the identified requests cause a race condition by reordering the requests and executing them.

7 Conclusion

In this paper, we investigated 76 WordPress plugins for race condition vulnerabilities. As a result, we found race condition vulnerabilities in 29 evaluations. The vulnerabilities are likely to be introduced when functions are used to retrieve and update values related to metadata and options, which are shared resources provided by WordPress, and when SQL is directly executed to retrieve and update values in the database. As a countermeasure, it is necessary to ensure consistency in processing so that there is no difference in the state at the time of getting and updating values from shared resources. As concrete countermeasures, we have discussed using SQL transaction and exclusive lock and exclusive processing by the `flock` function.

Plug-in developers need to be aware of secure-by-design by carefully considering the design of the logic of their programs. Additionally, when implementing important processes, it is necessary to take the utmost care for mixing race condition vulnerability and to pay attention to whether it is acceptable to use functions provided by WordPress.

In this study, we have focused on plug-ins with more than 10,000 active installations, but it is also necessary to investigate other plug-ins. Additionally, since plugins are classified arbitrarily, an objective classification method should be considered. For this purpose, we are considering using tools such as RaqRacer to conduct a comprehensive survey of plug-ins that may have race condition vulnerabilities [23]. In the future, we will measure the request interval at which attacks succeed and investigate the specific conditions and logic for successful attacks because the request interval for a successful attack was not measured at this time. We also need to investigate the race condition vulnerabilities of systems and frameworks other than WordPress.

The vulnerabilities identified in this study have been reported to Patchstack and Wordfence, both of which are CVE Numbering Authorities (CNAs) and accept the reports of WordPress plugin vulnerabilities, as well as to the plugin developers, and are being addressed in turn [24, 25]. Some of them are publicly available, e.g., CVE-2023-6109 [26].

References

1. Wordpress.org. https://wordpress.org
2. 2022 CWE Top 25 Most Dangerous Software Weaknesses. https://cwe.mitre.org/top25/archive/2022/2022_cwe_top25.html
3. 2023 CWE Top 25 Most Dangerous Software Weaknesses. https://cwe.mitre.org/top25/archive/2023/2023_top25_list.html
4. Race conditions | Web Security Academy. https://portswigger.net/web-security/race-conditions
5. Vulnerability assessment methodology documents that are too detailed but should be communicated (in Japanese). https://webapppentestguidelines.github.io/newtechtestdoc/docs/toctou/
6. OWASP TimeGap Theory. https://timegaptheory.com/
7. Wget Vulnerability Conflict Condition (in Japanese). https://timegaptheory.com/
8. CVE-2016-7098 Detail – NVD. https://nvd.nist.gov/vuln/detail/CVE-2016-7098
9. CWE-362: Concurrent Execution using Shared Resource with Improper Synchronization ('Race Condition'). https://cwe.mitre.org/data/definitions/362.html
10. Paleari, R., Marrone, D., Bruschi, D., Monga, M.: On race vulnerabilities in web applications. In: Zamboni, D. (ed.) DIMVA 2008. LNCS, vol. 5137, pp. 126–142. Springer, Heidelberg (2008). https://doi.org/10.1007/978-3-540-70542-0_7
11. Race Condition Exploit in Starbucks Gift Cards. https://www.schneier.com/blog/archives/2015/05/race_condition_.html
12. Accommodation reservation system disrupted Travel support spikes access to the system (in Japanese). http://www.nikkei.com/article/DGXZQOUC13CHJ0T11C22A0000000
13. CWE-367: Time-of-check Time-of-use (TOCTOU) Race Condition. https://cwe.mitre.org/data/definitions/367.html
14. TOCTOU/Race condition | WebApp Testing. https://webapppentestguidelines.github.io/newtechtestdoc/docs/toctou/
15. Turbo Intruder. https://portswigger.net/bappstore/9abaa233088242e8be252cd4ff534988
16. get_user_meta() – Function - WordPress Developer Resources/. https://developer.wordpress.org/reference/functions/get_user_meta/
17. update_user_meta() – Function. https://developer.wordpress.org/reference/functions/update_user_meta/
18. wpdb – Class - WordPress Developer Resources. https://developer.wordpress.org/reference/classes/wpdb/
19. 7.2.2 autocommit, Commit, and Rollback. https://dev.mysql.com/doc/refman/8.0/en/innodb-autocommit-commit-rollback.html
20. flock – Manual. https://www.php.net/manual/en/function.flock.php
21. wp_cache_get() – Function - WordPress Developer Resources. https://developer.wordpress.org/reference/functions/wp_cache_get/

22. Smashing the state machine: the true potential of web race conditions. https://portswigger.net/research/smashing-the-state-machine
23. Qiu, Z., Shao, S., Zhao, Q., Jin, G.: Understanding and detecting server-side request races in web applications. In: Proceedings of the 29th ACM Joint Meeting on European Software Engineering Conference and Symposium on the Foundations of Software Engineering, pp. 842–854 (2021). https://doi.org/10.1145/3468264.3468594
24. Patchstack: Fastest protection for WordPress security vulnerabilities. https://patchstack.com/
25. Wordfence: WordPress Security Plugin. https://www.wordfence.com/
26. YOP Poll <= 6.5.26 - Race Condition to Vote Manipulation. https://www.wordfence.com/threat-intel/vulnerabilities/wordpress-plugins/yop-poll/yop-poll-6526-race-condition-to-vote-manipulation

Finding (and Exploiting) Vulnerabilities on IP Cameras: The Tenda CP3 Case Study

Dario Stabili[1(✉)], Tobia Bocchi[2], Filip Valgimigli[2], and Mirco Marchetti[2]

[1] Department of Computer Science and Engineering, Alma Mater Studiorum - University of Bologna, Bologna, Italy
dario.stabili@unibo.it
[2] Department of Engineering "Enzo Ferrari", University of Modena and Reggio Emilia, Modena, Italy
{tobia.bocchi,filip.valgimigli,mirco.marchetti}@unimore.it

Abstract. Consumer IP cameras are now the most widely adopted solution for remote monitoring in various contexts, such as private homes or small offices. While the security of these devices has been scrutinized, most approaches are limited to relatively shallow network-based analyses. In this paper, we discuss a methodology for the security analysis and identification of remotely exploitable vulnerabilities in IP cameras, which includes static and dynamic analyses of executables extracted from IP camera firmware. Compared to existing methodologies, our approach leverages the context of the target device to focus on the identification of malicious invocation sequences that could lead to exploitable vulnerabilities. We demonstrate the application of our methodology by using the Tenda CP3 IP camera as a case study. We identified five novel CVEs, with CVSS scores ranging from 7.5 to 9.8. To partially automate our analysis, we also developed a custom tool based on *Ghidra* and *rhabdomancer*.

1 Introduction

This paper discusses the application of a classical methodology for conducting in-depth security analysis with a focus on consumer IP cameras. IP cameras are popular IoT devices, and their cybersecurity has been scrutinized by the scientific community in recent years. Related works [11,12] have already identified several vulnerabilities, but their analysis has mainly focused on network traffic. The discussed methodology takes an in-depth approach and requires physical disassembly of the device. While this attacker model may seem more powerful than the one used in related literature, we argue that it is more realistic and allows for the identification of a higher number of more relevant software vulnerabilities. Consumer IP cameras are inexpensive, making it easy for attackers to purchase one or more devices to experiment on. Moreover, our results demonstrate that this kind of analysis enables attackers to extract sensitive information and devise attack strategies that can be weaponized against other IP cameras of the same make and model, even without physical access. The adopted methodology comprises five main steps.

The first step involves gathering information from open and public sources related to the IP camera under analysis. This step does not require the camera itself and can be performed by checking public data records from the *FCC ID Search* web service [7]. This information proves to be extremely useful, as it often includes high-resolution pictures of the printed circuit boards, which can be used to identify diagnostic and programming interfaces. Additionally, valuable information can be obtained from firmware repositories. Depending on the camera manufacturer and model, it is often possible to download a copy of the firmware from official or unofficial repositories. This step may enable an attacker to focus on a limited number of IP cameras that are more likely to exhibit interesting vulnerabilities.

The second step requires physical access to a specimen of the IP camera under analysis. Within this step, the camera is disassembled to gain physical access to the inner printed circuit board. The primary objective is to visually inspect it and identify one or more vulnerability surfaces that enable direct and low-level interaction with the camera. In our experience, it is highly likely to identify internal USB ports that have no external connectors, as well as simpler debugging and diagnostic interfaces based on standard JTAG or UART protocols. Having physical access allows us to connect and probe these interfaces to confirm that they are active and explore the related attack surfaces. At this step, it is usually possible to interact with the bootloader and potentially gain access to a command-line interpreter as a privileged user.

The third step begins by extracting the firmware deployed on the IP camera. This task can be accomplished either by exploiting low-level read access to the memory of the IP camera through a diagnostic interface or by physically connecting an external reader to the memory chip soldered to the PCB. In some cases, a chip-off might be necessary, although it has not been required in our experience. The extracted firmware is then subjected to common static analysis procedures aimed at identifying relevant partitions, configuration files, scripts, executable files, and cryptographic material.

The fourth step complements the static analysis of the firmware with a dynamic analysis of the network behavior of the IP camera under test. The peculiarity of our approach is that, instead of applying a general approach for static analysis we focus on the main services exposed on the network by the device, thus considering its use-case scenario. By considering the classical usage scenario of the target device, we demonstrate how existing classical tools for static analysis can be tweaked to quickly identify vulnerabilities exposed by the target device, thus preventing the security researcher to manually analyze different potential sources of vulnerabilities that wouldn't lead to exploits.

The fifth and final step builds upon the information gathered in the previous steps to perform a detailed reverse-engineering process of all executables that implement services available from the network. To partially automate this complex step, we developed a novel tool based on *Ghidra* [14] and *rhabdomancer* [13] that identifies the functions responsible for handling data received from network connections, builds the invocation sequence list and correctly identifies the thread responsible for each invocation sequence. This allows security researchers to quickly analyze the whole function call sequence of a target network handler to identify potential vulnerabilities in its code, thus helping them to demonstrate potential exploits and identify possible mitigation.

In this paper, we demonstrate the effectiveness of the proposed methodology by focusing on a popular consumer IP camera, the Tenda CP3, as a use case. Our analysis has already led to the publication of five new CVEs, two of which have a CVSS score of 7.5 and the remaining three have a CVSS score of 9.8.

1.1 Related Work

The scientific literature already contains several research papers focusing on the cybersecurity of IoT devices, IP cameras, and video surveillance systems. However, most of this work limits itself to network-based security analysis, either by sniffing and analyzing network traffic or by interacting with exposed network services. Notable contributions in this field include the analysis of the attack surface of IP-based surveillance systems [10], as well as wide-ranging analysis of IoT devices [12] and the exposed network services of IP cameras belonging to a given nation [3]. These papers demonstrate that connected IoT devices present many vulnerabilities; however, in many cases, the analysis is limited to relatively simple scanning and probing activities.

Other papers more related to our proposal focus on the in-depth analysis of network communications of a given IP camera [1,4]. In particular, the authors of [4] managed to exploit network-based attacks, such as Man-in-the-Middle, to eavesdrop on and interact with network communications between the IP camera (a TP-Link Tapo C200) and other devices on the same local network, thus identifying three novel vulnerabilities. We remark that these papers only based their analysis on network interactions, without identifying relevant vulnerabilities (such as remote code execution) that require an in-depth reversing of executables extracted from the firmware of IP cameras.

In relevant related work, Shwartz et al. [16] perform firmware extraction from 16 different IoT devices, with the final goal of extracting and cracking passwords that would allow remote access to the compromised devices. They demonstrate the effectiveness of their approach, as well as the widespread vulnerability related to password management of IoT devices, by creating a modified version of the Mirai botnet that utilized these passwords to compromise vulnerable devices. The authors discuss the possibility of conducting a more comprehensive static analysis and reverse engineering of the analyzed devices but do not undertake these tasks themselves.

On the other hand, this paper introduces a methodology for the security analysis of consumer IP cameras, demonstrated through the examination of the Tenda CP3 as a case study, and the development of a novel tool. To our knowledge, this is the first paper to delve into such an in-depth analysis of IP cameras.

1.2 Outline

The remainder of this paper is organized as follows. Section 2 presents the IP camera that we use to demonstrate the application of our analysis methodology, while Sect. 3 presents the detailed analysis of the firmware extracted from our device. Section 4 analyses and describes the two main programs responsible to handle all external connections to the camera, demonstrating a practical method to identify potential vulnerability and to design their related exploit. Finally, Sect. 5 highlights the main strengths of this work and describes future development.

2 Analysis of the Tenda CP3 IP Camera

In this section, we present the analysis of the Tenda CP3 connected camera and provide details of the hardware platform. Although we had full access to the IP camera during our analysis, our primary focus was on outlining the steps necessary for gathering as much information as possible using OSINT sources and firmware analysis. Consequently, we describe a methodology that could be applied not only to other IP cameras but also to various IoT devices.

2.1 Hardware Analysis

The Tenda CP3 connected camera is based on a single PCB platform to which the lens and all extension PCBs are connected. We conducted an analysis of the camera's internals using its FCC ID, a unique identifier required for devices transmitting over radio frequencies in the United States. Upon locating the FCC ID on one of the labels attached to the camera, we entered its value into the FCC ID search form available on the Federal Communications Commission website. The FCC ID of the Tenda CP3 cameras is V7TCP3, with V7T representing the grantee code (i.e., Shenzen Tenda Technology Co., Ltd.) and CP3 being the product code assigned by the grantee. By examining the internal pictures of the V7TCP3 product (Fig. 1) we identified the main components of the main PCB.

The Tenda CP3 is equipped with a Fullhan FH8626 V100 System on Chip designed for HD IP cameras, capable of multi-stream encoding in *H.264* format at 1080p resolution and 15 frames per second. Additionally, it features a Realtek *8188FTV* Network Interface Controller, providing support for *802.11b/g/n 2.4 GHz* connectivity. On the top side of the main PCB, we also identified a UART serial interface, indicated by the two *tx* and *rx* pads located at the top of the image, as well as a flash chip (partially visible on the left side of the picture).

2.2 UART Serial

After the initial hardware analysis, we decided to access the internals of the camera available to us to verify the information found via OSINT. Although the labels *tx* and *rx* were not printed on the PCB found inside our device, all the

(a) Top side of the main PCB. (b) Bottom side of the main PCB.

Fig. 1. Internal pictures of the Tenda CP3 accessed via the FCC ID public repository.

other components and their locations were exactly the same. We proceeded by connecting to the UART serial interface using a USB TTL adapter and minicom configured with a baud rate of 115200 (8N1).

During the first boot of the device we only connected to the *tx* pad of the UART interface with the *rx* pin of our USB TTL adapter to log the output of the system boot process. After analyzing the recorded log of the boot process, we identified several useful information about the bootloader (U-Boot 2010.06-dirty, with the possibility to interrupt the autoboot process by pressing 'E'), the OS (a Linux-3.0.8 ARMv7 Linux Kernel Image), the number and mapping of the partitions on the *spi_flash*, the name of some demons and applications started by the system (one of them being *telenetd*), and some configurations saved by the device, including the configured WiFi credentials printed in clear.

We then connected the *tx* pin of our USB TTL adapter to the *rx* pad of the PCB to interrupt the autoboot sequence, only to encounter a password-protected login prompt. Later, we will discuss how the password was recovered to access the U-Boot console.

CVE-2023-30354: Physical access and WiFi credentials disclosure - Tenda IP Camera CP3 does not defend against physical access to U-Boot via the UART; the Wi-Fi password is shown, and the hard coded boot password can be inserted for console access.

Base Score: **9.8 Critical**
Vector: CVSS:3.1/AV:N/AC:L/PR:N/UI:N/S:U/C:H/I:H/A:H

2.3 Firmware Extraction and Analysis

We extracted the firmware from the SOIC8 chip by directly connecting to the pins of the chip via a dedicated clip, as depicted in Fig. 2. We took care to isolate the processor from the flash memory to prevent any modifications during the firmware extraction procedure, thus enabling us to work with the corresponding image of the data found on the flash memory.

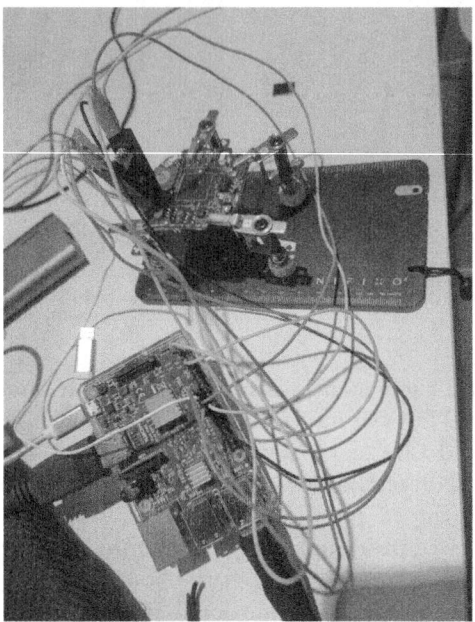

Fig. 2. Firmware extraction procedure.

We extracted the firmware image using the flashrom utility [8], and we modified the permissions on the saved image to be *read-only*. Additionally, we computed a fresh checksum of the saved flash image to ensure that we always had a clean image available.

After obtaining the firmware image, we manually extracted the partitions described in the boot process, resulting in 6 different files (one for each partition). Here, we provide a high-level analysis of the content of the partitions extracted from the flash image:

- **bootstrap** and **uboot-env:** partitions containing the configuration of the bootstrap and uboot environment;
- **uboot:** partition containing the uboot bootloader of the device;
- **kernel:** partition containing the root file system of the device. The root file system is stored in a compressed format.
- **data:** partition containing the user data used by the applications being executed on the device. This partition is formatted in a *jff2* file system.
- **app:** partition containing the file system on which all scripts, applications and configuration file of the Tenda CP3 IP camera. This partition is formatted in a *squashfs* file system

3 Detailed Analysis of the Tenda CP3 System

The detailed analysis of the Tenda CP3 camera combines both dynamic and static analysis on the content of the *app* partition of the extracted firmware image. Specifically, we are primarily interested in mapping all services being executed on the camera that accept any incoming traffic, and in enumerating interesting files found in the *app* partition of the camera via the firmwalker utility [6]. These files include UNIX configuration files (such as /etc./passwd and /etc./shadow files), bash scripts, and all executable files found in the partition.

In this section, we present the results of the analysis of the UNIX configuration files, the service mapping, and the bash scripts responsible for the initialization of the system. In Sect. 4, we provide a detailed analysis of the main programs found active on the camera.

The scripts used the steps outlined below are available on GitHub [2].

3.1 UNIX Configuration Files

We identified several different configuration files available in the *app* partition of the extracted file system. While some configuration files are related to the behavior of the applications executed by the system at start up (more on this in Sect. 3.3), by examining certain well-known strings in the text files, we were able to identify two extremely interesting files.

The first file is ap_mode.cfg (located at the root directory), which contains the default configuration for the access point exposed by the device while in configuration mode. This includes the interface label, the SSID type and prefix, the default IP address (192.168.55.1), DHCP range, and default password in plain text.

The second file is shadow (also located at the root directory), which serves as a modified version of the /etc./shadow file found in all UNIX systems that will be copied in the /etc. folder at start up (see Sect. 3.3). The *shadow* file contains a single user (root) and the hash (generated with *descrypt*) of the password associated with the root user. Since the length of the hash is limited to only 13 bytes, we attempted to reverse-engineer the password via a brute-force attack, eventually succeeding in recovering it. The recovered password has a length of 8 characters and is likely generated following a pre-defined scheme used by the vendor. Upon successful authentication with the recovered credentials via UART shell, we were also able to access the U-Boot shell after a couple of easy and intuitive modifications to the password.

3.2 Service Mapping

We conducted a network mapping on our device to identify all services accepting incoming traffic from external hosts. This mapping was performed from both an external attacker's perspective (e.g., by mapping the ports from a host connected to the same network as the device) and by accessing the internal shell of the camera (made possible by the recovered password found in Sect. 3.1) to identify the services handling incoming traffic.

External Mapping Report. We performed the external mapping using the *nmap* utility [9] to identify all listening ports accepting both TCP and UDP connections. The results of the network mapping procedure indicate that the camera is accepting *telnet* connections on port 23/TCP, *rtsp* (Real-Time Streaming Protocol) connections on port 8554/TCP, and exposes other unknown services on ports 843/TCP, 1300/TCP, 6688/TCP, 8699/TCP, 9876/TCP, 3702/UDP, 5012/UDP, 5683/UDP, and 19966/UDP.

We were able to access the camera via the *telnet* protocol using the `root` credentials recovered in the previous step, and via *rtsp* using the default credentials associated with the service, stored in plain text in the `ap_mode.cfg` configuration file. It is worth noting that these credentials are hard-coded and identical in all IP cameras from the same vendor, and cannot be modified via the corresponding smartphone application. Therefore, by accessing a network where a camera from the same vendor as the one used in our analysis is installed, anyone can access its live video stream using the same set of credentials.

CVE-2023-30351: Remote access via hard-coded credentials - Tenda IP Camera CP3 was discovered to contain a hard-coded default password for root which is stored using weak encryption. This vulnerability allows attackers to connect to the TELNET service (or UART) by using the exposed credentials.

Base Score: **7.5 High**
Vector: CVSS:3.1/AV:N/AC:L/PR:N/UI:N/S:U/C:H/I:N/A:N

CVE-2023-30352: RTSP feed access via hard-coded credentials - Tenda IP Camera CP3 was discovered to contain a hard-coded default password for the RTSP feed.

Base Score: **9.8 Critical**
Vector: CVSS:3.1/AV:N/AC:L/PR:N/UI:N/S:U/C:H/I:H/A:H

Internal Mapping Report. Following the mapping of services accepting incoming connections from outside the device, we exploited the previously found access via telnet to discover other potentially interesting services running on the device that could lead to further vulnerability findings. Initially, we analyzed the processes active on the device after gaining root access through the exploited telnet service. We found that only slightly more than 50 processes were active on the device, many of which were observed starting as system processes via the UART serial interface logs.

Upon observing the list of active threads on the device, we discovered that the vast majority were spawned from two different applications, namely *noodle* and *apollo*, which were also found in our copy of the flash memory in the *app* partition.

We then proceeded with the identification of processes associated with the open ports found in the external network mapping. The results of the netstat command highlighted that the *telnet* connection is managed by *inetd* (as expected), while all other connections are managed by either *noodle* or *apollo*. Specifically, *noodle* listens on ports 843/TCP, 1300/TCP, and 5012/UDP, while *apollo* serves all other ports, including 8554/TCP (RTSP). Since these two binaries serve as the main entry points for any external connection (including communication with the vendor's servers and the vendor's application), we will focus on their analysis in Sect. 4.

3.3 Bash Scripts

We analyzed the content of the bash scripts found in the /etc./init.d folder, which contains 5 different scripts:

- **S01udev:** responsible for creating some system folders and run the udevd demon and to start the *udevstart* program;
- **S02init_rootfs:** responsible for mounting the *data* file system partition;
- **S03network:** responsible for configuring the network interface;
- **S04app:** responsible for mounting the *app* file system, initializing different applications, and starting the *noodles* application;
- **rcS:** responsible for executing all the scripts found in the /etc./init.d folder starting with the S[0-9][0-9] regex expression.

Since the *S04app* script is the most interesting initializing script, we decided to analyze it in detail to recreate the entire initialization process of the applications being executed on the device and to find any potential vulnerabilities. The *S04app* script invokes another script (chk_ver.sh) that is responsible for updating any script found in the /usr/bin folder with newer versions found in the /app folder, if available. While it is possible to exploit this script to overwrite system applications with another file with the same name placed in the /app folder, it is worth noting that obtaining access to the system is necessary to perform this exploit. Given that the only user available on the device is the *root* user, the process of modifying a script is trivial and of little interest in our case study.

The *S04app* then proceeds to invoke three hard-coded scripts (patch.sh, sys_init.sh, and app_init.sh) from the /app directory, if available. Unfortunately, in both our device and flash image, we were unable to locate these scripts, as they are most likely related to the installation of a patch downloaded from the vendor's website.

After executing the *noodles* application, the *S04app* script identifies and mounts the SD card on the /mnt/sd mount point. If the SD card is mounted correctly, it then executes another script (iu.sh), which appears to be an update script. Upon further analysis, the iu.sh script copies the content of a file named *Flash.img* found in the root directory of the SD card to a temporary working folder (*/home*) and proceeds by copying its content to replace the entire flash memory. It is worth noting that since the entire system boot process does not check the integrity of the loaded flash image, it is possible to overwrite the system simply by inserting a properly formatted SD card with the malicious firmware image, without the necessity of accessing the device through the network.

> **CVE-2023-30356:** Missing support for Integrity Check - Tenda IP Camera CP3 was discovered missing Support for an Integrity Check, allowing attackers to update the device with crafted firmware.
>
> Base Score: **7.5 High**
> Vector: CVSS:3.1/AV:N/AC:L/PR:N/UI:N/S:U/C:N/I:H/A:N

4 Binary Analysis: Noodles and Apollo

In this section, we present a detailed analysis of the two main binaries responsible for managing network connections on the Tenda CP3 camera, namely *noodles* and *apollo*. The primary objective of the analysis presented in this section is to outline the methodology we adopted in identifying vulnerabilities that could potentially allow for remote code execution on the device.

Our analysis is based on the reverse-engineered representation of the two binaries obtained with Ghidra [14], upon which we applied a customized version of the *rhabdomancer* script [13] to identify insecure functions handling external connections (recv, recvfrom, and recvmsg). Rhabdomancer is a Ghidra script designed to assist with vulnerability research tasks based on a candidate point strategy against software written in C/C++. It locates all calls to potentially insecure functions (the candidate points), which can be used to find insecure input access to the process. Additionally, we developed a tool on top of rhabdomancer that automates the entire process of reconstructing the function call sequence from the main function to the specified entry points [2], enabling us to easily map all the threads of the two processes to the different ports they use. Subsequently, we proceeded with a manual analysis to identify potential security vulnerabilities and design exploits to achieve remote code execution on our device.

4.1 The *Noodles* Binary

By executing our modified version of the rhabdomancer script, which specifically targeted functions relevant to our analysis (primarily *recv*, *recvfrom*, and *recvmsg*), we identified three candidate points in the decompiled binary. These points were labeled as FUN_00014e68, FUN_0001fc14, and FUN_00012b7c.

FUN_00014e68. This function is referenced in 5 other functions within the *noodles* binary. We will refer to these different invocations using the memory addresses of our reversed binary for simplicity.

1. 0x00011b04. The first reference is inside the main function, and is related to a socket listening on port 1300 (one of the ports already identified in the previous analysis step). In this invocation, FUN_00014e68 is used to receive commands from the client, as confirmed by the string `receive_cmd from client<%d>: <%s> len = %d \n` found a couple of instructions later. The available commands (hard-coded in the binary) through this interface include some suspicious strings like `ELFEXEC`, `DOWNLOAD`, and `SYSTEM`.

2. 0x000123bc. The second reference to our target function is inside the `FUN_00012110` function, which is referenced by 3 other functions: `FUN_000128a0` (invoked by the `main` function after the `ELFEXEC` command is received), `FUN_00014674` (invoked by the `main` function after the `DOWNLOAD` command is received), and `FUN_000147ac` (invoked by the `main` function after the `UPGRADE` command is received). Upon further investigation, we confirmed that these references are all related to the previously discussed functionalities, and they can be used to trigger the execution of different scripts available on the camera.

3. 0x0001272c. The third reference is found inside two different functions: `FUN_000146e4` (invoked by the `main` function after the `UPLOAD` command is received) and `FUN_00014748` (invoked by the `main` function after the `FLASHDUMP` command is received). While via the former invocation it is possible to upload a specific file to the camera, by exploiting the latter invocation we demonstrated that it is possible to remotely upload a modified version of the firmware that will be copied to the flash memory on the next restart. This enables the exploitation of the vulnerability identified in Sect. 3.3 (**CVE-2023-30356**) without requiring physical access to the camera to upload a modified firmware version on the SD card.

4. 0x00013cbc. The fourth reference is found inside the function `FUN_00013c30`, which happens to be the *policy_thread* spawned by the function `FUN_00013df4` (directly called in the `main` function). The *policy_thread* is listening on port 843, accepts a fixed string (`policy-file-request`), and responds with a fixed XML structure.

5. 0x000144f8. The final reference is found inside `FUN_000143c0`, which is another function associated with the management of external commands accepted by *noodles*. Specifically, this function is called upon the reception of the `SYSTEMEX` command, which has already been exploited by other researchers in **CVE-2023-23080** to achieve remote code execution.

`FUN_0001fc14`. The second function containing a `recv` invocation is referenced only once in function `FUN_0001d2c8` in the *noodles* binary. However, this latter function is referenced three times.

The first reference (`FUN_0001d2c8`) is related to some WiFi connection tests and extends up to the `main` function (invoked after receiving a `SYSTEM` command containing the *STATUS* keyword). We analyzed the entire activation graph of this invocation, composed of 6 different functions, and established that this set of functions is used to test the status of a known WiFi SSID by the camera on system boot.

The second reference (`FUN_0001d1f8`) is also related to WiFi communication and is also invoked indirectly by the `main` function after a `SYSTEM` command is received. However, this second function accepts a different system command (*SCAN*) and performs a network scan on the wlan0 (hard-coded) network interface.

The third reference (FUN_0001d3b0) is once again related to WiFi communication and invoked via the SYSTEM handler of the main function. This time, the function accepts a *SCAN_RESULTS* command and prints the output of the last saved network scan on the serial interface. We remark that all three of these handlers return the same value (<SYSTEMEX_ACK>ok</SYSTEMEX_ACK>), which is the default response for any successful connection via the SYSTEM command. Additionally, we note that all of these commands are vulnerable to remote code injection, and that any received command is executed on the device with root privileges without requiring authentication.

FUN_00012b7c. The third function containing a recvfrom function is actually the *multicast_thread* spawned by the main function and attached to port 5012/UDP. The *multicast_thread* is configured to accept two commands, namely YGMP_SVR and YGMP_CMD.

Upon reception of the former command, *noodles* opens different configuration files to read the current settings of the device, which are then returned as an XML structure to the caller. These settings include the *IP* and *MAC* addresses of the camera, its *serial number*, the value encoded in the *QR Code*, the *hardware version*, and other information.

The latter command (YGMP_CMD), however, is far more interesting in the scope of our work, as it allows unauthenticated remote code execution on the camera by sending a formatted XML payload. In particular, the payload accepts 3 different tags for parsing: *TARGET*, *MAC*, and *CMD*. Although the content of both *TARGET* and *MAC* are apparently not used except in some printing functions, the content of the *CMD* tag is compared to the *reboot* string. If the strcmp returns 0, the FUN_00016ea8 function is called with the argument /app/bin/cmd reset; otherwise, the content of the *CMD* tag is passed directly to the same function.

Upon further inspection, we verified that the FUN_00016ea8 function is a simple wrapper for the system function, with the arguments passed to the function being forwarded directly to system without proper sanitization. This allows unauthenticated remote code execution on the camera by simply passing a command different from *reboot*.

> **CVE-2023-30353:** Unauthenticated RCE - Tenda IP Camera CP3 allows unauthenticated remote code execution via an XML document.
>
> Base Score: **9.8 Critical**
> Vector: CVSS:3.1/AV:N/AC:L/PR:N/UI:N/S:U/C:H/I:H/A:H

We emphasize that by following the described methodology, which is based on the analysis of the recv functions and their activation path, we were able to find all handlers for incoming connections managed by the *noodles* application. Furthermore, we demonstrated how to exploit these handlers to obtain unauthenticated RCE with root privileges on the device.

4.2 The *apollo* Binary

We employed the same methodology applied on the *noodles* binary to analyze the *apollo* binary. In particular, we want to remark that the vanilla rhabdomancer script on the whole *apollo* binary resulted in more than 128000 candidate points, while our tool returned less than 100 points, which we further reduced with a simple duplicate removal of different points on the same function calls.

The *apollo* binary utilizes 65 different threads to perform various tasks based on commands received from 7 different ports. Each of these threads eventually leads to one or more of the 25 recv functions. These functions containing the recv calls are solely responsible for managing incoming data, while the parsing of the received data structure is handled by the calling functions.

After thorough analysis, we successfully mapped each thread to a specific port listened to by the *apollo* process and identified the exposed functionalities.

- **3702/TCP** exposes ONVIF [15] *discovery, notification* and *hello* threads as required by the ONVIF Core Specification [3 threads];
- **6688/TCP:** exposes an HTTP server [3 threads];
- **8554/TCP:** exposes the *RTSP* service, which is used to access the camera video and audio [2 threads]
- **8699/TCP:** exposes a set of threads related to manage different functionalities of the camera [52 threads];
- **9876/TCP:** exposes the *yserver* TCP handler for incoming connections [3 threads];
- **5683/UDP:** exposes the *COAP* (COnstrained Application Protocol [5]) functionalities [1 thread];
- **19966/UDP:** exposes the *yserver* UDP handler for incoming connections [1 thread].

We proceeded with a more in-depth analysis of the main handler of port **8699/TCP** (ut_cmd_server_init) due to the significant number of threads directly associated with this port. We discovered that this connection is utilized for direct communication with the user application within the same network or via cloud services when in a different network. It accepts all possible commands that the user can provide through the application interface.

The incoming packets are handled by a dedicated thread (ut_rcmd_server_proc) and then passed to a parser function to identify the received command (FUN_0007cb00). In this function, the parser only checks that the received command starts with the character ! and then proceeds to compare the remainder of the received string with hard-coded commands. If the received string matches one of the commands, then a thread is spawned and the desired function is executed on the camera. We identified 148 different commands (147 plus the help command, which returns the description of all the other commands), which are mapped to 50 different threads. As an example, the audio_output_proc manages various functionalities related to recording audio from the microphone (e.g., *audio_vol_in*, used to set the audio input volume, or *capture_audio*, used to capture audio from the microphone) and setting different speaker parameters. Meanwhile, functionalities related to playing audio on the camera are managed by the audio_output_proc (e.g., *loop_audio* and *play_audio*). However, if the string received by the ut_rcmd_server_proc thread and parsed by the FUN_0007cb00 function is not recognized as one of the commands directly managed by the process, the system function is executed by passing the remaining string as the only parameter. By supplying a correctly formatted string to the service, we were able to achieve another instance of unauthenticated remote code execution on the camera.

Finally, we note that we also identified potential exploits on the other ports handled by the *apollo* process. While the methodology presented in this paper has proven effective in identifying vulnerabilities on our device, we emphasize that the process of behavior reconstruction (i.e., the detailed analysis presented on the *noodles* binary) and the subsequent crafting of exploits to verify a security vulnerability still heavily rely on human skill and experience.

5 Conclusions

This paper analyzes the process of vulnerability discovery on a consumer IP camera to demonstrate the effectiveness of the approach in the identification of security vulnerabilities. The methodology comprises five steps:

1. gathering relevant information from open sources;
2. physical access to a IP camera specimen aiming at identifying low-level attack vectors;
3. firmware extraction and static analysis of the whole file system, including configuration files, scripts and executables;
4. dynamic analysis of the network behavior, aiming at identifying all remote attack surfaces (such as open TCP and UDP port) of the connected IP camera;
5. in-depth reversing of all executables that implement network-facing services.

We provide a detailed example of the application of the proposed methodology by applying it on the widespread Tenda CP3 IP camera as a relevant use case. Our methodology allowed us to identify five new CVEs with a CVSS score ranging from 7.5 to 9.8.

We remark that the proposed methodology differs from the approaches that are commonly proposed in many related works, which only perform network-based analysis and fall short from executing a complete reversing of relevant executables.

To partially automate our approach we also developed a novel tool [2] based on Ghidra and rhabdomancer that is able to identify the functions managing incoming connection, to reconstruct their call tree from the *main* function for a fast identification of critical points in large binary executables.

Responsible Disclosure

Before publication of this work we contacted Shenzen Tenda Technology Co., Ltd. (May 2023) and disclosed our initial findings to them. We informed their representative that we had discovered several vulnerabilities in one of their products and mutually agreed to proceed with the responsible disclosure procedure once the CVE IDs for the vulnerabilities were assigned. We obtained 5 CVE IDs (out of the 7 initially requested, with 2 CVE IDs covering two vulnerabilities each) at the beginning of June 2023, and promptly reached out to their representative. As of time of submission of the camera ready of this work (July 2024), all details of our findings have been shared with the Tenda representative, who also assured that a patch resolving all these vulnerabilities is currently being developed and will be available in the next months.

Acknowledgments. This work was partially supported by project SERICS (PE00000014) under the MUR National Recovery and Resilience Plan funded by the European Union - NextGenerationEU.

References

1. Abdalla, P.A., Varol, C.: Testing IoT security: the case study of an IP camera. In: 2020 8th International Symposium on Digital Forensics and Security (ISDFS), pp. 1–5 (2020). https://doi.org/10.1109/ISDFS49300.2020.9116392
2. ACES - Automotive, Cyber-Physical, Embedded and Security research laboratory. IWSec 2024 - Scripts and materials. https://github.com/SECloudUNIMORE/ACES/tree/master/IWSec2024. Accessed April 2024
3. Bathich, P., Malli, M., Hazimeh, H.: Exploiting vulnerabilities of IP cameras: lebanon case study. In: 2021 9th International Symposium on Digital Forensics and Security (ISDFS), pp. 1–6 (2021). https://doi.org/10.1109/ISDFS52919.2021.9486324
4. Biondi, P., Bognanni, S., Bella, G.: Vulnerability assessment and penetration testing on IP camera. In: 2021 8th International Conference on Internet of Things: Systems, Management and Security (IOTSMS), pp. 1–8 (2021). https://doi.org/10.1109/IOTSMS53705.2021.9704890
5. COAP: COnstrained Application Procotol. https://datatracker.ietf.org/doc/html/rfc7252. Accessed March 2024
6. craigz28: Firmwalker. https://github.com/craigz28/firmwalker. Accessed April 2024
7. Federal Communications Commission: FCC ID Search. https://fccid.io/. Accessed March 2024
8. Flashrom: Flashrom. https://flashrom.org/. Accessed March 2024
9. Fyodor: NMAP - Network Mapper. https://nmap.org/. Accessed April 2024
10. Kalbo, N., Mirsky, Y., Shabtai, A., Elovici, Y.: The security of IP-based video surveillance systems. Sensors **20**(17) (2020). https://doi.org/10.3390/s20174806, https://www.mdpi.com/1424-8220/20/17/4806
11. Li, J., Li, Z., Tyson, G., Xie, G.: Your privilege gives your privacy away: an analysis of a home security camera service. In: IEEE INFOCOM 2020 - IEEE Conference on Computer Communications, pp. 387–396 (2020). https://doi.org/10.1109/INFOCOM41043.2020.9155516

12. Li, Y., Mandalari, A.M., Straw, I.: Who let the smart toaster hack the house? An investigation into the security vulnerabilities of consumer IoT devices (2023)
13. Marco Ivaldi: Rhabdomancer. https://github.com/0xdea/ghidra-scripts/blob/main/Rhabdomancer.java. Accessed April 2024
14. National Security Agency: Ghidra SRE. https://ghidra-sre.org/. Accessed April 2024
15. ONVIF: Open Network Video Interface Forum. https://www.onvif.org/. Accessed April 2024
16. Shwartz, O., Mathov, Y., Bohadana, M., Elovici, Y., Oren, Y.: Opening Pandora's box: effective techniques for reverse engineering IoT devices. In: Eisenbarth, T., Teglia, Y. (eds.) CARDIS 2017. LNCS, vol. 10728, pp. 1–21. Springer, Cham (2018). https://doi.org/10.1007/978-3-319-75208-2_1

Malware Countermeasure

File System Shield (FSS): A Pass-Through Strategy Against Unwanted Encryption in Network File Systems

Arash Mahboubi[1(✉)], Seyit Camtepe[2], Keyvan Ansari[3], Marcin Pawłowski[4], Paweł Morawiecki[5], Jarek Duda[4], and Josef Pieprzyk[2]

[1] Charles Sturt University and Artificial Intelligence and Cyber Futures Institute, Port Macquarie, Australia
amahboubi@csu.edu.au
[2] CSIRO, Canberra, Australia
{seyit.camtepe,josef.pieprzyk}@data61.csiro.au
[3] Murdoch University, Murdoch, Australia
Keyvan.Ansari@murdoch.edu.au
[4] Jagiellonian University, Kraków, Poland
[5] Polish Academy of Sciences, Warsaw, Poland

Abstract. This study introduces the Digital Immunity Module (DIM), a novel pass-through file system gateway, positioned strategically between storage and endpoints to enhance the security of files accessed via network protocols such as NFS and SMB on SharePoint. DIM serves as a protective layer against ransomware, designed with dual objectives: (1) detecting statistical anomalies that may indicate potential encryption within the network file system, and (2) proactively expanding under-attack files using a reverse source-coding algorithm to deprive ransomware of the resources it needs to operate. For practical deployment, we have developed a proxy gateway that connects endpoints to Azure storage using the SMB protocol. This setup effectively differentiates between benign and malicious activities without needing to identify specific processes at the endpoints, i.e., a critical advantage in combating fileless ransomware, which often eludes conventional security mechanisms such as behavioral analysis. Upon detecting malicious encryption, DIM reacts by expanding the size of buffer blocks, preventing ransomware from accessing subsequent files and frequently causing the ransomware to self-terminate. Our comprehensive evaluation, involving a benign dataset of 11,928 files against 75 ransomware families, including fileless types, demonstrates that DIM significantly impedes and often terminates ransomware operations early in the attack life cycle. This confirms the practicality and effectiveness of this pass-through defence strategy.

Keywords: Ransomware · Information Theory · Filesystem in Userspace · Arithmetic encoding · Fileless

1 Introduction

Ransomware, often classified as cryptoviruses, poses a significant threat to cybersecurity through its use of unauthorised encryption processes to render data inaccessible. Complications like ransomware attacks can also emerge when organisational files stored on shared systems are inadvertently encrypted by employees using legitimate cryptographic tools, creating situations that resemble ransomware activities, particularly when decryption keys are mismanaged or lost. Presently, machine learning (ML) techniques are at the vanguard of ransomware detection, employing predictive models that discern behaviour characteristics of ransomware. These models analyse patterns such as distinctive API calls, system library interactions, and file system dynamics, including the frequency of file read and write operations. Although these methodologies demonstrate efficacy against known ransomware types, they encounter limitations in identifying novel, characterised strains of ransomware. The evolving nature of ransomware enables it to mimic the behaviour of benign software, thereby challenging the sustained accuracy and effectiveness of ML detection models.

The relentless evolution of ransomware introduces substantial challenges in its detection, as adversaries refine their tactics to engineer ransomware that closely imitates the behaviour of legitimate software. This deceptive similarity significantly complicates the task of ML systems in distinguishing between malicious and benign programs. Emerging methodologies, such as unsupervised learning and anomaly detection, offer potential advancements in identifying a typical behaviour pattern without relying exclusively on predefined threat databases. These approaches indicate a prospective paradigm shift in the methodologies employed for ransomware detection, enhancing the ability to detect novel threats that evade traditional detection frameworks. Despite the promising advances in ML techniques, the complexity and adaptability of ransomware necessitate further innovations in detection and prevention strategies. This need has lead us to developing the Digital Immunity Module (DIM), a targeted solution designed to address the unique challenges posed by modern ransomware.

This paper presents the Digital Immunity Module (DIM), an innovative framework designed to safeguard data at the file-system level from unauthorised encryption, with applicability to networked and cloud-based environments. DIM proactively intervenes by scrutinising and manipulating file write operations, thereby markedly impeding the encryption process through the expansion of data blocks, which in turn disrupts ransomware activities and enhances attack traceability. This approach underscores the enhancement of resilience against ransomware, especially targeting novel and adaptive variants, by concentrating on the protection of remotely stored critical data. Utilising a custom FUSE (Filesystem in Userspace) file system, DIM thoroughly monitors and controls data transfers between endpoints and network storage, actively identifying and mitigating malicious encryption attempts. This strategy not only fortifies the security of files on network and cloud storage but also supports organisational cybersecurity policies that emphasise the protection of critical data assets over endpoint device data. As a result, the implementation of DIM represents a significant shift in how cybersecurity defences are conceptualised and applied within organisational frameworks.

The structure of this paper is organised as follows: In Sect. 2, we review related work and provide the necessary background. Section 3 is dedicated to a detailed description of the DIM concept. In Sect. 4, we elaborate on the experimental setup, evaluation methods, and assess the efficacy and performance of DIM. Section 5 engages in a comparative analysis of DIM with state-of-the-art solutions. Finally, Sect. 6 summaries our findings and outlines future research directions.

2 Related Works and Background

File System-Oriented Solutions: This section compares our purpose-built model with related storage-level works that use file system features to detect and prevent ransomware operations. We highlight the differences between our approach and most existing results, focusing on the I/O patterns analysis. Kharraz et al. in [19] focuses on analyzing the behavior of ransomware attacks from a file system perspective, describing common characteristics of ransomware attacks by investigating their file system activity. The authors developed a minifilter driver to monitor I/O requests generated by the I/O manager on behalf of user-mode processes to access the file system. They analyzed the file system activity of multiple ransomware samples, identified their attack strategies, and categorized the malicious activities. One such category involves encryption mechanisms, mainly composed of customized and standard cryptosystems. The paper provides insights into the encryption process, other malicious activities, and how a malicious process interacts with the file system during a ransomware attack.

ShieldFS [9] builds upon the work of [19], introducing a forward-looking file system that can prevent the harmful effects of ransomware attacks on data in a transparent manner. ShieldFS proposes to achieve this through automatic detection and transparent file recovery capabilities at the file system level. The detection system designed by the authors is based on entropy analysis involving write operations, frequency of read, write, and folder-listing operations, dispersion of per-file writes, the fraction of files renamed, and file-type usage statistics. ShieldFS then looks for indicators of cryptographic primitives and scans the memory of any process considered "potentially malicious", searching for traces of typical block cipher key schedules.

UNVEIL [18] is a system that employs a file system monitor with direct access to data buffers involved in I/O requests, providing complete visibility into all file system modifications. UNVEIL's monitor establishes callbacks on all I/O requests to the file system generated by any user-mode process. For performance reasons, the system aims to set only one callback per I/O request while maintaining comprehensive visibility into I/O operations. UNVEIL analyzes access patterns in I/O traces, which include sequences of user-mode processes, available files, I/O operations, and the entropy of read or write data buffers. It identifies distinctive I/O fingerprints for file locker ransomware samples by detecting repetitive I/O access patterns indicative of a ransomware strategy to deny access to user files. Additionally, UNVEIL computes the entropy of read and write requests to and from the same file offset, which is a common indicator of crypto-ransomware behavior. This pattern arises when ransomware reads the original file data, encrypts it, and then overwrites it with the encrypted version. However, this approach is not universally adopted across modern ransomware families and variants. Shannon entropy is used for this computation, assuming a uniform random distribution of bytes in a data block.

Paik et al. [27] proposed a method for detecting ransomware in flash-based storage, involving an access-pattern-based detector coupled with a buffer management policy designed for solid-state drives (SSDs). This method monitors read and write operations at the same location to identify instances where ransomware encrypts and then overwrites original files. However, its effectiveness may be limited if the read-write buffers on the SSD are small, and it may not always detect ransomware if the malicious software doesn't store files at the same location.

Baek et al. [2] introduced the SSD-Insider method, designed to detect and protect NAND flash-based SSDs from ransomware attacks. This approach scrutinizes unique attributes of I/O requests, such as block address, size, and type, to detect the presence of ransomware. It employs an Iterative Dichotomiser 3 (ID3) based binary decision tree for detailed analysis of these characteristics. The authors also propose an innovative Flash Translation Layer (FTL) design capable of restoring infected files by leveraging the delayed deletion feature inherent to NAND flash. Despite its ingenuity, this method incurs significant additional overhead on the SSD system.

Non-File System Oriented Solutions: This section reviews various ransomware detection and mitigation strategies, ranging from rule-based frameworks to those that use machine learning (ML) techniques. The focus of these strategies is on vigilant monitoring of process behaviors, meticulous analysis of network traffic, and scrupulous examination of system calls to detect any signs of suspicious or anomalous activities. These activities encompass various aspects such as OS log entries [8], changes to the Windows Registry [28], arbitrary file modifications [29], and the entropy of files [17,20,28].

The literature also discusses various machine learning approaches [4], including detection based on API/System Calls [30], file I/O operations [9], and network traffic features. These features include the average packet size, the number of packets exchanged between the host and other machines, and the source or destination IP addresses contained within packet headers [10].

Several research studies have explored process actions, referring to the event sequences occurring while a program or application runs. Researchers have also used process mining techniques to identify file system metrics and conducted Ransom Note Analysis to study instances of ransomware attacks [3,14,18]. Despite the advancement in detection techniques, recent ransomware variants such as DoppelPaymer, Sodinokibi, Hades, Ryuk, and Conti continue to pose significant challenges, including business disruption, data loss, reputational damage, remediation costs, and legal liabilities. These challenges primarily arise due to frequent changes in ransomware behavior, complicating the detection process. We have summarized related work in Table 1.

Table 1. Summary of ransomware detection techniques.

Detection techniques	Reference
Behaviour Based	[1, 12, 15, 17, 18, 29, 30]
I/O Request Packer Monitoring	[2, 9]
Network Traffic Monitoring	[5, 6, 10, 24, 26]
Storage Level	[2, 9, 27]
Opcode-Bytecode Sequences	[3]
Process mining identifying file system metrics	[22]
Ransom Note Analysis	[18]
File and Binary Entropy checking	[17, 20, 28]
API Call	[13]
File types extension analysis	[29]
Others (Autonomous Backup and Recovery SSD)	[23]
Others (Windows Registry, log files, sdhash)	[3, 8, 11, 14, 28, 29]

3 Digital Immunity Module

This section introduces the concept and approach of our proposed Digital Immunity Module (DIM). The primary role of DIM is to actively prevent ransomware from encrypting files under its protection. DIM focuses on file security with two main objectives: (1) Identify DIM-protected files undergoing encryption, and (2) Prevent malicious encryption of DIM-protected files.

Encryption Detection – Shannon Entropy Approach: to achieve its objectives, DIM needs to effectively distinguish between encrypted and unencrypted files. Unencrypted files can be text files (such as PDFs, Microsoft Word documents, and LaTex files), multimedia files (like images, music, and videos), and other commonly used formats. We propose using Shannon's entropy concept as a natural method to differentiate between these file types. Consider a random variable X representing n events $x_1, \ldots, x_n$, with each event x_i occurring with a probability $P(x_i)$. In this context, entropy is defined as follows:

$$H(X) = -\sum_{i=1}^{n} P(x_i) \log_2 P(x_i). \quad (1)$$

We consider the events of our random variable X to be characters of the Unicode standard, including non-printable ones. Entropy is a useful measure to gauge the randomness of a file's content. High entropy is indicative of randomness, whereas redundant (correlated) content results in low entropy. To calculate the entropy $H(f)$ of a file $f = \{x\}_1^N$ with N characters from X, we count the occurrences ℓ_x of each character x in f, as follows:

$$H(f) = -\sum_{x \in f} \frac{\ell_x}{N} \log_2 \frac{\ell_x}{N},$$

where $\frac{\ell_x}{N}$ denotes the probability of character x occurring in file f. For instance, consider a file $f = \{aaaaaaaaa\}$. Here, $\ell_a = 9$, $N = 9$, and thus $\frac{\ell_a}{N} = 1$, leading to $H(f) = 0$. Another file $f' = \{aeaieou!\}$, with varied occurrences, will have $H(f') = 2.5$.

Each type of unencrypted file, treated as a source of symbols/characters, is assumed to have a specific probability distribution characterizing its source program. For sufficiently long files f generated by a PDF source, for example, the probability of a symbol x can be approximated by its occurrence ℓ_x in f:

$$P(x) \approx \frac{\ell_x}{N},$$

where N is the total number of characters in file f. Thus, $H(f)_{PDF} = H_{PDF}$, where $H(f)_{PDF}$ is the entropy of f generated by a PDF source and H_{PDF} is the entropy of the PDF source. However, this approximation is ineffective for "short" files. Since sources of unencrypted files typically generate byte characters, the maximum entropy H_{max} of a file equals 8 bits, occurring when source characters are uniformly distributed.

Entropy of Encrypted Files: We expect sufficiently long encrypted files to have entropy levels approaching $H_{\max}$. Cryptographically robust encryption typically produces cryptograms that are virtually indistinguishable from truly random sequences. To test this hypothesis, we conducted experiments on various file types. Initially, we measured the entropy of a representative sample for each specific file type. Then, we encrypted these samples using three different open-source encryption tools: AESCrypt, GnuPG, and Challenger, and repeated the entropy measurement. The results, depicted in Table 2, confirm with high confidence that a file f is encrypted if its entropy $H(f)$ satisfies $7.99 < H(f) \leq 8$.

However, it is important to remember that compressed files can also exhibit entropy values near $H_{\max}$, which necessitates careful interpretation in such cases.

Table 2. Entropy of encrypted and un-encrypted files

File Format	Unencrypted	Challenger	GnuPG	AESCrypt
.pptx	7.90786434941	7.99993409023	7.99992547868	7.99992691156
.bmp	6.38231379202	7.99994411725	7.99969271027	7.99994075204
.jpg	7.96841466702	7.99969969991	7.99972370710	7.99964407683
.docx	7.82881687843	7.99564129666	7.99531941975	7.99383985158
.pdf	7.85009879424	7.99998526860	7.99997917863	7.99998576992
.xlsx	7.93289273016	7.99846117766	7.99844636333	7.99869412812
.png	7.98653176951	7.99983209472	7.99978322342	7.99982432301
.tex	4.81546551317	7.99832884790	7.99416858853	7.99793348066
.sql	5.14310355930	7.99991774345	7.99949416462	7.99992064505

The above observations lead to the following conclusions: (a) Entropy can be used to characterize redundancy in files generated by specific applications, such as PDF creators, Microsoft Word, and PowerPoint. The entropy of plain or unencrypted files typically falls below 7.99. (b) Encrypted files generally exhibit a uniform probability distribution of characters, resulting in an entropy close to $H_{\max}$. However, a notable caveat is that compressed files may also display high entropy values, necessitating distinct consideration.

Measuring Entropy in Practice: Calculating file entropy typically requires fetching the entire file from the HDD into RAM, which is both computationally expensive and time-consuming, especially for large files. Detection processes that are time- and computation-intensive have proven inefficient in dealing with ransomware attacks. This inefficiency arises from the rapid pace at which ransomware can encrypt target files once an attack is initiated.

A practical solution involves determining a *'minimum threshold length of bytes'* whereby a portion of the target file can be used to approximate its entropy. This approximation aims to yield a value that closely mirrors the file's actual entropy, enabling DIM to make rapid decisions about potential encryption. To test this approach, we used 436 PDF documents containing historical Federal Reserve projections of the U.S. economy, commonly referred to as *Greenbook projections* (or Board of Governors Datasets). These documents consist of text, tables, and graphs. Our experiments suggest that setting a minimum threshold length of 25,000 bytes achieves an acceptable confidence level for approximating a file's entropy. The entropy approximation for 15,000 bytes is presented in Table 3, and for 25,000 bytes in Table 4, using the Greenbook PDF Dataset encrypted by specified ransomware. The bold values in Table 4 indicate the threshold value of 7.99. Note that only a subset of the files is displayed in this table.

Table 3. The first 15000 bytes of the file are read and the entropy is computed.

File Name	Total File Entropy	GandCrab	locked	OFFWHITE	az3zg	avdn	eswasted	WNCRY
GS-1966-01-11.pdf	7.7787168	7.98654117	7.9871808	7.98838185	7.98779854	7.98884194	7.9877807	7.98771588
GS-1966-02-08.pdf	7.7957867	7.98679319	7.98813517	7.98663561	7.98738209	7.98744374	7.98915027	7.98577155
GS-1966-03-01.pdf	7.71154378	7.98849562	7.98780239	7.98756999	7.98761761	7.98670168	7.9885083	7.98640685
GS-1966-03-22.pdf	7.70743395	7.98853245	7.98775498	7.98745479	7.98805904	7.98589657	7.98739649	7.98965494
GS-1966-04-12.pdf	7.70909013	7.9864649	7.98792679	7.98629035	7.98944624	7.98654917	7.98642588	7.9882894
GS-1966-05-10.pdf	7.71872743	7.9873719	7.98942611	7.9889985	7.98769273	7.98756768	7.98744401	7.98777511
GS-1966-06-07.pdf	7.71313681	7.98778132	7.98508746	7.9872488	7.98805607	7.9876873	7.98932451	7.98676996
GS-1966-06-28.pdf	7.7869504	7.98654693	7.98843465	7.98801858	7.98777954	7.98756831	7.98874163	7.98857874
GS-1966-07-26.pdf	7.78627432	7.98702218	7.9866608	7.98770975	7.98996563	7.98626002	7.98707602	7.98900321
GS-1966-08-23.pdf	7.72829092	7.98679314	7.98909114	7.98884781	7.98636617	7.9893225	7.98484725	7.9857893

Entropy of Compressed Files: *JPEG files:* Compressed files like JPEGs, which employ lossy compression, inherently have high entropy due to the reduction of character redundancy in image files. For our experiments, we utilised the *INRIA Holidays JPG dataset* [16], comprising 812 JPG images occupying 1.1GB of storage. The entropy of each file in this dataset was calculated, revealing that the highest entropy value, 7.95245506, was derived from the initial 25,000 bytes of a file. Notably, although JPG files exhibit high entropy values, they are not as high as those of encrypted files. This difference is attributed to non-uniform character distribution probabilities in JPG files. For example, the *Null* (or 00) character is the most frequent in most JPG files, while in others, the *nbsp* (or 255) character predominates.

Table 4. The first 25000 bytes of the file are read and the entropy is computed.

File Name	GandCrab	locked	OFFWHITE	az3zg	avdn	eswasted	WNCRY
GS-1966-01-11.pdf	**7.99**338252	**7.99**245514	**7.99**215868	**7.99**127136	**7.99**254762	**7.99**140233	**7.99**28472
GS-1966-02-08.pdf	**7.99**100436	**7.99**313812	**7.99**253868	**7.99**211495	**7.99**210098	**7.99**252393	**7.99**172881
GS-1966-03-01.pdf	**7.99**22206	**7.99**283364	**7.99**205808	**7.99**274639	**7.99**110681	**7.99**350538	**7.99**23769
GS-1966-03-22.pdf	**7.99**364135	**7.99**293043	**7.99**278268	**7.99**234747	**7.99**238042	**7.99**19224	**7.99**362411
GS-1966-04-12.pdf	**7.99**20972	**7.99**251146	**7.99**17135	**7.99**382699	**7.99**163157	**7.99**097479	**7.99**184339
GS-1966-05-10.pdf	**7.99**399683	**7.99**291601	**7.99**391016	**7.99**315747	**7.99**326597	**7.99**235577	**7.99**343543
GS-1966-06-07.pdf	**7.99**248154	**7.99**199274	**7.99**239283	**7.99**317553	**7.99**241421	**7.99**336579	**7.99**261136
GS-1966-06-28.pdf	**7.99**300174	**7.99**353394	**7.99**285691	**7.99**322543	**7.99**293433	**7.99**270476	**7.99**301798
GS-1966-07-26.pdf	**7.99**31377	**7.99**344906	**7.99**250657	**7.99**272543	**7.99**232356	**7.99**183047	**7.99**371094
GS-1966-08-23.pdf	**7.99**218428	**7.99**356795	**7.99**311067	**7.99**240853	**7.99**295244	**7.99**21548	**7.99**167112

TIFF Files: TIFF file compression uses adaptive dictionary algorithms, like LZW compression. Our experiments aimed to explore the statistical properties of TIFF files. We used a sample of 87 TIFF images from a medical database, specifically the OME-TIFF dataset. The results showed that the highest file entropy was 5.20967171, significantly lower than the $H_{\max}$ value of 8. This outcome suggests a non-uniform probability distribution of characters in TIFF images. For example, the *Null* character frequently appears with the highest probability in these files.

High-performance compression algorithms, such as those used in TAR and ZIP applications, effectively reduce character redundancy to the extent that the file entropy approaches $H_{\max}$. This resemblance creates a significant challenge in distinguishing compressed files from those encrypted by ransomware, particularly if entropy is the sole characteristic under consideration. To address this issue, user applications and DIM can negotiate an acceptable level of compression quality. This can be achieved by slightly skewing the byte probability distribution, thereby introducing a small redundancy ε. Consequently, the file entropy is adjusted to $H(f) - \varepsilon$, where $H(f)$ represents the entropy of the compressed file. The introduced redundancy ε should be minimal to avoid compromising compression quality, yet substantial enough to enable DIM to differentiate between compressed and encrypted files.

Distribution of Symbols in Encrypted Files: In encrypted files, characters behave as if they are random, making it impossible to extract any sensitive information from them. Essentially, any two adjacent characters should be regarded as independent random variables X and Y, where X does not reveal any information about Y and vice versa. Consequently, characters in encrypted files tend

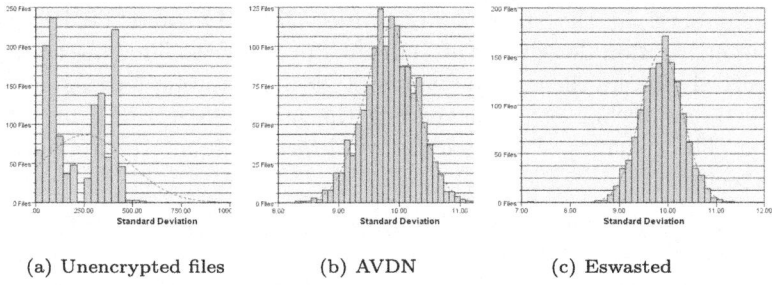

(a) Unencrypted files   (b) AVDN   (c) Eswasted

Fig. 1. The Standard Deviation (σ) of PDF, JPG, and TIFF files was computed from the first 25 kilobytes (KB) of each file. Sub-Figure (a) illustrates that symbols in unencrypted files appear loosely distributed, whereas in encrypted files, symbols are more uniformly distributed (b) and (c)

Table 5. Average Confidence Interval of the first 25000 Bytes of 8010 encrypted and 1335 unencrypted files. The data set is encrypted by six different ransomware families.

	Encrypted files			Unencrypted files		
	Lower bound	Mean	Upper bound	Lower bound	Mean	Upper bound
Confidence Interval 99%	96.02748789	97.65625	99.31896542	35.4255017	97.65625	159.8869983
Confidence Interval 95%	96.38530503	97.65625	98.92719497	50.43465809	97.65625	144.8778419
Confidence Interval 90%	96.590831	97.65625	98.721669	58.07091603	97.65625	137.241584
Confidence Interval 85%	96.72440466	97.65625	98.58809534	63.03380651	97.65625	132.2786935
Confidence Interval 80%	96.8330564	97.65625	98.4794436	66.84643556	97.65625	128.4660644

to follow a uniform probability distribution. To test this theory in the context of ransomware encryption, we selected six prevalent ransomware variants and used them to encrypt a collection of three datasets: Greenbook projections, INRIA Holidays, and OME-TIFF. We then computed the standard deviations of characters for the first 25 kilobytes (KB) of each encrypted file.

Figure 1 shows the distribution of symbols in both unencrypted and ransomware-encrypted files, confirming that characters in encrypted files are indeed uniformly distributed. Additionally, Table 5 presents the confidence intervals for both encrypted and unencrypted files, calculated for the first 25 KB of the 8010 encrypted and 1335 unencrypted files, corresponding to confidence levels ranging from 99% to 80%.

Ransomware with Low Entropy: Modern ransomware variants achieve higher throughput and lower latency by employing parallel threads, allowing them to fetch data from the HDD and encrypt it concurrently without waiting for other threads to complete. A notable example of such ransomware is Dharma (also known as CrySIS), which has been active since 2016. With over a hundred different versions, our analysis reveals that this multi-threaded ransomware encrypts eight files simultaneously. Additionally, it writes 256 KB of the *null* character at the start of image files (like JPG and TIFF), likely to circumvent encryption detection through entropy analysis. This insertion of null bytes effectively lowers the entropy values of files. To counteract this, we employ a sliding window technique while reading the initial 25 KB of a file to detect encryption. The specifics of this sliding window technique are explained in the following section.

Context Triggered Piecewise Hashing: Similarity-preserving hashing, also known as fuzzy hashing, has been used in malware analysis [21]. In this study, we propose employing fuzzy hashing to detect buffers containing malicious content. Consider a collection of files $F = \{f_1, f_2, \ldots, f_m\}$, with each file f_m requiring a finite set of buffers $\{b_1, b_2, \ldots, b_n\}$, where each buffer b_n is 4096 bytes in size. Let $f_{\text{hash}}(f_m(b_n))$ represent the hashing signature (digest) of the b_n buffer contents of f_m. Algorithm 1 computes similarity-preserving hash signatures for all files in the collection F stored on the HDD. This approach allows us to: (1) Detect files with correct similarity-preserving hash signatures before writing them to the HDD. (2) Identify padding data added by ransomware to reduce file entropy. (3) Make it difficult for ransomware to predict which buffers (hash signatures) DIM uses to identify encrypted contents. (4) Determine if ransomware has deleted and rewritten all buffers of a file, indicating that the original file is irreversibly damaged and no ransom should be paid. (5) Update buffers' fuzzy signatures after each legitimate file write operation. (6) Distinguish existing files from new ones, even if the new files exhibit high entropy (such as ZIP or encrypted files).

4 Experimental Setup for DIM Efficacy and Performance Evaluation

To validate the DIM concept, a proof-of-concept setup was created to assess its efficacy and performance. The system consists of a Dell desktop with an Intel Core i7-4770 CPU @ 3.40 GHz, 16 GB RAM, and 4 cores with 8 logical processors. It hosts two virtual machines on a VMware hypervisor, each configured with 4 GB RAM and 4 processor cores. The VMs run on Ubuntu 20.04 Desktop and Windows 10 Education N. The first VM, representing a typical ransomware target, runs Windows 10, chosen for its prevalence in ransomware attacks due to its widespread use. The second VM uses Ubuntu with Samba (SMB protocol) to simulate network storage, protected by DIM, and contains a shared folder with 1335 files of various types, including PDF, JPG, and TIFF. This setup is designed to evaluate DIM's potential in a controlled environment that mimics real-world conditions.

A key component of our setup is the FUSE (Filesystem in Userspace) framework. FUSE is widely used, with at least 100 different FUSE-based file systems available online. It has two main components: a kernel module and a user-level daemon. Once the kernel module is loaded, it registers with the Linux Virtual File System (VFS) as a FUSE file system driver, enabling the creation of file systems in user space rather than kernel space. FUSE is popular for custom file system development.

Algorithm 1 collects buffers at random for files and computes their fuzzy hashing signatures. There is a collection of fuzzy signatures for each file that exists on storage.

1: **Input**: $F = \{f_1, f_2, \ldots, f_m\}$ {#All files on HD}
2: **Output**: Collection of all files fuzzy signatures
3: $FuzzyCollection[]$ {#Global}
4: $files[] \leftarrow f_m$
5: $b_n := 4096$
6: $n := 1$
7: **for** f_m in $files$ **do**
8:    {#7 buffers need for entropy}
9:    $Random \leftarrow range(1, 7)$
10:    $Read\ f_m$:
11:    **while** $Not\ EOF$ **do**
12:      $temp \leftarrow read\ f_m(b_n)$ {# Read file 4096 }
13:      **if** $n = Random$ **then**
14:         $FuzzyCollection := f_{hash}(temp)$
15:         $break$
16:      **end if**
17:      $n := +1$
18:    **end while**
19:    $Close f_m$
20:    $n := 1$
21: **end for**

Several FUSE-based file systems have been developed by various vendors, such as Google Cloud Storage FUSE and s3fs-fuse. The FUSE kernel module, integrated into the Linux kernel, serves as an intermediary for specific file systems implemented by different user-level daemons. When a user application accesses a FUSE file system, the Linux VFS directs the request to the FUSE kernel driver. This driver creates a FUSE request, adds it to a queue, and typically pauses the requesting process while the request is processed. The user-level FUSE daemon retrieves the request from the kernel queue via /dev/fuse and handles it [31]. FUSE is also available for Windows systems under the name WinFsb.

DIM Pass-Through Module for Encryption Detection: *(Question: Where can DIM be embedded in a resilient system?)* To address this question, we developed a pass-through module that interfaces with the FUSE file system. This module is designed to intercept and examine the read/write buffers within the network share file that is under DIM protection. It has all necessary permissions to manipulate files, including access, chmod, open, create, read, and write, making it a fully functional file system.

Three principal directories **A** ⇔ **B** ⇔ **C** interact with the pass-through module. Directory **A** contains all files but is not directly accessible to users. Directory **B**, configured as a shared mounting point (user-level daemon) with the Samba protocol, is accessible to users over the network. Directory **C** is located in the user environment. Note that while both **A** and **B** are on the Ubuntu VM, **C** resides on the Windows VM, representing the user's machine. When a process, initiated by a user or ransomware, opens or writes to a file, the module inspects the file's write buffers.

(Next question: How can DIM detect and identify encrypted write buffers, regardless of the encryption algorithm used?) The pass-through module inspects

all write buffers of files originating from directory **C**. It determines whether the contents of a buffer are encrypted before these contents are written to the HDD. Our analysis shows that at least 25 KB of a file is needed to compute reliable file entropy. To achieve this, the module reads seven buffers (each 4096 bytes) to identify encrypted content and calculates the file's entropy, standard deviation, and confidence interval.

Consider a scenario where ransomware reads a 100 KB file, encrypts its contents, and stores it in memory, i.e., the buffer cache. The system then writes these encrypted bytes to the HDD using a default block size, which in this case is 4 KB. Let $\Omega = \{b_1, b_2, \ldots, b_n\}$ represent a collection of n buffers. The process of encryption detection employed by the pass-through module is outlined in Algorithm 2.

Algorithm 2 identifies encrypted buffers. It reads seven buffers (chosen at random) to determine whether their signatures belong to the fuzzy hashing collection. It also measures the entropy of the seven buffers.

1: **Input**: An encrypted buffer $b_i \in \{b_1, b_2, \ldots, b_n\}$
2: **Input**: Cumulative buffer $byte[] \ Buffers$
3: **Input**: n the number of encrypted buffers arrived
4: $i := 0$
5: **for** $n := 1 \ to \ 7$ **do** { # Count for 7 buffer arrivals}
6:     $temp := FuzzyHash(b_n)$
7:     { # From Fuzzy }
8:     **for** $item \leftarrow FuzzyCollection[i]$ **do**
9:       $Compare := FuzzyHash.compare(temp, item)$
10:       { # No match at FuzzyHash}
11:       **if** $Compare = 0$ **then**
12:         $i := i + 1$
13:       **end if**
14:       **if** $i = length \ of \ FuzzyCollection[]$ **then**
15:         {#the file is new}
16:         $i := 0$
17:         $break$
18:       **end if**
19:     **end for**
20:     Insert b_n to $Buffers[]$ {#Accumulate buffers}
21: **end for**
22: $X := H(Buffers[b_1, .., b_7])$
23: **if** $(X \geq 7.99)$ & (no match in $FuzzyCollection$) **then**
24:     buffers are encrypted...
25:     start expanding buffers...
26:     break
27: **else**
28:     write buffer to HDD if conditions are not met
29: **end if**

DIM Encoding Expansion Module: Compression is a process that assigns shorter bit encodings to more probable symbols, while less probable symbols receive longer bit encodings [25]. There's extensive literature on coding schemes for lossless compression, such as Huffman, arithmetic, the Lempel-Ziv family (refer to [25]), and the asymmetric numeral system (ANS) [7], which has been found to be up to 30 times faster than earlier methods.

How can DIM Obstruct the Functionality of Ransomware? Compression is not only crucial for shortening transmission times, saving storage space, and accelerating encryption, but it also presents an interesting defensive mechanism against ransomware. When symbol occurrences in a file do not adhere to expected statistical distributions, compression can inadvertently expand the file. This expansion, typically undesirable, can be leveraged as a defense against ransomware. For instance, if DIM is requested by ransomware to store an encrypted file on the HDD, DIM can apply a compression algorithm using non-uniform symbol statistics, potentially derived from or similar to the file before encryption. This DIM-induced compression expands the file, thereby occupying the ransomware encryption engine. The extent of this expansion can be regulated by altering symbol probabilities, growing significantly when more frequent symbols are assigned very low probabilities. In theory, this expansion can reach sizes of gigabytes (GBs) or even terabytes (TBs), effectively slowing down the ransomware encryption engine without needing to locate the elusive ransomware process. This delay facilitates the triggering of an alarm for system or human intervention. Increasing symbol probabilities could potentially disable the ransomware functionality through excessive I/O load or insufficient storage on a DIM-controlled volume.

The primary function of the encoding expansion module is to engage a ransomware encryption engine by supplying it with an ever-expanding bitstream. To demonstrate this, we developed a simple algorithm that transforms a stream of uniformly distributed symbols (as in an encrypted file) into an exceedingly long bitstream. Suppose ransomware requests to write an encrypted file to a victim's HDD. Before proceeding, let's define some notations. Let $C = \Delta = \{c_1, c_2, \ldots, c_m\}$ represent a collection of characters (Unicode). For a sequence $S = (s_1, \ldots, s_n)$, where $s_i \in \Delta$, $|S|_{c_i}$ denotes the number of occurrences of c_i in S. The probability of occurrence of c_i in S is given by $P(c_i) = \frac{|S|_{c_i}}{n}$.

Algorithm 3 operates within the interval $[0, 1)$ of real numbers. As the set C expands, the interval needed to represent it decreases, while the number of bits required to specify the interval increases. Symbols $\{c_1, c_2, \ldots, c_m\}$ from the set of encrypted symbols reduce the interval size in accordance with their probabilities. The algorithm is designed to allow error-free decoding, even when the expansion encoding module has encoded unencrypted symbols. To ensure this, we enhanced the precision of the symbol distribution range table.

Let's consider two examples to illustrate the algorithm. For a set of random unencrypted symbols $\{a, e, i, n, t\}$, arithmetic encoding is demonstrated in Table 6. Each symbol s is allocated a unique interval, the length of which is proportional to the symbol's probability. Suppose our encoding expansion module receives the sequence (e, a, i) of symbols. Upon encountering the first symbol e, the module narrows the initial interval $[0, 1)$ to $[0.2, 0.5)$. For the second symbol a, it proportionally shortens the current interval $[0.2, 0.5)$ to $[0.2, 0.26)$. The lower interval bound is $p_{s_{1_{(low)}}}$, while the upper interval bound is $p_{s_{1_{(low)}}} + p_{s_0} \cdot p_{s_1}$. For the final symbol i, the current interval $[0.2, 0.26)$ is further narrowed to $[0.23, 0.236)$. The lower interval bound becomes $p_{s_{1_{(low)}}} + p_{s_1} \cdot p_{s_2}$, and the upper interval bound is $(p_{s_{1_{(low)}}} + p_{s_1} \cdot p_{s_2}) + p_0 \cdot p_1 \cdot p_2$. Ultimately, the module stores the lower bound 0.23 as the encoding of the sequence (e, a, i).

Algorithm 3 Buffer encryption expansion encoding module.

Input: $C = \{c_1, c_2, ..., c_m\}$ be a sequence of n random encrypted symbols
1: **Initialize:** precision := 1000000
2: **Initialize:** $S[] := null$
3: **Initialize:** $S_{c_i}[] := 0$
4: **for** $(n := 0 \text{ to } C.length)$ **do**
5:    $key := C[n]$
6:    $S_{c_i}[key]+ = 1$
7:    **if** $(key \text{ not in } S[])$ **then**
8:      $S[]+ = C[n]$
9:    **end if**
10: **end for**
11: $low := 0$
12: $high := 1/S_{c_i}[key]$
13: **for** $(key \text{ in sorted } S[])$ **do**
14:    $cdf\_range[key] := [low, high]$
15:    $low := high$
16:    { # increasing bitstream exponentially.}
17:    $high := high + (\frac{1}{S_{c_i}[key]^{precision}})$
18: **end for**
19: {# Compute probability distribution function (pdf)}
20: **for** $(key \text{ in sorted } S[])$ **do**
21:    $pdf[key] := \frac{1}{S_{c_i}[key]}$
22: **end for**
23: $LowerBound := 0$
24: $UpperBound := 1$
25: **while** (there are still symbols in $S[]$ to encode) **do**
26:    $CurrentRange := UpperBound - LowerBound$
27:    $UpperBound := LowerBound + (CurrentRange * cdf\_range[key])$
28:    $LowerBound := LowerBound + (CurrentRange * cdf\_range[key-1])$
29:    {#Update the probability tables}
30:    **for** $(key \text{ in sorted } pdf)$ **do**
31:      $pdf[key] := \frac{1}{S_{c_i}[key]}$
32:    **end for**
33:    **for** $(key \text{ in sorted } cdf\_range)$ **do**
34:      $pdf[key] := [low, high]$
35:      $low := high;$
36:    **end for**
37: **end while**
38: {# write repeat encoded LowerBound.}
39: $\prod_{LowerBound}^{i=1000}$

Table 6. Example of fixed normal symbols distribution range model.

Symbols	Probability	Range	
S	p_{s_n}	$p_{s_{(low)}}$	$p_{s_{(high)}}$
a	$p_{s_0} \leftarrow 0.2$	[0.0,	0.2)
e	$p_{s_1} \leftarrow 0.3$	[0.2,	0.5)
i	$p_{s_2} \leftarrow 0.1$	[0.5,	0.6)
n	$p_{s_3} \leftarrow 0.3$	[0.6,	0.9)
t	$p_{s_4} \leftarrow 0.1$	[0.9,	1.0)

Now, consider a sequence of symbols $\{x, y, z, k, !, \text{Space}\}$. Let's assume the probability distribution of these symbols is detailed in Table 7. Figure 2-A depicts the probability density function range table with a precision of 15, as outlined in Algorithm 4. We also present the result of expanding encrypted symbols $S = \{x, y, z, k, !, Space\}$, which are 6 bytes in length. Using a precision of 500, the compression output increases to 672 bytes, as shown in Fig. 2-B. A larger precision can inflate the compression output to file sizes on the order of gigabytes (GB). We tested a precision of one million, which expanded a 5-byte file into a 10-GB file before the system crashed-an outcome potentially beneficial during a ransomware attack. In theory, it's possible to expand a short file into a much larger one, potentially on the order of terabytes (TB).

Algorithm 4 computes encoding table with higher precision with the longer bitstream.

1: **Precision:** 15
2: **Input:** $S = [x, y, z, k, !, Space]$
3: **Initialize:** $S_{c_i}[]$ {# Algorithm 4 defines it}
4: $low := 0$
5: $high := 1/S_{c_i}[key]$
6: **for** (key in sorted S[]) **do**
7: $\quad cdf\_range[key] := [low, high)$
8: $\quad low := high$
9: $\quad high := high + (\frac{1}{S_{c_i}[key]precision})$
10: **end for**

Table 7. Probability density function range table for each symbol with equal distribution probability $(p_0, \cdots, p_5 = 0.166667)$.

Symbols	Probability	Range ← 1/|S|	
		ps_{low}	ps_{high}
S	p_s		
Space	p_0	[0.000000,	0.166667)
!	p_1	[0.166667,	0.333334)
k	p_2	[0.333334,	0.500001)
x	p_3	[0.500001,	0.666668)
y	p_4	[0.666668,	0.833335)
z	p_5	[0.833335,	1.000000)

Recovery of Corrupted Files: Modern ransomware variants overwrite original files upon encryption, deleting the originals and saving encrypted copies to storage. DIM addresses this by storing files being accessed in a secure temporary directory, protecting them from immediate encryption. This module reads file buffers and compiles statistics to facilitate file recovery. If the files are unencrypted, DIM deletes the temporary directory; if they are encrypted, it retains the directory to recover the files. This design ensures minimal impact on HDD storage and computational load, providing an effective defense against current and future ransomware tactics without focusing on the specific coding of the ransomware.

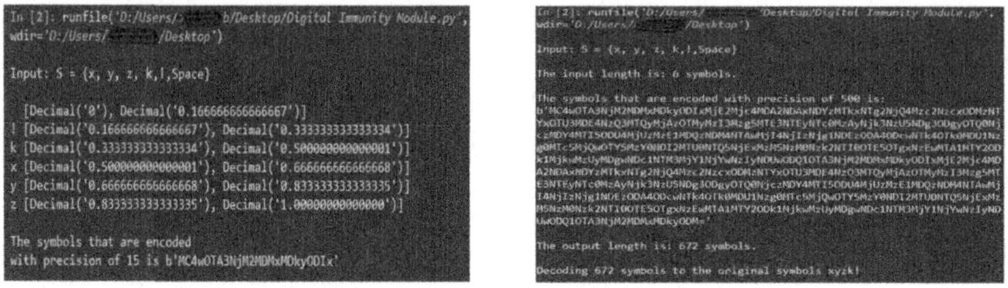

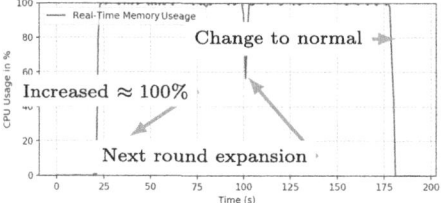
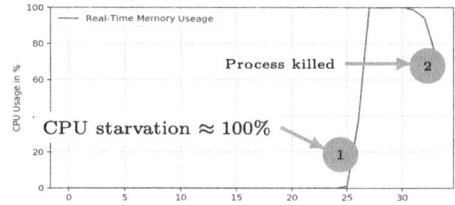

Fig. 2. Left: The probability density function range table with precision of 15. Right: Manipulating the PDF range table at a 500 precision level increases input from 6 to 672 symbols.

Fig. 3. CPU starvation resulting from the manipulation of the probability density function range table (precision of 100,000) during a ransomware attack, permitting the expansion of buffers without terminating the overwriting process by the ransomware.

Fig. 4. CPU and memory starvation resulting from the manipulation of the probability density function range table (precision of 10,000,000) during a ransomware attack, killing the malicious process.

Evaluation and Results: We gathered a substantial collection of ransomware variants, totaling 1,182 instances across multiple families, from databases like VirusShare, MalwareBazaar, and Kaggle. We selected 100 executable variants from 75 different families for repeated testing against our Defense Mechanism (DIM). The effectiveness of DIM in preventing file encryption was evaluated against a dataset comprising 32.6 GB and 11,928 different file types. Our approach to halt ransomware involves inducing CPU and memory resource starvation by manipulating the probability density function (PDF) to significantly increase resource demands, as shown in Figs. 3 and 4, leading to ransomware process termination depicted in Figs. 5a and 5b. DIM analyzes file buffers using a sliding window technique, effectively detecting encryption, particularly for complex variants like Dharma, by extending its analysis to more windows.

False Positive and False Negative Evaluation: DIM's file expansion strategy effectively combats ransomware by transforming small files into significantly larger ones, stopping encryption and facilitating recovery in cases of false positive detections. Our evaluations reveal no false negatives with the latest ransomware variants. The entropy of encrypted data usually exceeds 7.99, with DIM ensuring effective file protection on shared drives as well. Resource usage analysis shows that DIM maintains minimal CPU usage during idle states, with consistent performance under load, detailed in Fig. 7. A video demonstration of DIM's capabilities is available *here*.

5 Comparison and Discussion

Existing ransomware detection models, focusing on system-level I/O behaviors, face significant challenges, including high false positives due to similarities between ransomware and legitimate applications like file compressors and backup software, leading to unwanted disruptions [2,9,19,27]. These models also suffer from performance overhead, particularly when monitoring high I/O operations, which affects system performance and user experience [9,27]. Additionally, ransomware can employ evasion techniques like memory mapped I/O or fileless attacks, complicating detection [2,9]. Traditional approaches are generally reactive, providing a window for ransomware to inflict damage [18,27], and struggle with scalability in large environments [2,9,19]. In contrast, **DIM** utilizes a FUSE file system with a statistical analysis approach via sliding windows to identify encryption activities, effectively reducing false positives and eliminating false negatives during ransomware tests. Despite causing some delays in file system operations, DIM does not interrupt benign activities and adapts to detect evasion techniques in real-time. Its scalability and responsiveness make it suitable for large-scale deployments and capable of adapting to new ransomware tactics [19,27].

6 Conclusion, Limitations and Future Work

This paper presents the Digital Immunity Module (DIM), which effectively counters encrypted buffers in file systems using real-time analysis and inverse arithmetic coding. Tested against 75 ransomware families, DIM had no false negatives and provided recovery options for false positives. It protected data against Black Basta ransomware's encryption techniques. Future work will enhance anomaly detection in file encryption using online machine learning to minimize entropy and handle Base-64 encoding, with early tests showing a 33.33% increase in file size for lowered entropy. Findings support the efficacy of online learning classifiers in detecting statistical anomalies, leading to further development of a hybrid model.

Acknowledgment. The work has been supported by the Cyber Security Research Centre Limited (Grant number C22-00255) whose activities are partially funded by the Australian Government's Cooperative Research Centre Program.

A Resource Overload and Process Termination Approach

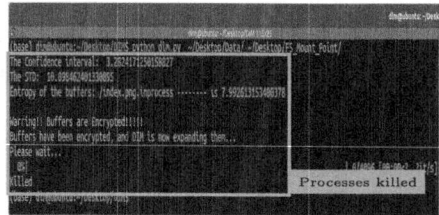

(a) DIM's response to illegal encryption: Memory usage surged from 79MB to 1.61GB, with CPU utilization peaking at 89.1%, leading to abrupt process termination.

(b) Killing of a malicious process because of resource starvation - read together with Figure 5a.

Fig. 5. Comparison between two scenarios.

B Sliding Approach and CPU Overheard Analysis

Figure 6 illustrates the sliding windows concept of the DIM, which utilizes this technique to effectively manage ransomware activities. This method is particularly effective in detecting ransomware's attempts to obfuscate its presence by inserting characters that artificially reduce entropy.

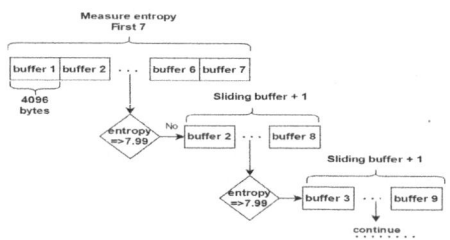
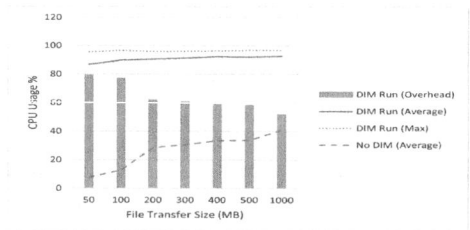

Fig. 6. DIM uses sliding windows to deal with ransomware, which may insert characters to reduce entropy.

Fig. 7. The results illustrate the server CPU overhead (DIM) during file transfers between a client and a server.

References

1. Al-rimy, B.A.S., Maarof, M.A., Prasetyo, Y.A., Shaid, S.Z.M., Ariffin, A.F.M.: Zero-day aware decision fusion-based model for crypto-ransomware early detection. Int. J. Integr. Eng. **10**(6) (2018)
2. Baek, S., Jung, Y., Mohaisen, A., Lee, S., Nyang, D.: SSD-insider: internal defense of solid-state drive against ransomware with perfect data recovery. In: 2018 IEEE 38th International Conference on Distributed Computing Systems (ICDCS), pp. 875–884 (2018). https://doi.org/10.1109/ICDCS.2018.00089
3. Baldwin, J., Dehghantanha, A.: Leveraging support vector machine for opcode density based detection of crypto-ransomware. In: Dehghantanha, A., Conti, M., Dargahi, T. (eds.) Cyber Threat Intelligence. AIS, vol. 70, pp. 107–136. Springer, Cham (2018). https://doi.org/10.1007/978-3-319-73951-9_6
4. Bijitha, C.V., Sukumaran, R., Nath, H.V.: A survey on ransomware detection techniques. In: Sahay, S.K., Goel, N., Patil, V., Jadliwala, M. (eds.) SKM 2019. CCIS, vol. 1186, pp. 55–68. Springer, Singapore (2020). https://doi.org/10.1007/978-981-15-3817-9_4
5. Cabaj, K., Gregorczyk, M., Mazurczyk, W.: Software-defined networking-based crypto ransomware detection using http traffic characteristics. Comput. Electr. Eng. **66**, 353–368 (2018). https://doi.org/10.1016/j.compeleceng.2017.10.012, https://www.sciencedirect.com/science/article/pii/S0045790617333542
6. Cabaj, K., Mazurczyk, W.: Using software-defined networking for ransomware mitigation: the case of cryptowall. IEEE Netw. **30**(6), 14–20 (2016). https://doi.org/10.1109/MNET.2016.1600110NM
7. Camtepe, S., et al.: Compcrypt-lightweight ANS-based compression and encryption. IEEE Trans. Inf. Forensics Secur. **16**, 3859–3873 (2021). https://doi.org/10.1109/TIFS.2021.3096026
8. Chen, Q., Bridges, R.A.: Automated behavioral analysis of malware: a case study of wannacry ransomware. In: 2017 16th IEEE International Conference on Machine Learning and Applications (ICMLA), pp. 454–460 (2017). https://doi.org/10.1109/ICMLA.2017.0-119
9. Continella, A., et al.: ShieldFS: a self-healing, ransomware-aware filesystem. In: Proceedings of the 32nd Annual Conference on Computer Security Applications, ACSAC 2016, pp. 336–347. Association for Computing Machinery, New York (2016). https://doi.org/10.1145/2991079.2991110
10. Cusack, G., Michel, O., Keller, E.: Machine learning-based detection of ransomware using SDN. In: Proceedings of the 2018 ACM International Workshop on Security in Software Defined Networks & Network Function Virtualization. SDN-NFV Sec 2018, pp. 1–6. Association for Computing Machinery, New York (2018). https://doi.org/10.1145/3180465.3180467
11. Genç, Z.A., Lenzini, G., Ryan, P.Y.A.: No random, no ransom: a key to stop cryptographic ransomware. In: Giuffrida, C., Bardin, S., Blanc, G. (eds.) DIMVA 2018. LNCS, vol. 10885, pp. 234–255. Springer, Cham (2018). https://doi.org/10.1007/978-3-319-93411-2_11
12. Gómez-Hernández, J., Álvarez González, L., García-Teodoro, P.: R-locker: thwarting ransomware action through a honeyfile-based approach. Comput. Secur. **73**, 389–398 (2018). https://doi.org/10.1016/j.cose.2017.11.019, https://www.sciencedirect.com/science/article/pii/S0167404817302560
13. Harikrishnan, N., Soman, K.: Detecting ransomware using GURLS. In: 2018 Second International Conference on Advances in Electronics, Computers and Com-

munications (ICAECC), pp. 1–6 (2018). https://doi.org/10.1109/ICAECC.2018.8479444
14. Homayoun, S., et al.: DRTHIS: deep ransomware threat hunting and intelligence system at the fog layer. Futur. Gener. Comput. Syst. **90**, 94–104 (2019). https://doi.org/10.1016/j.future.2018.07.045, https://www.sciencedirect.com/science/article/pii/S0167739X17328467
15. Honda, T., Mukaiyama, K., Shirai, T., Ohki, T., Nishigaki, M.: Ransomware detection considering user's document editing. In: 2018 IEEE 32nd International Conference on Advanced Information Networking and Applications (AINA), pp. 907–914 (2018). https://doi.org/10.1109/AINA.2018.00133
16. Jegou, H., Douze, M., Schmid, C.: Hamming embedding and weak geometric consistency for large scale image search. In: Forsyth, D., Torr, P., Zisserman, A. (eds.) ECCV 2008. LNCS, vol. 5302, pp. 304–317. Springer, Heidelberg (2008). https://doi.org/10.1007/978-3-540-88682-2_24
17. Jung, S., Won, Y.: Ransomware detection method based on context-aware entropy analysis. Soft Comput. **22**(20), 6731–6740 (2018). https://doi.org/10.1007/s00500-018-3257-z
18. Kharaz, A., Arshad, S., Mulliner, C., Robertson, W., Kirda, E.: UNVEIL: a large-scale, automated approach to detecting ransomware. In: 25th USENIX Security Symposium (USENIX Security 2016), pp. 757–772. USENIX Association, Austin (2016). https://www.usenix.org/conference/usenixsecurity16/technical-sessions/presentation/kharaz
19. Kharraz, A., Robertson, W., Balzarotti, D., Bilge, L., Kirda, E.: Cutting the Gordian knot: a look under the hood of ransomware attacks. In: Almgren, M., Gulisano, V., Maggi, F. (eds.) DIMVA 2015. LNCS, vol. 9148, pp. 3–24. Springer, Cham (2015). https://doi.org/10.1007/978-3-319-20550-2_1
20. Lee, K., Lee, S.Y., Yim, K.: Machine learning based file entropy analysis for ransomware detection in backup systems. IEEE Access **7**, 110205–110215 (2019). https://doi.org/10.1109/ACCESS.2019.2931136
21. Li, Y., Sundaramurthy, S.C., Bardas, A.G., Ou, X., Caragea, D., Hu, X., Jang, J.: Experimental study of fuzzy hashing in malware clustering analysis. In: 8th Workshop on Cyber Security Experimentation and Test (CSET 15). USENIX Association, Washington, D.C. (2015). https://www.usenix.org/conference/cset15/workshop-program/presentation/li
22. Mahboubi, A., Ansari, K., Camtepe, S.: Using process mining to identify file system metrics impacted by ransomware execution. In: Bouzefrane, S., Laurent, M., Boumerdassi, S., Renault, E. (eds.) MSPN 2020. LNCS, vol. 12605, pp. 57–71. Springer, Cham (2021). https://doi.org/10.1007/978-3-030-67550-9_5
23. Min, D., et al.: Amoeba: an autonomous backup and recovery SSD for ransomware attack defense. IEEE Comput. Archit. Lett. **17**(2), 245–248 (2018). https://doi.org/10.1109/LCA.2018.2883431
24. Morato, D., Berrueta, E., Magaña, E., Izal, M.: Ransomware early detection by the analysis of file sharing traffic. J. Netw. Comput. Appl. **124**, 14–32 (2018). https://doi.org/10.1016/j.jnca.2018.09.013, https://www.sciencedirect.com/science/article/pii/S108480451830300X
25. Nelson, M., Gailly, J.L.: The Data Compression Book, vol. 2. M&t Books, New York (1996)
26. Netto, D.F., Shony, K.M., Lalson, E.R.: An integrated approach for detecting ransomware using static and dynamic analysis. In: 2018 International CET Conference on Control, Communication, and Computing (IC4), pp. 410–414 (2018). https://doi.org/10.1109/CETIC4.2018.8531017

27. Paik, J.Y., Choi, J.H., Jin, R., Wang, J., Cho, E.S.: A storage-level detection mechanism against crypto-ransomware. In: Proceedings of the 2018 ACM SIGSAC Conference on Computer and Communications Security, CCS 2018, pp. 2258–2260. Association for Computing Machinery, New York (2018). https://doi.org/10.1145/3243734.3278491
28. Ramesh, G., Menen, A.: Automated dynamic approach for detecting ransomware using finite-state machine. Decis. Support Syst. **138**, 113400 (2020). https://doi.org/10.1016/j.dss.2020.113400, https://www.sciencedirect.com/science/article/pii/S016792362030155X
29. Scaife, N., Carter, H., Traynor, P., Butler, K.R.B.: CryptoLock (and drop it): stopping ransomware attacks on user data. In: 2016 IEEE 36th International Conference on Distributed Computing Systems (ICDCS), pp. 303–312 (2016). https://doi.org/10.1109/ICDCS.2016.46
30. Takeuchi, Y., Sakai, K., Fukumoto, S.: Detecting ransomware using support vector machines. In: Proceedings of the 47th International Conference on Parallel Processing Companion, ICPP 2018. Association for Computing Machinery, New York (2018). https://doi.org/10.1145/3229710.3229726
31. Vangoor, B.K.R., Tarasov, V., Zadok, E.: To FUSE or not to FUSE: performance of user-space file systems. In: 15th USENIX Conference on File and Storage Technologies (FAST 2017), pp. 59–72. USENIX Association, Santa Clara (2017). https://www.usenix.org/conference/fast17/technical-sessions/presentation/vangoor

Implementation for Malicious Software Using ChatGPT-4

Nobuyuki Sugio(✉) and Hokuto Ito

Hokkaido University of Science, Sapporo 006-8585, Japan
sugio-n@hus.ac.jp

Abstract. Large language models, including ChatGPT, have become widely available and have been used in various fields. This study attempts to create malicious software using ChatGPT-4 with minimal coding effort to demonstrate that they can be created even by non-expert security professionals. We also show whether obfuscating the source code of the created malicious software can reduce the malware detection rates by security analysis tools.

Keywords: Large language models (LLMs) · ChatGPT · Malicious software · Implementation

1 Introduction

The advent of deep learning has revolutionized the field of artificial intelligence. A significant milestone was the breakthrough victory of Krizhevsky et al.'s model in the 2012 ImageNet Large Scale Visual Recognition Challenge (ILSVRC) [1]. This achievement led to a surge of research in deep learning for image recognition, speech recognition, and natural language processing.

Among these, the emergence of large language models (LLMs) has been a major advancement in natural language processing, with ChatGPT reaching over one hundred million users by 2023. The release of ChatGPT-4[1] in March 2023 marks a leap forward in artificial intelligence technology. It possesses significantly enhanced comprehension and response capabilities compared to previous models, enabling it to provide high-precision answers to a wide range of questions. It is now used in various fields, and its potential looks like limitless.

However, the advancement of LLMs also has negative aspects. One of them is the potential for malicious software to be created using the advanced generative capabilities of ChatGPT-4. Pa Pa et al. demonstrated the feasibility of creating malwares by injecting the jailbreak prompts into ChatGPT [2].

While previous research [2] has shown that researchers with advanced security skills can create malwares by jailbreaking ChatGPT, the OpenAI's ethical guidelines prohibit malicious activities such as malware creation. Therefore, the aims of this study were to create malicious software by instructing ChatGPT-4

---

[1] https://chatgpt.com/.

without jailbreaking, and to investigate whether it was possible to create sophisticated malicious software even without being a skilled security professional. Additionally, this study examines whether obfuscating the source code of the created malicious software can reduce the malware detection rates by security analysis tools.

1.1 Ethical Considerations

The purpose of this study was to demonstrate the possibility of generating malicious software with minimal coding effort using ChatGPT. The prompts we used to create our malicious software were designed to contribute to a broader discussion with a generalized approach.

We adhere to the Checklist for ethical considerations in cybersecurity research[2]. It should be stated clearly that our research does not endorse the use of ChatGPT or similar techniques for the purpose of creating malicious software. We recognize the ethical implications associated with such actions and strongly advocate the responsible use of AI techniques in security research. Our focus is on exploring the potential use of these tools to promote the understanding of LLMs and the effective use of technology, not on compromising security or privacy.

1.2 Organization

The remainder of this paper is organized as follows. Section 2 discusses previous research on malware generation using ChatGPT. Section 3 and Sect. 4 describe the overview of the created malicious software and the procedures for their creation using ChatGPT-4. Section 5 evaluates the behavior of the created malicious software and investigates the impact of source code obfuscation on the results of security analysis tools. Finally, Sect. 6 summarizes the study and discusses future work.

2 Related Works

According to the OpenAI's ethical guidelines, the prompts instructing the creation of malware are rejected. However, several studies have reported successfully creating malware using ChatGPT-4. The methods used in previous studies can be categorized into two types: (1) creating malware with jailbreak, and (2) creating malware without jailbreak.

(1) Creating malware with Jailbreak [2–5]. The Jailbreak involves bypassing the system's inherent limitations and constraints to enable functionalities or actions that are typically unavailable. This method has been successful in prompting ChatGPT to generate the source codes for malware by the following techniques:

---

[2] https://www.iwsec.org/csec/ethics/checklist.html

- **DAN (Do Anything Now) Technique**:
  This method commands ChatGPT forcefully. It involves giving clear and absolute instructions to trigger the jailbreak.
- **SWITCH Technique**:
  This method causes the jailbreak by prompting ChatGPT to take opposite actions (switching on/off) in scenarios where it would normally refuse to respond.
- **CHARACTER PLAY Technique**:
  This method lets ChatGPT to play a specific character. Defining a character and demanding responses consistent with that character's setting triggers the jailbreak.

(2) Creating malware without Jailbreak [6,7]. This method generates a source code for each function separately and then concatenates them to create a malware without violating the OpenAI's ethical guidelines. Even if ChatGPT refuses to create a malware, the functions that compose a malware are not against the ethical guidelines, so their creation is not rejected.

3 Overview of the Malicious Software Implementation

Kramer introduced that malware was software that harmfully attacks other software [8]. In this study, we use *malicious software* to denote software which harm data processed on a target's computer. This study describes the overview of the malicious software and the procedures used for attacks employing them. We develop the following three types of malicious software in Python code without jailbreak:

1 Hashing User Files
2 Steganography
3 Extraction and Auto-Execution

3.1 Hashing User Files

This malicious software hashes all files in 'Desktop', 'Downloads', 'Documents', and 'Pictures' directories on Windows OS, including their subdirectories, and deletes the original files. The structure of this program is shown in Fig. 1.

The file access is based on relative paths starting from the home directory, allowing attacks without prior knowledge of the target's computer username. The desktop.ini file, a hidden file in Windows OS defining folder display settings and behavior, is excluded from operations to prevent alerting the target. Hashing and deleting this file would invalidate the settings, changing the display names from Japanese to English, which might reveal the malware's presence.

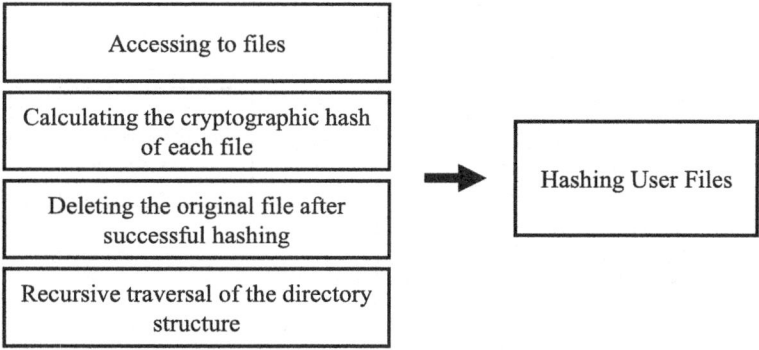

Fig. 1. Structure of Hashing User Files

3.2 Steganography

This program embeds malicious software into an image file to conceal it. Two types of steganography program were developed: (A) Steganography by Appending Data at the End of an Image and (B) LSB Steganography.

In the former program, the malicious software and the image file are concatenated by appending the malicious software's binary data directly at the end of the image's binary data. This program is fast and does not require size calculations for the image file and the malicious software. However, the concealed data can be easily discovered upon binary analysis.

The latter program converts the malicious software into a bitstream and replaces the least significant bits of each pixel in the image file with the malicious software's bitstream. This program makes data discovery more challenging upon image analysis, though it is significantly slower and requires the image size to exceed the size of malicious software.

3.3 Extraction and Auto-Execution

This software extracts the malicious software embedded in an image file and configures it for auto-execution. The structure of this program is shown in Fig. 2. This malicious software creates the folder named 'sample' in the target's computer home directory. After creating the folder, this program extracts the malicious software from the image file and places it in the folder. After placing the malicious software in the folder, this program ensures its automatic execution every system startup by rewriting the registry data.

3.4 Attack Procedure

The attack procedure is organized by the following four steps:

1 Python script conversion to executable files
2 Embedding malicious software using steganography

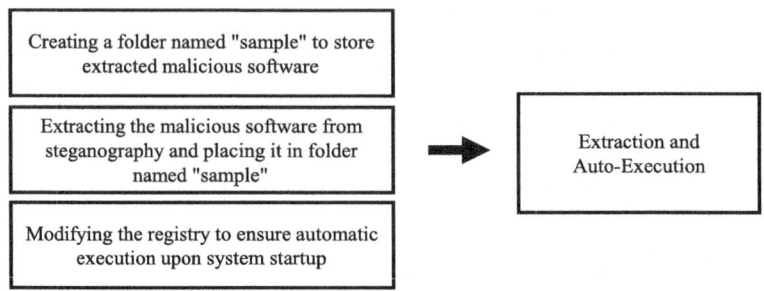

Fig. 2. Structure of Extraction and Auto-Execution

3 Icon disguise for enhanced deception
4 Malicious software distribution

Python Script Conversion to Executable Files. The attacker utilizes PyInstaller to transform the Python codes for "Hashing User Files" and "Extraction and Auto-Execution" into executable files (EXEs). The `onefile` option creates a single executable, incorporating all required libraries and dependencies. This option eliminates the need for a pre-installed Python environment on the target's computer. The `noconsole` option prevents a conspicuous console window from appearing when the malicious software is executed, thus reducing the likelihood of detection by the target.

Embedding Malware Using Steganography. The attacker employs the steganography program to conceal the malicious software in the prepared image file.

Icon Disguise for Enhanced Deception. Using tools like the Icon Wizard[3] and the Resource Hacker[4], the attacker masks "Extraction and Auto-Execution" with an enticing icon and filename (e.g., disguised as a PDF file) to increase the chances of the target executing it.

Malicious Software Distribution. The attacker delivers the malicious software-embedded image file and the disguised "Extraction and Auto-Execution" to the target. Upon receiving them, if the target inadvertently executes the disguised "Extraction and Auto-Execution", the following occurs:

- The folder named 'sample' is created in the target computer's home directory.
- The embedded malicious software is extracted from the image file.
- The malicious software is configured to automatically execute upon every system startup.

---

[3] https://www.naporitansushi.com/iconwizard/.
[4] https://resource-hacker.softonic.jp/.

4 Malicious Software Implementation Using ChatGPT-4

4.1 Methodology

We employ ChatGPT-4 as an assistive tool in the malicious software development process. The workflow is as follows:

1. **Functional Decomposition**: The malicious software capabilities are broken down into discrete, implementable functions.
2. **Prioritization**: The functions are prioritized based on criticality and feasibility.
3. **Iterative Development**: The Python code for each function is generated using ChatGPT-4. Feedback and code refinements if necessary.
4. **Functionality Expansion**: Subsequent functions are added and enhanced using a similar iterative approach.

4.2 System Architecture

In this study, we establish a controlled environment with two distinct roles: the attacker and the target. Two virtual machines (VMs) running Windows 11 are constructed using VirtualBox to simulate these roles. The system architecture is illustrated in Fig. 3.

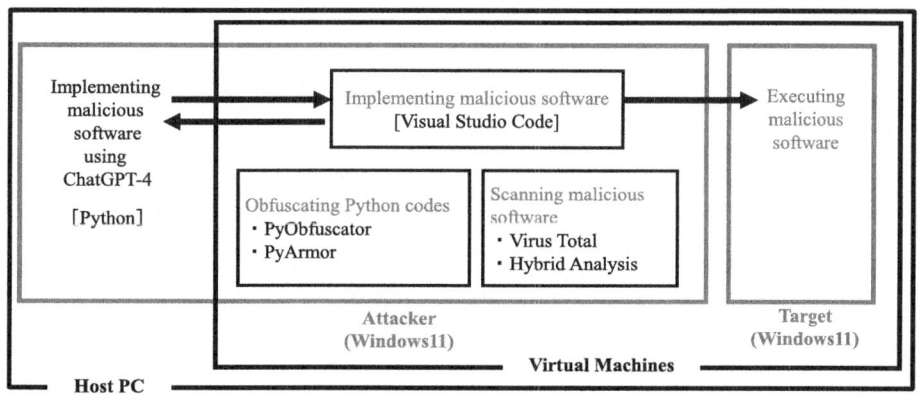

Fig. 3. System Architecture

Implementing and assessing the malicious software are conducted on the attacker's computer. While WinSCP/OpenSSH were used to transfer the malicious software in this study, realistic attack scenarios often leverage less conspicuous methods like an email or a cloud storage.

4.3 Example: Hashing User Files

Due to space limitations, this paper introduces the implementation of "Hashing User Files" as an example. The core functionalities are listed below.

1. **Hashing Files**: This function calculates cryptographic hashes (e.g., SHA-256) of all files in user-specified directories 'Desktop', 'Downloads', 'Documents', and 'Pictures'.
2. **Original File Deletion**: This function deletes the original files without user warnings after successful hashing.
3. **Supporting Relative Paths**: This function supports the target directories using relative paths from the user's home directory.
4. **Recursive Subdirectory Processing**: This function applies hashing and deleting all files in subdirectories.
5. **Error Handling**: This function manages the errors such as file access errors, path errors, and other potential runtime exceptions.
6. **Exclusion Handling**: This function excludes the specific files (e.g., 'desktop.ini') based on predefined criteria.

The prompts for "Hashing User Files" are shown in Table 1. The results are respectively illustrated in Fig. 4 and Fig. 5.

Table 1. Prompts for each function

Functions	Prompt for each function
Hashing Files	*Create a Python program to hash files in the Desktop, Downloads, Documents, and Pictures directories.*
Original File Deletion	*Add the function to delete the original files after hashing them.*
Supporting Relative Paths	*Please specify the path as a relative path, starting from the user's home directory.*
Recursive Subdirectory Processing	*Add a function to recursively perform the same process on subdirectories in the directory.*
Error Handling	*Strengthen the error handling.*
Exclusion Handling	*Exclude the desktop.ini file from being processed.*

5 Evaluation and Discussion

In this section, we evaluate the malicious software and investigate their detection rates using the security analysis tools. Furthermore, we examine whether obfuscating the source code of the malicious software reduces their detection rates when reanalyzed with security analysis tools.

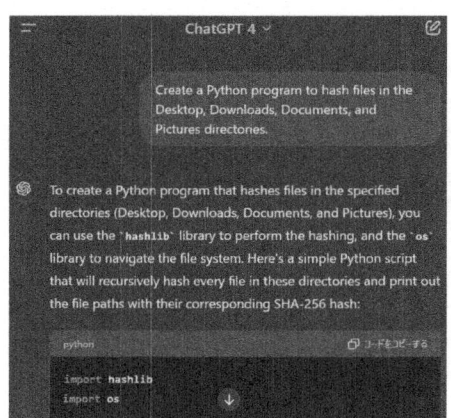

Fig. 4. Prompt for filehashing **Fig. 5.** The result of file hashing prompt

5.1 Hashing User Files

When this program is executed on the target's computer, it is confirmed that all files in 'Desktop', 'Downloads', 'Documents', and 'Pictures' including subdirectories are hashed. After hashing, it is confirmed that the original files are deleted.

5.2 Extraction and Auto-Execution

The icon-disguised "Extraction and Auto-Execution" and the steganography-treated image file are transferred to the target's computer. This program creates the folder named 'sample' in the home directory where the malicious software is extracted as 'test.exe'. Restarting the target's computer triggers the automatic execution of "Hashing User Files".

5.3 Malware Analysis

The created malicious software were uploaded to the Hybrid Analysis[5] for both static and dynamic analysis. The results revealed that the executable file format "Hashing User Files" and "Extraction and Auto-Execution" were detected as malware in both static and dynamic analysis. The results are shown in Fig. 6. However, the Python codes for "Steganography" evaded all tools, not detected as malwares and assessed as programs without any security risk.

These results suggest that the security analysis tools might apply stricter detection criteria to executable files than to Python codes. Additionally, the lack of digital signatures might have influenced the results. Normally, the commercial

---

[5] https://www.hybrid-analysis.com/.

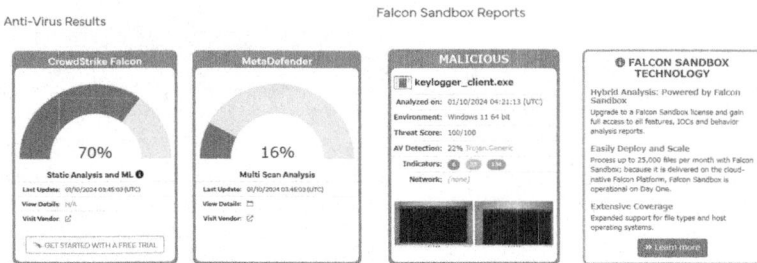

Fig. 6. Results by Hybrid Analysis

software is digitally signed, ensuring it comes from a trusted source and is free from viruses or malware. The malicious software created in this study did not have digital signatures, which might have impacted the results.

5.4 Source Code Obfuscation

Following the malicious software analysis, we investigate whether obfuscating the source codes of "Hashing User Files" and "Extraction and Auto-Execution", which were deemed threats and high security risks in both static and dynamic analysis, reduces their detection rates in static analysis. The obfuscations were performed using **PyObfuscator**[6] and **PyArmor**[7], followed by conversion into executable files to evaluate for reduced detection rates.

- **PyObfuscator**: We used level 6 (Base64 encoding of the entire source code) for obfuscation. Subsequently, the codes were converted into the executable files for evaluation experiments and malware analysis. Despite functioning correctly, the malware detection rates by the security analysis tools did not change.

- **PyArmor**: The source codes were compiled into bytecode and subjected to irreversible transformation. After conversion into executable files, the evaluation experiments and malware analysis were conducted. Similar to PyObfuscator, PyArmor did not reduce the malware detection rates in security analysis tools.

6 Conclusion

This study has demonstrated the feasibility of creating malicious software using ChatGPT with minimal coding effort by non-expert security professionals. However, the executable files were detected as malicious by the security analysis tools, indicating the inability to create advanced malware that can evade these tools. Additionally, attempts to reduce the detection rate in static analysis through

---

[6] https://pypi.org/project/PyObfuscator/.
[7] https://pypi.org/project/pyarmor/.

source code obfuscation using PyObfuscator and PyArmor were not successful in this study.

To evade malware detection in dynamic analysis, one potential method is adding sleep variables to the malicious software's source code, delaying its operation, and causing sandbox-based analysis to terminate prematurely. For evading static analysis, repeatedly applying tools like PyObfuscator and PyArmor to make the source code analysis more challenging can be considered.

Future work will be to apply our methods to other LLMs, such as Gemini[8], and compare the results obtained with ChatGPT-4.

References

1. Krizhevsky, A., Sutskever, I., and Hinton, G.: Imagenet classification with deep convolutional neural networks. In: Advances in Neural Information Processing Systems, pp. 1097–1105 (2012)
2. Pa Pa, Y.M., Tanizaki, S., Kou, T., Eeten, M., Yoshioka, K., Matsumoto, T.: An attacker's dream? exploring the capabilities of ChatGPT for developing malware. In: Proceedings of the 16th Cyber Security Experimentation and Test Workshop, CSET 2023, pp. 10–18 (2023)
3. Mulgrew, A.: I built a Zero day virus with undetectable exfiltration using only ChatGPT prompts Forcepoint. https://www.forcepoint.com/blog/x-labs/zero-day-exfiltration-using-chatgpt-prompts. Accessed 24 June 2024
4. Derner, E., Batistič, K.: Beyond the safeguards: exploring the security risks of ChatGPT, arXiv:2305.08005 (2023)
5. Chat GPT DAN and other Jailbreaks. https://gist.github.com/coolaj86/6f4f7b30129b0251f61fa7baaa881516. Accessed 24 June 2024
6. Botacin, M.: Gpthreats-3: is automatic malware generation a threat?. In: IEEE Security and Privacy Workshops, pp. 238–254 (2023)
7. Roy, S., Naragam, K., Nilizadeh, S.: Generating phishing attacks using ChatGPT, arXiv:2305.05133 (2023)
8. Kramer, S., Bradfield, J.C.: A general definition of malware. J. Comput. Virol. **6**, 105–114 (2010)
9. Liu, Y., et al.: Jailbreaking ChatGPT via prompt engineering: an empirical study, arXiv:2305.13860v1 (2023)
10. Deng, Y., Zhang, W., Pan, S.J., Bing, L.: Multilingual jailbreak challenges in large language models, arXiv:2310.06474 (2023)
11. Shi, J., Liu, Y., Zhou, P., Sun, L.: BadGPT: exploring security vulnerabilities of ChatGPT via backdoor attacks to InstructGPT, arXiv:2304.12298 (2023)
12. Al-Hawawreh, M., Aljuhani, A., Jararweh, Y.: Chatgpt for cybersecurity: practical applications, challenges, and future directions. Cluster Comput. **26**, 3421–3436 (2023)

---

[8] https://gemini.google.com/app.

A Markov Game Model for Evaluating Cybersecurity Attacks on Cloud

Hooman Alavizadeh[1](✉) [iD], Julian Jang-Jaccard[2] [iD], Hootan Alavizadeh[3], and Tansu Alpcan[4] [iD]

[1] School of Computing, Engineering and Mathematical Sciences, La Trobe University, Melbourne, Australia
h.alavizadeh@latrobe.edu.au
[2] Cyber-Defence Campus, armasuisse Science and Technology, Thun, Switzerland
[3] Department of Computer Science, Wright State University, Dayton, USA
[4] Department of Electrical and Electronic Engineering, The University of Melbourne, Parkville, Australia
tansu.alpcan@unimelb.edu.au

Abstract. Cyber threats have become increasingly sophisticated and prevalent, posing significant risks to cloud environments. Designing a robust threat model is essential to effectively defend cyber threats in the cloud. Modeling cyber threats using game theory can help the defender to select optimal strategies against the attacks and can help the defender to make effective decisions to mitigate the attack's impact. In this paper, we model a cyber threat strategy in which the attackers can utilize various methods to launch attack effectively. Then, we present a Markov game model to evaluate the efficiency of different attacker's strategies against cyber defense from attacker's perspective in a cloud system scenario. We then conduct experiments based on CVSS metrics to quantify the outcomes of this zero-sum game model for both attack and defense strategies such as the shortest attack path, random, and greedy attack.

Keywords: Security modeling · Markov Games · Cyber threats · Cloud computing · Attack models

1 Introduction

A resilience cyber defense system should be able to defend against different strategies of cyber attacks, such as adaptive attacks [4]. Game-theoretic models have been extensively applied to cybersecurity problems and have shown to be very effective in the evaluation of defensive systems and addressing the security of networks and systems [2,3]. In this initial paper, we model advanced attack strategy in which an attacker can leverage subtle techniques to estimate the shortest attack path in a networked model [6]. We then propose a cloud system and attack model based on an Attack Graph (AG) representing the states of the game. We then define a zero-sum Markovian game model that captures the capabilities of the attacker and defender. In this case, the attacker can choose the actions that exploit the real-world vulnerabilities reported in the Common Vulnerabilities and Exploits (CVEs) through National Vulnerability Database (NVD). Then, the defender's actions are modeled based on a dynamic defense consisting of the placement of detection systems such as Intrusion Detection System (IDS) to the hosts in the cloud. We design the rewards of this game by leveraging the widely used Common Vulnerability Scoring Systems (CVSS) values such as attack impact and exploitability. This helps the defender to select appropriate strategies using the limited number of monitoring actions for each state of the game. The defender action is the placement of an IDS in a host in the cloud to monitor and detect any prospective threats. The main contributions of this paper are as follows:

- We propose a graph-based attack model for a cloud system and model an attack scenario in which attacker is able to find the shortest attack path.
- We define a Markov game model that can evaluate the effectiveness of defense mechanisms against different attack strategies. We quantify the resulting zero-sum game parameters based on CVSS values.
- We offer the formal mathematical definitions for the proposed game model. We also determine the probabilistic values of the states of the game. Finally, we clearly formalize, analyze, and quantify actions and states transition probabilities for the game model based on three different attacker's strategies.

The rest of the paper is organized as follows. The related work is given in Sect. 2. Section 3 discusses the cybersecurity threat model. In Sect. 4, we define the necessary concepts, definitions, mathematical notations, and propose our Markovian game model. In Sect. 5, we evaluate our proposed game model and provide numerical results. Finally, we conclude the paper in Sect. 6.

2 Related Work

Various cyber attack techniques have been proposed in the literature that leverage different techniques to discover the fastest, shortest, cheapest, or more efficient attack paths in a networked system using attack graphs, such as Deep Learning [6] and so forth. Finding the attack path from source to target in a graphical attack model is an important capability for the attackers [7]. This enables the attacker to reach the target with minimum effort and cost. Game theory, Markov processes, and neural networks have long been applied to study network security [2]. Alpcan and Basar [1] proposed a security game between attacker and IDS in the sensor network. They modeled their solution based on a finite Markov chain, Markov decision process, and Q-learning. In [5], the authors proposed a novel generative adversarial network anomaly detection scheme using a min-max game played locally on each device and collaboration between devices using the Nash equilibrium and Machine Learning models. In [3], the authors proposed the game-theoretic models based on the attack graph for cyber deception. Their method could capture the players' uncertainties using the dynamic game models.

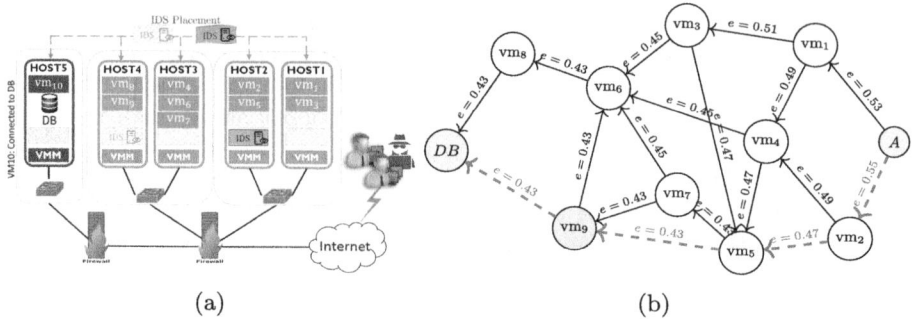

Fig. 1. (a) The cloud-model including 10 VMs in different hosts (servers). (b) Attack graph model corresponding to the cloud-model.

Table 1. VMs vulnerabilities information ($|V|$ is the number of vulnarabilities and e is the maximum exploitability of all vulnerabilities for a host)

VM	Current Host	$|V|$	e	Impact	VM	Current Host	$|V|$	e	Impact
vm_1	h1	4	0.53	10	vm_6	h3	1	0.45	9
vm_2	h2	3	0.55	8	vm_7	h3	1	0.43	10
vm_3	h2	3	0.51	8	vm_8	h4	1	0.43	9
vm_4	h2	3	0.49	8	vm_9	h4	1	0.43	10
vm_5	h2	2	0.47	9	DB	h5	1	0.43	10

3 Cybersecurity Threat Model

3.1 Cloud System and Threat Model

We modeled a cloud system consisting of 10 Virtual Machines (VMs) distributed in five different physical servers or hosts in the cloud. We assume that only the VMs vm_1 and vm_2 are connected to the internet and they are the entry point of the cloud. The cloud model is demonstrated as in Fig. 1. Each VM has a number of vulnerabilities associated with the Operating System (OS) it uses as in Table 1. Thus, the attack model can be represented as a directed attack graph. Let $AG = (V, E)$ be a graph, where V is a set of all the nodes and E is a set of all the edges. The aim of the attacker is to obtain the shortest attack path (SAP) which is a path between two nodes without considering the weight of the attack path. Note that the weight of the edges determines the exploitability (e) of the connected VM based on Table 1.

We assume that an intelligent attacker can analyse the target system and gain valuable information about the system, targets, and attack paths. We assume that the attacker can leverage methods to estimate the shortest attack path in the modeled cloud system. The shortest attack path for the cloud model, Fig. 1b. We assume that the attacker can estimate the shortest path attack from the entry point of the system (i.e., Internet) to the target (DB) in the cloud. The attacker can exploit the vulnerabilities existing on each host with the probabilities defined based on the CVSS metrics. However, for each attack step in an attack path, the attacker incurs some expenses such as costs and time (Table 2).

4 A Game-Theoretic Analysis of Attacks Strategies

4.1 Game Model Definition

Markovian Game Model. We model the attacker and a defender scenario as a two-player zero-sum Markov game leveraging the information in the cloud model and corresponding AG represented in Fig. 1b. Moreover, the transition from each state and consequently the corresponding reward for each state depends on players' actions for that specific state (this also can be modeled based on previous states and actions which are beyond the scope of this paper). We formally define a zero-sum Markov Game model based on obvious Markovian assumption and explain how each of these parameters are obtained in our cloud model. A Markov game for two players can be defined by a tuple (S, $\mathcal{A}_A$, $\mathcal{A}_D$, T, R) where,

- $S = \{s_0, s_1, s_2, \ldots, s_r\}$ denoted the finite states of the game where in here $|S| = max(len(ap_i \in AP))$.
- $\mathcal{A}_A = \{a_0^A, a_1^A, a_2^A, \ldots\}$ is the attacker's set of actions. The defender can have a set of actions as $\mathcal{D}_A = \{a_0^D, a_1^D, a_2^D, \ldots\}$.
- $T = (s, a^A, a^D, s')$ is a States' transition where the current state $s \in S$ is changed to $s' \in S$ upon the actions come from both attacker and defender respectively. However, each transition has a probability denoted by $tp(T)$.
- $R^A(s; a^A; a^D)$ is the reward obtained by attacker if in state s, attacker and defender take the actions a^A and a^D respectively. However, based on the zero-sum game definition, the reward can be negative if the attacker choose a wrong action $(-R^A(s; a^A; a^D))$.

Reward Function. To quantify reward values we use the important variables such as the impact of an attack and cost of defense (C_{def}), we used CVSS metrics that provide the Impact (I) for a specific VM (I_{vm_i}), Exploitability Scores (e), and other relevant metrics. I_{vm_i} is a metric that computes the damage imposed to the VM by computing all impacts on the resources through an attack. For instance, $I_{vm_4} = 8$ is the attack impact value on the VM vm_4 based on the related impact metrics of vulnerabilities in CVSS represented in Table 1. The rewards matrix for attackers is formulated as Eq. 1.

$$R^{\mathcal{A}}_{a^A, a^D} = \begin{cases} 0 & \text{if } a^A \subset \emptyset \\ C_{def} & \text{if } a^A \subset \emptyset, a^D \not\subset \emptyset \\ I_{vm_i} + C_{def} & \text{if } a^A = E(vm_i), a^D \not\subset \emptyset, vm_i \notin H(ids) \\ I_{vm_i} & \text{if } a^A = E(vm_i), a^D \subset \emptyset \\ -(I_{vm_i} - C_{def}) & \text{if } a^A = E(vm_i), a^D \not\subset \emptyset, vm_i \in H(ids) \end{cases} \quad (1)$$

Table 2. Payoff matrix formalization based on a^A, a^D for the game states s_0–s_4

s_0: Initial State (no exploit)			
A/D	No-act	Def-h_1	Def-h_2
No-att	$0,0$	$C_{def}, -C_{def}$	$C_{def}, -C_{def}$
$E(vm_1 \in h_1)$	$I_{vm_1}, -I_{vm_1}$	$-(I_{vm_1} - C_{def}), I_{vm_1} - C_{def}$	$I_{vm_1} + C_{def}, -(I_{vm_1} + C_{def})$
$E(vm_2 \in h_2)$	$I_{vm_2}, -I_{vm_2}$	$I_{vm_2} + C_{def}, -(I_{vm_2} + C_{def})$	$-(I_{vm_2} - C_{def}), I_{vm_2} - C_{def}$
s_1: Transition State ($vm_2 \in h_2$ exploited)			
A/D	No-act	Def-h_3	Def-h_2
No-att	$0,0$	$C_{def}, -C_{def}$	$C_{def}, -C_{def}$
$E(vm_4 \in h_3)$	$I_{vm_4}, -I_{vm_4}$	$-(I_{vm_4} - C_{def}), I_{vm_4} - C_{def}$	$I_{vm_4} + C_{def}, -(I_{vm_4} + C_{def})$
$E(vm_5 \in h_2)$	$I_{vm_5}, -I_{vm_5}$	$I_{vm_5} + C_{def}, -(I_{vm_5} + C_{def})$	$-(I_{vm_5} - C_{def}), I_{vm_5} - C_{def}$
s_2: Transition State ($vm_5 \in h_2$ exploited)			
A/D	No-act	Def-h_3	Def-h_4
No-att	$0,0$	$C_{def}, -C_{def}$	$C_{def}, -C_{def}$
$E(vm_7 \in h_3)$	$I_{vm_7}, -I_{vm_7}$	$-(I_{vm_7} - C_{def}), I_{vm_7} - C_{def}$	$I_{vm_7} + C_{def}, -(I_{vm_7} + C_{def})$
$E(vm_9 \in h_4)$	$I_{vm_9}, -I_{vm_9}$	$I_{vm_9} + C_{def}, -(I_{vm_9} + C_{def})$	$-(I_{vm_9} - C_{def}), I_{vm_9} - C_{def}$
s_3: Transition State ($vm_9 \in h_4$ exploited)			
A/D	No-act	Def-h_3	Def-h_5
No-att	$0,0$	$C_{def}, -C_{def}$	$C_{def}, -C_{def}$
$E(vm_6 \in h_3)$	$I_{vm_6}, -I_{vm_6}$	$-(I_{vm_6} - C_{def}), I_{vm_6} - C_{def}$	$I_{vm_6} + C_{def}, -(I_{vm_6} + C_{def})$
$E(DB \in h_5)$	$I_{DB}, -I_{DB}$	$I_{DB} + C_{def}, -(I_{DB} + C_{def})$	$-(I_{DB} - C_{def}), I_{DB} - C_{def}$
$\bar{s}_4$: Final State (DB exploited)			

$H(ids)$ is a function that returns the host in which ids has been located. For instance, if the defender locates the IDS in Host h_4, then $H(ids)$ returns h_4. As the game is a zero-sum game the reward for the defender is as Eq. 2.

$$R^{\mathcal{D}}_{a^A, a^D} = -1 * R^{\mathcal{A}}_{a^A, a^D} \qquad (2)$$

As stated earlier, the formulation of the reward function is based on CVSS values and mainly the impact of the attack on a targeted VM. If the defender and the attacker do not take any action such that $a^A \subset \emptyset, a^D \not\subset \emptyset$ both get zero rewards. Moreover, if the attacker doesn't attack (*no-att*) while the defender places the IDS to any host in the cloud to secure any hosts, the defender incurs a cost for the defense $(-C_{def})$ and gets a negative reward. However, if the attacker attacks on a VM vm_i while the defender place the IDS to detect attacks on the host in which the targeted VM vm_i is located such that $vm_i \in H(ids)$, then the defender gets the reward for avoiding the attack impact on that VM (I_{vm_i}), but as the defender incurs some costs for the defense the total reward of successful defense is formulated as $I_{vm_i} - C_{def}$. For instance, suppose that the cost of defense is 2 units (for both successful and unsuccessful defense). Then, if attacker exploits VM vm_1 and defender put IDS on the host $h1$ ($vm_1 \in h_1$), the

Table 3. Payoff Matrix quantifying based on zero-sum game and CVSS values

s_0: Initial State (no exploit)				s_2: Transition State ($vm_5 \in h_2$ exploited)			
A/D	No-act	Def-h_1	Def-h_2	A/D	No-act	Def-h_3	Def-h_2
No-att	0,0	2,−2	2,−2	No-att	0,0	2,−2	2,−2
$E(vm_1 \in h_1)$	10,−10	−8,8	12,−12	$E(vm_7 \in h_3)$	10,−10	−8,8	12,−12
$E(vm_2 \in h_2)$	8,−8	10,−10	−6,6	$E(vm_9 \in h_4)$	10,−10	12,−12	−8,8
s_1: Transition State ($vm_2 \in h_2$ exploited)				s_3: Transition State ($vm_9 \in h_4$ exploited)			
A/D	No-act	Def-h_3	Def-h_2				
No-att	0,0	2,−2	2,−2	No-att	0,0	2,−2	2,−2
$E(vm_4 \in h_3)$	8,−8	−6,6	10,−10	$E(vm_6 \in h_3)$	9,−9	−7,7	11,−11
$E(vm_5 \in h_2)$	9,−9	11,−11	−7,7	$E(DB \in h_5)$	10,−10	12,−12	−8,8

defender gains a total reward of 7 which is as $R^D = I_{vm_1} - C_{def} = 9 - 2$ while the attacker is penalized by -7 unit. In contrast, if the attacker attacks on a VM vm_i while the defender place the IDS to detect attacks on the host in which the targeted VM vm_i is not located such that $vm_i \notin H(ids)$, then the defender gets the penalty for wrong defense and incurs the impact of the attack on that VM plus the cost of wrong defense which is $-(I_{vm_i} + C_{ids})$ while the attacker reward would be as $I_{vm_i} + C_{ids}$ based on the zero-sum definition. For instance, if attacker exploits VM vm_1 and defender put IDS on the host $h2$ ($vm_1 \notin h_2$), the defender gets a negative reward of -11 which is as the sum of the impact of attack on that VM and the cost of defense as $R^D = -1 * (I_{vm_1} + C_{def}) = -1 * (9 + 2)$. Then, the attacker gets rewards of 11 which is $R^A = -R^D$. Lastly, if the attacker attacks on a VM and the defender takes no action then the attacker gains the reward for the successful attack which is equivalent to the impact of the attack on exploited VM vm_i as $R^A = I_{vm_i}$ while the defender gets a negative reward as $R^D = -I_{vm_i}$. A normal-form zero-sum reward matrix for the four states of the game in the Markov game is shown in Table 3 which is quantified based on the CVSS values and the reward function formulation explained before.

States, Actions and Transitions. The Markov model of the proposed game is illustrated in Fig. 2 that captures the transitions and associated probabilities in which the attacker tries to find the shortest attack path to exploit DB.

States. It represents the state attacker/defender currently have in the cloud over different preformed actions. We extract the information from the shortest path in the cloud attack graph to define the states. For instance, for the attacker, initial state $s_0 = (Host; User)$, if the successful execution of the exploit of VM vm_2 is performed by the attacker $E(vm_2)$, the attacker can transition to another state $s_1 = (H_1; Attacker)$.

Actions and State Transitions. Based on the system model represented in Fig. 1b, the attacker has at most three possible actions in each state and can choose no attack (*no-att* or ∅) or attack to another adjacent VM by exploiting the vulnerabilities of targeted VM. Thus, for each state the maximum actions can be defined as $Max(Deg(vm_i \in H)) + 1 = 3$. For instance, in s_0, the action space for the attacker can be as $a^A_{0,s_0} = \emptyset$, $a^A_{1,s_0} = E(vm_1)$, $a^A_{2,s_0} = E(vm_2)$. Similarly, the defender has its own possible actions to defend (Def) hosts. For instance, the defender can perform no defense (*No-act* or ∅). All possible actions for the defender in state s_0 is as $a^D_{0,s_0} = \emptyset$, $a^D_{1,s_0} = D(h_1)$, $a^D_{2,s_0} = D(h_2)$.

5 Player Strategies and Numerical Evaluation

We assume that the defender uses Uniform Random Strategy (URS) where the defender selects the actions $a^D_s \in \mathcal{D}_A$ based on a uniform probability distribution over its possible actions in the corresponding state. The decision-making process can be viewed as randomization that chooses the next valid state based on a specific probability distribution over states $s_q \in S$, then choosing the next host for IDS placement from a uniform distribution to become specific instances of randomization. We choose URS as the baseline of the defender's strategy.

The actions for attackers and defender are considered separately for each state. For instance, the attacker action space in the initial state S_0 is as $\mathcal{A}_{A,s_0} = \{a^A_{0,s_0}, a^A_{1,s_0}, a^A_{2,s_0}\}$ where $a^A_{0,s_0} = \emptyset$ which indicates the attacker takes no action/attack (*No-att*) to avoid detection, $a^A_{1,s_0} = E_1$ which implies that the attacker exploits VM vm_1 (note that $E(vm_i)$ is shortly denoted as E_i that means exploiting of ith VM), and $a^A_{2,s_0} = E_2$ which means exploiting of VM vm_2 or $E(vm_2)$. The probability of attack access through considering all possible actions for each state s_j, denoted as $p(AS_{s_j})$, can be defined as the Eq. (3). This means the attacker can launch a successful attack by taking only one successful action in that state (note that the action *No-att* is not considered as a successful attack action).

$$p(AS)_{s_q} = 1 - \prod_{a^A_{j,s_q} \in \mathcal{A}_{A,s_q} - \{\emptyset\}} \left(1 - e(a^A_{j,s_q})\right) \tag{3}$$

Note that $e(a^A_{j,s_q})$ is the probability of attack success by taking the specific action a^A_j in a state s_q which is the exploitability of the targeted VM based on Table 1. For instance, exploiting of vm_1 is an action of the attacker $a^A_{1,s_0} = E_1$, then $e(a^A_{1,s_0})$ is $e(E_1) = e(vm_1) = 0.53$.

Now we define the probability that the attacker chooses a specific action a^A_z in a current state S_q as Eq. (4).

$$p(a^A_{z,s_q}) = \frac{e(a^A_{z,s_q})}{\sum_{a^A_{j,s_q} \in \mathcal{A}_{A,s_q}} \left(e(a^A_{j,s_q})\right)} \tag{4}$$

For instance, the probability that attacker takes action a_{1,s_0}^A in state s_0 which means that the attacker prefers to exploit vm_1 (denoted as $p(a_{1,s_0}^A)$ or $p(E_1)$) is calculated as:

$$p(a_{1,s_0}^A) = \frac{e(a_{1,s_0}^A)}{e(a_{1,s_0}^A) + e(a_{2,s_0}^A)} = \frac{e(E_1)}{e(E_1) + e(E_2)}$$

Based on the above equation, the result of $p(E_1)$ is as $\frac{0.53}{1.08} \approx 0.49$. Similarly, the probability of the attacker choose the second action $p(E_2)$ is computed as $p(a_{2,s_0}^A) = p(E_2) \approx 0.51$.

We then define the transition probability for attackers only for a specific attack action (a_z^A) as Eq. (6).

$$\tau(a_{z,s_q}^A) = \begin{cases} p(a_{z,s_q}^A).e(a_{z,s_q}^A) & \text{if } a_{z,sq}^A \not\subset \emptyset \\ 1 - \sum_{a_{j,s_q}^A \in A_{A,s_q}} \left(p(a_{j,s_q}^A).e(a_{j,s_q}^A) \right) & \text{otherwise} \end{cases} \quad (5)$$

For instance, the $\tau(a_{2,s_0}^A) = \tau(E_2) = 0.51 * 0.55 = 0.28$ which is the product of the probability that the attacker choose action a_{2,s_0}^A and the attack success probability of the related attack action $e(a_{2,s_0}^A)$. We then assume that the probability of defender's actions for each state of the same are uniformly distributed. Thus, the transition probability for defender only for a specific defend action (a_z^D) for the state s_q is defined as:

$$\tau(a_{z,s_q}^D) = \frac{1}{|\mathcal{D}_{A,s_q}|}, \quad (6)$$

where $|\mathcal{D}_{A,s_q}|$ is the numbers of actions for defender. For instance, if the defender has three actions such as no action (no-act), defend host h_1, and defend host h_2, then $\tau(a_{2,s_0}^D) = \tau(D_2) \approx 0.33$. Note that $D_2 \in \mathcal{D}_A$ indicates the defend of host h_2 (placement of IDS in host h_2). Now we define the transition probability based on both attacker's and defender's actions as Eq. (7).

$$tp(s, a_z^A, a_z^D, s') = \tau(a_{z,s}^A).\tau(a_{z,s}^D) \quad (7)$$

For example, the transition probability for $T_{0,1} = (s_0, a^A, a^D, s_1)$ can be computed as:

$$tp(T_{0,1}) = tp(s_0, a^A, a^D, s_1) = \tau(E_2).\tau(D_2) \cup \tau(E_2).\tau(\emptyset)$$

which yields $p(T_{0,1}) \approx 0.18$. Similarly, the transition from state s_0 to s_0 can be defined as $T_{0,0} = (s_0, a^A, a^D, s_0)$ and its probability is computed as:

$$\begin{aligned} tp(T_{0,0}) = tp(s_0, a^A, a^D, s_0) &= \tau(\emptyset).\tau(\emptyset) \cup \tau(\emptyset).\tau(D_1) \\ &\cup \tau(\emptyset).\tau(D_2) \end{aligned} \quad (8)$$

Figure 2 illustrates the Markovian model transition including transition probability distribution for different states of the game based on the shortest attack path described in Sect. 3.

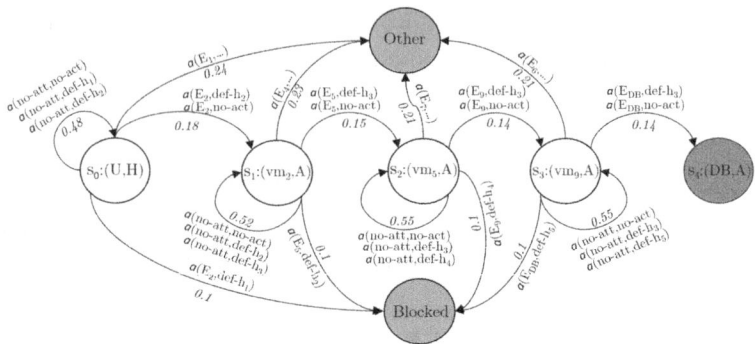

Fig. 2. Markov model of the game with finite states and deterministic probabilities based on the shortest attack path.

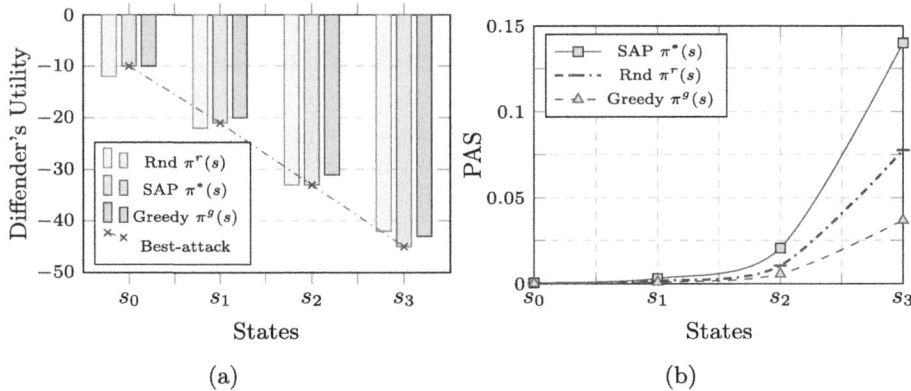

Fig. 3. Comparing the results of the (a) defender's utility and (b) the probability of attack success, against various attacks' strategies.

Numerical Results. Table 4 compares different policies such as random $\pi^r(s)$ or greedy policy $\pi^g(s)$ alongside with SAP strategy. It can be observed that the cumulative attack utility denoted by $U^A_{\pi(s)}$ is the highest for SAP policy $\pi^*(s)$ that is 45. The attacker reaches target in state s_3. However, if the attacker follows different strategies such as a random strategy or a greedy strategy, the attacker can gain less cumulative utility in state s_3 as $U^A_{\pi^r(s)}$ and $U^A_{\pi^g(s)}$ for random and greedy policies respectively. Moreover, the attacker cannot exploit the target in state s_3 in both random and greedy strategy. The defender's utility based on the attacker's successful strategies is presented in Fig. 3a. The vertical axis shows the defender's utility based on each state of the game according to the attacker's action and strategies. As it can be seen, the SAP strategy incurs more utility loss to the defender in the final state s_3 of the game compared to both random and greedy strategies. Figure 3 illustrates the probability of attack success based on different state of the Markov model. Based on the Fig. 3, the SAP attack

Table 4. Game states probabilities and utilities for three different attack strategies: best SAP policy $\pi^*(s)$, random $\pi^r(s)$ and greedy exploit policy $\pi^g(s)$.

Game State	Transition	tp	PAS	$U^A_{\pi(s)}$	Target
$\pi^*(s): s_0 \xrightarrow{e(E_2)} s_1 \xrightarrow{e(E_5)} s_2 \xrightarrow{e(E_9)} s_3 \xrightarrow{e(DB)} s_4$					
$s_0 \xrightarrow{\pi^*(s)} s_1$	$T_{0,1}$	0.18	4.8×10^{-4}	10	✗
$s_1 \xrightarrow{\pi^*(s)} s_2$	$T_{1,2}$	0.15	2.7×10^{-3}	21	✗
$s_2 \xrightarrow{\pi^*(s)} s_3$	$T_{2,3}$	0.14	1.8×10^{-2}	33	✗
$s_3 \xrightarrow{\pi^*(s)} s_4$	$T_{3,4}$	0.14	1.4×10^{-1}	45	✓
$\pi^r(s): s_0 \xrightarrow{e(E_1)} s_1 \xrightarrow{e(E_4)} s_2 \xrightarrow{e(E_6)} s_3 \xrightarrow{e(E_8)} s_4 \xrightarrow{e(DB)} \bar{s}_5$					
$s_0 \xrightarrow{\pi(s)} s_1$	$T_{0,1}$	0.17	2.6×10^{-4}	12	✗
$s_1 \xrightarrow{\pi(s)} s_2$	$T_{1,2}$	0.15	1.6×10^{-3}	22	✗
$s_2 \xrightarrow{\pi(s)} s_3$	$T_{2,3}$	0.14	1.1×10^{-2}	33	✗
$s_3 \xrightarrow{\pi(s)} s_4$	$T_{3,4}$	0.28	7.8×10^{-2}	42	✗
$\pi^g(s): s_0 \xrightarrow{e(E_2)} s_1 \xrightarrow{e(E_4)} s_2 \xrightarrow{e(E_5)} s_3 \xrightarrow{e(E_9)} s_4 \xrightarrow{e(DB)} \bar{s}_5$					
$s_0 \xrightarrow{\pi(s)} s_1$	$T_{0,1}$	0.18	1.6×10^{-4}	10	✗
$s_1 \xrightarrow{\pi(s)} s_2$	$T_{1,2}$	0.16	0.9×10^{-4}	20	✗
$s_2 \xrightarrow{\pi(s)} s_3$	$T_{2,3}$	0.15	5.6×10^{-3}	31	✗
$s_3 \xrightarrow{\pi(s)} s_4$	$T_{3,4}$	0.14	3.7×10^{-2}	43	✗

policy yields the highest chance of attack success while the greedy strategy has the lowest rate in the state s_3. However, note that if the defender opts a correct action to correctly place defensive mechanism in any state, the states of the game goes to blocked state as represented in Fig. 2 and the defender win the game. The defender has a high chance of winning by deploying defensive strategy in the hosts of the cloud holding the VMs in a shortest attack path.

6 Conclusion

This paper first discusses different attack strategies against a cloud model including shortest attack path in an attach graph. We then formulized a zero-sum Markov Game model to evaluate different attack strategies. Our proposed model can further help the defender to make appropriate decision to mitigate the attack impact by placing the IDS in an appropriate cloud's host. The initial results of this paper show the potential of Markov game theory models for strengthening the decision-making to encounter the capabilities of cyber threats and find optimized defense strategies.

References

1. Alpcan, T., Basar, T.: An intrusion detection game with limited observations. In: 12th International Symposium on Dynamic Games and Applications, Sophia Antipolis, France, vol. 26 (2006)
2. Alpcan, T., Vorobeychik, Y., Baras, J.S., Dán, G. (eds.): GameSec 2019. LNCS, vol. 11836. Springer, Cham (2019). https://doi.org/10.1007/978-3-030-32430-8
3. Anwar, A.H., Kamhoua, C.: Game theory on attack graph for cyber deception. In: Zhu, Q., Baras, J.S., Poovendran, R., Chen, J. (eds.) GameSec 2020. LNCS, vol. 12513, pp. 445–456. Springer, Cham (2020). https://doi.org/10.1007/978-3-030-64793-3_24
4. Hu, P., Li, H., Fu, H., Cansever, D., Mohapatra, P.: Dynamic defense strategy against advanced persistent threat with insiders. In: Proceedings of the IEEE INFOCOM, pp. 747–755 (2015)
5. Katzef, M., Cullen, A.C., Alpcan, T., Leckie, C., Kopacz, J.: Distributed generative adversarial networks for anomaly detection. In: Zhu, Q., Baras, J.S., Poovendran, R., Chen, J. (eds.) GameSec 2020. LNCS, vol. 12513, pp. 3–22. Springer, Cham (2020). https://doi.org/10.1007/978-3-030-64793-3_1
6. Rizi, F.S., Schloetterer, J., Granitzer, M.: Shortest path distance approximation using deep learning techniques. In: 2018 IEEE/ACM International Conference on Advances in Social Networks Analysis and Mining (ASONAM), pp. 1007–1014. IEEE (2018)
7. Zimba, A., Chen, H., Wang, Z.: Bayesian network based weighted APT attack paths modeling in cloud computing. Futur. Gener. Comput. Syst. **96**, 525–537 (2019)

Network Security and Privacy

Few Edges are Enough: Few-Shot Network Attack Detection with Graph Neural Networks

Tristan Bilot[1,2,3(✉)], Nour El Madhoun[3,4], Khaldoun Al Agha[1], and Anis Zouaoui[2]

[1] Université Paris-Saclay, CNRS, Laboratoire Interdisciplinaire des Sciences du Numérique, Gif-sur-Yvette, France
tristan.bilot@universite-paris-saclay.fr, alagha@lisn.fr
[2] Iriguard, Puteaux, France
anis.zouaoui@adservio.fr
[3] LISITE Laboratory, ISEP (Institut Supérieur d'Electronique de Paris), Issy-les-Moulineaux, France
nour.el-madhoun@isep.fr
[4] Sorbonne Université, CNRS, LIP6, Paris, France

Abstract. Detecting cyberattacks using Graph Neural Networks (GNNs) has seen promising results recently. Most of the state-of-the-art models that leverage these techniques require labeled examples, hard to obtain in many real-world scenarios. To address this issue, unsupervised learning and Self-Supervised Learning (SSL) have emerged as interesting approaches to reduce the dependency on labeled data. Nonetheless, these methods tend to yield more anomalous detection algorithms rather than effective attack detection systems. This paper introduces *Few Edges Are Enough* (FEAE), a GNN-based architecture trained with SSL and Few-Shot Learning (FSL) to better distinguish between false positive anomalies and actual attacks. To maximize the potential of few-shot examples, our model employs a hybrid self-supervised objective that combines the advantages of contrastive-based and reconstruction-based SSL. By leveraging only a minimal number of labeled attack events, represented as attack edges, FEAE achieves competitive performance on two well-known network datasets compared to both supervised and unsupervised methods. Remarkably, our experimental results unveil that employing only 1 malicious event for each attack type in the dataset is sufficient to achieve substantial improvements. FEAE not only outperforms self-supervised GNN baselines but also surpasses some supervised approaches on one of the datasets.

Keywords: Attack Detection · Network Security · Few-shot Learning · Self-Supervised Learning · Graph Neural Networks

1 Introduction

In our interconnected and digitalized world, cybersecurity is of utmost importance, impacting our society and technological infrastructure. As technology advances rapidly, cyber threats become more sophisticated, emphasizing the need for strong defense systems to combat these evolving challenges.

With the recent advancements in Machine Learning and Deep Learning, researchers are increasingly turning to these techniques to reinforce computer systems against complex attacks. The abundance of data in network environments makes Deep Learning an attractive approach to uncover hidden patterns within malicious communications occurring in the network. The emergence of Graph Deep Learning and Graph Neural Networks (GNNs) has generated significant interest in fields where interconnected data is prevalent. Cybersecurity researchers have notably adopted these graph-based models to detect attacks in network data [2,21,25], which inherently possess interconnected structures. Consequently, multiple variants of message-passing GNNs [11] have been successfully applied to diverse network datasets, including network flows, packets and authentication logs, to detect specific attacks such as DDoS attacks [5,18] and Botnet attacks [21,38], relying heavily on labeled training examples. However, the reliance on numerous labeled attacks presents significant challenges for real-world scenarios, as reliable labels are often difficult to obtain from enterprise networks. Furthermore, training a model to detect specific attacks in a supervised manner inherently limits its ability to generalize to unseen attacks [8]. Consequently, researchers are increasingly exploring unsupervised and self-supervised techniques that do not require pre-labeled attacks [2]. While these methods are effective at detecting anomalies and unusual events, their application to attack detection can result in a high number of false positives, particularly in highly imbalanced real-world data. The model might struggle to distinguish between an actual attack and an unprecedented but benign action, such as a first-time SSH connection between two hosts, in the absence of labeled attack data for training.

Therefore, we encounter a dual trade-off between the complexity of obtaining a multitude of labeled attacks and the requirement of having some labels to effectively distinguish between anomalies and attacks. To address this trade-off, we propose a viable solution using Few-Shot Learning (FSL), employing a minimal number of labeled examples in conjunction with the Self-Supervised Learning (SSL) loop. Motivated by this idea, we introduce *Few Edges Are Enough* (FEAE), a GNN-based detection system that leverages FSL to more accurately identify attacks while relying on only a very small number of labeled examples. FEAE employs contrastive learning along with a few-shot aware reconstruction-based objective, allowing it to cluster similar unlabeled attack edges while requiring only few malicious edges.

This paper introduces the following contributions:

- We propose FEAE, which, to the best of our knowledge, is the first approach that leverages GNNs with few-shot learning and hybrid SSL for network attack detection. Other similar works typically rely on either supervised, self-supervised, or fully unsupervised methods.

- We introduce a few-shot aware reconstruction loss that successfully integrates the knowledge of few-shot malicious samples within the self-supervised training of the GNN encoder. This capability allows the model to directly cluster various attack families within the embedding space, enabling the downstream decoder to distinctly separate them from benign activities.
- We evaluate the detection capabilities of FEAE on two well-known network datasets and across a variety of attack families.

The main achievement of this research reveals that the performance of fully-supervised methods can be approached or even exceeded by using merely one few-shot malicious edge per attack family. This result is encouraging as it reduces the need for extensive labeling and reliance on noisy dataset labels.

The paper is organized as follows: Sect. 2.2 presents some background knowledge and related works. Section 3 introduces the architecture of FEAE. Section 4 presents the model configurations, used datasets and baselines, along with a performance analysis of FEAE. Section 5 benchmarks the performance of the model compared to the baselines and discusses future research directions, whereas Sect. 6 concludes this work.

2 Background

We introduce the background knowledge and essential definitions in Sect. 2.1, and present related works in Sect. 2.2.

2.1 Definitions

Network Graph. Networks can be inherently represented using graph structures. We define a network graph as a type of graph where nodes represent hosts characterized by their IP addresses, and edges represent network flows, typically associated with features obtained through monitoring tools. Mathematically, a graph is represented as $G = (V, E)$, where V denotes the set of nodes (or hosts), and E denotes the set of edges (or events) that connect pairs of nodes within the set V. Network graphs are represented in memory as adjacency lists of shape $(2, |E|)$, constructed from netflow logs by creating an edge between any pair of connected nodes and integrating optional flow features as edge attributes.

Graph Neural Networks. Graph Neural Networks (GNNs) [27,34] are a class of neural networks designed to operate on graph-structured data. They leverage the graph structure along with integrated features to learn robust structural representations of nodes and edges. GNNs iteratively aggregate and transform node features from their neighbors, enabling tasks such as the detection of malicious nodes and edges in network graphs [2,37], provenance graphs [8,14] or code-based graphs [3,4,9].

Graph Self-supervised Learning. Graph Self-Supervised Learning (Graph SSL) aims to learn node and edge representations using the graph structure itself as label, eliminating the need for manually labeled data [20]. A prominent approach is graph contrastive learning [1,36], which generates multiple augmented views $\{G_i\}$ of a graph G and trains a model f to maximize the mutual information between the representations $f(G_i)$ and $f(G_j)$ of these views for positive pairs (i, j), while minimizing it for negative pairs generated through augmentation methods.

Few-Shot Learning. Few-shot learning (FSL) aims to train models that perform well with only a limited number of labeled instances per class [29,33]. Given a support set $S = \{(x_i, y_i)\}_{i=1}^{k}$ with k labeled examples per class, the goal is to accurately classify instances in a query set Q. Unlike traditional supervised learning, which requires a large labeled dataset, FSL leverages the few available examples to generalize across new tasks.

2.2 Related Works

Since the emergence of Graph Neural Networks (GNNs) across various disciplines, these methods have demonstrated significant efficacy in the domain of network attack detection. Consequently, there has been a substantial increase in research efforts dedicated to this area.

E-GraphSAGE [22] is a model inspired by GraphSAGE [12], specifically designed for edge-level tasks on network graphs. The message-passing function has been adapted to incorporate edge features before updating the node embeddings, with edge embeddings obtained by concatenating connected pairs of nodes. Due to its simplicity and remarkable performance, this model has become a fundamental building block for numerous other works.

In another study [17], authors introduced an improvement to E-GraphSAGE by implementing a pre-sampling step before training. This technique reduces graph size, enhancing scalability, and has shown slight performance improvements on the UNSW-NB15 dataset [23].

Another innovative approach, E-ResGAT [7], operates on a line graph instead of an edge-attributed graph. Consequently, the detection task transforms into a node classification problem, where edges and their features are converted into nodes. The GAT model [31] serves as the GNN encoder to derive node embeddings, and residual connections are incorporated for propagating original edge features. To achieve greater scalability, the authors propose a neighbor sampling strategy, which uniformly samples neighboring nodes during aggregation.

Beyond these advancements, E-GraphSAGE has also been adapted into a self-supervised method known as Anomal-E [6]. Anomal-E utilizes the same graph structure but does not require any labels during the training of the GNN encoder. Deep Graph Infomax (DGI) [32] is employed to generate embeddings for positive and negative graph samples, maximizing local-global mutual information by comparing embeddings to a summarized version of the graph. Negative graphs are created using a corruption function, involving shuffling all edges. E-GraphSAGE functions as the encoder and is trained in a self-supervised manner to distinguish between positive and negative edges. Following training, edge embeddings are classified using an Isolation Forest (IF) [19], using all benign embeddings as the training set. We elaborate further in Sect. 3 on the challenges posed by the requirement of all these benign labels in the classifier and how FSL can mitigate this problem.

Authors in [30] introduce a few-shot malicious IoT traffic detection system based on a GNN. This method visualizes binary traffic flows as color images and extracts features of nodes using a GCN model [16]. By employing FSL, the model is trained to generalize and detect new types of attacks with minimal labeled samples. The evaluation demonstrates that this approach achieves high F1 scores on a dataset containing benign traffic and six different types of attack, outperforming traditional detection methods.

3 Design of FEAE

In this section, we provide a comprehensive overview of our proposed **FEAE** model. Section 3.1 outlines the challenges associated with current models and introduces the innovative solutions implemented in **FEAE**. Section 3.2 offers a comparative analysis with other state-of-the-art approaches. Sections 3.3 to 3.6 detail the technical design and implementation of the model.

3.1 Intuition

Our proposed framework leverages a GNN-based SSL method enhanced with FSL for the detection of network attacks, such as Distributed Denial of Service (DDoS), brute force, and botnets. The primary objective of our framework is to achieve high precision in detecting these attacks using minimal labeling. To this end, the input network flow data are first converted into a large graph representation, where nodes correspond to hosts, identified through their IP addresses, and edges represent the network flows. This graph is enriched with additional flow features, such as the count of packets within a Netflow record and the mean packet size, represented as a vector of edge features.

FEAE comprises three key components illustrated in Fig. 1: (i) the **GNN encoder**, (ii) the **SSL module**, and (iii) the **few-shot decoder**.

The GNN encoder, presented in Sect. 3.4, is designed to compute node and edge embeddings that capture the intrinsic relationships between hosts by leveraging the graph topology and the flow features within the network. It operates by training in a self-supervised manner through the SSL module, which ensures that the generated embeddings preserve the original network structure and semantics.

The SSL module, introduced in Sect. 3.5, employs hybrid self-supervised strategies, making use of both contrastive-based and reconstruction-based objectives. The contrastive objective is designed to differentiate between original (positive) and augmented (negative) edges, while the reconstruction objective, combined with few-shot samples, aims to produce dissimilar embeddings for benign and malicious edges identified in the few-shot context, also called malicious few-shot edges. The training of the encoder is conducted end-to-end with the SSL module, enabling the generation of embeddings that are aware of the topology and features associated to malicious activity.

Lastly, the few-shot decoder is trained separately on the learned edge embeddings. It uses a supervised learning approach focused on edge classification and takes advantage of the few-shot labels related to network attacks. The design of the decoder is explained in Sect. 3.6.

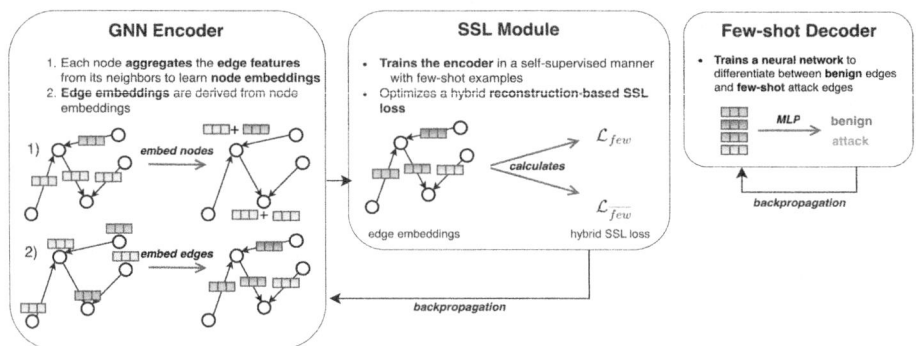

Fig. 1. Overall architecture of FEAE.

3.2 Comparison with Other Works

Other SSL techniques, such as Anomal-E [6], necessitate the inclusion of both benign and attack samples to train the GNN encoder, and exclusively benign samples to train the Isolation Forest decoder. This indirectly leads to a supervised learning paradigm as it requires prior identification of which samples are benign or malicious. In contrast, our few-shot approach requires only a minimal number of malicious samples, thereby obviating the need for identifying benign samples beforehand.

Moreover, fully self-supervised or unsupervised approaches primarily serve as anomaly detection mechanisms rather than cyberattack detection systems [2,10,15,24]. The lack of training labels prevents these models from accurately differentiating between legitimate cyberattacks and false positive anomalies. Conversely, models trained solely under supervised conditions may become excessively tailored to the attack patterns observed during training, limiting their generalizability to unseen attacks. Therefore, FSL is proposed as a balanced intermediary, merging the advantages of both paradigms to enhance the precision in detecting diverse network attacks.

3.3 Notations

The subsequent sections of this paper will elaborate on each of the components within FEAE using the scientific notations summarized in Table 1.

Table 1. Notations

E	Training edges
X	Training edges' features
k	Number of selected few-shot edges in each attack family
m	Number of attack families
$\mathcal{E}$	Few-shot edges (benign and malicious)
$\mathcal{E}_{\text{mal}}$	Few-shot edges (only malicious)
$Y_{\mathcal{E}}$	Few shot edges' labels
$\mathbf{H}$	Positive edge embeddings matrix
$\widetilde{\mathbf{H}}$	Negative edge embeddings matrix

3.4 GNN Encoder

In this paper, we propose a simple and lightweight GNN encoder to perform message-passing between nodes in the network graph. Our proposed GNN encoder first computes node embeddings by leveraging the flow numerical flow features attributed to neighboring edges. Precisely, each node aggregates its neighboring edge features in such a way that both the local neighborhood topology and the flow features are captured. Formally, we compute the aggregation of neighboring edges such that:

$$h_{\mathcal{N}(u)} = \sum_{v \in \mathcal{N}(u)} e_{uv}, \quad u \in N, \tag{1}$$

where e_{uv} denotes the feature vector of the edge (u,v), $\mathcal{N}(u)$ represents the neighboring nodes of node u, and $h_{\mathcal{N}(u)}$ represents the sum aggregation u's neighboring edges. We employ here a sum aggregation as it offers interesting injective capabilities. As detailed in the original Graph Isomorphism Network (GIN) paper [35], the sum aggregation is characterized by its injectivity concerning node features, meaning that a unique combination of features will produce a distinctive sum. Through the use of a similar sum aggregation on the neighboring edge features, the model effectively preserves a greater amount of the structural features within the graph when contrasted with other aggregations like the mean or maximum.

Following the aggregation of node features, these features are then processed by a linear layer with activation function, as described by the following formula:

$$h_u = \sigma \left(h_{\mathcal{N}(u)} \mathbf{W}_{\text{agg}} \right), \tag{2}$$

where h_u represents the embedding of node u, σ is the ReLU activation function, and $\mathbf{W}_{\text{agg}}$ is a trainable weight matrix.

Following the calculation of node embeddings, our objective is to generate specific edge embeddings from these node representations. These edge embeddings are intended for the subsequent identification of network attacks, characterized here by malicious edges. To achieve this, embeddings from each pair of connected nodes are concatenated. This concatenated output is then multiplied by a distinct trainable matrix, which aims to learn edge embeddings given the concatenated source and destination node embeddings.

$$h_{uv} = [h_u, h_v] \mathbf{W}_{\text{edge}}, \tag{3}$$

where [,] designates the concatenation operation and $\mathbf{W}_{\text{edge}}$ is the edge-level trainable matrix.

Our experiments have shown that a single-layer of this GNN encoder yields superior results in learning representations from positive and negative edges during the self-supervised phase.

3.5 SSL Module

The SSL technique employed to train the edge encoder plays a crucial role in obtaining meaningful embeddings, essential for effective classification by the few-shot decoder. To address this, we propose a hybrid SSL objective that merges contrastive- and reconstruction-based losses. By integrating both methods, the model gains the ability to distinguish between positive edges and negatively augmented edges, while maximizing the reconstruction error for the malicious few-shot edges. This hybrid approach enhances the discriminative power of the embeddings and contributes to the overall detection performance.

Contrastive-Based Loss. The recent success of contrastive learning in network intrusion detection [2,6] and many other domains [20], motivated us to adopt it in the SSL training. Deep Graph Infomax (DGI) is the first attempt to apply contrastive learning to graphs, aiming to maximize the mutual information between patch and global representations of the original graph while minimizing it with negative augmentations. Initially designed for node-level tasks, DGI leverages node features when creating node embeddings. However, Anomal-E has demonstrated the successful application of DGI to edge-level tasks, utilizing edge features. In this version, an edge-level encoder such as E-GraphSAGE, computes the edge embeddings for the original graph G and its negatively augmented version $\widetilde{G}$:

$$\mathbf{H} = \text{enc}(G), \tag{4}$$
$$\widetilde{\mathbf{H}} = \text{enc}(\widetilde{G}), \tag{5}$$

where $\mathbf{H}$ and $\widetilde{\mathbf{H}}$ correspond to the edge embedding matrix for the original graph and its negative augmentation, respectively. Graph $\widetilde{G}$ is defined by $\widetilde{G} = \mathcal{A}(G)$ with $\mathcal{A}$ an augmentation function that generates a modified version of G. The edge embeddings will then be compared to a compact version of the original graph to measure the similarity. This compact version, also known as global summary, is represented by a single vector s that preserves global graph information, achieved through a readout function given by:

$$s = \sigma\left(\mathcal{R}(\mathbf{H})\right), \tag{6}$$

where $\mathcal{R}$ is the mean readout operation and σ is the sigmoid function. For each edge in both the original and augmented graphs, the local-global similarity is measured by calculating the dot product between the corresponding edge and the global summary. Additionally, a weight matrix $\mathbf{W}$ is utilized during training to either maximize or minimize these similarities. The sigmoid activation function σ is then applied to convert the similarity scores into probabilities, indicating whether the input edge is positive or negative:

$$\mathcal{D}(\mathbf{H}_{uv}, \boldsymbol{s}) = \sigma(\mathbf{H}_{uv}\mathbf{W}\boldsymbol{s}), \tag{7}$$

$$\mathcal{D}(\widetilde{\mathbf{H}}_{uv}, \boldsymbol{s}) = \sigma\left(\widetilde{\mathbf{H}}_{uv}\mathbf{W}\boldsymbol{s}\right), \tag{8}$$

where $\mathcal{D}$ is called the discriminator function, which returns the probability of an edge being either positive or negative, whereas $\mathbf{H}_{uv}$ and $\widetilde{\mathbf{H}}_{uv}$ respectively represent the positive and negative embeddings for the edge uv.

Ultimately, the encoder is trained using the Binary Cross-Entropy (BCE) loss function on the positive and negative edges:

$$\mathcal{L}_{\text{DGI}} = -\frac{1}{|E|+|\widetilde{E}|}\sum_{uv\in E}\mathbb{E}_G\left[\log\mathcal{D}(\mathbf{H}_{uv},\boldsymbol{s})\right] + \sum_{uv\in\widetilde{E}}\mathbb{E}_{\widetilde{G}}\left[\log\left(1-\mathcal{D}\left(\widetilde{\mathbf{H}}_{uv},\boldsymbol{s}\right)\right)\right], \tag{9}$$

where $|E|$ and $|\widetilde{E}|$ represent the number of edges in the positive graph and negative graph, respectively. The loss is optimized by comparing the probabilities of positive and negative edges to all-ones and all-zeros vectors. Minimizing this loss enables the model to learn to distinguish between original and fake edges, thus producing meaningful edge embeddings that preserve the original graph information. These embeddings can be used as valuable input vectors for the downstream task, which here is a few-shot classifier.

Reconstruction-Based Loss. While the contrastive-based loss method effectively learns edge representations through self-supervision, it overlooks the potential of leveraging the few-shot labeled samples available in the FSL context. Recognizing the value of these limited labeled edges, we introduce a novel loss function intended to capitalize on these few labeled instances during the SSL phase. Our goal is to create distinct embeddings specifically for the labeled few-shot examples. To achieve this, we propose an approach inspired by reconstruction-based SSL methods, where we aim to reconstruct edge features from edge embeddings, thereby ensuring that the embeddings of few-shot labeled edges can be easily identified in embedding space. Formally, given an edge embedding $\mathbf{H}_{uv}$, the reconstructed edge feature of (u,v) is defined as:

$$\hat{\mathbf{X}}_{uv} = \sigma(\mathbf{H}_{uv}\mathbf{W}_{\text{rec}}) \tag{10}$$

where σ is the sigmoid function and $\mathbf{W}_{\text{rec}}$ is a weight matrix with same output dimension as the number of original edge features. The Mean Squared Error (MSE) loss is used to measure the reconstruction error between the reconstructed and the original edge features. We specifically divide this problem in two separate

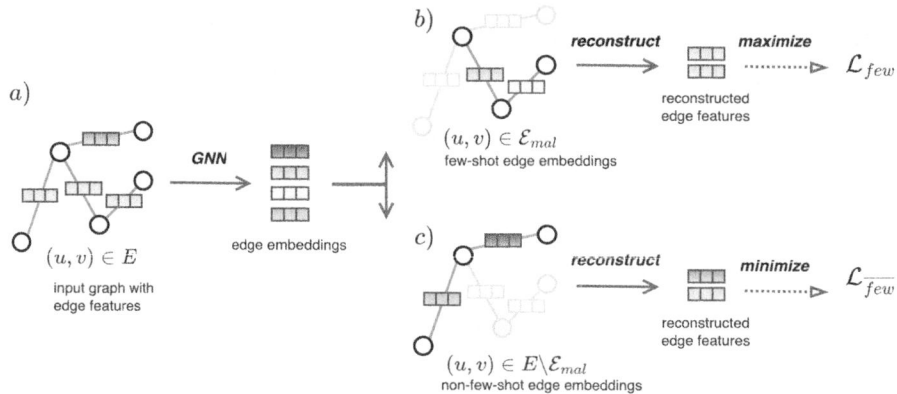

Fig. 2. Illustration of the few-shot aware reconstruction-based loss. a) The GNN encoder first compiles features from the local neighborhood edges to produce edge embeddings. Here, red edges represent malicious few-shot edges, whereas green edges symbolize non-few-shot edges, presumed to contain a high rate of benign edges. b) The SSL module leverages the few-shot edges by maximizing the loss associated with these malicious events. This action compels the encoder to create dissimilar edge embeddings for the malicious few-shot edges, ensuring they are easily distinguishable from benign edges. c) The loss function is also designed to minimize the loss for all non-malicious edges. (Color figure online)

loss functions $\mathcal{L}_{\text{few}}$ and $\mathcal{L}_{\overline{\text{few}}}$, which correspond to the reconstruction loss of the few-shot and non-few-shot examples, respectively:

$$\mathcal{L}_{\text{few}} = \sum_{uv \in \mathcal{E}_{\text{mal}}} \left(\mathbf{X}_{uv} - \hat{\mathbf{X}}_{uv} \right)^2, \quad (11)$$

$$\mathcal{L}_{\overline{\text{few}}} = \sum_{uv \in E \setminus \mathcal{E}_{\text{mal}}} \left(\mathbf{X}_{uv} - \hat{\mathbf{X}}_{uv} \right)^2, \quad (12)$$

where $\mathcal{E}_{\text{mal}}$ is a set of k malicious edges selected among each of the m attack families present in the dataset, $E \setminus \mathcal{E}_{\text{mal}}$ is the set of remaining (unlabeled) non-few-shot edges, and $\mathbf{X}_{uv}$ represents the original features of edge (u, v). As illustrated in Fig. 2, our aim is to maximize the reconstruction loss of the $k * m$ malicious few-shot edges while simultaneously minimizing the reconstruction loss of the other non-few-shot edges. This dynamic of maximizing loss for a few malicious instances while minimizing loss for many benign edges fosters the creation of edge embeddings that are distinctively separable in the embedding space. This separation is achievable provided the dataset exhibits significant imbalance, with the majority of edges being benign, thereby statistically ensuring that non-few-shot edges predominantly consist of benign examples.

The resulting loss function presented in Eq. 13, integrates the contrastive-based and reconstruction-based objectives presented previously:

$$\mathcal{L}_{\text{FEAE}} = \mathcal{L}_{\text{DGI}} + \alpha \mathcal{L}_{\overline{\text{few}}} - \beta \mathcal{L}_{\text{few}} \tag{13}$$

where $\mathcal{L}_{\text{DGI}}$ is the loss from DGI presented in Eq. 9. α and β are trade-off coefficients to balance the reconstruction error of few-shot and non-few-shot examples. We recommend to set $\alpha < \beta$, particularly when the dataset contains a significant number of malicious edges. Indeed, $\mathcal{L}_{\overline{\text{few}}}$ should be controlled by α to avoid minimizing the reconstruction error of unlabeled malicious edges present in the non-few-shot edges $E \backslash \mathcal{E}_{\text{mal}}$. Conversely, special attention should be directed towards maximizing $\mathcal{L}_{\text{few}}$ over the malicious few-shot edges, as they have a more significant impact than all other unlabeled edges.

3.6 Few-Shot Decoder

The decoder is responsible for the classification of the edge embeddings computed by the encoder and the SSL module; therefore, its training is separate from theirs. It consists of a 2-layer Multi-Layer Perceptron (MLP) trained using BCE in a supervised manner on the few-shot edge embeddings. The decoder outputs a prediction $\hat{\mathbf{y}}$ for every edges such that:

$$\hat{\mathbf{y}} = \sigma \left(\text{MLP} \left(\mathbf{H} \right) \right), \tag{14}$$

where σ is the sigmoid function. To mitigate overfitting on the malicious few-shot edges, we introduce a new set $\mathcal{E}$ that supplements $\mathcal{E}_{\text{mal}}$ such that $\mathcal{E}_{\text{mal}} \subset \mathcal{E}$, by randomly selecting benign edges from the dataset while attempting to maintain the same class distribution. However, in the few-shot scenario, information on labels and their distribution is considered unavailable. As a result, we only select a fixed percentage of benign edges, which varies based on the original dataset distribution. For datasets recognized to be highly imbalanced, primarily consisting of benign samples, as exemplified in this paper, we assume the selection of random edges as the benign few-shot edges for the encoder.

The decoder is trained over all edges in $\mathcal{E}$ by computing the BCE loss between the prediction $\hat{y}$ and the actual few-shot label such that:

$$\mathcal{L}_{\text{DEC}} = \frac{\sum_{uv \in \mathcal{E}} \text{BCE} \left(\hat{\mathbf{y}}_{uv}, \mathbf{y}_{uv} \right)}{|\mathcal{E}|}, \tag{15}$$

where $|\mathcal{E}|$ represents the number of select few-shot edges and $\mathbf{y}_{uv} \in Y_{\mathcal{E}}$ denotes the label of an edge (u, v), which is set to a malicious label if $(u, v) \in \mathcal{E}_{\text{mal}}$ and a benign label otherwise.

4 Experiments

In this section, we present the configuration and datasets used to evaluate FEAE, along with a comprehensive evaluation of the model using different numbers of few-shot edges and comparing it against multiple baselines. We also discuss the scalability of the proposed method.

4.1 Configurations and Datasets

The `FEAE` architecture consists of one encoder layer, described in Sect. 3), trained for a maximum of 600 epochs, with early stopping set to 150 epochs. For all experiments, we utilized the sum aggregation method, as it provided better performance than the mean aggregation, which led to smoother embeddings. Both the encoder and SSL module were implemented with a hidden size of 128 neurons. To train the encoder, we used a learning rate of 0.001 with the Adam optimizer. Additionally, we applied a weight decay of 0.0001 to the optimizer to better control large gradients generated by the sum aggregation. Regarding the SSL module, the trade-off parameters α and β were set to 0.2 and 0.8, respectively, and 5% of edges in E were randomly selected as benign samples to create $\mathcal{E}$, the full set of selected few-shot edges. The few-shot decoder was trained for a maximum of 4000 epochs, and we applied early stopping at 1500 epochs. We used the Adam optimizer for training, setting the learning rate to 1×10^{-3} and the weight decay to 1×10^{-5}.

Our experiments were conducted on two network datasets [26] commonly used in GNN-based detection methods [2].

NF-CSE-CIC-IDS2018-v2. This dataset is a Netflow version of the original CSE-CIC-IDS2018 dataset [28], containing approximately 18.9 million network flows. Among these flows, around 12% correspond to attack samples, which are divided into 6 attack families including BruteForce, Bot, DoS, DDoS, Infiltration, Web attacks.

NF-UNSW-NB15-v2. Also converted to Netflow format, this version of the UNSW-NB15 dataset [23] comprises 2.3 million flows, with attack samples accounting for 4% of the dataset, distributed across 9 attack families including Fuzzers, Analysis, Backdoor, DoS, Exploits, Generic, Reconnaissance, Shellcode, Worms.

Both datasets have been standardized using the Netflow format to facilitate ease of use and benchmarking across different detection methods. They offer 43 standardized network flow features [26] such as the duration of a flow or the number of packets and bytes within a flow, which we employed as edge features in our experiments. Similar to the approach used in Anomal-E, we used only 10% of each dataset for scalability concerns, with 70% used as the train set and 30% as the test set. The GNN encoder and SSL module are trained end-to-end on a graph containing both benign and malicious edges. Subsequently, the few-shot decoder is trained separately using these embeddings to classify edges.

The forward and backward steps were performed on an NVIDIA Tesla V100 GPU with 32 GB of memory and an Intel Xeon Gold 6148 CPU with 20 cores and 60 GB of memory. The `FEAE` architecture along with the different baseline models were developed in PyTorch using the DGL library.

4.2 Baselines

To evaluate the performance of `FEAE`, we conducted a benchmark using multiple GNN baselines that follow different learning paradigms.

Supervised Baselines. We introduced four supervised baselines to compare the performance of fully-supervised and few-shot approaches. The first baseline chosen was E-GraphSAGE, as detailed in Sect. 2.2. This model is foundational for malicious edge classification in network graphs. The remaining three baselines-LineGAT, LineGCN, and LineSAGE-are adaptations of the GAT, GCN, and GraphSAGE models, respectively, applied to a line graph [13]. Given that these GNNs are originally designed for node features, their direct application to scenarios leveraging edge features is impractical. To accommodate this, we converted each edge into a node within a line graph, thus framing it as a node-classification problem where edge features are embodied within nodes. A comparable approach employing a line graph was also utilized in E-ResGAT. However, the complex architecture of this model precluded experiment replication due to memory exhaustion, even when employing the sampling strategy recommended in the original publication. For E-GraphSAGE, a single layer configuration with 128 hidden neurons yielded best results, whereas all line graph-based baselines were implemented with two layers, each comprising 128 hidden neurons.

Benign-Supervised Baselines. We propose multiple variants of the Anomal-E model, as it is the main framework leveraging self-supervised learning to detect network attacks using flow features. Anomal-E consists of the E-GraphSAGE model as the encoder, DGI as the SSL module, and an Isolation Forest (IF) as the decoder. Anomal-E falls under the benign-supervised category as it requires knowledge of all benign edges to train the IF classifier. We evaluate two variants of this model, using different positive and negative augmentations in the SSL training. Findings in [1] reveal that employing different augmentation techniques for the positive and negative graphs can improve the prediction accuracy. DGI and Anomal-E both use the original graph as the positive graph and the original graph with randomly permuted edges as the negative graph. However, using different augmentations can improve detection performance of such self-supervised techniques depending on the underlying dataset. Consequently, we propose a variant of this baseline denoted as aug_1 that uses the same random edge permutation as the negative graph, but builds a positive graph by randomly dropping 30% of the nodes along with all connected edges. This augmentation aims to simulate a graph with fewer hosts while conserving the same topology between the remaining hosts.

Few-Shot Baselines. Given the absence of established few-shot GNN baselines for attack detection, we introduce a modified version of Anomal-E. In this adaptation, the IF classifier is substituted with the few-shot classifier from **FEAE**. The SSL module incorporating DGI remains unaltered to enable a direct comparison with the SSL module employed in our methodology. Moreover, we assess two variations of **FEAE**: one adheres to the same positive and negative data augmentations as used in DGI, while the other applies the augmentation discussed earlier. This decision to use a single attack edge among several potential edges aims to circumvent the need for extensive labeling and analysis of attacks within

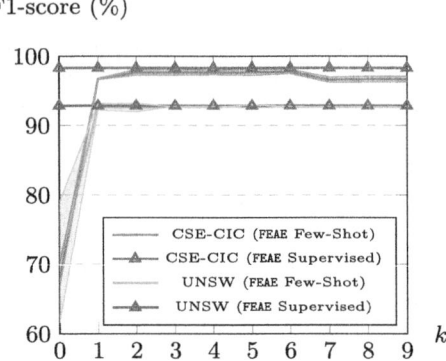

Fig. 3. FEAE performance with respect to k. Setting $k = 0$ indicates that only benign edges are used for training, without any labeled malicious edge.

the training set by analysts, who may not have prior knowledge of the specific edges involved in the attack. Consequently, this approach results in the use of 6 labeled malicious edges for the NF-CSE-CIC-IDS2018-v2 dataset and 9 labeled malicious edges for the NF-UNSW-NB15-v2 dataset.

4.3 Experimental Results

Evaluation with Respect to k. The effectiveness of FEAE across the two presented datasets, with respect to varying k values, is showed in Fig. 3. Here, k denotes the count of malicious few-shot edges per each attack family used in training both the SSL module and the few-shot decoder. Additionally, we compare the performance to the supervised variants of FEAE that leverage all available supervised examples for training. The evaluation metrics chosen for this analysis are the precision and the macro F1-score, presented in Eq. 16. The F1 metric is particularly suitable as it provides a balanced measure of the precision and recall across all classes, which is crucial in imbalanced datasets where attack events are significantly less frequent than benign events.

$$F1 = 2 \times \frac{\text{precision} \times \text{recall}}{\text{precision} + \text{recall}} \qquad (16)$$

This metric takes into account both false positives and false negatives, providing a comprehensive evaluation that is particularly valuable in scenarios where class distributions are skewed.

On the NF-CSE-CIC2018-v2 dataset, the results in the figure indicate a remarkable 96.40% F1-score with only $k = 1$, and the performance further improves to 97.65% with $k = 4$. This demonstrates the ability of the few-shot aware reconstruction loss function to learn effective representations using a minimal number of malicious labels.

For the NF-UNSW-NB15-v2 dataset, a 92.60% F1-score is reached starting from $k = 1$, and the performance remains nearly linear for $k > 1$.

In the two outlined scenarios, employing merely one or two malicious samples within this model's framework suffices to reach performance levels comparable to those of fully supervised baselines, which leverage the entirety of available labels. To guarantee a detailed evaluation, the ensuing sections will detail a comparative analysis against various baseline models.

Evaluation Against Baselines. The experimental results are summarized in Table 2, highlighting the performance of the different approaches described in Sect. 4.

Table 2. Performance benchmark between FEAE and other baselines.

Data	Model	NF-CSE-CIC-IDS2018-v2			NF-UNSW-NB15-v2		
		F1	Precision	Time	F1	Precision	Time
A, X, Y	E-GraphSAGE	96.02	98.82	0.31	95.35	92.49	0.32
A, X, Y	LineGAT	93.84	96.84	4.3	95.33	91.81	14.2
A, X, Y	LineGCN	89.29	95.42	0.43	95.35	91.83	0.58
A, X, Y	LineSAGE	94.94	97.10	1.00	**95.90**	93.11	2.08
A, X, Y_{ben}	Anomal-E (IF)	94.46	96.86	85.1	91.14	85.78	9.2
A, X, Y_{ben}	Anomal-E (IF) + aug$_1$	96.53	98.84	81.3	87.38	84.13	7.9
A, X, Y_{few}	Anomal-E (Few-Shot)	95.3	97.28	24.5	92.47	86.42	1.45
A, X, Y_{few}	FEAE	96.40	99.05	19.6	92.64	87.69	1.22
A, X, Y_{few}	FEAE + aug$_1$	**97.44**	98.71	18.4	92.64	87.69	1.19

Data refers to the input data required to train a specific **Model**. The first group of baselines represents supervised approaches, whereas the second group represents benign-supervised methods (with Y_{ben} corresponding to all benign labels) and the last group is dedicated to the few-shot baselines (with Y_{few} corresponding to the malicious few-shot labels). **Time** corresponds to the overall training time in minutes, to reach the score of the corresponding baseline. For both datasets, the performance is measured using the macro **F1** score and the **Precision** over 5 iterations, with the notation mean ± standard deviation

On the NF-CSE-CIC-IDS2018-v2 dataset, the variant of FEAE employing the augmentation strategy variant achieves the highest performance. This result demonstrates the effectiveness of FSL methods on this dataset, as it surpasses the results of fully supervised approaches by using merely one label per attack family. Additionally, FEAE exhibits enhanced performance compared to Anomal-E in the few-shot scenario, highlighting the capabilities of the hybrid SSL objective incorporated in FEAE. For a deeper insight into the learning mechanisms

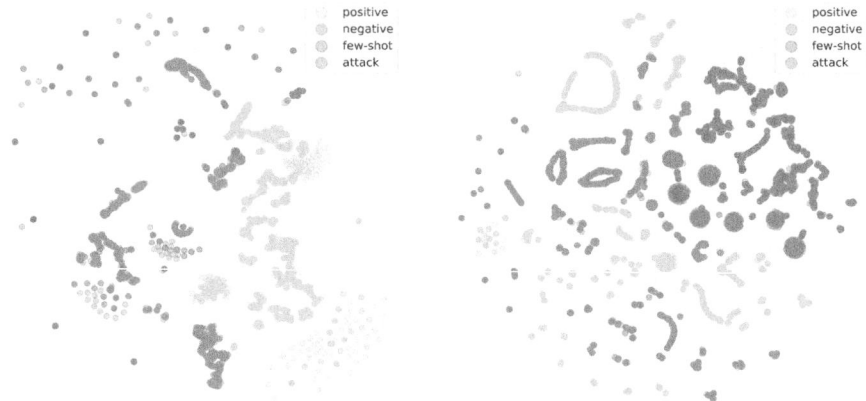

Fig. 4. Left: Some edge embeddings produced by Anomal-E. Note that the few-shot edges are just for comparison as they are not leveraged in the original Anomal-E. **Right:** Edge embeddings generated by **FEAE**.

of the model, we direct attention to Fig. 4, which illustrates 5000 edge embeddings produced by the encoder within **FEAE**. On the left are embeddings from E-GraphSAGE trained with DGI in Anomal-E, highlighting the model's ability to separate positive and negative edges without specifically focusing on attack edges (purple). On the right, **FEAE**'s embeddings using DGI's augmentations are displayed, offering insights into its differentiation strategy. In the case of Anomal-E, the model successfully separates positive and negative edges without giving special attention to attack edges (denoted in purple). Furthermore, attack edges do not naturally cluster within a common region in the embedding space since the loss function does not specifically enforce this clustering. However, when examining the **FEAE** edge embeddings, we observe a distinct cluster of attack edges, including the labeled few-shot edges used during the encoder training. By directly clustering these attack edges in the SSL training, **FEAE** assists the downstream classifier in more effectively distinguishing between benign and malicious edges. Furthermore, in the embeddings from Anomal-E, attack edges do not aggregate into a unified region within the embedding space, due to the absence of a specific requirement in the loss function for such clustering. In contrary, the **FEAE** edge embeddings exhibit a notable clustering of attack edges. This cluster encompasses the few-shot labeled edges used during the training of the encoder. By directly clustering these attack edges in the SSL training phase, **FEAE** successfully clusters benign and malicious edges, which facilitates the classification by the downstream decoder.

On the NF-UNSW-NB15-v2 dataset, the observed performance surpasses that of Anomal-E but falls short of the results achieved by supervised baselines. This suggests that the model may not have been optimally trained on this dataset. It underscores the need for further experimentation and exploration of SSL methodologies specific to this dataset.

The experiments also highlight the importance of using different graph augmentations, as these techniques lead to an improvement of up to 1% in the F1-score for `FEAE` and up to 2% for Anomal-E. However, we also notice that one augmentation pair may not perform well on both datasets, suggesting that this strategy requires a prior understanding of the underlying data to be applied.

4.4 Scalability

The `FEAE` model demonstrates a significant reduction in computation time compared to the computationally intensive IF classifier used in Anomal-E baselines. Indeed, the IF classifier used in Anomal-E accounts for a significant portion of the computational time, thus serving as a primary bottleneck. Furthermore, experimental evidence suggests that the integration of few-shot examples within the learning process reduces the total number of training epochs, as an extended training on the few-shot examples may induce overfitting. This effectively reduces training time compared to fully self-supervised methods like Anomal-E.

Despite their advantages, both `FEAE` and Anomal-E incur higher computational costs than simpler supervised GNN models, which benefit from simpler end-to-end training. Indeed, self-supervised models based on DGI are inevitably slower than the supervised ones, which do not require any SSL module. Nonetheless, the trade-off between computational expense and the ability to efficiently handle few-shot scenarios with `FEAE` justifies its application, particularly in the cybersecurity domain where dataset labeling is scarce.

5 Discussion

This section discusses the advantages, limitations and research directions of `FEAE` and FSL methods for network attack detection.

5.1 Benefits of Few-Shot Learning

The conducted experiments have demonstrated the interesting capability of detecting attacks using only one malicious example per attack class through few-shot learning. In a real-world scenario, this labeling strategy could reduce the reliance on benign-supervised methods, which require the assumption of training the model solely using benign examples. However, it is often challenging to ensure that the labeled examples are genuinely benign, which can be a costly and time-consuming process. Few-shot learning, on the other hand, offers a promising alternative, as it requires only a small number of labeled malicious examples to be effective. Furthermore, using graphs in network attack detection offers a significant benefit: cybersecurity analysts can leverage the predictions of the `FEAE` model to approximate the initial structure of an attack graph. This is achieved by gathering and analyzing the edges that `FEAE` identifies as malicious. Through this process, analysts can gain insights into the attack's topology and understand how different nodes (potentially representing users, servers, endpoints, or other network entities) are interconnected in a malicious campaign. This capability not only aids in understanding the attack but also in devising targeted countermeasures by revealing the path of the attack within the network.

5.2 Limitations and Further Works

A limitation of FEAE and similar few-shot learning approaches is their dependency on requiring some malicious activity data, which may not exist in the historical data of many enterprise networks. To address this challenge, future research might focus on integrating malicious activities from synthetic sources or datasets with known malicious content into real-world datasets. Such an approach could reduce the necessity for labeling, as labels from these enriched datasets would suffice. This strategy not only promises to alleviate the labeling burden but also verifies that the performance of the model remains unaffected by new attack types. Moreover, exploring the influence of flow features on prediction accuracy and conducting studies on datasets limited to topological data, devoid of additional features, could provide deeper insights into the model's operational dynamics in varied environments.

Moreover, substantial effort should be dedicated to enhancing the scalability of such models, especially when dealing with large graphs that may undergo structural changes over time. As networks evolve and grow, the model's ability to adapt and handle dynamic structures efficiently becomes crucial. Research into developing scalable approaches for few-shot learning on large and dynamic graphs would greatly benefit practical deployment in real-world environments.

6 Conclusion

In this study, we undertake the first analysis of applying few-shot learning to network-based attack detection with GNNs. Through the introduction of the FEAE architecture and the conducted experiments, it has been demonstrated that merely one labeled attack example per attack family is sufficient to achieve competitive detection capabilities when compared to fully-supervised or benign-supervised approaches. These encouraging results open up exciting possibilities for reducing the reliance on fully supervised methods and addressing the challenges of limited labeled data in the field of attack detection. The integration of few-shot learning in attack detection represents a promising research direction, offering more efficient solutions that can adapt well to real-world scenarios.

References

1. Bilot, T., El Madhoun, N., Al Agha, K., Zouaoui, A.: A benchmark of graph augmentations for contrastive learning-based network attack detection with graph neural networks. In: 2023 7th Cyber Security in Networking Conference (CSNet), pp. 53–56. IEEE (2023)

2. Bilot, T., El Madhoun, N., Al Agha, K., Zouaoui, A.: Graph neural networks for intrusion detection: a survey. IEEE Access **11**, 49114–49139 (2023)
3. Bilot, T., El Madhoun, N., Al Agha, K., Zouaoui, A.: A survey on malware detection with graph representation learning. ACM Comput. Surv. **56**, 1–36 (2023)
4. Bilot, T., Geis, G., Hammi, B.: PhishGNN: a phishing website detection framework using graph neural networks. In: 19th International Conference on Security and Cryptography, pp. 428–435. SCITEPRESS-Science and Technology Publications (2022)
5. Cao, Y., Jiang, H., Deng, Y., Wu, J., Zhou, P., Luo, W.: Detecting and mitigating DDoS attacks in SDN using spatial-temporal graph convolutional network. IEEE Trans. Dependable Secure Comput. **19**(6), 3855–3872 (2021)
6. Caville, E., Lo, W.W., Layeghy, S., Portmann, M.: Anomal-E: a self-supervised network intrusion detection system based on graph neural networks. Knowl.-Based Syst. **258**, 110030 (2022)
7. Chang, L., Branco, P.: Graph-based solutions with residuals for intrusion detection: the modified E-graphSAGE and E-ResGAT algorithms. arXiv preprint arXiv:2111.13597 (2021)
8. Cheng, Z., et al.: KAIROS: practical intrusion detection and investigation using whole-system provenance. arXiv preprint arXiv:2308.05034 (2023)
9. Fang, Y., Huang, C., Zeng, M., Zhao, Z., Huang, C.: JStrong: malicious JavaScript detection based on code semantic representation and graph neural network. Comput. Secur. **118**, 102715 (2022)
10. Fang, Y., Wang, C., Fang, Z., Huang, C.: LMTracker: lateral movement path detection based on heterogeneous graph embedding. Neurocomputing **474**, 37–47 (2022)
11. Gilmer, J., Schoenholz, S.S., Riley, P.F., Vinyals, O., Dahl, G.E.: Neural message passing for quantum chemistry. In: International Conference on Machine Learning, pp. 1263–1272. PMLR (2017)
12. Hamilton, W., Ying, Z., Leskovec, J.: Inductive representation learning on large graphs. In: Advances in Neural Information Processing Systems, vol. 30 (2017)
13. Harary, F., Norman, R.Z.: Some properties of line digraphs. Rendiconti circolo matematico palermo **9**, 161–168 (1960)
14. Jia, Z., Xiong, Y., Nan, Y., Zhang, Y., Zhao, J., Wen, M.: MAGIC: detecting advanced persistent threats via masked graph representation learning. arXiv preprint arXiv:2310.09831 (2023)
15. King, I.J., Huang, H.H.: Euler: detecting network lateral movement via scalable temporal link prediction. ACM Trans. Priv. Secur. (2023)
16. Kipf, T.N., Welling, M.: Semi-supervised classification with graph convolutional networks. arXiv preprint arXiv:1609.02907 (2016)
17. Lan, J., et al.: E-minBatch graphSAGE: an industrial internet attack detection model. Secur. Commun. Netw. **2022** (2022)
18. Li, Y., et al.: Graphddos: Effective DDoS attack detection using graph neural networks. In: 2022 IEEE 25th International Conference on Computer Supported Cooperative Work in Design (CSCWD), pp. 1275–1280. IEEE (2022)
19. Liu, F.T., Ting, K.M., Zhou, Z.H.: Isolation forest. In: 2008 Eighth IEEE International Conference on Data Mining, pp. 413–422. IEEE (2008)
20. Liu, Y., et al.: Graph self-supervised learning: a survey. IEEE Trans. Knowl. Data Eng. **35**(6), 5879–5900 (2022)
21. Lo, W.W., Kulatilleke, G., Sarhan, M., Layeghy, S., Portmann, M.: XG-BoT: an explainable deep graph neural network for botnet detection and forensics. Internet Things **22**, 100747 (2023)

22. Lo, W.W., Layeghy, S., Sarhan, M., Gallagher, M., Portmann, M.: E-graphSAGE: a graph neural network based intrusion detection system for IoT. In: NOMS 2022-2022 IEEE/IFIP Network Operations and Management Symposium, pp. 1–9. IEEE (2022)
23. Moustafa, N., Slay, J.: UNSW-NB15: a comprehensive data set for network intrusion detection systems (UNSW-NB15 network data set). In: 2015 Military Communications and Information Systems Conference (MilCIS), pp. 1–6. IEEE (2015)
24. Paudel, R., Huang, H.H.: Pikachu: temporal walk based dynamic graph embedding for network anomaly detection. In: NOMS 2022-2022 IEEE/IFIP Network Operations and Management Symposium, pp. 1–7. IEEE (2022)
25. Pujol-Perich, D., Suárez-Varela, J., Cabellos-Aparicio, A., Barlet-Ros, P.: Unveiling the potential of graph neural networks for robust intrusion detection. ACM SIGMETRICS Perform. Eval. Rev. **49**(4), 111–117 (2022)
26. Sarhan, M., Layeghy, S., Portmann, M.: Towards a standard feature set for network intrusion detection system datasets. Mobile Netw. Appl. 1–14 (2022)
27. Scarselli, F., Gori, M., Tsoi, A.C., Hagenbuchner, M., Monfardini, G.: The graph neural network model. IEEE Trans. Neural Netw. **20**(1), 61–80 (2008)
28. Sharafaldin, I., Lashkari, A.H., Ghorbani, A.A.: Toward generating a new intrusion detection dataset and intrusion traffic characterization. ICISSp **1**, 108–116 (2018)
29. Sung, F., Yang, Y., Zhang, L., Xiang, T., Torr, P.H., Hospedales, T.M.: Learning to compare: relation network for few-shot learning. In: Proceedings of the IEEE Conference on Computer Vision and Pattern Recognition, pp. 1199–1208 (2018)
30. Thein, T.T., Shiraishi, Y., Morii, M.: Few-shot learning-based malicious IoT traffic detection with prototypical graph neural networks. IEICE Trans. Inf. Syst. **106**(9), 1480–1489 (2023)
31. Veličković, P., Cucurull, G., Casanova, A., Romero, A., Lio, P., Bengio, Y.: Graph attention networks. arXiv preprint arXiv:1710.10903 (2017)
32. Veličković, P., Fedus, W., Hamilton, W.L., Liò, P., Bengio, Y., Hjelm, R.D.: Deep graph infomax. arXiv preprint arXiv:1809.10341 (2018)
33. Wang, Y., Yao, Q., Kwok, J.T., Ni, L.M.: Generalizing from a few examples: a survey on few-shot learning. ACM Comput. Surv. (CSUR) **53**(3), 1–34 (2020)
34. Wu, Z., Pan, S., Chen, F., Long, G., Zhang, C., Philip, S.Y.: A comprehensive survey on graph neural networks. IEEE Trans. Neural Netw. Learn. Syst. **32**(1), 4–24 (2020)
35. Xu, K., Hu, W., Leskovec, J., Jegelka, S.: How powerful are graph neural networks? arXiv preprint arXiv:1810.00826 (2018)
36. You, Y., Chen, T., Sui, Y., Chen, T., Wang, Z., Shen, Y.: Graph contrastive learning with augmentations. In: Advances in Neural Information Processing Systems, vol. 33, pp. 5812–5823 (2020)
37. Zhong, M., Lin, M., Zhang, C., Xu, Z.: A survey on graph neural networks for intrusion detection systems: methods, trends and challenges. Comput. Secur. 103821 (2024)
38. Zhou, J., Xu, Z., Rush, A.M., Yu, M.: Automating botnet detection with graph neural networks. arXiv preprint arXiv:2003.06344 (2020)

Information Leakage Through Packet Lengths in RTC Traffic

Jaiden Fairoze(✉) and Peitong Duan

University of California, Berkeley, Berkeley, CA 94709, USA
{fairoze,peitongd}@berkeley.edu

Abstract. Modern real-time communication (RTC) depends on efficient audio and video compression to minimize bandwidth requirements. While the codecs are certainly up to the task, the combined effect of live data, lossy compression, and length-preserving encryption leads to the possibility of leakage: the lengths of encrypted packet sequences can leak information about the underlying, unencrypted data. In this work, we measure leakage in real-world RTC platforms and analyze whether information is recoverable. We survey a range of real-world RTC platforms (along with various configurations of each platform) for their propensity to leak data through encrypted packet lengths. We then conduct an in-depth study on Zoom and collect 268,392 network traces amounting to over 786.8 h of recorded media. We use this data to train models to automatically recover information from packet lengths. This is achieved by leveraging existing action recognition datasets, along with a new dataset of virtual meeting recordings. We train neural networks for action recognition over encrypted packet lengths rather than the source data itself. We find that under certain conditions, our models significantly outperform random selection, in effect quantifying leakage for the given learning problem.

Keywords: Information leakage · Real-time communication · Measurement

1 Introduction

Internet-based communication is more prevalent than ever. As a result of the COVID-19 pandemic, audio and video conferencing tools saw unprecedented growth [25]. Real-time communication (RTC) platforms have been widely adopted for corporate use, healthcare visits, recreational purposes, and beyond. In other words, the data handled by RTC platforms has ballooned in size and sensitivity, and platform security is paramount. For instance, conversation confidentiality is particularly critical given the prevalence of telehealth. If information about the plaintext can be extracted in any way, the consequences for compliance (e.g., HIPAA) would be severe.

Current Security Practices. The usual defense mechanisms include encrypting data at rest and in transit. Encryption of static data in transit is usually straightforward because the plaintext is entirely *known*. Encryption is more challenging when the plaintext is dynamic or freshly streamed, as is the case in RTC. This problem is compounded by codecs that exaggerate information leakage through packet lengths. In fact, such attacks are known to be theoretically feasible in specific codec and encryption configurations in both the audio [1,27,30,31] and video [2,10,19] domains.

These attacks are possible because encrypting data as it comes produces burst patterns [19] that reveal bits of information about the plaintext. Even more concerning, our formal notions of security break down in the streaming setting. Standard security definitions assume the plaintext and ciphertext are the same length: this is clearly violated if the plaintext is not entirely known at the time of encryption.

In standard secure encryption, the adversary chooses two plaintext messages m_1 and m_2 such that $|m_1| = |m_2|$ and receives the encryption of one of them. The adversary's goal is to determine which message was encrypted. Alternative security notions exist such as "real-or-random"-style definitions where the adversary instead distinguishes between an encryption of a chosen m and a random string of the same length. Another variant is simulation-based security, where security is implied by the existence of an efficient simulator that produces the same distribution of ciphertexts as the real encryption scheme. Critically, all of these definitions require that the ciphertext length is the same as the plaintext length, which does not hold in the streaming setting.

In the RTC context, the direct composition of variable bit rate (VBR) encoded data and length-preserving encryption (LPE) (say, the Advanced Encryption Standard [5]) is known to be particularly devastating. Prior work has demonstrated that under simulated conditions, the language spoken in a conversation [31], the identity of speakers [1], and even transcript extraction [27,30] is possible from only network-level data (i.e., encrypted packets) under VBR encoding and LPE.

Our Work. In this project, we initiate the study of real-world RTC leakage. We ask the following question:

Can we extract information about the underlying plaintext from ciphertext packets produced by live RTC applications?

Our key approach toward answering this question is to emulate pairwise RTC communication exactly: we set up *real* RTC calls upon which we perform our experiments. This (re)produces the network packets that the RTC platform would generate if the communication occurred naturally. We do this by spoofing both the audio and video devices in software and feeding the pre-recorded media into the respective devices. From the RTC client's perspective, it is as if the audio and video comes live from a recording device (i.e., microphone or camera). This means the packets we capture are genuine encrypted packets from a given RTC platform and the source data of our choosing. While our emulation is exact for pairwise communication, we use the same setup to analyze data that involves more than two participants: we discuss the implications of this in addition to the setup's limitations in Sect. 3.2.

1.1 Our Contributions

We explore the possibility of leakage through packet lengths—for the question above, we find that the answer is "yes": we can extract information about plaintext data from sequences of ciphertext packets. Our contributions include:

1. **Semi-automated packet collection pipeline.** We first develop a semi-automated data collection framework to repeat our experiments across different datasets and platforms. We gathered 268,392 network traces (capture files) across 7 datasets and 9 platforms, amounting to over 786.8 total hours (334.6 GiB) of raw packet data.
2. **Characteristic analysis.** Using the data gathered from our pipeline, we provide a heuristic security analysis for nine major RTC platforms (listed in Table 1). We stress test each platform (under specific settings) with high- and low-entropy synthetic data to evaluate the audio and video codecs' responses. The test results serve as an indicator of each platform's vulnerability to audio and video leakage. Ultimately, we select Zoom for targeted analysis due to the video codec's response to our tests (see Fig. 2), coupled with the platform's widespread use. Refer to Sect. 4 for more detail about the characteristic analysis experiment.
3. **Information leakage analysis.** We focus on Zoom for in-depth leakage analysis along two lines of investigation:
    (a) *How well can we classify human actions from existing ML datasets streamed over Zoom?* The relevant datasets are HMDB51 [13], UCF101 [22], Charades [20], and Something-Something [9]. For each dataset, we find that standard neural networks (LSTM, GRU) trained on the dataset learn non-trivial information from packet sequences. The largest advantage over random (i.e., the most leakage) we measure is 27.3% test accuracy over 101 classes (vs. baseline of 0.99%) (see Table 2). Note that with strong security, one should not be able to use packet lengths to gain any classification advantage.
    (b) *How well can we classify natural video conferencing data on Zoom?* We scraped public recordings of work calls from YouTube, re-streamed them over Zoom, and collected the encrypted packets. We use this custom dataset to again train standard neural networks (LSTM, GRU) to predict classes on unseen data. In this case, the classifier is trained to assign a class out of: screen sharing, single participant speaking, and a gallery view of all participants. Again, we identified leakage was present: we were able to obtain test accuracy of 65.23% (vs. baseline of 33%).

2 Background

Using Packet Lengths for Fingerprinting. Prior work has shown fingerprinting is possible for video-based encrypted streams. We refer the reader to Sect. 6.1, a survey of major fingerprinting applications. These attacks are made possible by a varying bitrate. Previously, video fingerprinting was conducted on platforms that use Dynamic Adaptive Streaming over HTTP (DASH) [10,14,19] or HTTP adaptive streaming (HAS) [2]—these protocols are optimized for one-way data streaming. This is often appropriate for applications with a public or readily-accessible stream source such as YouTube, Netflix, or Twitch. A malicious actor observing the network could launch the following attack: Say the actor wishes to know whether her target is watching Video A, Video B, or Video C. She can observe the sequence of encrypted packets delivered to her own machine when viewing or streaming each source herself. Then, to spy on her target, she can compare the known packet sequences to the target's current network activity and deduce whether it matches A, B, C, or none. This fingerprinting attack functions for two key settings that we define below: *public-static* and *public-dynamic*.

Public-static. In this setting, e.g. a YouTube video [19], the source data is both public and static. Public data implies the attacker has the ability to produce encrypted packet sequences for the source data, i.e., she has access to the raw fingerprint of each video of interest. Static data implies the fingerprint is stable: it does not change over time. Once a fingerprint is obtained, the attacker can simply look for it "in the wild."

Public-dynamic. In this setting, e.g. a Twitch stream [11], the source data is still public, but it is now dynamic. The attacker can still access raw fingerprints by viewing the livestream herself, thereby observing the live encrypted packet sequence (fingerprint). The dynamic setting is more difficult because the attacker must now monitor her targets and the source data simultaneously.

Private-dynamic. In both scenarios above, it is relatively straightforward to launch a fingerprinting attack given the publicly accessible source data. In this paper, we tackle a harder variant of the problem under the private-dynamic setting: we attempt to learn information from encrypted packets without knowing what source produced it. Intuitively, private data changes the problem from matching exact fingerprints to clustering similar fingerprints: since the attacker is no longer able to view the target data herself, she must now learn from similar media to make predictions about encrypted data she has not seen before.

We set out to tackle this classification task in the private-dynamic setting over RTC platforms.

3 Experimental Pipeline

Terminology. Throughout the paper, we use the following terms. *Dataset* refers to a collection of *source* files: for example, the UCF101 dataset contains a source

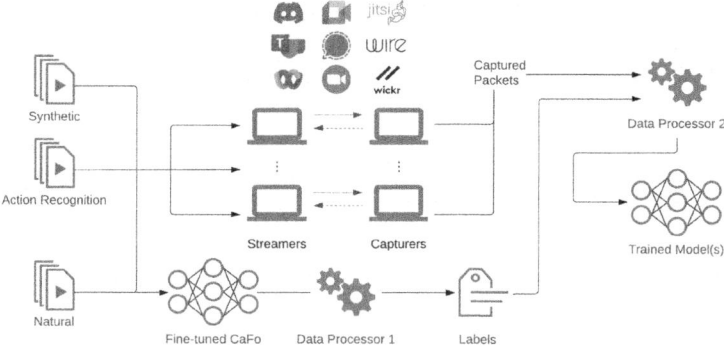

Fig. 1. High-level overview of our end-to-end evaluation pipeline. Synthetic data depicts our high- and low-entropy multimedia. Action recognition depicts the ML datasets that we transformed for our leakage study. Natural depicts our custom Zoom conferencing dataset and requires an extra inference step to generate labels.

v_Kayaking_g22_c03.mp4. Each source within each dataset is streamed over an *app*, where an app is a configuration of an RTC platform specified in Table 1. For example, zoom-auto for Zoom with automatic noise cancelling enabled.

Overview. We designed and implemented a semi-automated end-to-end pipeline to collect and analyze encrypted packets from an array of RTC platforms for our experiment. The pipeline is extendable to any RTC platform that runs a desktop operating system. We describe the primary components of the pipeline at a high level and refer the reader to Fig. 1 for a visual overview.

(1) **Dataset preparation.** The first step is preprocessing input datasets. This ensures that (a) metadata is consistent across different datasets and (b) multimedia is encoded efficiently for the experimental environment. This step is omitted from Fig. 1 for brevity.

(1.1) **Automatic labeling.** Our natural dataset consisting of recordings of real meetings requires an additional processing step: a purpose-built neural network is used to automatically break up and label long network captures into manageable labeled chunks. This is represented by "Fine-tuned CaFo" and "Data Processor 1" in Fig. 1.

(2) **Encrypted packet streaming and capturing.** For a given RTC platform, automated scripts stream and capture encrypted packets for each source in each dataset. This is performed between two distinct physical devices over a wireless network. This step is depicted by the "Streamers" and "Capturers" in the middle section of Fig. 1.

(3) **Encrypted packet processing.** Once all encrypted packets are captured, various filters are applied to de-noise and normalize network captures such that packets unrelated to the RTC platform are removed, and RTC-related packets are signal-processed to emphasize bitrate changes (i.e., emphasize

burst patterns). At this point, the data is ready for analysis. This step is represented by "Data Processor 2" in Fig. 1.

(4) **Model training.** We train DL models to perform specific classification tasks depending on the input dataset. We use the training results to compare leakage across platforms for each dataset. The model's ability to learn (measurable via validation loss) is correlated with leakage. This step is represented by "Trained Model(s)" in Fig. 1.

3.1 RTC Platform Selection

Table 1. Summary of RTC platforms evaluated. Version numbers represent the earliest version used—applications were kept up-to-date through our data gathering period. The protocol for a given platform comes from public documentation. If none was available, we leave the cell blank. The audio and video codec columns are not exhaustive: only primary and default codecs listed. Namely, some platforms support other legacy codecs such as G.711 and G.722. We exclude these for brevity. Smaller platforms have limited documentation regarding codec support. Note that Satin is a superset of Opus.

	Capturer Version	Streamer Version	Protocol	Audio Codec	Video Codec
Discord	Stable 147045 (6ba38a9)	Stable 147045 (6ba38a9)	DTLS-SRTP [26]	Opus	H.264
Google Meet	Unknown	Unknown	DTLS-SRTP [8]	Opus	VP9, VP8 (screen sharing)
Jitsi Meet	2.0.7648	2.0.7648	Custom SFrame [4]	Opus	VP8 (default), VP9, H.264
Microsoft Teams	1.0.0.22073101005	1.0.0.22073101005	DTLS-SRTP [15]	Satin (Opus)	H.264
Signal	5.58.0 production	5.58.0 production	Custom SFrame [6,24]	Opus	VP8
Cisco WebEx	42.9.0.23494	42.9.0.23494	Custom SFrame [3]	Opus	H.264, AV1
Wickr	Windows v5.106.15 build 1	Linux v5.106.14 build 1	—	Opus	—
Wire	Version 2022.06.30.13.51	Version 2022.06.30.13.51	DTLS-SRTP [28]	Opus	—
Zoom	Version 5.11.10 (4400)	Version 5.11.1 (6602)	DTLS-SRTP [33]	Opus	H.264

We cast a large net over a wide range of RTC platforms as presented in Table 1. These platforms were selected for their popularity (e.g. Zoom) and/or their focus on security (e.g. Signal). Recall we define different configurations of the same RTC platform as an *app*, and consider them independently in the experiment. We do not tweak or constrain the operation of any RTC platform beyond what can be achieved through the honest "Settings" interface. In particular, we assess each platform for settings with direct impact on audio or video bandwidth, such as noise cancellation or VBR/CBR toggles. Overall, we streamed over 786.8 h of multimedia during the experiment, resulting in 334.7 GiB worth of network packets.

3.2 Automated Packet Collection

We define two entities: the *Streamer* machine and *Capturer* machine. The Streamer is responsible for streaming encrypted multimedia data to the Capturer, whose job is to capture the relevant packets. For a given app, Streamer and Capturer join a "call." The Streamer's job is to spoof the video and audio devices (i.e., the native microphone and webcam feed) with custom multimedia. The Capturer's job is to capture the packets generated by the spoofed data.

Streamer. We developed a custom OBS Studio [21] script for the Streamer device. OBS, armed with the script, allows us to feed the desired video media through a virtual webcam and control it systematically. For audio, we use the PulseAudio sound server on Linux to reroute system monitoring audio into a virtual microphone, meaning audio playback (such as the OBS playback) is rerouted into the virtual microphone. The script is written in Python and coordinates with a Capturer-side program using `asyncio` and `websockets`. The Streamer signals to the Capturer when to capture packets (i.e., once streaming starts) and sends relevant metadata. For each app, we establish a connection between the Streamer and Capturer to perform automated packet collection for every dataset.

Capturer. In tandem with OBS on the Streamer side, a corresponding headless program runs on the Capturer side to automate packet collection. It is a Python program that listens for signals from the Streamer to start or stop capturing packets. It additionally receives metadata to allow the Capturer script to appropriately label captures. The program captures network packets using the `tshark` command line tool from the Wireshark [29] suite.

Experimental Procedure. Before we started the experiments, we installed a fresh copy of Ubuntu 22.04 on both the Streamer and Capturer machines along with our tooling. We then do the following for each app and dataset combination:

1. Upload the relevant dataset sources to the Streamer device.
2. Pair the two devices over the RTC platform of choice, i.e., place them in a call. If the dataset has one stream (only audio or only video), mute the unused channel.
3. Start the capturer script on the Capturer device.
4. Run the OBS script on the Streamer device. Ensure that OBS's virtual camera is the default webcam and that system sound is in monitor mode, guaranteeing the RTC platform will use the virtual inputs. This begins the capture process. It will run automatically until all sources in the dataset have a corresponding network capture.

Limitations. The primary goal of our emulation setup is to reproduce genuine packets for selected source data. While the emulation is accurate for all action recognition datasets, there are limitations with our Zoom conferencing dataset.

First, our data collection pipeline only supports unidirectional data streaming, i.e., streaming from a single source device to a single destination device. In a real Zoom call between two participants, data is bidirectional and each individual stream is selectively forwarded. We claim the unidirectional setup is sufficient due to the following approximation: for two media streams A and B where $\mathsf{encode}(x)$ returns the size of x's encoding in bits and $\oplus$ denotes side-by-side (i.e., stacked) concatenation, if $|(\mathsf{encode}(A) + \mathsf{encode}(B)) - \mathsf{encode}(A \oplus B)| < \delta$ for a sufficiently small δ (meaning the encoder doesn't have "too many" opportunities to compress both streams together), then $\mathsf{encode}(A) + \mathsf{encode}(B) \approx \mathsf{encode}(A \oplus B)$.

To reproduce a bidirectional and selectively forwarded RTC stream in a unidirectional manner, we mix the streams by concatenating them "side-by-side".

By the approximation above, we are still able to measure burst patterns so long as the burst signal of any one stream is not completely eliminated by reencoding: the bidirectional case corresponds to the LHS, and our unidirectional (mixed) setup corresponds to the RHS.

Second, many of the Zoom recordings that we use are from calls that involve more than two participants. Since our setup only involves two devices, it is an imperfect reproduction. However, we claim this discrepancy is minimal due to the same reasoning as above—only this time, we mix more than two streams.

In summary, our collection architecture is faithful to packets produced by server mixing: as long as the mixing approach does not eliminate the burst signal of any one stream, the burst contribution of any individual stream is measurable through packet lengths. However, other architectures exist, such as selective forwarding. We leave it to future work to design and implement a collection framework that is closer to these architectures. This, we expect, should allow for more accurate measurement of leakage through packet lengths.

4 Phase 1: Platform Leakage Characteristic Analysis

The goal of Phase 1 is to identify real-world RTC platforms that are likely to leak significant information through packet lengths. Suppose we have two videos: Video A and Video B. The key idea is: if no information is leaked from encrypted packet lengths, then the total packet size from streaming A then B should be equal to that of streaming B then A. We formalize this idea and systematically evaluate a wide range of RTC platforms.

Media Generation. Many prior works studied length leakage in an idealized setting [1,27,30,31]—they analyzed the output of (mostly audio) codecs under *chosen* conditions. On real RTC platforms, we do not have fine-grained control over codec choice, codec parameters, or how codec payloads are encrypted. In Phase 1, we analyze the packets produced by live RTC applications by leveraging synthetic data (as opposed to genuine media input such as webcam footage or microphone capture) designed to test various aspects of the underlying codecs. For both audio and video media, we generate extreme synthetic data that makes use of (a) minimal entropy data (a white background for video and silence for audio) and (b) maximal entropy data (uniformly random video and audio). We use this data to empirically measure the codec's response to rapidly changing bitrates. This is done by concatenating high entropy data and low entropy data (and vice versa). At the point of concatenation, the media codec is "shocked" by a rapid change in bitrate and its response can be measured. The codec goes through an adjustment period in which it optimizes itself for the new bitrate data—this optimization process can leak information. That is, the fact that bitrate has rapidly changed says something about the underlying plaintext.

Let H_t^{media} denote the $H \in \{U, W\}$-entropy media file of duration t seconds and type $\mathsf{media} \in \{\mathsf{audio}, \mathsf{video}\}$. Note that U denotes maximum entropy (uniformly random) media and W denotes minimum entropy (white or silent) media.

Let $H_t^{\text{media}} \parallel H'^{\text{media}'}_{t'}$ denote the head-to-tail concatenation of two media files. The $\parallel$ operator preserves order. Then, for media $\in \{\text{audio}, \text{video}\}$, we specify our synthetic data accordingly:

$$\text{U} := U_{120}^{\text{media}} \qquad \text{UWUW} := U_{30}^{\text{media}} \parallel W_{30}^{\text{media}} \parallel U_{30}^{\text{media}} \parallel W_{30}^{\text{media}}$$

$$\text{W} := W_{120}^{\text{media}} \qquad \text{WUWU} := W_{30}^{\text{media}} \parallel U_{30}^{\text{media}} \parallel W_{30}^{\text{media}} \parallel U_{30}^{\text{media}}$$

$$\text{UW} := U_{60}^{\text{media}} \parallel W_{60}^{\text{media}} \qquad \text{WU} := W_{60}^{\text{media}} \parallel U_{60}^{\text{media}}$$

Later in the paper, we drop media when it is inferable from context.

All synthetic audio sources were encoded with WAV [12] – a lossless audio codec. All synthetic video sources were encoded with VP9 [18] in lossless mode with FFmpeg using the following configuration: `ffmpeg -i {input} -c:v libvpx-vp9 -lossless 1 -async 1 {output}`

Data Collection. We set up pairs of RTC devices to programatically stream the synthetic datasets over the nine RTC platforms mentioned in Table 1 following the procedure described in Sect. 3.2.

For each platform, we tested the following apps (different configurations of the same RTC platform):

1. `discord-noise-supp`: Discord with Krisp noise suppression enabled.
2. `google-meet-(noise-canc|no-canc)`: Google Meet with noise cancellation enabled and disabled, respectively.
3. `jitsi-meet`: Jitsi Meet with performance setting at highest quality.
4. `signal`: Signal with default configuration.
5. `teams`: Microsoft Teams with default configuration.
6. `webex`: Cisco WebEx with default configuration.
7. `wickr-(TCP|nonTCP)`: Wickr with TCP mode enabled and disable, respectively. Note that TCP disabled means that UDP mode is used.
8. `wire-(agc|no-agc)-(cbr|vbr)`: Wire with automatic gain control turned on (off), CBR enabled (disabled), and VBR disabled (enabled), respectively.
9. `zoom-(low|med|high|auto)`: Background noise filtering set to low, med, high, and auto.

For all platforms, we enable HD video and preserve aspect ratios when possible.

Results. With the captured packets for each app, we are able to see the total length of data transmitted over the network and measure the magnitude of information loss from the codec's compression. This is shown in Fig. 2.

Recall that we expect a horizontal line for an app if it does not leak any information through its encrypted packets. Examining Fig. 2 more closely, we can see two categories of lines:

1. Relatively stable lines for the majority of apps, which indicates low leakage. Additionally, these apps have total bandwidth close to their mean bandwidth over the four UW, WU, UWUW, and WUWU sources. At best, `signal` has all four bandwidth values within 0.51% of its mean in the audio setting, and `wire-agc-cbr` has all four within 0.10% in the video setting.

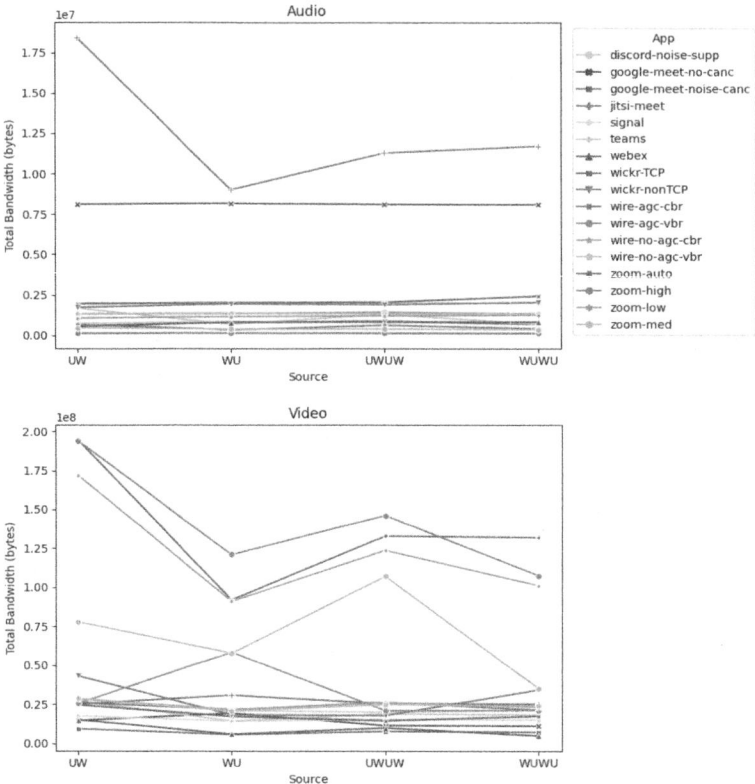

Fig. 2. Total bandwidth measurements for various permutations of high-and low-entropy audio (left) and video (right) over a range of RTC apps. The expectation for an app with zero leakage is a perfect horizontal line. Refer to the "Data collection" paragraph in Sect. 4 for app descriptions.

2. Jagged lines for a handful of apps. These indicate higher leakage and suggest the apps are compressing data in an asymmetrical, lossy fashion.
   (a) Among the jagged lines, it is common that sources prefixed with U result in larger-than-expected total packet lengths, indicating that it takes considerable time for the codec to adjust between high and low bitrate data. In the audio setting, `jitsi-meet` and `teams` exhibit this pattern, deviating by 46% and 55% from their respective means. In the video setting, all `zoom` variations exhibit this pattern: even the flattest `zoom` line deviates from the mean by 37%, and the others even moreso. In general, the audio graph is more stable than its video counterpart, which is expected due to the larger amount of data transferred over video. This further emphasizes the effect of codec sensitivity.
   (b) In `jitsi-meet` audio and `zoom-auto` video, we see that UW and WU have significant bandwidth magnitude differences, whereas we see relatively equal bandwidth totals for UWUW and WUWU. This suggests the codec

may be able to better adapt when there are repeated bitrate shocks (three bitrate transitions rather than one).

(c) There are a few outlying, less-pronounced jagged lines in the video graph which do not exhibit the pattern described above: `wickr-nonTCP` and `wire-agc-vbr`. The largest difference from the mean across all apps was 86% for `wire-agc-vbr`.

Next, we discuss the effect of different settings across the apps. We tested each setting with all other parameters held equal.

1. **Background noise reduction.** We see a large average bitrate reduction for Google Meet in the audio setting when noise cancellation is enabled: the total packet length mean across the four audio sources was 8.13 MB vs. 0.73 MB. Similarly, Zoom decreases in bandwidth as noise filtering strength increases. Notably, the bandwidths of `zoom-auto` and `high` were close (124.20 MB vs. 129.49 MB respectively), suggesting that, given the choice, Zoom automatically selects the high noise filtering preset for our synthetic data. `zoom-med` used 389.93 MB of bandwidth and `zoom-low` used 1,162.32 MB total bandwidth. The results are shown in the dominant `google-meet-no-canc` line over its `noise-canc` counterpart, as well as the increasing order of `zoom-high`, `med`, and `low`. These observations suggest the noise filters are effective—on both platforms, the respective filters are able to detect the presence of uniform noise and remove it from the signal.

2. **TCP vs. UDP.** Compared to Wickr with TCP enabled, we expect Wickr over UDP to reduce total bandwidth since the platform does not need to spend as much bandwidth for non-payload packets. We find the audio setting is consistent with this expectation: UDP uses less data (1,896.46 MB) than TCP (2,104.48 MB). However, in the video setting, we saw the opposite effect: UDP used 28,240.65 MB vs. 18,314.24 MB for TCP. We conjecture the UDP option may support a larger maximum bitrate, and the uniform video streaming would likely reach the limit.

3. **CBR vs. VBR.** Wire enables users to toggle between CBR and VBR—it was the only RTC platform that provided such a control. In the audio setting: (a) With AGC enabled, switching from VBR used 1,343.67 MB vs. CBR's 505.45 MB. (b) With AGC disabled, bandwidth costs are relatively unchanged: 1,324.75 MB for VBR vs. CBR's 1,342.19 MB. In the video setting: (a) With AGC enabled, switching from VBR to CBR significantly reduces bandwidth costs: from 31,388.27 MB to 23,676.94 MB, respectively. This was unexpected since AGC should, in theory, have no effect on the amount of transmitted data. We again conjecture that another variable may have been at play. (b) With AGC disabled, bandwidth costs are relatively unchanged with 24,371.11 MB for VBR and 24,594.48 MB for CBR.

4. **Automatic gain control vs. manual gain control.** We tested the effect of automatic gain control (AGC) for audio on Wire under both VBR and CBR conditions. Examining the data from Item 3 along the AGC axis, we observe that in the VBR case, toggling AGC had little to no effect on bandwidth: both VBR with and without AGC used on the order of 1,300 MB bandwidth.

However, in the CBR case, turning AGC on reduced total bandwidth from 1,342.19 MB for CBR without AGC to 505.45 MB with AGC.

Our findings from Phase 1 show us the magnitude of leakage in the video setting is far larger than the that of the audio setting. Hence, we focus on video for our Phase 2 analysis since it is easier to measure burst patterns. Zoom exhibits the strongest indication of leakage in the video setting, so we proceed with targeted leakage analysis on this platform.

5 Phase 2: Learning from Lengths

We focus on Zoom for video-based analysis and begin Phase 2 to thoroughly assess the information leakage. We measure leakage by training neural networks to see whether and how much they can learn from encrypted packet lengths alone: if they perform better than random, leakage is present.

5.1 Experimental Setup

Media Generation and Data Collection. We use a range of well-studied action recognition datasets in addition to a custom dataset containing labeled Zoom conference recordings. They are:

1. HMDB51: Kuehne et al. [13] manually annotated around 7,000 video segments of movies and YouTube clips in 2011. They were classified into 51 categories that represent common verbs such as "jump," "run," and "sit" to name a few examples.
2. Something-Something V2 (S-S): Goyal et al. [9] curated a dataset designed to help neural networks learn about trivial physical phenomena in 2017. Their database contains over 100,000 video clips classified into 174 classes. Each class is a descriptive English caption. For example, "Pushing a green chili so that it falls off the table."
3. UCF101: Soomro, Zamir, and Shah [22] compiled a dataset of 101 action classes. It contains over 13,000 distinct clips totaling to around 27 h of video data. The data is user-uploaded footage to YouTube. It includes varying camera motions and background footage per class.
4. Charades: Sigurdsson et al. [20] annotated 9,848 common daily human actions. The authors claim the actions are not commonly found in public sources such as YouTube because they are mundane actions. The videos are, in general, longer than the other action recognition datasets; their average length is about 30 s.
5. Conferencing: In addition to using existing datasets, we also construct a new dataset consisting of recorded conference calls over Zoom. We scraped the data from YouTube and labeled it automatically using a fine-tuned Transformer model [32]. We defined three scenarios that are likely to cover all frames of an active Zoom call, i.e., the call is always in one of the three scenarios. In particular, we labeled instances of screen sharing, participants speaking, and gallery view of all participants.

Classification Tasks. For the existing action recognition datasets, we attempt the same action recognition task for which the dataset was designed, except we perform it over encrypted packets that form the dataset's training instances. For our custom Conferencing dataset, the goal is to classify the meeting scenario for a given timeframe. We design three unified neural net architectures to perform classification over encrypted packets. We retrain each model for each specific dataset and classification problem.

5.2 Model Architecture and Training

We use sequence-to-one models to classify sequences of video packet lengths. Specifically, we use three different encoders, each with a recurrent architecture, to embed the packet sequences of varying lengths. Each encoder then generates a fixed-length embedding of the packet sequence for input to a classifier that predicts the label for the video sequence.

Capture Processing. We filter the captures to retain only the packets that travel from the Streamer to the Capturer over UDP. We throw away packets that do not originate from the known IP addresses of the Streamer or Capturer.

Our goal is to train on sequences of packet length data. Let $S = \{(p_i, t_i) | i = 0, \ldots, n\}$ denote the $(n+1)$-long sequence of (packet length, timestamp) pairs corresponding to a single label, i.e., it is a single training instance. Rather than training on sequence S directly, we instead train on $S' = \{(\delta_{p_i}, \delta_{t_i}) | i = 1, \ldots n\}$ where $\delta_{p_i} = p_i - p_{i-1}$ and $\delta_{t_i} = t_i - t_{i-1}$ respectively. We do this to assist the model in learning generic patterns among network traces and prevent it from memorizing specific sequences of packets for a given arrival sequence. We find this approach improves performance on unseen data and reduces overfitting.

Preparing the Conferencing Dataset for Training. We use 20-shot fined-tuned CaFo [32], a state-of-the-art low-shot image classifier, to automatically label frames spaced one second apart in long Zoom recordings. The Zoom recordings (often greater than 30 min) are much longer than media from other datasets (less than 1 min), so we algorithmically split up long packet captures into smaller chunks. The quality of the chunks relies on the quality of CaFo's predictions. While fine-tuned CaFo had perfect test accuracy on 294 hand-labeled frames from our dataset, misclassifications are still possible. These errors would propagate to the final model—to minimize their effect, we look for long contiguous sections of the same CaFo-assigned class and drop sections that are below a threshold. This is a heuristic filter based on the relative stability of a Zoom conference call: each class (e.g., screen sharing) is likely to last for many frames (seconds to minutes). In practice, we drop all frames that are not in a contiguous section of at least 5 s—the probability that the model misclassifies all frames in the section is low. Another option for mitigation would be to increase the number of shots when fine-tuning CaFo, but we found this to be unnecessary.

Models. We explored three different model architectures for the encoder:

1. **LSTM with Attention.** This model uses an encoder with two stacked LSTM layers. After reading in the entire sequence, all the hidden states of the second LSTM are passed to an attention layer to generate a weighted mean that better captures the entire sequence. This is used as the embedding of S' and is fed into the classifier.
2. **LSTM.** This model also uses two stacked LSTM layers for the encoder. We drop the attention layer described above.
3. **GRU.** This model replaces the two stacked LSTM layers with two stacked GRU layers.

GRUs have a simpler architecture, so they have faster training time and less memory usage. However, they generalize worse than LSTMs, and we wanted to see how their performance compares. Finally, attention has been shown to improve performance, especially in long sequences, as it enables the model to focus on relevant parts of the sequence when making predictions.

Each encoder reads in one element of S' at a time, and takes in its δ_p and δ_t values as features. Each classifier consists of a single feed-forward layer followed by the final output layer, corresponding to the set of classes. The size and number of layers for both models were tuned via a hyperparameter sweep. All models were implemented and trained with PyTorch [16].

For each model and dataset, we use 80% for training, 10 for validation, and 10 for test. We train the entire model end-to-end with the Adam optimizer, a learning rate of $3e$-4, and a batch size of 64. We save the model with the best validation loss and evaluate it on the test set.

5.3 Results

Table 2. Maximized datasets have been optimized for the number of training instances at the cost of distinct classes. S-S (relabeled) denotes an alternative labeling for the S-S dataset—it groups similar motion labels into larger sets. Baseline performance is the expected performance for a classifier that assigns classes randomly (i.e. the inverse of the number of classes). This is the best possible performance if there is no leakage. We define advantage as the difference between baseline performance and test accuracy.

Dataset	Class Count	Baseline	LSTM with Attention		LSTM		GRU	
			Accuracy	Advantage	Accuracy	Advantage	Accuracy	Advantage
HMDB51	51	1.96%	9.02%	7.06%	7.10%	5.14%	8.45%	6.48%
UCF101	101	0.99%	27.30%	26.31%	6.17%	5.18%	22.39%	21.40%
Charades	157	0.64%	1.16%	0.52%	0.19%	-0.44%	0.58%	-0.06%
Charades (maximized)	91	1.10%	2.70%	1.60%	2.08%	0.98%	2.12%	1.03%
S-S	174	0.57%	0.90%	0.32%	1.45%	0.87%	0.85%	0.27%
S-S (maximized)	105	0.95%	4.47%	3.52%	3.81%	2.86%	4.61%	3.65%
S-S (relabeled)	48	2.08%	5.07%	2.99%	4.43%	2.35%	4.51%	2.43%
S-S (relabeled, maximized)	13	7.69%	18.49%	10.80%	16.89%	9.20%	16.71%	9.02%
Conferencing	3	33.33%	64.62%	31.29%	65.23%	31.90%	61.30%	27.97%

Table 2 shows each model's performance on each dataset. The baseline performance shown in the table is computed from $\frac{1}{\text{classcount}}$. This baseline is the expected performance for a random assignment of classes, i.e., no leakage. We study performance via an advantage measure: the difference between the model's performance and random class assignment—the higher the advantage is, the better the model is relative to its baseline. Of our three models, LSTM with Attention performed the best across the board, with the exception of Conferencing where LSTM was better by a slim margin. This suggests the attention mechanism is useful in identifying which parts of the packet sequence are learnable.

Action Recognition Results. Our models outperform the baseline for most datasets, with accuracy improvements up to 26.31% more than that of the baseline for UCF101. For UCF101, we report test accuracy of 27.30%—the baseline action recognition model in the original paper [22] achieved 44.5% in 2012 when trained on the *unencrypted* data. While performance on the unencrypted data is likely to be much higher than 44.5% with current ML techniques, it is striking that we are able to achieve more than half of the original performance on encrypted data. We hypothesize the high performance is due to a combination of (a) the dataset's higher-than-average resolution and (b) the diversity of movement across the classes (e.g., soccer juggling vs. playing cello). This diversity would manifest as different signatures in the packet sequences, making it easier to classify. Higher resolution data may have the effect of emphasizing the signature.

Next, we describe two methods of boosting training instances that slightly improved the advantage measure for some datasets:

1. One approach is to create *maximized* variants of certain datasets. Let N_c denote the number of training instances for class $c \in C$, where C is the set of all classes in a given dataset. Without maximizing, we balance the training set by taking $\min_{c \in C} N_c$ training instances from each class. With maximizing, we take a subset $D^* \subseteq C$ of classes such that D^* maximizes $|D| \cdot \min_{d \in D} N_d$ over all possible subsets $D \subseteq C$. That is, D^* is constructed by removing classes from C until the total number of training instances in the balanced dataset is maximized over all possible subsets $D \subseteq C$.
2. We also saw advantage improvements after simplifying class labels based on class similarity. For example, the S-S dataset has many classes of the form "Holding X..." and "Holding Y..."—we truncate these classes to their root verb, in this case "Holding."

We observe negligible performance gain for the Charades and S-S datasets. We hypothesize this low performance is attributed to two key factors:

1. These datasets are highly unbalanced to begin with. They have a lot of classes and high variation between the number of samples for each class. However, with some boosting of these datasets (maximizing and relabeling), performance gain improves to a degree—this suggests there may be a lack of data. Boosting improved performance the most with the LSTM with Attention model. After maximizing Charades and S-S, we measure advantage improvements from 0.52% to 1.60% for the former, and 0.32% to 3.52% for the latter. After relabeling S-S, we see an advantage improvement from 0.32% to

2.99%. After maximizing the relabeled S-S dataset, we see an even larger advantage increase: from the aforementioned 0.32% (for pure dataset), 3.52% (maximized only), and 2.99% (relabeled only), to the maximized, relabeled dataset's 10.80%. As expected, we find that more data leads to better performance and believe that further improvements are tractable.
2. These datasets consist of highly similar videos: whereas the UCF101 and HMDB51 datasets have highly varied movements and backgrounds (e.g., as mentioned before for UCF101, soccer juggling vs. playing cello), the Charades and S-S datasets have near-identical movements with a static background (e.g., "Holding something next to something" vs. "Holding something in front of something"). We are able to learn when there are distinguishable burst patterns for each class; this holds for UCF101, HMDB51, and our Zoom conferencing dataset. On the other hand, it is difficult to learn when the classes are too similar.

Zoom Conferencing Results. Our custom Conferencing dataset had the lowest number of distinct classes (3), and we were able to achieve test accuracy of 65.23% (advantage of 31.90% over random) from 67 epochs of training. As mentioned previously, this relatively strong performance can be attributed to the distinct burst patterns across the screen sharing, single participant, and gallery view classes. We also had 438.12 h of Zoom conferencing data for three classes at our disposal–the most hours across the least classes among all our datasets. We believe model performance can be improved with a full emulation (See Section Sect. 3.2).

6 Related Work

We provide an overview of audio- and video-based fingerprinting in addition to relevant cryptographic works.

6.1 Fingerprinting

Fingerprinting tasks generally involve two stages: First, a dataset is constructed from label-trace pairs of known data. Second, this dataset is leveraged by a model to map labels in new packet traces (not contained in the original dataset) to the known dataset. This is effectively a constrained form of ML classification. Importantly, fingerprinting is designed to identify new traces to *known* labels (e.g., a website), not to perform predictive tasks. We section fingerprinting literature into a number of key subareas: audio-stream, voice-command, video-stream, and website fingerprinting (WF).

Audio Stream Fingerprinting. Wright et al. [31] showed in 2007 that VBR-encoded VoIP traffic leaks the language of the underlying plaintext. Their classifier leverages packet lengths and was able to extract a range of language-based information from encrypted traffic. In subsequent work, Wright et al. [30] further showed that VBR-encoded VoIP traffic directly leaks fragments of the plaintext. They were able to identify specific phrases from a standard speech corpus (i.e., a closed set of phrases) with an average accuracy of 50%, but greater than 90% for certain phrases.

White et al. [27] extended the phrase identification techniques of Wright et al. [30], showing that we can extract approximate transcripts without making closed set assumptions. They take a bottom-up approach, first identifying specific phonemes, then reconstructing words, and finally reconstructing sentences. Note their approach only works for the VoIP configuration analyzed in their paper, namely speech-specific VBR-encoded audio over SRTP.

Backes et al. [1] showed how to recover the identity of speakers participating in encrypted voice communication. They exploited the fingerprint produced by certain speakers and the times at which their voice would activate. In essence, speaker-specific speech patterns were reflected in how often their voice activated for a given voice activity detection (VAD) algorithm. This work again relies on speech-specific codecs and makes closed set assumptions. In particular, they analyzed the output of Speex (the codec) directly and did not simulate the encryption step that would happen in practice. They addressed the latter point by stating that LPE preserves length except for a constant offset, so the analysis of plain packets is equivalent to that of real traffic. In practice, their claim may not always hold: for example, the encryption algorithm may pad short inputs up to a minimum length.

Video Stream Fingerprinting. Schuster, Shmatikov, and Tromer [19] were able to fingerprint video footage over a range of DASH streaming platforms. They observed that the bitrate produced by DASH when streaming a video encoded activity in source data, i.e., a "burst pattern." The burst pattern of a video was found to be a strong fingerprint, meaning ML models can be trained to recognize a video's fingerprint "in the wild" with reasonable robustness against different streaming platforms and environmental variance. The authors made heavy use of CNNs in their models.

In a similar pursuit, Gu et al. [10] also proposed a video identification method for network streaming over DASH traffic. The key difference in their approach was using a bespoke, bitrate-based feature extraction technique. This added robustness to their models.

Li et al. [14] took video fingerprinting a step further, showing that it is possible over sniffed Wi-Fi traffic (i.e., packets obtained "from the air") as opposed to packets obtained directly at the IP layer. They used MLP- and RNN-based models that could identify streamed YouTube videos from a closed set. They compared their results to prior on-the-wire attacks that used CNNs, showing performance was roughly the same with about three-times-lower computation power and time.

More recently, Bae et al. [2] studied video identification attacks in the context of HAS over Long Term Evolution (LTE) networks. They showed an unprivileged device with the ability to broadcast radio signals can identify, with accuracy up to 98.5%, that a mobile user is watching a known video. Their attack relies on

CNNs trained on features extracted from LTE traces, so it is highly coupled to LTE network architecture.

6.2 Cryptography

Tezcan and Vaudenay [23] showed that in general, hiding message lengths is impossible for arbitrary message distributions. They proved that an exponentially-long padding is needed to ensure a negligible distinguisher advantage.

LHE attempts to overcome this impossibility. Paterson, Ristenpart, and Shrimpton [17] introduce a length-hiding parameter that is specified at encryption time. Naturally, it determines the amount of padding to be used for the encryption step. LHE is considered secure if for challenge messages m_0 and m_1, it holds that $0 \leq ||m_0| - |m_1|| \leq \Delta$ where Δ depends on the length-hiding parameter.

Importantly, LHE does not solve the problem of how to choose the length-hiding parameter in practice. Gellert et al. [7] explore the possibility of automatically updating the length-hiding parameter in LHE. They proposed new security definitions to capture the leakage through message lengths. Their definitions allowed them to quantify the effectiveness of various countermeasures (such as padding) for specific plaintext distributions. They found that even a 2–5% bandwidth overhead from padding significantly reduced the effectiveness of fingerprinting attacks for known message distributions.

7 Conclusion

We empirically study leakage in the RTC context by measuring the learnability of neural networks on encrypted packets. In our results, we observe a spectrum upon which some video sources are more learnable than others: those that have well-defined classes with clear differences (burst patterns) lead to more measurable leakage. In these cases (HMDB51, UCF101, S-S relabeled and maximized, and Conferencing), our models outperform random by a non-negligible advantage. On the other hand, we were unable to learn on the datasets with highly similar classes (Charades, S-S).

Disclosure of Interests. We do not believe there is an urgent need for changes to Zoom or other platforms. However, our work is important to consider for future design choices in RTC. We have notified Zoom of our findings and will assist however needed.

References

1. Backes, M., Doychev, G., Dürmuth, M., Köpf, B.: Speaker recognition in encrypted voice streams. In: Gritzalis, D., Preneel, B., Theoharidou, M. (eds.) ESORICS 2010. LNCS, vol. 6345, pp. 508–523. Springer, Heidelberg (2010). https://doi.org/10.1007/978-3-642-15497-3_31

2. Bae, S., et al.: Watching the watchers: practical video identification attack in LTE networks. In: 31st USENIX Security Symposium (USENIX Security 22), pp. 1307–1324. USENIX Association, Boston, MA (2022)
3. Cisco.: Zero-trust security for webex (2021). https://www.cisco.com/c/en/us/solutions/collateral/collaboration/white-paper-c11-744553.pdf. Accessed 19 Oct 2022
4. Corretgé, S.I., Ivov, E.: End-to-end encryption in jitsi meet (2021). https://jitsi.org/wp-content/uploads/2021/08/jitsi-e2ee-1.0.pdf. Accessed 19 Oct 2022
5. Daemen, J., Rijmen, V.: Reijndael: the advanced encryption standard. Dr. Dobb's J. Softw. Tools Prof. Program. **26**(3), 137–139 (2001)
6. Foundation, S.: Ringrtc (2022). https://github.com/signalapp/ringrtc. Accessed 19 Oct 2022
7. Gellert, K., Jager, T., Lyu, L., Neuschulten, T.: On fingerprinting attacks and length-hiding encryption. In: Galbraith, S.D. (ed.) CT-RSA 2022. LNCS, vol. 13161, pp. 345–369. Springer, Cham (2022). https://doi.org/10.1007/978-3-030-95312-6_15
8. Google: Google meet security & privacy for users (2022). https://support.google.com/meet/answer/9852160?hl=en#zippy=%2Cencryption. Accessed 19 Oct 2022
9. Goyal, R., Ebrahimi Kahou, S., Michalski, V., et al.: The "something something" video database for learning and evaluating visual common sense. In: Proceedings of the IEEE International Conference on Computer Vision, pp. 5842–5850 (2017)
10. Gu, J., Wang, J., Yu, Z., Shen, K.: Walls have ears: traffic-based side-channel attack in video streaming. In: IEEE INFOCOM 2018 - IEEE Conference on Computer Communications, pp. 1538–1546 (2018)
11. Hasselquist, D., Vestlund, C., Johansson, N., Carlsson, N.: Twitch chat fingerprinting. In: Ensafi, R., Lutu, A., Sperotto, A., van Rijswijk-Deij, R. (eds.) 6th Network Traffic Measurement and Analysis Conference, TMA 2022, Enschede, The Netherlands, 27–30 June 2022. IFIP (2022)
12. Kabal, P.: Wave file specifications (2022). https://www.mmsp.ece.mcgill.ca/Documents/AudioFormats/WAVE/WAVE.html. Accessed 30 Aug 2023
13. Kuehne, H., Jhuang, H., Garrote, E., Poggio, T., Serre, T.: HMDB: a large video database for human motion recognition. In: 2011 International Conference on Computer Vision, pp. 2556–2563. IEEE (2011)
14. Li, Y., et al.: Deep content: unveiling video streaming content from encrypted WIFI traffic. In: 2018 IEEE 17th International Symposium on Network Computing and Applications (NCA), pp. 1–8 (2018)
15. Microsoft: Security and microsoft teams (2022). https://learn.microsoft.com/en-us/microsoftteams/teams-security-guide. Accessed 19 Oct 2022
16. Paszke, A., et al.: Pytorch: an imperative style, high-performance deep learning library. In: Advance Neural Information Processing System, vol. 32 (2019)
17. Paterson, K.G., Ristenpart, T., Shrimpton, T.: Tag size *Does* matter: attacks and proofs for the TLS record protocol. In: Lee, D.H., Wang, X. (eds.) ASIACRYPT 2011. LNCS, vol. 7073, pp. 372–389. Springer, Heidelberg (2011). https://doi.org/10.1007/978-3-642-25385-0_20
18. Project, W.: Vp9 video codec (2023). https://www.webmproject.org/vp9/. Accessed 4 May 2023
19. Schuster, R., Shmatikov, V., Tromer, E.: Beauty and the burst: remote identification of encrypted video streams. In: 26th USENIX Security Symposium (USENIX Security 17), pp. 1357–1374 (2017)

20. Sigurdsson, G.A., Varol, G., Wang, X., Farhadi, A., Laptev, I., Gupta, A.: Hollywood in homes: crowdsourcing data collection for activity understanding. In: Leibe, B., Matas, J., Sebe, N., Welling, M. (eds.) ECCV 2016. LNCS, vol. 9905, pp. 510–526. Springer, Cham (2016). https://doi.org/10.1007/978-3-319-46448-0_31
21. Software, O.B.: Obs studio (2023). https://obsproject.com/. Accessed 4 May 2023
22. Soomro, K., Zamir, A.R., Shah, M.: UCF101: a dataset of 101 human actions classes from videos in the wild (2012). arXiv preprint. http://arxiv.org/abs/1212.0402 arXiv:1212.0402
23. Tezcan, C., Vaudenay, S.: On hiding a plaintext length by preencryption. In: Lopez, J., Tsudik, G. (eds.) ACNS 2011. LNCS, vol. 6715, pp. 345–358. Springer, Heidelberg (2011). https://doi.org/10.1007/978-3-642-21554-4_20
24. Thatcher, P.: How to build large-scale end-to-end encrypted group video calls. (2021). https://signal.org/blog/how-to-build-encrypted-group-calls/. Accessed 19 Oct 2022
25. Tudor, C.: The impact of the COVID-19 pandemic on the global web and video conferencing SaaS market. Electronics **11**(16), 2633 (2022)
26. Vass, J.: How discord handles two and half million concurrent voice users using webrtc (2018). https://discord.com/blog/how-discord-handles-two-and-half-million-concurrent-voice-users-using-webrtc. Accessed 19 Oct 2022
27. White, A.M., Matthews, A.R., Snow, K.Z., Monrose, F.: Phonotactic reconstruction of encrypted VoIP conversations: HOOKT on FON-IKS. In: 2011 IEEE Symposium on Security and Privacy, pp. 3–18 (2011)
28. Wire: Wire security whitepaper (2021). https://wire-docs.wire.com/download/Wire+Security+Whitepaper.pdf. Accessed 19 Oct 2022
29. Wireshark: The world's most popular network protocol analyzer (2023). https://www.wireshark.org/. Accessed 4 May 2023
30. Wright, C.V., Ballard, L., Coull, S.E., Monrose, F., Masson, G.M.: Spot me if you can: uncovering spoken phrases in encrypted VoIP conversations. In: 2008 IEEE Symposium on Security and Privacy (SP 2008), pp. 35–49 (2008)
31. Wright, C.V., Ballard, L., Monrose, F., Masson, G.M.: Language identification of encrypted VoIP traffic: Alejandra y Roberto or Alice and bob? In: 16th USENIX Security Symposium (USENIX Security 07). USENIX Association, Boston, MA (2007)
32. Zhang, R., et al.: Prompt, generate, then cache: cascade of foundation models makes strong few-shot learners. In: Proceedings of the IEEE/CVF Conference on Computer Vision and Pattern Recognition, pp. 15211–15222 (2023)
33. Zoom: Zoom cryptography whitepaper (2022). https://raw.githubusercontent.com/zoom/zoom-e2e-whitepaper/master/zoom_e2e.pdf. Accessed 24 Jan 2023

A Study on Anonymization Through Participation in iPWS Cup 2023

Kabuto Okajima and Koji Chida[✉]

Gunma University, Maebashi, Gunma 371–8510, Japan
{j2100031,chida}@gunma-u.ac.jp

Abstract. This paper presents a comprehensive review and further development of the anonymization and re-identification attack methods proposed during the international anonymization competition, iPWS Cup 2023, which was a part of IWSEC 2023. The primary contributions of this research are threefold: (1) Proposing the *minimum frequency attack* method against "Yamaoka anonymization," which has increased the complexity of previous anonymization competitions. (2) Introducing a straightforward yet robust anonymization method that combines overlapped record swapping with the addition of noise while enhancing data protection. (3) The effectiveness and practicality of the aforementioned methods have been demonstrably assessed through extensive experimentation.

Keywords: iPWS Cup · Anonymization competition · Privacy enhancing technologies

1 Introduction

PETs (Privacy Enhancing Technologies) have received significant attention across research, practice, and policy domains for their role in ensuring the secure use of personal data while preserving privacy. For instance, the G7 Data Protection and Privacy Authorities highlight that PETs may help entities/organizations to integrate the necessary data protection safeguards into various data processing activities [1]. The US White House's Privacy-Preserving Data Sharing and Analytics Strategy Report also states that PETs will require close international collaboration on technology standards, norms, and R&D [2].

Anonymization is recognized as a fundamental technical approach for PETs. However, the emergence of advanced and potent re-identification and attribute inference attacks has made achieving high privacy and utility in anonymization ever more challenging. In such a context, the anonymization competition *iPWS Cup 2023* [3] took place last year as part of IWSEC 2023. The iPWS Cup 2023 was designed to identify effective anonymization methods and cultivate expertise by engaging each team in practical anonymization and subsequent attack simulations.

This paper reviews and further develops the anonymization and re-identification attack methods proposed in the iPWS Cup 2023. The iPWS Cup was first held in 2023 as an international version of the anonymization competition PWS Cup [4], which has been conducted in Japan since 2015. Since the PWS Cup began, a countermeasure against "Yamaoka anonymization" has been an issue for the rule designers every year. Re-identification attacks typically rely on similarities between the original and anonymized data. Yamaoka anonymization, which shuffles records within the original dataset, aims to disguise these similarities with randomization. While this method can defend against basic re-identification attacks and retains statistical utility due to preserving the original data distribution, it is insufficient for practical anonymization as it merely shuffles the original data.

We propose a *minimum frequency attack* against Yamaoka anonymization, alongside a novel anonymization method based on overlapped record swapping with noise addition. Furthermore, the efficacy of both methods has been experimentally validated through comprehensive experimentation.

2 iPWS Cup

2.1 Overview

The iPWS Cup 2023 (iPWS Cup for short) consists of two parts: an anonymization phase and an attack phase as described below.

- Anonymization phase
  1. The organizer distributes the original data $B^{(i)}$ to each participating team (called the anonymizer) i.
  2. Each anonymizer i creates anonymized data $C^{(i)}$ from $B^{(i)}$ and submits it to the organizer.
- Attack phase
  1. The organizer randomly samples a certain number of records from $C^{(i)}$ and distributes the sampled data $D^{(i)}$ along with $B^{(i)}$ to each participating team (called the attacker) j.
  2. Each attacker j conducts a re-identification attack on $D^{(i)}$ and submits $E^{(i,j)}$ to the organizer.

Each participating team assumes dual roles as both anonymizer and attacker. As anonymizers, they enhance the data's anonymity and utility described in Sects. 2.2 and 2.3. Concurrently, as attackers, they execute a re-identification attacks aimed at compromising the anonymity of data anonymized by the other teams.

The original data $B^{(i)}$ provided to anonymizer i comprises 3,985 records, including two numerical attributes (age, BMI value) and eight categorical attributes. In practice, ten sets of candidate $B^{(i)}$ are distributed and the anonymizer i can select one to anonymize from a fairness perspective. The k-th record of anonymized data $C^{(i)}$ corresponds one-to-one to the k-th record of $B^{(i)}$ (i.e. the record of the same person), and the attacker guesses the correspondence from $B^{(i)}$ and randomly sampled data $D^{(i)}$ of $C^{(i)}$, which is called the re-identification attack. Please refer to [5] for more details.

2.2 Anonymity

Let $E^{(i,j)}$ be the result of the attacker j estimating the sequence $X^{(i)}$ of row indices in $B^{(i)}$ corresponding to $D^{(i)}$. Here, $X^{(i)}$ represents the correct mapping or row indices, as determined by organizer, linking $D^{(i)}$ to $B^{(i)}$. The success rate of the re-identification attack on $D^{(i)}$ by attacker j, $\alpha_{i,j}$, is defined as the number of matched rows in $X^{(i)}$ and $E^{(i,j)}$ divided by the number of rows in $D^{(i)}$, $|D^{(i)}|$. The anonymity of $C^{(i)}$ against the attacker j is evaluated as $1-\alpha_{i,j}$. As a result, the *privacy score* of $C^{(i)}$ is quantified as

$$PS^{(i)} = 1 - \max_{j} \alpha_{i,j}. \qquad (1)$$

2.3 Utility

In the iPWS Cup, the utility of $C^{(i)}$ is evaluated based on the maximum difference value of age in each record of $B^{(i)}$ and $C^{(i)}$, $\Delta age^{(i)}$, the maximum difference value of BMI value in each record, $\Delta bmi^{(i)}$, the maximum discrepancy number of eight category attribute values in each record, $\Delta cat^{(i)}$, the maximum difference value for each element of the cross tabulation table, $\Delta rate^{(i)}$, the maximum difference value for each element of the covariance matrix, $\Delta cor^{(i)}$, and the maximum difference value for each element of the odds ratio, $\Delta or^{(i)}$. Define $\Delta^{(i)} = (\Delta age^{(i)}, \Delta bmi^{(i)}, \Delta cat^{(i)}, \Delta rate^{(i)}, \Delta cor^{(i)}, \Delta or^{(i)})$. Suppose that all elements of $\Delta^{(i)}$ are normalized to a value between 0 and 1. Then the *utility score* of $C^{(i)}$ is quantified as

$$US^{(i)} = \left(\prod_{u \in \Delta^{(i)}} (1-u) \right)^{1/6}. \qquad (2)$$

Hereafter, a superscript for anonymizer i and attacker j (e.g., (i)) may be omitted for simplicity.

In the iPWS Cup, Δage, Δbmi, and Δcat are included in the utility score as a countermeasure to Yamaoka anonymization, which involves insufficiently anonymizing datasets through simple record shuffling, to ensure a reduced overall score for such data. In practice, however, several teams submitted the anonymized data using Yamaoka anonymization with (almost) $\Delta rate = \Delta cor = \Delta or = 0$ and small Δage, Δbmi, Δcat values.

3 Proposed Method

In this section, we present the anonymization method and re-identification attack tequnique that we utilized in the iPWS Cup. In particular, the proposed re-identification attack is regarded as an effective measure against Yamaoka anonymization.

3.1 Re-identification Attack

Each attacker knows B, D and Δ. Using the values of Δage, Δbmi, and Δcat, the candidate records in B corresponding to each record in D can be narrowed down. If there are k candidates, the expected probability of a successful attack is $1/k$.

The similarity between the two records, SR, follows the measure used in the iPWS Cup. That is,

$$SR = \left(1 - \frac{\min(\delta_{age}, 20)}{20}\right) \times \left(1 - \frac{\min(\delta_{bmi}, 20)}{20}\right) \times \left(1 - \frac{\delta_{cat}}{8}\right) \quad (3)$$

where δ_{age} and δ_{bmi} are the difference of the age values and bmi values respectively, and δ_{cat} is the Hamming distance of the cat 1 to 8 values. The SR takes values between 0 and 1. If two records are identical, $SR = 1$, indicating the highest level of similarity. Conversely, if $\delta_{age} \geq 20$, $\delta_{bmi} \geq 20$ or $\delta_{cat} = 8$, then $SR = 0$, resulting in a utility score of zero. The basic re-identification attack described above can be easily avoided when multiple candidate records are present. In particular, Yamaoka anonymization is effective in this situation.

The proposed algorithm is shown in Algorithm 1. MinElement in line 2 is a function that returns the index u of a set with minimum elements greater than 1 for $S_1, \ldots, S_m$. MinFreq in line 3 is a function that returns the element $c_{u,*} \in S_u$ of the minimum frequency except b_u in $S_1, \ldots, S_m$. In the iPWS Cup, Algorithm 1 achieved the highest success rate in re-identifying the anonymized data using Yamaoka anonymization among the participating teams, with success rates ranging from 11% to 22%.

Algorithm 1 Proposed re-identification attack.

Require: $S_k = \{b_k, c_{k,1}, \ldots, c_{k,n_k}\}$ for $k = 1, 2, \ldots, m$
Ensure: $S_k = \{c_k^*\}$ for $k = 1, 2, \ldots, m$
1: **while** $\exists u : |S_u| > 1$ **do**
2:     $u \leftarrow \mathsf{MinElement}(S_1, \ldots, S_m)$
3:     $c_{u,*} \leftarrow \mathsf{MinFreq}(u, S_1, \ldots, S_m)$
4:     $S_u \leftarrow \{c_{u,*}\}$
5:     **for all** $v \neq u$ **do**
6:         **if** $c_{u,*} \in S_v$ **then**
7:             $S_v \leftarrow S_v - \{c_{u,*}\}$
8:         **end if**
9:     **end for**
10: **end while**
11: **return** S_k

3.2 Anonymization

Our anonymization method is detailed below.

1. Set $b_k \in B$ as the initial value $c_k \in C$.
2. Determine the values of $\Delta age, \Delta bmi, \Delta cat$ while considering their impact on utility.

3. For each record c_k in C, randomly select one record in B satisfying

$$\delta_{age} \leq \Delta age,$$
$$\delta_{bmi} \leq \Delta bmi,$$
$$\delta_{cat} \leq \Delta cat \qquad (4)$$

and replace c_k with the selected record.

4. Repeat the process by randomly selecting a record from C and randomizing it to satisfy Eq. (4) and increase utility.

For step 2, the larger the values of $\Delta age, \Delta bmi, \Delta cat$, the more records in B satisfying Eq. (4), the more anonymity is expected. However, there is a trade-off, as utility decreases. Therefore, appropriate values must be chosen to maintain a good balance between anonymity and utility. Through this step, we carefully determine the number s of k such that $|S_k| = 1$, where the sole record in S_k is deemed high risk. Consequently, the probability that t records with $|S_k| = 1$ are included in D can be estimated from the hypergeometric distribution

$$f(t) = \frac{\binom{s}{t}\binom{|B|-s}{|D|-t}}{\binom{|B|}{|D|}} \qquad (5)$$

where $|B|$ is the number of records in B (= 3,985) and $|D|$ is the number of records in D (= 300). Our strategy was to identify values of $\Delta age, \Delta bmi, \Delta cat$ that would make the probability of $t \geq 20$ sufficiently small based on Eq. (5). We chose $(\Delta age, \Delta bmi, \Delta cat) = (0.15, 0.27, 0.375)$ where the probability of $t \geq 20$ was about 0.544%.

3.3 Summary of the iPWS Cup

The result of the iPWS Cup is available to the public [6].

In summary, out of the 10 teams, it is evident that Teams 06, 08, and 10 performed Yamaoka anonymization, as indicated by their $\Delta rate, \Delta cor$, and Δor values being close to zero. Our team, 04, successfully attacked Teams 06 and 08 using the proposed attack method against Yamaoka anonymization, whereas the other participating teams encountered considerable difficulties.

In terms of the Privacy Score, although our team tied for second place, the leading team exhibited significantly higher $\Delta age, \Delta bmi$, and Δcat values compared to our team. This indicates that the leading team sacrifices more utility than we do, ultimately leading to our team's victory in the overall score.

The effectiveness of our anonymization method will be assessed in an experimental setting in the next section.

4 Experimental Results

4.1 Extension Experiment for the iPWS Cup

To assess our anonymization method, we have implemented our anonymization method presented in Sect. 3.2 and a Yamaoka anonymization algorithm for comparative experiments, shown in Algorithm 2. Cand in line 2 is a function that returns all candidate records in B satisfying Eq. (4) for b_k. Rand in line 6 is a function that returns an element except b_u randomly from S_u.

Algorithm 2 A Yamaoka anonymization algorithm.

Require: $b_k \in B$ for $k = 1, \ldots, m$ ($|B| = m$), Δage, Δbmi, Δcat
Ensure: c_k for $k = 1, \ldots, m$
1: **for all** $b_k \in B$ **do**
2:     $S_k \leftarrow \mathsf{Cand}(b_k, B, \Delta age, \Delta bmi, \Delta cat)$
3: **end for**
4: **while** $\exists u : |S_u| > 1$ **do**
5:     $u \leftarrow \mathsf{MinElement}(S_1, \ldots, S_m)$
6:     $c_{u,*} \leftarrow \mathsf{Rand}(S_u)$
7:     $S_u \leftarrow \{c_{u,*}\}$
8:     **for all** $v \neq u$ **do**
9:         **if** $c_{u,*} \in S_v$ **then**
10:             $S_v \leftarrow S_v - \{c_{u,*}\}$
11:         **end if**
12:     **end for**
13: **end while**
14: **return** $c_k \in S_k$

Figure 1 shows the result. The "noise size" in the top and bottom axes indicates the number of times step 4 of our anonymization method has been performed. The "baseline" and "our strategy" refer to the results of Algorithm 2 and our anonymization method, respectively. In this experiment, $B^{(8)}$ and $(\Delta age, \Delta bmi, \Delta cat) = (0.15, 0.2, 0.375)$ of Team 08 was used. To mitigate the effects of randomization, three sets of anonymized data were generated, and the utility and privacy scores were calculated as the averages of these sets.

Figure 1 illustrates that Algorithm 2 has a high utility score of 0.85 before adding noise, but a low privacy score of approximately 0.915. As noise is incrementally added, there is a gradual increase in the privacy score, while the utility score declines significantly. In contrast, our anonymization method begins with a relatively high privacy score even before the addition of noise, though its initial utility score is inferior to Algorithm 2. However, as noise is introduced, both the utility and privacy scores slowly increase. Notably, our anonymization method consistently achieves a superior privacy score, and with a slight addition of noise, our utility score surpasses that of Algorithm 2.

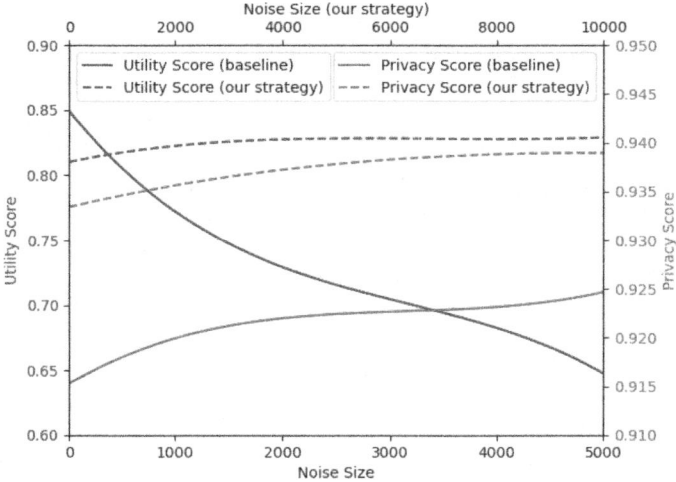

Fig. 1. Comparison between Yamaoka anonymization and ours.

4.2 Additional Experiments

We further evaluated the privacy level of our method using TAPAS[1] (a Toolbox for Adversarial Privacy Auditing of Synthetic Data) [7]. TAPAS is an open-source software (OSS) that implements several typical attacks against synthetic data. Many of the attacks implemented in TAPAS can be applied to generic anonymized data, not just synthetic data. To the best of our knowledge, it is one of the best OSS tools for experimentally assessing the security of anonymized data. TAPAS takes a target anonymization code, an evaluation dataset, and some parameter values as input, generates a large amount of anonymized data to be attacked, and outputs various privacy scores.

In TAPAS, some attack types, attack methods, and attacker's knowledge of the original data can be selected for the threat modeling. Attack types include *Membership Inference Attack* (MIA). Attack methods [8] are seven types of attacks, ClosestDistanceMIA, ClosestDistanceAIA, LocalNeighbourhoodAttack, ShadowModellingAttack, GroundhogAttack, ProbabilityEstimationAttack, SyntheticPredictorAttack including recent research findings. Attacker's knowledge of the original data consists of ExactDataKnowledge, where all the original data is known, or AuxiliaryDataKnowledge, where the data is restricted.

We introduce an example of the TAPAS attack procedure using MIA. First, d records are sampled from the input dataset, and a dataset D^+ containing the target record t and a dataset D^- not containing it are set up. Then, for each D^+, D^-, m, and n anonymized datasets are generated for training and testing, respectively. Note that the training data has been used to build a generative model for the attack. In Experiment 2 of [7], $d = 500$, $m = 1,000$ and $n = 2,500$

---
[1] https://github.com/alan-turing-institute/tapas.

are selected. A target record t is sampled from d records in the input dataset (in general, the more specific the data, the more likely it is to be attacked).

Next, an attack is attempted to generate a model from m training anonymized datasets and identify n testing datasets. The attack is based on the attack methods and the knowledge of the original data. The result of the attack is given as the proportion of D^- correctly identified (true positive rate : TP), the proportion incorrectly identified (false negative rate : FN $= 1 - $ TP), the proportion of D^+ correctly identified (true negative rate: TN) and the proportion incorrectly identified (false positive rate: FP $= 1 -$ TN). Finally, TAPAS outputs the accuracy of prediction, privacy gain [9], AUC, ROC curve and so on.

Figures 2, 3 and 4 show the results for MIA using TAPAS, where the number of noise additions is 0, 100, and 300. For simplicity, noise is only added for eight categorical data. We set $(d, m, n) = (500, 100, 100)$ for the number of sampled data, d, training datasets, m, and testing datasets, n, and selected ExactData-Knowledge as an attacker's knowledge of the original data. Note that the impact of 100 and 300 noise additions is relatively large because the data is sampled to $d = 500$. We used the original data $B^{(8)}$ and the attack methods 1 to 8 in the TAPAS below.

- GroundhogAttack: It is a variant of the *shadow modeling attack* using a random forest classifier over simple features extracted from datasets proposed in [9]. The shadow modeling attack trains a set classifier from D^+, D^- to predict membership or the sensitive attribute for the sensitive data.
  1. NaiveGroundhog, 2. HistGroundhog, 3. CorrGroundhog, 4. LogisticGroundhog
- ClosestDistanceMIA: It is a membership inference attack that uses the minimal distance between the target record and records in the anonymized dataset B as score $s(B, x) = -\min_{y \in B} distance(x, y)$.
  5ClosestDistance − Hamming, 6DirectLookup, 7ClosestDistance − L2
- ProbabilityEstimationAttack: It is a membership inference attack that uses a density estimator fit to the anonymized data. The score used by the attack is the density estimated at the target point. 8KernelEstimator

The number of noise additions generally increases the privacy level, however, our method is not always correct because it adds noise in a way that increases the utility. Figures 2, 3 and 4 show the change in privacy levels due to noise addition. The graphs on the right in the figures represent the ROC curve, where the greater the difference between the true positive rate (TP) and the false positive rate (FP), the more significant the attack. Attacks 3, 4, and 8 appear to be relatively successful attacks in Fig. 2. However, whether they are significant attacks or not needs to be determined by appropriate criteria, which is an issue for the future. On the other hand, Fig. 3 seems that the noise additions don't reduce the privacy level, but rather improve it, as shown in Fig. 1. Figure 4, where noise is added 300 times, shows that Attacks 2, 4, and 8 are relatively effective. In Sect. 4, noise was added during evaluation using our attack method, however, it is necessary to add noise during evaluation with other attack methods, such as the attack methods implemented in TAPAS.

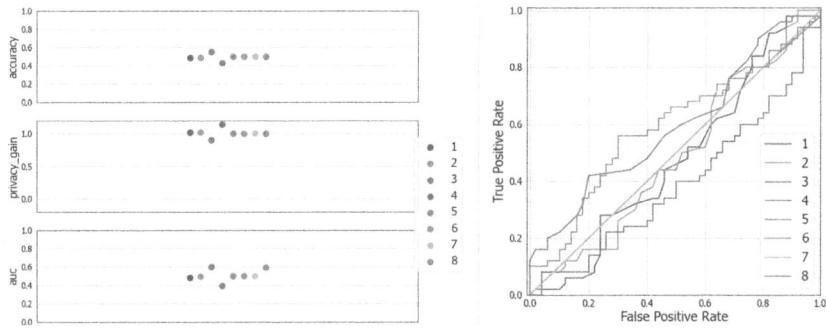

Fig. 2. Privacy level of our method for MIA from TAPAS (0 noise additions).

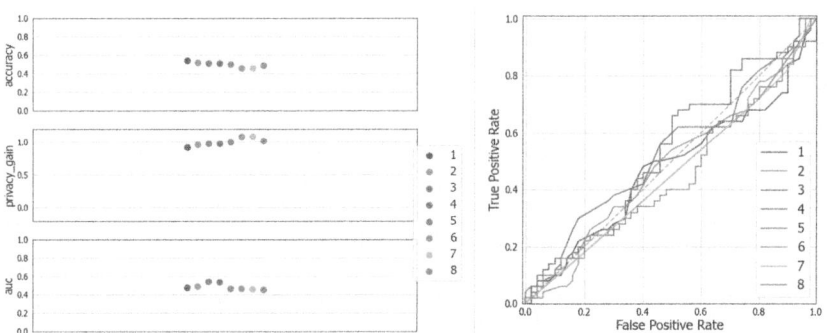

Fig. 3. Privacy level of our method for MIA from TAPAS (100 noise additions).

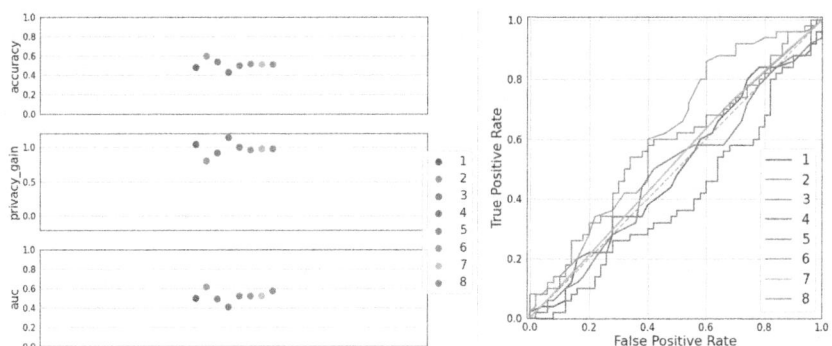

Fig. 4. Privacy level of our method for MIA from TAPAS (300 noise additions).

5 Conclusion

This paper proposed novel approaches to anonymization and re-identification attack methods within the context of the iPWS Cup 2023 competition. The proposed methods contribute to the field of PETs and address challenges associated with Yamaoka anonymization. The introduction of the minimum frequency attack method provides a new perspective in overcoming the previous challenges of re-identification attacks against Yamaoka anonymization. Additionally, the proposed overlapped record swapping with the noise addition method offers a straightforward yet robust approach to anonymization. These methods have been assessed, demonstrating potential in advancing the secure use of personal data while preserving privacy. As the demand for robust PETs increases, these contributions pave the way for further research and development in this domain.

Acknowledgments. We would like to thank the iPWS Cup 2023 committee members for their efforts in planning and organizing the iPWS Cup 2023. This work was supported in part by JSPS KAKENHI Grant Number JP23K11097.

References

1. The G7 Data Protection and Privacy Authorities. G7 DPAs' communiqué : Roundtable of G7 Data Protection and Privacy Authorities – Working toward Operationalizing Data Free Flow with Trust and Intensifying Regulatory Cooperation, 21 June 2023. https://www.ppc.go.jp/files/pdf/G7roundtable_202306_communique.pdf
2. National Science and Technology Council. National Strategy to Advance Privacy-Preserving Data Sharing and Analytics (2023). https://www.whitehouse.gov/wp-content/uploads/2023/03/National-Strategy-to-Advance-Privacy-Preserving-Data-Sharing-and-Analytics.pdf
3. iPWS Cup Committee. Data Anonymization Competition - iPWS Cup 2023 (2023). https://www.iwsec.org/pws/ipws2023/
4. PWS Organizing Committee. Privacy Workshop (PWS) (2015). https://www.iwsec.org/pws/index_e.html
5. iPWS Cup Committee. iPWS Cup 2023 rules Ver 1.0 - "diabetes challenge" (2023). https://github.com/kikn88/ipwscup2023/blob/main/iPWSCup2023-rule3.pdf
6. PWS Organizing Committee. iPWS Cup 2023: Diabetes Challenge (2023). https://codalab.lisn.upsaclay.fr/competitions/13907
7. Houssiau, F., et al.: TAPAS: a toolbox for adversarial privacy auditing of synthetic data. In: NEURIPS 2022 Workshop on Synthetic Data for Empowering ML Research. Neural Information Processing Systems Foundation (2022). https://openreview.net/pdf?id=9hXskf1K7zQ
8. Houssiau, F., Jordon, J., Elliott, A., Geddes, J., Mole, C., Smith, C.R.: Library of attacks (2022). https://tapas-privacy.readthedocs.io/en/latest/library-of-attacks.html
9. Stadler, T., Oprisanu, B., Troncoso, C.: Synthetic data - anonymisation groundhog day. In: 31st USENIX Security Symposium, USENIX Security 2022, pp. 1451–1468. USENIX Association (2022)

Author Index

A
Aikawa, Yusuke 158
Al Agha, Khaldoun 257
Alavizadeh, Hooman 244
Alavizadeh, Hootan 244
Alpcan, Tansu 244
Ansari, Keyvan 213
Auzemery, Aurélien 142

B
Belel, Anushree 101
Bille, Alexander 23
Bilot, Tristan 257
Bocchi, Tobia 195

C
Camtepe, Seyit 213
Chida, Koji 297

D
Duan, Peitong 277
Duda, Jarek 213
Dutta, Ratna 101

E
El Madhoun, Nour 257

F
Fairoze, Jaiden 277

H
Honda, Yoshiaki 85
Hwang, Vincent 125

I
Isobe, Takanori 3
Ito, Hokuto 234
Ito, Norimitsu 65

J
Jang-Jaccard, Julian 244

K
Katayama, Akira 142

L
List, Eik 45

M
Mahboubi, Arash 213
Marchetti, Mirco 195
Miyachi, Rin 179
Morawiecki, Paweł 213

N
Nagashima, Konan 179

O
Okajima, Kabuto 297
Okano, Takako 65

P
Pawłowski, Marcin 213
Pieprzyk, Josef 213

S
Saito, Taiichi 179
Sakamoto, Kosei 3
Sato, Arata 142
Shinagawa, Kazumasa 85
Shiraya, Takuro 3
Stabili, Dario 195
Sugio, Nobuyuki 234

T
Taga, Bungo 65
Takagi, Tsuyoshi 158
Tischhauser, Elmar 23

V
Valgimigli, Filip 195

Y
Yasuda, Masaya 142
Yoshiguchi, Naoki 158

Z
Zouaoui, Anis 257

SPRINGER NATURE

GPSR Compliance

The European Union's (EU) General Product Safety Regulation (GPSR) is a set of rules that requires consumer products to be safe and our obligations to ensure this.

If you have any concerns about our products, you can contact us on ProductSafety@springernature.com

In case Publisher is established outside the EU, the EU authorized representative is:

Springer Nature Customer Service Center GmbH
Europaplatz 3
69115 Heidelberg, Germany

The manufacturer's authorised representative in the EU is Springer Nature Customer Service Centre GmbH, Europaplatz 3, 69115 Heidelberg, Germany. If you have any concerns regarding our products, please contact ProductSafety@springernature.com

Printed and bound by CPI Group (UK) Ltd, Croydon, CR0 4YY
25/03/2026
02078194-0013